Publications of

Scholars Book Co.

Kenneth MacNeal, *Truth in Accounting*

George Staubus, *A Theory of Accounting to Investors*

Robert R. Sterling (editor), *Asset Valuation and Income Determination: A Consideration of the Alternatives*

ACCOUNTING

ACCOUNTING

ITS PRINCIPLES AND PROBLEMS

BY

HENRY RAND HATFIELD, PH.D.

PROFESSOR OF ACCOUNTING IN THE UNIVERSITY
OF CALIFORNIA; AUTHOR OF "MODERN ACCOUNTING"

SCHOLARS BOOK CO.

BOX 3344

LAWRENCE, KANSAS 66044

Reprinted by special arrangement with
Appleton-Century-Crofts, Educational Division,
Meredith Corporation.

REPRINTED 1971 BY
SCHOLARS BOOK CO.

PRINTED IN THE UNITED STATES OF AMERICA

TO

R. M. H.

IN GRATEFUL ACKNOWLEDGMENT

OF ASSISTANCE RENDERED

EDITOR'S FOREWORD

Hatfield's *Accounting* is a welcome addition to the Accounting Classics Series. The purpose of the series is to make available certain out of print works that have made significant contributions to accounting thought. As the Foreword to the Reissue points out, Hatfield's *Accounting* occupies a special niche in the development of accounting thought.

The economics of publishing is such that the price of this volume would have been prohibitive had it not been for a grant from Arthur Andersen & Co. In keeping with their policy of encouraging the free flow of ideas, they have provided the funds necessary to make this book available at a reasonable price. In keeping with this same policy, they suggested that "all editorial decisions be made on campus by the editor." Therefore, the responsibility for such decisions, chiefly the selection of the books to be reissued, rests solely with me.

We are indebted to Stephen Zeff for writing the Foreword; to John Hatfield and Appleton-Century-Crofts for permission to reprint; and especially to AA for making the series possible.

ROBERT R. STERLING

University of Kansas

FOREWORD TO THE REISSUE

After more than four decades, Henry Rand Hatfield's *Accounting: Its Principles and Problems* is being reissued. Why does this book stand apart from its contemporaries, and why should it command our attention today?

Unlike the great majority of his brethren, Hatfield was not a certified public accountant, had not taken a course in accounting, and had never practiced the profession. At Northwestern University he studied classics and at the University of Chicago his fields were political economy and political science. He earned a bachelor's degree from the former and a doctorate from the latter. His first fulltime teaching assignment was in, of all things, psychology. Those were the days of the Renaissance Man.

At around the turn of the century, he happened into accounting. Evidently he enjoyed the subject, and especially its history. An avid bibliophile, he unearthed many historical documents and treatises during his frequent visits to Great Britain and the Continent.

Well known are Hatfield's pungent humor, sly wit, and incisive criticism. Though we are entertained by "An Historical Defense of Bookkeeping" (1924), his points are deftly made. His eye for the ironic and the incongruous is evident throughout the critical essay, "What They Say About Depreciation" (1936).

Yet only in Hatfield's *Accounting* are readers referred to *Mother Goose* to repair "a deplorable ignorance of our heritage of English Literature" among college students (p. 268). And who else would have answered his editor's plea for a more comprehensive index with the entry, "Mike, love of, 256"? There, on page 256 of *Accounting*, we find the most famous Mike in the accounting literature enshrined in footnote.

Hatfield is rare among accounting writers for his alertness

and sensitivity to the literature about him. An eclectic who duelled with others' opinions, he preferred the rapier to the bludgeon. His faculty for keen and perceptive criticism is evident on almost every page of *Accounting*, a book brought out in his 61st year. By 1927, the year of its publication, Hatfield had earned the respect of academicians and practicing accountants alike for his aversion to dogma, his attentiveness to other's views, and the care and precision of his analysis. An accounting writer who was active in the 1930s once said that Hatfield's influence was more strongly felt through the scholarliness he brought to accounting discussions than for the specific opinions he held.

As for *Accounting* itself, its enduring value is twofold. First, are the qualities of clarity and balance, freshness and sanity that characterize the presentation. His two chapters on depreciation remain among the most lucid and thoughtful treatments in the literature, and they are commendably succinct. Much may still be learned today from his thorough and critical survey of statutes, case law, and opinions of accounting writers on the relation between dividends and profits, a subject that intrigued Hatfield for many years. In his chapter on consolidated balance sheets, one finds a brief but interesting suggestion which may be regarded as a precursor of the "entity theory" of adjusting goodwill, developed in the 1940s by Moonitz.

A second and yet more valuable attribute of *Accounting* is its perspectives into the evolution of accounting thought and practice during the first three decades of the century.

Accounting reveals an author whose mind is genuinely open to all ideas, however radical. To read Hatfield, especially his *Accounting*, is to be shaken loose from one's prejudices and preconceptions by an author whose objectivity and intellectual honesty are welcome antidotes to a literature replete with briefs and summary judgments. Hatfield approaches his subject as a student and beckons his reader to join in the quest. In the Preface, he writes:

> Although the science of accounting has made marked progress, it is still in a formative stage, and it were indeed a daring or foolhardy accountant who would attempt a categorical and dogmatic treatment

> of the subject. In accounting there is no person or academy whose pronouncement can be accepted as having unquestioned authority. Those who write on the subject must, in general, express opinions and formulate arguments rather than render decisions. (p. viii)

Although such an invocation might be interpreted as license to ignore what others are saying, Hatfield sets out to marshal informed opinions from a broad array of sources, a task he achieves with intelligence and an absence of pedantry.

It is precisely because of Hatfield's sensitive sampling of diverse views and judgments that *Accounting* is itself a work of considerable historical interest for students of accounting. Hatfield not only draws on the standard American accounting authorities of the period, to wit Kester, Montgomery, Paton, Cole, Finney, and Esquerré, he also invokes the opinions of jurists, economists, and many writers on accounting from both sides of the Atlantic.[1] To Hatfield, the literature does not end at the water's edge. Fluent in German and French, he frequently compares U.S. practices and laws with those in France, Germany, Austria and Great Britain.[2] He gently reminds us that accounting is not unique to America.

It is not the volume or variety of quotations and references that make the work. What truly impresses the reader is Hatfield's deep understanding of the diverse literatures and authors from whom he borrows a pithy line here, a lengthy quote there. He traces an author's thinking through successive editions, pointing out ironies and inconsistencies. He juxtaposes apparently contradictory authorities, exposing curious anomalies to close examination. Above all, he demonstrates a comprehension and insight into domestic and foreign case law as it pertains to accounting that is exceptional for one who has not had the advantage of formal legal education. It is true that he cites Prosper Reiter on key points, but Reiter, after all, was one of Hatfield's students.

---

[1] Two Englishmen, Dickinson and Pixley, are among Hatfield's most respected sources.

[2] See the recent publication of his 1911 paper, "Some Variations in Accounting Practice in England, France, Germany and the United States," *Journal of Accounting Research*, Autumn, 1966, pp. 169–82.

Hatfield's extensive review of English and American cases on dividend law led him to the following observation, which while perhaps not original with him, deserves greater emphasis in the literature.

> Much of the discussion of realized profits is confused by an uncertainty as to whether the writer, perhaps a judge rendering a decision, means that profits are not in existence until realized, or that profits are not available for distribution unless they have been realized. The economist is more likely to take the former ground, the jurist even when his language refers in more general terms to profits, is probably thinking of profits available for dividends. . . . (pp. 251–52)

Hatfield himself recommended that while assets might properly be revalued upward, the corresponding credit should not be made to profits until realized.

Oft-quoted is the following Hatfieldian wisdom:

> The denial that profit can exist without a sale and the simultaneous recognition of accruing interest as profit is another of the many inconsistencies in accounting practice. The exception in favor of accruing interest probably rests upon the idea that it is definitely calculable, its amount may be accurately determined. But if this is a satisfactory basis for differentiation, the rule for recognizing profits should be expressed in terms of calculability or certainty rather than made dependent upon the existence of a contract. (p. 257)

Hatfield the historian was not content with mere description and enumeration: he often interpolated cause and consequence. Montgomery's view that the balance sheet should show current values was traced by Hatfield to Montgomery having "been influenced by the startling changes in price level which have accompanied the Great War" (p. 284). Systematic accounting for depreciation and wasting assets, writes Hatfield, was largely a product of the Federal income tax law (pp. 140, 279).

Hatfield's *Accounting* transcends the bounds of a normal textbook, for it is no less than a critical annotation of the literature. Decidedly not a work for the untutored student, it might best be studied at the "intermediate" and "advanced" levels.

Hatfield does not dally with the routine. He heads straight for the topics most susceptible to debate. Authorities, though cited often, are not suffered gladly. No authority is spared, none is sacrosanct.

Besides earning the unanimous praise of reviewers in the leading accounting and economics journals, *Accounting* was honored with the Award of Merit by Beta Alpha Psi as "the most outstanding contribution to the literature of accountancy for the year ended May 1, 1928." It remained in print for three decades.

In 1937, John B. Canning, whose *Economics of Accountancy* was a critique of a different genre, wrote the following lines in a letter to Hatfield on the occasion of the latter's retirement from active teaching:

> When I say you are an economist I mean it in a special, private sense. Disguised as a professor of accounting, you go prying into people's secrets. You peep into their account books. You ferret out the kind of things men use for information in their affairs. You stare rudely at their less than algebraic reasoning about simultaneous impossibilities.
>
> It would be bad enough if you had kept all this to yourself. But you did not. Ten years ago you published 474 pages of shameless gossip about it. You even called attention to the innumerable contradictions in it. This you excused by saying 'The student may thus get a broader view of the subject, . . .' You held out the solemn nonsense of judicial opinions, commission rulings, and statutory provisions so that anyone could see the intellectual sores and scar tissue. You referred to them as 'these somewhat carefully prepared statements.' You called the book *Accounting: Its Principles and Problems* instead of *Follies in Economic Behavior*. Problems, yes: but principles, no. Could anything be more unprincipled?

All this and Mother Goose too.

STEPHEN A. ZEFF

PREFACE

Much has occurred in the field of accounting since the publication, some eighteen years ago, of the forerunner of this treatise, entitled *Modern Accounting*. During that period more books have been written on the subject, and more serious study has been given to its scientific aspects, than in any other period of similar length, perhaps more than in the preceding centuries since Pacioli.

Several causes have contributed to this progress in accounting. One of these is the increase in the number of large corporations, for as ownership and management become severed, the need of uniform and correct accounting procedure is imperative. The influence of the Interstate Commerce Commission, multiplied by the generally concurring state commissions, has been another potent factor. And the enactment of the Federal income tax law has, more than any other single event, emphasized the necessity of keeping accounts that will exhibit with approximate accuracy the annual income.

In these circumstances it has seemed desirable, in revising *Modern Accounting,* practically to rewrite the entire book drawing upon the wealth of material which recent years have brought forth. While the changes made in rewriting the treatise justify a change of title, it is hoped that the present work has retained enough of the features of *Modern Accounting* to insure that the generous treatment accorded the earlier work will be granted its supplanter.

Some few chapters not really pertinent to the subject have been omitted, while chapters on the consolidated balance sheet (largely a recent development) and on the interpretation of accounts have been added. There is added also a collection of questions and problems suited to classroom work.

Although the science of accounting has made marked progress, it is still in a formative stage, and it were indeed a daring or foolhardy accountant who would attempt a categorical and dogmatic treatment of the subject. In accounting there is no person or academy whose pronouncement can be accepted as having unquestioned authority. Those who write on the subject must, in general, express opinions and formulate arguments rather than render decisions. Hence in this treatise there are presented the somewhat divergent, and at times perhaps contradictory, statements of recognized authorities. The student may thus get a broader view of the subject, and have a better opportunity to arrive at a reasoned conviction, than if the author had adopted the easier method of expounding only his personal views. For a similar reason much reference is made to the opinions of courts, the rulings of commissions, and even to the formulations of statute law. So long as accounting is still mobile, the somewhat carefully prepared statements of such public authorities are surely worthy of careful attention and sympathetic study, even though the accountant may feel free to criticize the conclusions reached.

To attempt to render full acknowledgment to all those whose views may have influenced the writer would require an altogether too formidable list of names. The footnotes must be accepted as an indication of the indebtedness of the author. Thanks are extended alike to those who are criticized and to those approved.

H. R. H.

CONTENTS

APPENDIX

ACCOUNTING

ACCOUNTING

CHAPTER I

THE BALANCE SHEET

Double Entry Bookkeeping

Accounting, in so far as it is based on double entry bookkeeping, is essentially an attempt to present two aspects of business affairs concerning which every business man needs to be informed. This is true whether the person concerned is the owner of the business, a creditor of the business, a prospective investor, or the public interested in regulating prices and profits. There is, in the first place, an exhibit in such detail as may seem appropriate, of the wealth owned and the debts for which the proprietor is liable; a showing of what one owns and what one owes. In technical language this is an exhibit of assets and liabilities.

The other aspect of business, which accounting attempts to exhibit, is the amount the proprietor is worth, and how his wealth increases or decreases from time to time. This exhibit does not concern itself with the concrete embodiments of wealth, not with the various things owned or the different debts due, but with the abstract quantity of wealth, and how, and why that net wealth changes in amount. This information is set forth primarily in the profit and loss statement.

It is always a matter of discretion as to the amount of detail to be set forth in either of these fundamental exhibits. The merchandise handled may all be shown in a single amount, or there may be separate showings of an indefinite number of different kinds of merchandise. Debts due to the concern, or those owed by it may be classified in accordance with the security back of the loan (*e.g.*, as mortgage loans, collateral loans, unsecured loans) or by the time when the loan matures (*e.g.*, short time, long time, past due), or they may be classed by the character of the debtor or creditor (*e.g.*, due to depositors, due to other banks). The essential is that the categories shall be all-comprehensive and mutually exclusive so that every asset and liability shall be set forth in a reasonably definite and intelligible manner.

Similarly in the exhibit of proprietorship there is practically unlimited scope for discretion in determining the details to be shown. The sources of increased wealth may be shown in a few or in many categories. Expenses, which are, *pro tanto*, a reduction of proprietorship, may be shown in a few comprehensive subdivisions (*e.g.*, wages, rent, miscellaneous expenses) or they too may be indefinitely subdivided, making manifest the effect of wages paid to each class of labor, the rent paid for each facility, the almost infinite variety of items going to make up miscellaneous expense.

A characteristic merit of double entry bookkeeping is that in the keeping of this twofold set of accounts there is an imperfect but very valuable check against error. This is due to the fact that the sum obtained in the first set of accounts, by subtracting liabilities from assets, must at all times equal the net proprietorship shown in the second set of accounts. At the beginning of any business, it is true by definition that Assets — Liabilities = Proprietorship. Starting with this initial equation, it is obvious that any change in amount of net assets must at the moment of change effect an increase or a decrease in proprietorship. If the changes are promptly recorded in both sets of records, the equation remains. Accounting is then essentially the presentation of a statement in the form of an equation in which $A - L = P$. Subtraction is a somewhat less easy operation than addition. In preparing a statement of the condition of a business the arrangement of items is ordinarily changed so that the liabilities are added to proprietorship, instead of being subtracted from assets. The form of the bookkeeping equation is thus made: $A = L + P$.

The Balance Sheet

A systematic exhibit presenting this equation is known as a balance sheet. Such a statement is presumably made at the beginning of any business enterprise, or at the installation of its first systematic accounts. During the period of operations, changes from day to day, from moment to moment, are recorded in the accounts, always with a view of presenting at the end of the fixed fiscal period a new balance sheet, exhibiting anew the status of the business as it may have been altered by the transactions and mishaps of the year. The balance sheet has therefore been called by Sprague both the origin and the goal of all accounting. A slight exaggeration perhaps, as accounting has other aspects, but the balance sheet is certainly one of the goals of accounting. Through all the tedious recording of transactions, there is always in mind the effect which the transaction will have in altering the balance sheet. Always the record is made in a way to facilitate the preparation of that important statement.

In earlier times, the importance of the balance sheet was not fully realized. Where trading was largely in the nature of a series of separate ventures, the sending of a caravan to one place and a ship to another, no general reckoning was made at the end of each year. Each venture was treated separately and were a ship so fortunate as to return after a long and hazardous voyage to the Indies, the profits of that particular completed transaction were ascertained. The earlier treatises do not prescribe a final closing of the ledger each year; this in many instances was done only when the ledger was full. Thus of the old account books which have come down to us, one was not balanced until the end of nine years, another not until twenty-seven years had elapsed. The British East-India Company prepared a general balance sheet in 1665—but not again until 1685. But during the seventeenth century the custom of business men changed and a marked step was taken by the French Ordinance of 1673 requiring a balance sheet each two years. At the present time, an annual balance sheet is customary. In most of the European countries, this is required by law of all corporations. Accounting is less strictly regulated in the United States, but an annual balance sheet is required of those corporations which are more directly regulated by government; and the rules of the stock Exchange, the requirements of bankers, and the compelling power of business custom in this country make the annual balance sheet well-nigh universal.

Balance Sheet and Trial Balance

The balance sheet presents an abstract of all the accounts in the ledger. So too does a mere trial balance. But the trial balance ordinarily lists in one column all ledger accounts showing a debit balance, in another those showing a credit balance. The balance sheet, while also arranged in two columns, attempts to classify the items further, and in some way to bring out not merely the equation of debits and credits, but an equation between assets on one hand, and the sum of liabilities and proprietorship on the other. The balance sheet ordinarily implies that the ledger has been closed, so that the temporary accounts showing current modifications of proprietorship have been gathered into a Profit and Loss account, and in some cases, the balance carried to Capital. In this process, practically all of the accounts in the ledger which, after closing, show debit balances, represent assets. Practically all those showing credit balances represent either a liability or a part of proprietorship. The exceptions consist in the ledger account showing a net deficit if one exists, and in the balances of those accounts which have been called Valuation accounts (or offset accounts) such as Allowance (or Reserve) for Depreciation which are discussed later.

The Two Sides of the Balance Sheet

The first of these groups is ordinarily called assets or resources. Until quite recently the second group—while comprising proprietorship items as well as liabilities—has been labeled liabilities. Accounting practice at the present tends towards a more exact title and with increasing frequency there is substituted the phrase liabilities and capital, or liabilities and net worth.

Ordinarily the balance sheet places the asset items in the left, the liabilities and net worth in the right of two vertical parallel columns, thus:

Balance Sheet

Cash	$ 100	Notes Payable	$ 50
Merchandise	800	Mortgage Payable	250
Real Estate	500	Capital	1,000
		Profits	100
	$1,400		$1,400

English Form of Balance Sheet

A curious custom is, however, found in the balance sheets of English companies which, in contrast to those of the rest of the world, reverse the order, showing assets in the right-hand column. It suffices here to note this variation without attempting to discuss either its origin or its justification. Such a variation in accounting practice is a mild misfortune, but like the English custom of driving to the left, it must be recognized. Fortunately an English balance sheet may continue to circulate, although the accounting world in general is otherminded, without the disastrous wreckage which would mark the course of the Englishman who persisted in turning always to the left while driving on an American highway.

Report and Account Forms

Another variation in the mass arrangement of the balance sheet is frequently mentioned, although of even less significance. This consists in placing the two groups of accounts in a single vertical column, one above the other, rather than side by side. This variant is frequently described as the report form of the balance sheet, in contradistinction to the account form. Its usage has perhaps developed in connection with the limitations of the newspaper columns in which balance sheets are frequently published, in part perhaps as more easily handled in an ordinary typewriter. When published in the report form the assets generally come first.[1]

[1] See balance sheet of Sears, Roebuck & Co. below, Form 7.

Segregation of Liabilities

It is, however, desirable not merely to indicate by title that the second group of items contains those representing proprietorship as well as liabilities. There should be, as well, a segregation of liabilities from proprietorship items. This is a recent development in accounting practice. The almost unbroken custom in 1900 was to show the credit items in the balance sheet in about the following order: capital stock, funded debt, current liabilities, reserves, profit and loss. In this arrangement the various proprietorship items are not all grouped together, but are separated by the interjection of liabilities. It does not lend itself to easy interpretation, and in many cases, leaves the reader uncertain as to whether a given item, such as a reserve, is in reality a liability or a part of proprietorship. Accounting practice has by no means altogether changed in this respect, but there is a growing custom of listing first all the liabilities proper, with a subtotal showing their sum, followed by a list, similarly totaled, exhibiting all the items entering into proprietorship or net worth. An excellent example of such an arrangement is found in the model balance sheet recommended by the Federal Reserve Board as shown on page 48.[2]

An even more marked differentiation between liabilities and proprietorship is sometimes made in the balance sheet. This consists in showing the total liabilities as an actual subtraction made from the sum of the assets, listing in the second group of accounts only the items representing proprietorship. The balance then is one which shows the net assets as equivalent to the proprietorship, rather than one which makes an equation between the total assets and the sum of liabilities and proprietorship. This arrangement, although recommended by some authorities,[3] is almost never found in practice when the balance sheet is prepared in the account form. But where

---

[2] While such an arrangement is somewhat sparingly found in published balance sheets it has the approval of eminent accountants. See, *e.g.*, Montgomery, *Auditing, Theory and Practice*, 3d ed., I, pp. 368-9; Kester, *Accounting*, I, p. 232; Dickinson, *Accounting Practice and Procedure*, p. 51; Couchman, *The Balance Sheet*, p. 176.

[3] *E.g.*, Rehm, *Die Bilanzen*, p. 10.

the balance sheet is given in the report form the liabilities are not infrequently subtracted from the assets. The remainder, which is often entitled net worth, is followed by an explanation that the net worth is "made up of the following items," the several proprietorship items being then duly listed. Montgomery states that this form is his "conception of an ideal balance sheet."[4] A balance sheet prepared in this way is frequently called a financial statement. This phraseology is, however, not particularly happy, for it is only one of a vast array of financial statements, and its variation in form does not make it any less a balance sheet.[5]

Double Account Form

Another variation in the form of the balance sheet is that prescribed for the so-called parliamentary companies of England, and known as the double account balance sheet. An example is as follows:

Capital Account

Cost of Property	£195,000	Share Capital	£100,000
Balance	5,000	Debentures	100,000
	£200,000		£200,000

General Balance Sheet

Liabilities		*Assets*	
Capital Account, balance	£ 5,000	Materials, etc.	£ 4,000
Notes Payable	10,000	Cash	6,000
Profit and Loss	3,000	Accounts Receivable	8,000
	£18,000		£18,000

It is to be noticed that the balance sheet proper does not contain the entire outstanding capital but merely the portion of the capital receipts, including receipts from funded debts, which has not been expended in acquiring the company's plant. Nor does the balance sheet include the plant in the

[4] *Op. cit.*, p. 367. The form is printed *infra*, p. 52.
[5] *Cf.* Kester, *Accounting, Theory and Practice*, 2d ed., II, p. 73.

asset column. Information on these points is gained from the accompanying capital account, the balance of which is brought down as a liability in the general balance sheet.

The origin of this peculiar arrangement is that the law governing such companies provides that the money received on capital account (that is, from subscription to shares or from sales of debentures, etc.) may be used solely for investment in the plant of the company, and the double account balance sheet is designed to show how far this requirement has been fulfilled. This form is rarely used in American practice.[6]

The balance sheet of the company given above, if presented in the ordinary English form, would be:

Balance Sheet

Capital and Liabilities		*Assets*	
Share Capital	£100,000	Cost of Property	£195,000
Debentures	100,000	Materials, etc.	4,000
Notes Payable	10,000	Accounts Receivable	8,000
Profit and Loss	3,000	Cash	6,000
	£213,000		£213,000

In discussing the subject of the shrinkage in value of plant in reference to profits it will be shown that the double account form of balance sheet has had a considerable and perhaps baleful influence on the legal interpretation of accounts. It has indeed been argued that the placing of the capital in a separate account involves the principle that changes therein cannot affect the Profit and Loss appearing in the balance sheet. While the validity of this inference may be questioned it is true that the isolation of capital assets and capital liabilities in the Capital account has a tendency to cause them to be considered as isolated in fact, and has led to some far-reaching conclusions which otherwise might never have been reached.

Comparative Balance Sheets

This is a form in which the figures for two successive years are exhibited in parallel columns. It is in reality merely two

[6] It was, however, used by the Atchison, Topeka & Santa Fe Ry. Co. until 1922.

balance sheets printed on the same page. Such an arrangement is of value as it makes comparison easy and emphasizes changes which have taken place in the financial status of the corporation. Information regarding the changes which have taken place is of very great assistance in interpreting the balance sheet. The balance sheet of the General Motors Corporation printed below as Form 3 is in this form.

Consolidated Balance Sheets

In the complexity of modern business a new form has arisen known as the consolidated balance sheet. This, while in balance sheet form, is not the balance sheet of any existing corporation, nor does it present the balances obtained from any ledger. It is used where, through stock ownership, a consolidation of interests has been brought about without destroying the legal existence or independence of any of the affiliated corporations. In such a case it is desirable to present, in the form of a balance sheet, a statement which, so far as possible, represents the financial condition of the entire combination, but which is not an exact picture of any existing corporation. The published accounts of most of the large businesses of this country are presented in the form of a consolidated balance sheet. Several of these are printed later in this chapter. The problems connected with the formation and interpretation of a consolidated balance sheet are many and difficult and are reserved for fuller discussion in a later chapter.

Valuation or Offset Accounts

Until recent years it has been assumed that all the debit balances outstanding after the ledger has been closed are to be listed among the assets, all credits either as liabilities or as proprietorship. It is true that most of the debit and credit balances may thus be classified, but there is an important group of accounts which are exceptional. These have come to be called valuation (or offset) accounts and are typically represented by the accounts designed to show how much depreciation has taken place in some fixed asset. It is a well recognized convention, and one amply justified, that the inevitable decline, say in a machine, is not to be shown by a series of credit entries in the Machinery account. A credit in that account would, of course, indicate a subtraction from the original value, just as a credit to Cash indicates that the value of the cash on hand has suffered diminution. But, in the case of depreciation, it is thought desirable to continue to show, from year to year, the original value of the machine, as well as the depreciation which has taken place up to date. Accordingly, instead of crediting Machinery, some other account, perhaps entitled Allowance for Depreciation, is credited. This account would normally have a credit balance, and its value must somehow be shown in the balance sheet. It used to be customary to list such credit balances along with the liabilities or proprietorship items, which likewise are credits. But such an item is evidently not a liability, it is owed to no one. Even less is it a proprietorship item; an indication that a value is not in existence can by no hocus-pocus be transformed into an addition to the original capital. A credit to Allowance for Depreciation is merely a technical substitute for a credit to the Machinery account itself; its meaning is the same. It indicates, and indicates only, that a subtraction is to be made from the amount appearing as the debit balance of the Machinery account. Hence the better practice in recent years is to show, in the balance sheet, all valuation accounts as subtractions from the account to which they refer, thus:

Buildings	$100,000	
Less depreciation	20,000	$80,000
Machinery	$ 75,000	
Less depreciation	25,000	50,000

Accounts showing accrued depreciation have been mentioned as typical valuation accounts. Allowance for Doubtful Accounts is, however, an equally good example. Discount on Capital Stock is an example of a debit balance which is not an asset but logically a deduction to be made from the amount of capital stock, the capital stock having been listed at its par value. A common rule should be followed and the subtraction indicated by such accounts should be shown in an interior column of the balance sheet, the remainder being extended into the long column.

Occasionally, a balance sheet appears in which a debit represents a net deficit. This clearly is not an asset. Logically such an item is in reality a valuation account, and indicates that there is a subtraction to be made from the amount of nominal or original capital. The balance sheet, in such a case, should exhibit this item in a manner similar to depreciation.[7] In all such cases it is to be noticed that the balance sheet does not exactly correspond with the ledger. In the ledger the accounts are kept altogether distinct. In the balance sheet, while both accounts are shown, the actual subtraction is performed and the remainder only is set forth.

Marshaling Items

Additional clearness in the balance sheet is secured if the asset items are arranged somewhat in the order in which they will probably be turned into cash. The status of a concern is not indicated merely by the relation between the amount of the assets and the amount of the liabilities. It is important to know as well the relation between the various forms of liabilities to be met and the various kinds of assets available for meeting them. Even though assets far exceed the liabilities, forced liquidation may occur if these assets are not in a form suitable for payment of the maturing debts. Cash is the most available of assets. Other assets may be marshaled in a series in reference to their availability. Such a marshaling may not be altogether accurate in detail. One cannot always tell whether the notes receivable will be paid before or after the accounts receivable, nor whether the merchandise will be transformed into cash more easily than bonds can be sold. But a roughly satisfactory arrangement can be made, and present-day accounting clearly demands that this be attempted.

---

[7] For balance sheet showing the subtraction of a deficit see that of the Willys-Overland Co. and the model form recommended by the Federal Reserve Board printed below. For conflicting views on the propriety of this procedure, *cf.* Couchman, *The Balance Sheet*, pp. 35 and 207; and Bennett, *Advanced Accounting*, pp. 315-6.

Sequence of Items

Considerable discussion has taken place as to whether the list of assets should begin with cash and end with the least liquid asset, or should appear in somewhat the reverse order. Some have thought that the former arrangement appeals most to the banker, whose emphasis being always placed on the ability to meet current liabilities prefers to have cash appear as the first in the list of assets; but that the investor, who is interested in the much larger item of permanent investment, prefers to give precedence to plant and other fixed assets. Whichever order is adopted the liabilities should be somewhat similarly arranged so as to facilitate the comparison between current liabilities and the quick assets by which these debts are to be met. Owing, however, to the desirability of having all the proprietorship items appear in a single group, there is reason for preferring the arrangement running from liquid to fixed, rather than the reverse. In this way the liabilities, progressing from current liabilities to funded debt, are placed in close contrast to similar groups of assets. The capital, most permanent of the credit items, appears somewhat contrasted to the most permanent of the assets, and yet is not separated from surplus and undivided profits with which it is, logically, most closely related.

While the order, fixed to current, is still the more common, there is a marked change in accounting practice toward the other order. Many high authorities favor the newer arrangement; it is recommended by the Federal Reserve Board. An instance of change in this respect is found in the balance sheets of the General Motors Corporation. In its balance sheet for 1920 cash is placed as the first item among the assets; prior to that the list began with the fixed assets.

Subdivisions in the Balance Sheet

The balance sheet is even more serviceable if, in addition to marshaling the items in some regular sequence, subdivisions are made with subtitles and subtotals. The traditional grouping was under three heads, current assets, fixed assets, and deferred assets or deferred charges.[8] The precise definition of these terms is difficult. In general, current assets are cash and those assets "which in the regular course of business will be readily and quickly realized, together with such additional assets as may readily be converted into cash without impairing the business or enterprise."[9] Fixed or capital assets are those of a permanent nature or intended for long continued use or possession. Deferred assets or charges represent that portion of expense items which is applicable to a period subsequent to the date of the balance sheet.

Current Assets

There is, however, no perfect agreement among accountants as to the exact content of these terms. Current assets undoubtedly include cash, accounts receivable, notes receivable and similar items, all of which are expressed in terms of money, and which will presumably be turned into money without further negotiation. Slightly different from these are such items as merchandise, work in process, raw material, etc., which may indeed soon be transformed into money, but in order that this take place, further operations are necessary. Such items are frequently spoken of as working assets.[10] By many accountants, working assets are considered a subdivision of current assets, coördinate with cash and receivables, but by some they are erected into a separate category, coördinate with current assets.[11] To include working assets as a subdivision of current assets seems preferable as well as more customary in recent accounting practice.

---

[8] This is still found in the form recommended by the Federal Reserve Board (Form 12, below), and in the published balance sheet of the J. I. Case Threshing Machine Co. (Form 4, below).

[9] "Report of Committee on Terminology, A.I.A.," *Journal of Accountancy,* XXXV, p. 465.

[10] The Committee on Terminology of the American Institute of Accountants defines working assets as follows: "Assets which are consumed in the activities carried on without themselves forming an integral part of the product." (*Journal of Accountancy,* XXXV, p. 467.) This would include supplies used in operations but exclude raw material. This is an unfortunate definition from so authoritative a body, the differentiation being crudely materialistic and meaningless.

[11] See, *e.g.,* Dickinson, *Accounting Practice and Procedure,* pp. 34-5.

Investments

Difference of treatment has appeared in regard to investments in bonds and other securities. While the definition given above allows the inclusion of marketable securities among current assets, many accountants have excluded them, considering that only short-time items may be called current. It is, however, preferable to include such securities as Liberty bonds among current assets, not that they are already flowing along in a regular channel of business which will automatically arrive at cash (which is true of receivables and, to some extent, even of merchandise), but because they are so easily convertible and may indeed be held as a substitute for cash. Indeed the position of such securities is not very different from items generally called cash. Strictly speaking, cash means only currency. It is immediately available but not immediately productive if held in the till or the company's safe. Ordinarily cash is not left, in large amounts, in the till but is turned over to a bank. There is then in reality no cash on hand, there is really no "money on deposit," but the company has a claim on the bank which it is hoped will be immediately met on demand. It has something almost as available as cash, and at the same time something which may be yielding a low rate of interest instead of being entirely barren. Liberty bonds held as a resource against emergencies, or in anticipation of early demands, are almost identical. They are not cash, but a form of asset almost as available as cash. It seems then entirely proper to include them among current assets, although nominally they may run many years before maturity. But some accountants exclude long-time securities from current assets even when they are easily marketable, and this is the rule of the Interstate Commerce Commission.[12]

Where the securities are held, not as a more profitable substitute for cash but, as in the case of stock in an affiliated company, in order to secure control or to promote friendly relations, the securities partake rather of the nature of fixed assets. In some balance sheets such securities are included

[12] See Account 707 in balance sheet (Form 13, below).

under the general head of fixed assets, but there is an increasing tendency, despite the influence of the Interstate Commerce Commission, to establish an independent group entitled investments,[13] or even more specifically, so as to distinguish them from ordinary investments, under some such title as Investments in Controlled and Subsidiary Companies.

Fixed Assets

There is also divergence of opinion as to what constitutes fixed assets. In general they comprise those assets which are held for the purpose of conducting the business, in contradistinction to those assets which the proprietor holds for the purpose of converting into cash. They include real estate, buildings, machinery, and stock of other companies where this is held as a permanent investment for the purpose of controlling the activities of a subordinate company. Goodwill and franchises are, with some justification, frequently included among the fixed assets. In a way these two items are the most permanent of all investments, for while the sale of plant and machinery might restrict the company in its future activities, it is of course possible that all of the present plant could be sold and the business still continue in a new location. But the sale of goodwill implies the cessation of business activities, and the franchise of a company cannot be given up without preventing the continuance of the functions governed by the franchise. On the other hand, conservative accountants are apt to look somewhat askance upon the items of goodwill and franchise as they appear in the balance sheet. Their value is thought to be somewhat uncertain and problematical, and in marked contrast to the supposedly fixed value of plant and building. There is, therefore, an increasing tendency to list goodwill, franchises, and similar items, in a category distinct from fixed assets, either under these specific names or with the general heading of intangible assets. This seems the preferable procedure, and is favored by Montgomery in his model balance sheet[14] and by Couch-

[13] *Cf.* the balance sheets (Forms 3 and 7) of Sears, Roebuck & Co. and the General Motors Corporation.

[14] *Auditing, Theory and Practice,* 3d ed., I, p. 367.

man,[15] although goodwill is still included among fixed assets in the balance sheets of many corporations. Until recently it was almost universally the case that goodwill was not merely included among fixed assets, but was combined in a single item such as Plant, Machinery, and Goodwill. But this practice is now very generally condemned. In England it is even considered illegal to include goodwill with fixed tangible assets in a single item.[16] Improvement in this respect has been marked in the last twenty years.

Deferred Charges and Prepaid Expenses

The conventional grouping of certain items as deferred charges, or less satisfactorily as deferred assets, is a matter of somewhat greater difficulty. Under this heading quite different items have been included. These are: (1) payments that have been made for services to be rendered during the following fiscal period. Thus, for instance, insurance which covers the protection of one or more years in advance, and rent or interest paid in advance, all represent a claim against some outsider, not, indeed, for the payment of money, but for rendering some service (protection against fire, the continued use of borrowed funds without additional payment, or the use of rented property) and therefore may well be considered either as assets or as near assets. (2) Items representing the expense of a service already rendered, but one which it is thought should in part be allocated to future fiscal periods. A good example is the expense involved in the surface stripping of a mine. Here the service paid for has been rendered in full, but as this is an expense which appertains to many years' operation of the mine, it is customary to carry it as a deferred charge, gradually amortizing it somewhat proportionately to the amount of ore annually extracted. Discount upon capital stock or bonds is also not infrequently included in the group of deferred charges. (3) Items representing unusual losses, as, for instance, that due to an earthquake, which it is thought best to distribute over several years.

[15] *The Balance Sheet,* p. 138.

[16] Galloway *v.* Schill Seebohm & Co. [1912], 2 K.B. 354.

There is a tendency at the present time to break this group and to treat prepaid expenses, at least in so far as they pertain to operations of the near future, as a branch of current assets, while continuing to carry such items as the cost of stripping as a deferred charge. This is perhaps a better practice although by no means generally adopted. Neither the Federal Reserve Board nor the Interstate Commerce Commission includes prepaid expenses among current assets; but they are so treated in the balance sheet of the General Motors Corporation with the approval of the auditors, Haskins and Sells; and Montgomery [17] boldly expresses his belief "that within a short time good accounting practice will sanction the inclusion in current assets of all current prepayments." This would leave as deferred charges only such prepayments as cover a somewhat long period, and possibly items representing not the payment of an expense in the ordinary sense, but some unusual loss which it is desired to spread over many years, gradually writing it off against income. A still different use of the term, deferred assets, has somewhat unfortunately been established by the Interstate Commerce Commission. The term itself seems not to be specifically defined, but by illustration it includes advances made to agents and others for working funds, and the cash and securities set aside to constitute insurance, pension, and other similar funds. The items which are generally listed as deferred assets (charges), or as prepaid expenses are classified by the Commission under the heading, unadjusted debits.

Where only such prepayments as cover the operations of a somewhat extended future are included among deferred charges, they closely resemble fixed assets. The relation between such prepayments and the cost price of a machine, or other fixed asset, will be discussed later. Here it suffices to note that while the prevailing custom is to list such deferred charges as a separate subdivision of the balance sheet this usage is not universal. Thus the General Motors Corporation includes deferred expenses (in contradistinction to prepaid expenses listed as current assets) among the fixed assets.[18]

---

[17] *Op. cit.*, p. 393.

[18] See p. 30, below.

Attention has been called to the desirability of arranging assets somewhat in the order in which they become available for making payments. The position of deferred charges in such sequence is of peculiar difficulty. From one point of view they can never be converted into cash, and hence should be farthest removed from cash. But from another viewpoint they frequently represent prepayments which cover at most a relatively small number of years, and do not seem as fixed and permanent as land or buildings. From the examination of some hundreds of balance sheets, it appears that only rarely are deferred charges placed between fixed and current assets. The arrangement in general is either fixed, current, deferred, or current, fixed, deferred. As the arrangement in which cash begins the list of assets is only gradually coming into vogue, it is probable that the accepted form in the future will have fixed assets follow current, and deferred charges come after fixed assets. This is the form recommended by the Federal Reserve Board. No instance is recorded where the list of assets begins with deferred charges.

Other Subdivisions of Assets

From an examination of the balance sheets printed below, it is apparent that the simpler threefold division of assets into current, fixed, and deferred is no longer regarded as sufficient. Division into four classes is more common. The additional subdivisions to be introduced will naturally vary with the nature of the business transacted and the character of assets held. It seems desirable to list goodwill and other similar intangible assets separately; and where cash or securities are set aside as specific funds, either for retiring bonds or for other purposes, they should be separated from other fixed or current assets. Occasionally other subdivisions may seem desirable. In some cases, however, subdivisions which appear among the assets should properly appear not among the assets but as subtractions from items on the other side of the balance sheet. This is true of the item, Discount and Expenses on Capital Stocks, appearing in the balance sheet of the Pacific Gas and Electric Company. This would preferably be shown, not as an asset, but as a subtraction from the nominal amount of capital stock.

Subdivisions of Liabilities

Liabilities have customarily been subdivided along somewhat the same lines as the conventional subdivision of assets. Current liabilities include debts shortly maturing. While there is no definite agreement as to the time which separates long from short, it is customary to say that debts maturing within a year should be included in current liabilities. Some accountants show a separate category called accrued liabilities, which includes the obligation for wages, interest, rent, and the like, which have accrued up to the date of the balance sheet but which are not yet due. There is no reason whatever for distinguishing between current liabilities and accrued liabilities, for surely the pay roll, coming due on the following Saturday, or rent payable at the end of the month, rank among the more immediately pressing current debts. Better practice is, therefore, to include these items as a subdivision of current liabilities.

Deferred Credits

A group called deferred liabilities, deferred credits, or deferred items occasionally appears in the balance sheet. Strictly speaking, a deferred credit should be analogous to a deferred debit. It should represent income received but not yet earned, as for instance, money received by a landlord for rent in advance. Where used in this sense, the deferred item very closely approximates a current liability. It represents not an obligation to pay money to the tenant, and may be not even a contingent liability for such payment, but there is at least an obligation to allow the tenant the use of the property without further payment. Inclusion of this among the liabilities seems entirely proper. In so far as expenses paid in advance are treated as current assets, income received in advance might appropriately be treated as a current liability. It is, however, more customary, and doubtless preferable, to treat such items as a subdivision of liabilities, coördinate to current liabilities. The showing of premium received upon the issue of stock, or discount upon bonds purchased, as a deferred credit sometimes found in a balance sheet is, however, objectionable. Premium upon stock issued is clearly a part of the proprietorship, and should be shown with other proprietorship items. Discount upon securities purchased is nothing but a correction of an overvaluation due to listing the securities at their par rather than at their real value, and in the balance sheet should be shown as a subtraction on the asset side. Premium received on the company's own bonds should be included among the liabilities.[19] It is in fact, part of the money borrowed from the bond owners which is being returned in installments at the time that the coupons are paid. No very serious objection can, however, be made if it is listed as a deferred credit.

Reserves

So far it has been assumed that all items upon the right-hand side of the balance sheet represent either liabilities or proprietorship. This has been recognized even by those who have criticized the conventional heading, liabilities, and have insisted that the right-hand side of the balance sheet should be headed liabilities and capital. But the question is raised by some accountants as to whether there is not a third somewhat indeterminate grouping to be made, items which for the moment at least it is impossible to classify either as a liability or as an element of proprietorship. The best illustration of such an item is a reserve for contingencies. Events only can show whether this will ripen out to an actual liability because of some guaranty, or whether it will prove to be merely a conservative withholding of profits to provide against an eventuality which never arose. Accordingly in some balance sheets, as for instance that of the General Motors Corporation, three main classifications are recognized; liabilities, reserves, and capital, and the general heading for that side of the balance sheet is a triple one. Where such a threefold

---

[19] For discussion of the proper method of amortizing this premium, see below, p. 227.

division is made, care should be taken to include in the third group only items which are really ambiguous. To group together all reserves is apt to be misleading, for some, such as a reserve for extension, are clearly part of the proprietorship. Other reserves, such as a reserve for depreciation, while neither a liability nor proprietorship, are just as clearly an element of an asset account, and should appear as a subtraction from the asset to which it refers. A reserve for contingency may be really ambiguous in its nature, and if so there seems to be no ground for objection to its appearing in the balance sheet in a class by itself. By some accountants, deferred credits are similarly separated from liabilities and from proprietorship. But this is unnecessary. It is much better to have on the credit side of the balance sheet only the two groups, liabilities and proprietorship. The interjection of a third category may at times be justified, but it should be employed only sparingly, and that when there are items which it is practically impossible to classify.

Purpose of the Balance Sheet

The purposes of the balance sheet are twofold. Primarily it shows the financial status of the concern, giving information as to its solvency, and in a less degree it exhibits accumulated profits. The first purpose is on the face the more evident one. The balance sheet shows a cross section of the business; it presents the status at a given moment of time; it is ostensibly a showing of assets and liabilities, not of income and expenses. Yet the balance sheet is not without value as an exhibit of profits. Prepared, as it ordinarily is, at annual intervals, it serves at least by comparison, to show the flow of income during the period, as well as the financial status at the moment of its preparation. As Cole has so happily expressed it: "The two balance sheets give the terminals of the journey (the start and the finish), and the income sheet gives some of the details of the journey itself."[20] Indeed, some writers, noticeably Rehm, maintain that the prime function of the balance sheet is to show the profits of the year and

[20] *The Fundamentals of Accounting*, p. 47.

serve as a basis for the declaration of dividends. It may even be presented in such form as not only to show the profits of the past year, but also to indicate the proposed distribution of such profits. An illustration of such an arrangement is found in the balance sheet of the Union Oil Company, printed as Form 8. A somewhat similar treatment is found in the balance sheets of many English companies, as *e.g.*, that of J. & P. Coates, Limited.

For whichever use the balance sheet is designed it is evident that it must give, as far as possible, a correct showing of the facts. High standards have been set in this respect by statutes. Thus the English Companies Act provides that the balance sheet shall be "drawn up so as to exhibit a true and correct view of the state of the company's affairs,"[21] and the German Commercial Code prescribes severe penalties for "untruthfulness or unclearness" of the balance sheet. Nevertheless accountants generally deny the possibility of strict accuracy in the balance sheet. Thus Dicksee says: "A balance sheet is not a statement of facts, but rather an expression of opinion"; and another has said: "Not more than ten percent of the items in any average balance sheet are, or can possibly be, facts that are capable of being absolutely tested."

Misleading Balance Sheets

Unclearness and subsequent misunderstanding of balance sheets may be due to several different causes, the principal ones being: (1) The nature of accounting itself, which being at basis an estimate can never be absolute or free from error; (2) The vagueness of the terminology used and the liability that technical words will be misunderstood, even when used in good faith; (3) The purposeful misrepresentation of the condition of the company on the part of the directors or officers.

1. The uncertainty of all accounting can never be altogether avoided. It appears principally in connection with the valuation of assets. In many cases there is no outside criterion of value and no way of insuring against a wrong

[21] Companies (Consolidation) Act, 1908, sec. 113, 2b.

estimate. This subject is discussed in the chapters dealing with assets and their valuation.

2. The vagueness of terminology adds to the difficulty of presenting a lucid statement. Technical terms such as reserve, reserve fund, treasury stock, adjustment account, and others, are used with entirely different meanings by different companies and are given most divergent definitions by the courts and by the various textbook writers. Unfortunately there is at present no accepted authority to whom appeal can be made.

The likelihood of a serious misunderstanding is increased because of the fact that items so widely divergent in character stand together in the columns of the balance sheet. On the debit side items representing losses or expenses may be confused with assets. On the other hand, the credit column contains such antipodal items as profits and depreciation—that is, those showing that there has been an increase in the net value of the assets, and those indicating that the value of some of the assets has declined. Exactly the same term may be used to indicate these two categories, for both are frequently covered by what is called reserve. Much good will be accomplished by the action of the Interstate Commerce Commission in prescribing certain uniformities in railroad accounting. It would be well for the public accountants of the country to take even wider action in securing definite and uniform accounting terminology.

3. Purposeful misrepresentation in the balance sheet is secured in part by insidiously taking advantage of the inherent difficulties just referred to, in part by more palpable untruth. Of the latter little need be said. Evidently if a company deliberately states it has \$100,000 cash on hand when it really has only \$10,000 no knowledge of the principles of accounting will disclose the facts. More insidious are the less open misrepresentations. Sometimes a purposeful grouping together of certain items will conceal the real condition. Thus a company owning \$100 government bonds and \$100,000 bonds of some wildcat company lists them under the heading, Government and Other Bonds. Or it lists bonds and stocks together as Bonds and Other Investments.

More flagrant is the case where liabilities have been subtracted from the assets, as for instance where the balance sheet does not show both Notes Receivable and Notes Payable, but merely the excess of the former over the latter; or again shows only the equity in real estate instead of both the cost price and the purchase-money mortgage given in part payment. Even the improper division of an account may be resorted to in order to hide the fact that a company is too largely involved in a single line of investment. A striking example of this came up in connection with the disastrous failure of the Leipziger Bank, which divided up among various different accounts the advances which it had made to an industrial company, hoping thereby to conceal the extent to which the bank was involved in that ruinous enterprise.

Against the positive misstatements in the balance sheets, the outsider is of course defenseless. But assuming that amounts are correctly given and that there is no gross overstatement, he still needs to be on guard against a misunderstanding. He should be sure that the ambiguous titles are rightly understood, and that he does not confuse accounts of opposite nature. A most important aid in this matter is the careful indication of valuation accounts in the manner suggested. Further examination of the balance sheet and of the other statements which should accompany it is then possible. The difficult points, in theory and practice, relate to substance rather than to form and are discussed in the chapters following.

Understatement in the Balance Sheet

Reference has here been made to incorrectness in the balance sheet as being an admitted fault, or even a fraud. Attention should be called to the fact that many accountants and jurists draw a marked line between the incorrectness of statement which places the company in a more favorable light and one which understates its financial strength or minimizes its profits. To some the former is fraudulent, the latter almost a virtue. It suffices here to call attention to this point, which is discussed at some length in connection with the subject of secret reserves.

Does the Balance Sheet Record Costs or Exhibit Values?

The question of accuracy in the balance sheet involves a matter of fundamental theoretical importance which has perhaps received too little discussion and has never been satisfactorily settled. Accuracy may, indeed, be demanded but what constitutes accuracy depends on the purpose of the balance sheet. A statement is accurate if it correctly presents a record of past transactions as truly as if it records present values. It has generally been accepted by accountants as a truism, indeed exalted by them into a "principle of accounting" that the balance sheet professes to set forth present values. But this concept is by no means fully realized; it is in accounting very frequently set aside. In the next chapter are discussed certain conventionally accepted rules regarding the valuation of various kinds of assets. In some of these the implication is strong that, at least in some instances, no attempt is made to prepare a statement of present values, but rather to represent the facts as they occurred in the past. The double account balance sheet is even more clearly, so far as the capital account is concerned, a history of previous transactions and in no sense a statement of present values. It is just as accurate to state what a given piece of property cost twenty years ago as to give its present estimated value, provided, of course, that in either case it is clearly understood just what the figure given really means. The balance sheet is assumed to state present values, but it strangely halts and stumbles toward this goal. It might, and ordinarily does in part, disregard present values and present historic costs. Which of these concepts is proper may well be considered a fundamental question, but it is one on which accounting theory is unfortunately not quite clear.

Illustrative Forms of Balance Sheets

To illustrate the variations in form found in accounting practice, there are given below a number of balance sheets of different corporations. Descriptive notes are to be found on the pages following the forms.

FORM 1

AMERICAN AGRICULTURAL

INCLUDING SUBSIDIARY COMPANIES AND INVESTMENTS IN CHARLOTTE

Consolidated Balance

ASSETS

CURRENT ASSETS			
Cash		$ 3,359,496.48	
U. S. Government and Other Securities:			
U. S. Liberty Bonds	$ 43,400.00		
Mortgage Bonds of the Company	439,716.50	483,116.50	
Accounts and Notes Receivable from sales of 1921 and prior years	$11,275,154.55		
Less Reserves	9,275,154.55	2,000,000.00	
Accounts and Notes Receivable of 1922-1924	$22,389,507.28		
Less Reserves for Freights, Discounts and Doubtful Receivables	2,978,145.83	19,411,361.45	
Inventories (Manufactured Products, Materials and Supplies) at cost, or market if lower ...		9,628,762.05	
TOTAL CURRENT ASSETS			$34,882,736.48
DEFERRED CHARGES			
Unexpired Insurance, Prepaid Taxes and Other Deferred Charges to Future Operations			535,029.47
SINKING FUNDS FOR REDEMPTION OF MORTGAGE BONDS AND TRUST FUNDS			506,319.90
CAPITAL ASSETS			
Land, Buildings, Machinery and Equipment	$31,902,192.90		
Less Reserves for Depreciation and Adjustment of Property Values	9,523,114.47	$22,379,078.43	
Mining Properties, less Depletion		17,062,359.50	
Charlotte Harbor & Northern Railway Company and Other Investments, less Reserves		5,406,888.48	
Good-Will, Brands and Trade-Marks		1.00	
TOTAL CAPITAL ASSETS..			44,848,327.41
TOTAL ASSETS..			$80,772,413.26
DEFICIT			19,404,875.56
			$100,177,288.82

FORM 1

CHEMICAL COMPANY

HARBOR & NORTHERN RAILWAY COMPANY AND ASSOCIATED COMPANIES

Sheet as of June 30, 1924

LIABILITIES

CURRENT LIABILITIES			
Accounts Payable and Accrued Taxes		$ 1,068,821.95	
Notes Payable and Trade Acceptances		1,542,135.49	
Accrued Interest on Bonds		951,559.38	
TOTAL CURRENT LIABILITIES			$ 3,562,516.82
DEFERRED CREDITS			179,014.90
RESERVE FOR FEDERAL TAXES AND CONTINGENCIES			919,931.10
FUNDED DEBT			
First Mortgage 5% 20-year Convertible Gold Bonds, due October 1, 1928		$12,000,000.00	
Less Retired through Sinking Fund	$ 5,306,000.00		
Less Converted into Preferred Stock ..	1,213,000.00	6,519,000.00	
		$ 5,481,000.00	
First Refunding Mortgage 7½% 20-year Sinking Fund Gold Bonds, Series A, due February 1, 1941 ..	$30,000,000.00		
Less Retired through Sinking Fund	1,742,500.00	28,257,500.00	
TOTAL FUNDED DEBT			33,738,500.00
TOTAL CURRENT LIABILITIES, RESERVES AND FUNDED DEBT..			$38,399,962.82
CAPITAL STOCK			
Preferred Stock Authorized	$50,000,000.00		
Less Unissued	21,544,800.00	$28,455,200.00	
(Dividends Paid to April, 1921)			
Common Stock Authorized	$50,000,000.00		
Less Unissued	16,677,874.00	33,322,126.00	61,777,326.00
			$100,177,288.82

FORM 2

BETHLEHEM STEEL

Consolidated Balance Sheet

ASSETS

CAPITAL ASSETS:			
Property Account (Depletion and amortization deducted):			
As at January 1, 1923		$426,826,712.79	
Additions during year		172,941,054.26	
		$599,767,767.05	
Less—Reserve for depreciation, obsolescence, relining of furnaces, etc.		146,830,855.81	$452,936,911.24
INVESTMENTS IN AND ADVANCES TO AFFILIATED COMPANIES			7,944,425.25
SPECIAL FUNDS IN HANDS OF TRUSTEES:			
For payment or redemption of bonds or notes		$ 984,573.86	
Proceeds of mortgaged property released		301,806.22	1,286,380.08
CONTINGENT AND INSURANCE FUND ASSETS			3,958,703.44
STOCKS AND SUNDRY SECURITIES, INCLUDING REAL ESTATE MORTGAGES			4,520,141.14
CURRENT ASSETS:			
Inventories:			
Raw materials and supplies on hand and in transit...	$53,850,362.42		
Worked materials, and contracts in progress, less bills rendered on account	35,954,839.89	$ 89,805,202.31	
Accounts and notes receivable		36,379,148.13	
U. S. government securities		18,395,800.76	
Marketable securities		477,278.12	
Cash in banks and on hand		17,393,390.45	162,450,819.77
DEFERRED CHARGES TO OPERATIONS ...			3,803,791.12
			$636,901,172.04

FORM 2

CORPORATION

as of December 31, 1923

LIABILITIES

CAPITAL LIABILITIES:			
Capital Stock:			
8% Cumulative Convertible Preferred Stock:			
Authorized and issued		$ 30,000,000.00	
Less—Converted into 7% Cumulative Preferred Stock		11,337,700.00	$ 18,662,300.00
7% Cumulative Preferred Stock:			
Authorized		$ 77,000,000.00	
Less — Unissued (including $21,461,700 reserved for exchange)	$36,793,900.00		
Held by Corporation	92,000.00	36,885,900.00	40,114,100.00
Common Stock:			
Authorized		$270,000,000.00	
Less — Unissued (including $18,662,300 reserved for exchange)	$89,710,100.00		
Held by Corporation	138,000.00	89,848,100.00	180,151,900.00
			$238,928,300.00
Cambria Iron Company Stock—Dividend of 4% Guaranteed			8,465,625.00
Funded and Secured Debt Including Mortgage Payable			212,884,225.28
			$460,278,150.28
CURRENT LIABILITIES:			
Notes payable		$ 9,630,000.00	
Accounts payable, including advance payments on contracts, pay-rolls and accruing liabilities		30,185,404.86	
Bond interest accrued		2,911,241.75	42,726,646.61
SUNDRY RESERVES:			
Contingent and miscellaneous operating reserves		$ 5,379,918.63	
Insurance reserves		2,327,653,55	7,707,572.18
APPROPRIATED SURPLUS:			
Appropriated for, and invested in, additions to property and working capital			114,000,000.00
UNAPPROPRIATED SURPLUS			12,188,802.97
			$636,901,172.04

FORM 3

GENERAL MOTORS CORPORATION

Condensed Comparative Consolidated Balance

ASSETS

CURRENT AND WORKING ASSETS:	Dec. 31, 1922	Dec. 31, 1921
Cash in bauks and on hand	$ 27,872,722.92	$ 40,057,401.53
United States Government Bonds	3,950.00	5,228.04
Marketable securities	29,618.10	27,009.31
Sight drafts against B/L attached and C. O. D.	13,179,664.05	4,677,241.39
Notes receivable	4,455,042.33	4,794,978.99
Accounts receivable and trade acceptances, less reserve for doubtful accounts (in 1922, $1,431,143.55; in 1921, $1,078,772.26)	15,921,934.93	17,866.071.83
Inventories at cost or market, whichever is lower	117,417,823.05*	108,762,625.35
Prepaid expenses	1,358,404.98	1,944,988.35
TOTAL CURRENT AND WORKING ASSETS	$180,239,160.36	$178,135,544.79
FIXED ASSETS:		
Investments in allied and accessory companies, etc.	$ 57,293,864.72	$ 56,377,031.68
General Motors Corporation common and debenture stock held in treasury	3,275,432.65	3,889,799.51
Real estate, plants and equipment	255,207,970.82	248,593,751.60
Deferred Expenses	3,947,794.49	4,609,677.87
Goodwill, patents, copyrights, etc.	22,370,811.06	22,438,401.22
TOTAL FIXED ASSETS	$342,095,873.74	$335,908,661.88
TOTAL ASSETS	$522,335,034.10	$514,044,206.67

* At some plants demand for product precluded shut-down, for taking physical inventory. At such points book values are used, careful scrutiny having led to the conclusion that these values are conservative.

FORM 3

AND SUBSIDIARY COMPANIES

Sheet as of December 31, 1922 and 1921

LIABILITIES, RESERVE AND CAPITAL

	Dec. 31, 1922	Dec. 31, 1921
CURRENT LIABILITIES:		
Accounts payable	$ 34,812,441.20	$ 15,640,429.41
Notes payable	———	48,974,996.29
Taxes, payrolls and sundries accrued not due	16,166,563.70	15,894,778.40
Federal taxes	1,650,821.93	———
Accrued dividends on preferred and debenture stock, payable February 1	1,133,096.23	1,043,763.07
TOTAL CURRENT LIABILITIES	$ 53,762,923.06	$ 81,553,967.17
Purchase money mortgages ($100,602.12 due in 1923)	$ 1,279,750.12	$ 1,475,592.82
Purchase money notes, account Fisher Body Corporation stock purchase ($1,000,000.00 due August 1)	1,000,000.00	4,000,000.00
	$ 2,279,750.12	$ 5,475,592.82
RESERVES:		
For depreciation of real estate, plants and equipment	$ 50,827,907.11	$ 37,527,774.94
For employes' investment fund	1,143,962.50	2,171,885.00
For sundry contingencies	7,016,667.35	3,139,579.72
For bonus to employes	1,344,098.70	17,630.87
For anticipated losses and unforeseen contingencies of prior years	———	14,000,000.00
For completion of office building	———	2,499,261.00
TOTAL RESERVES	$ 60,332,635.66	$ 59,356,131.53
CAPITAL STOCK:		
Debenture stock 7%	$ 32,181,600.00	$ 26,931,600.00
Debenture stock 6%	60,801,000.00	60,801,000.00
Preferred stock 6%	16,183,400.00	16,183,400.00
Common stock, no par value: 20,557,750 shares issued and outstanding at $10.00 per share	205,577,500.00	206,456,575.25
Common stock ($100 par value)	700.00	7,400.00
TOTAL CAPITAL STOCK	$314,744,200.00	$310,379,975.25
Interest of minority stockholders in subsidiary companies with respect to capital and surplus	1,278,662.18	1,464,379.44
SURPLUS over and above $10.00 per share of no par value common stock	89,936,863.08	55,814,160.46
TOTAL CAPITAL STOCK AND SURPLUS	$405,959,725.26	$367,658,515.15
TOTAL LIABILITIES, RESERVES AND CAPITAL	$522,335,034.10	$514,044,206.67

FORM 4

J. I. CASE THRESHING

Balance Sheet,

Assets			
Properties:			
Land, Building, Plant and Equipment		$15,549,836.03	
Deduct:			
Reserve for Depreciation and Accruing Renewals		3,304,678.93	
		$12,245,157.10	
Patents Designs, Devices, etc.		1,044,422.71	$13,289,579.81
Current Assets:			
Inventories of Materials, Supplies and Finished Product		$12,720,454.87	
Customers' Notes Receivable Including Interest Accrued ..	$7,669,896.25		
Less: Commission Certificates outstanding	842,088.99	6,827,807.26	
Accounts Receivable, due by Dealers, etc.		432,262.88	
Investment in and Advances to Compagnie Case de France, Paris		276,504.18	
Notes Receivable due from Officers and Employes for Capital Stock Purchased		137,248.06	
Real Estate and Properties acquired under Foreclosure and held for sale		103,016.89	
Cash in Banks and on Hand........		683,356.72	21,180,650.86
Deferred Charges to Future Operations:			
Selling and Publicity Expenses on account of 1923 Season, Unmatured Advertising, Prepaid Interest and Insurance Premiums, etc			339,336.63
			$34,809,567.30

FORM 4

MACHINE COMPANY

December 31, 1922

LIABILITIES

CAPITAL STOCK:		
Authorized:		
7% Cumulative Preferred Stock—200,000 Shares of $100.00 each..	$20,000,000.00	
Common Stock—200,000 Shares of $100.00 each	20,000,000.00	
	$40,000,000.00	
Issued and Fully Paid:		
7% Cumulative Preferred Stock—130,000 Shares of $100.00 each..	$13,000,000.00	
Common Stock—130,000 Shares of $100.00 each	13,000,000.00	$26,000,000.00
CURRENT LIABILITIES:		
Bills Payable	$ 5,395,000.00	
Accounts Payable:		
Audited Vouchers	427,109.15	
Dealers, etc.	150,598.14	
Interest, Taxes, Wages and Royalties Accrued	419,486.60	6,392,193.89
RESERVES:		
For Contingencies and Future Collection Expenses	$ 1,000,000.00	
For Industrial Accident Liability....	100,000.00	1,100,000.00
SURPLUS		1,317,373.41
		$34,809,567.30

FORM 5

PACIFIC GAS AND ELECTRIC COMPANY

Consolidated Balance Sheet

ASSETS

PLANTS AND PROPERTIES			$249,178,251.62
DISCOUNT AND EXPENSES ON CAPITAL STOCKS			9,104,811.86
INVESTMENTS			1,355,849.97
TRUSTEES OF SINKING FUNDS (excluding Company Bonds in Sinking Funds):			
Cash		$ 86,888.05	
Accrued interest on bonds held in sinking funds		141,618.97	
TOTAL TRUSTEES OF SINKING FUNDS			228,507.02
CASH IN HANDS OF TRUSTEES FOR REDEMPTION OF NOTES MATURED			4,407.50
CURRENT ASSETS:			
Cash		$ 8,779,321.48	
Notes receivable	$ 69,761.84		
Accounts receivable	4,746,978.44		
TOTAL	$4,816,740.28		
Less reserve for doubtful accounts and notes	44,753.79		
REMAINDER		4,771,986.49	
Installments receivable from subscribers to First Preferred and Common Capital stocks		436,143.29	
Construction Funds in hands of trustees of First and Refunding Mortgage		2,705,846.79	
Materials and Supplies		4,983,996.11	
Accrued Interest on Investments		6,784.01	
TOTAL CURRENT ASSETS			21,684,078.17
DEFERRED CHARGES:			
Unamortized Bond Discount and Expenses		$ 8,148,977.33	
Prepaid Taxes and Undistributed Suspense Items		297,754.72	
TOTAL DEFERRED CHARGES			8,446,732.05
TOTAL			$290,002,638.19

FORM 5

AND SUBSIDIARY COMPANIES

December 31, 1924

LIABILITIES

CAPITAL STOCKS OF PACIFIC GAS AND ELECTRIC COMPANY, INCLUDING STOCKS SUBSCRIBED FOR BUT NOT FULLY PAID:			
First Preferred Capital Stock		$ 54,464,411.91	
Common Capital Stock	$74,502,798.33		
Less — Owned by Subsidiary Company	31,696,866.66	42,805,931.67	
TOTAL CAPITAL STOCKS			$ 97,270,343.58
CAPITAL STOCKS OF SUBSIDIARY COMPANIES not held by the Pacific Gas and Electric Company and Unpaid Dividends thereon			18,775.34
FUNDED DEBT:			
Pacific Gas and Electric Co. Bonds.		$111,542,000.00	
Bonds of Subsidiary Companies ...		41,815,300.00	
TOTAL FUNDED DEBT			153,357,300.00
CURRENT LIABILITIES:			
Accounts Payable		$ 2,041,555.88	
Drafts Outstanding		457,014.88	
Meter and Line Deposits		731,017.55	
Dividends		839,663.10	
Bond Interest Due		464,516.25	
Accrued Interest—not Due		1,818,303.99	
Accrued Taxes—not Due		2,189,469.73	
TOTAL CURRENT LIABILITIES ..			8,541,541.38
RESERVES:			
For Northern California Power Company Consolidated Plant Adjustments and Accrued Depreciation		$ 1,650,398.63	
Depreciation		17,062,383.64	
Insurance		520,801.10	
For amounts charged during 1913, 1914, 1915, 1916, and 1917 to Consumers in excess of rates allowed by City Ordinances		1,820,134.09	
TOTAL RESERVES			21,053,717.46
SURPLUS			9,760,960.43
TOTAL			$290,002,638.19

FORM 6

PACKARD MOTOR

AND SUBSIDIARY

Consolidated Balance Sheet

ASSETS

PROPERTY ACCOUNT:		
Land, Buildings, Machinery, Plant and Equipment—Depreciated values at beginning of year	$19,799,380.06	
Add—Expenditures for three months	766,046.38	$20,565,426.44
Less—Depreciation for three months		1,027,046.90
Balance as at Nov. 30, 1924.......		$19,538,379.54
Rights, Privileges, Franchises and Inventions		1.00
TOTAL PROPERTY INVESTMENT ...		$19,538,380.54
CURRENT ASSETS:		
Inventories at or below cost:		
Raw material, work in process, etc.	$ 6,151,867.14	
Finished Motor Carriages	2,638,730.88	$ 8,790,598.02
Accounts Receivable (net)		2,093,863.44
Deferred Installment Notes and Bills Receivable		1,729,290.71
Miscellaneous Marketable Securities..		1,470,504.00
U. S. Government Securities at cost..	$11,716,842.90	
Cash in Banks and on Hand	4,968,231.60	16,685,074.50
TOTAL CURRENT ASSETS		$30,769,330.67
DEFERRED CHARGES TO FUTURE OPERATIONS:		
Prepaid Insurance and Other Expenses		$ 426,763.40
TOTAL ASSETS		$50,734,474.61

FORM 6

CAR COMPANY

COMPANIES

as at November 30, 1924

LIABILITIES

CAPITAL STOCK:		
Authorized—		
7% Cumulative Preferred—200,000 Shares of $100.00 each	$20,000,000.00	
Common Stock—3,000,000 Shares of $10.00 each	30,000,000.00	
	$50,000,000.00	
Outstanding—		
7% Cumulative Preferred—110,575 Shares of $100.00 each	$11,057,500.00	
Common Stock—2,377,020 Shares of $10.00 each	23,770,200.00	
TOTAL CAPITAL STOCK		$34,827,700.00
CURRENT LIABILITIES:		
Current Accounts Payable and Payrolls	$ 740,933.48	
Provision for Federal Taxes and other Miscellaneous Liabilities not yet due	2,479,560.19	
TOTAL CURRENT LIABILITIES		3,220,493.67
RESERVE FOR CONTINGENCIES		3,000,000.00
SURPLUS:		
Balance at beginning of year		$ 9,488,442.71
Add—Net Profits for three months...		1,872,753.23
TOGETHER		$11,361,195.94
Deduct—Dividends Paid and Declared—		
On Preferred Stock	$ 248,703.00	
On Common Stock	1,426,212.00	1,674,915.00
Balance as at November 30, 1924		$ 9,686,280.94
TOTAL LIABILITIES		$50,734,474.61

FORM 7

SEARS, ROEBUCK AND COMPANY

Consolidated Balance Sheet December 31, 1924

ASSETS

FIXED ASSETS:		
Real Estate, Buildings, Fixtures and Machinery	$ 24,069,386.41	
Good Will, Patents, Etc.	30,000,000.00	
		$ 54,069,386.41
INVESTMENTS:		
Capital Stock of Other Companies..................		5,392,096.97
CURRENT ASSETS:		
Inventories: Raw Material, Goods in Process, Supplies and Merchandise *	$ 35,510,954.29	
Accounts Receivable	20,021,821.34	
Purchase Money Mortgage Notes	12,000,000.00	
Marketable Securities	1,019,200.00	
Liberty Bonds	857,980.35	
Cash in Banks and on Hand	12,666,010.80	
		82,075,966.78
DEFERRED ASSETS:		
Insurance, Interest, Advertising Paid in Advance and Other Deferred Charges		2,865,657.65
TOTAL		$144,403,107.81

Liabilities and Capital

Current Liabilities:			
Accounts Payable		$ 10,588,487.90	
Accrued Taxes, Not Yet Due, including Reserve for Federal Taxes		3,158,530.22	
Preferred Capital Stock not presented for redemption		154,071.00	
			$ 13,901,089.12
Reserves		$ 4,061,566.70	
Common Capital Stock	$105,000,000.00		
Less 50,000 Shares in Treasury	5,000,000.00		
		100,000,000.00	
Surplus		26,440,451.99	130,502,018.69
TOTAL			$144,403,107.81

Surplus Account

Balance December 31, 1923		$ 17,575,017.16
Profit for the Year 1924		14,354,397.07
		$ 31,929,414.23
Deduct:		
Premium on Preferred Stock Redeemed November 15, 1924	$ 2,000,000.00	
Preferred Stock Dividend	489,203.74	
Common Stock Dividend	2,999,758.50	5,488,962.24
Balance December 31, 1924		$ 26,440,451.99

* Cost or Market, Whichever is Lower.

FORM 8

UNION OIL COMPANY

AND OWNED

Balance Sheet,

ASSETS

PROPERTIES:			
Oil Lands, Rights and Leases *		$ 95,300,636.69	
Oil Wells and Development		21,551,517.65	
Absorption Plants and Gas Facilities		2,316,762.15	
Pipe Lines and Storage System		16,144,524.59	
Steamships and Marine Equipment		13,508,300.95	
Refineries		12,724,106.16	
Marketing Stations		20,464,422.08	
		$182,010,270.27	
Less: Reserve for Depletion	$43,062,327.03		
Reserve for Depreciation	33,448,832.33	76,511,159.36	$105,499,110.91
INVESTMENTS:			
Controlled and Affiliated Companies:			
In Stocks		$ 872,895.96	
Advance Accounts		173,990.53	1,046,886.49
CURRENT ASSETS:			
Cash Resources:			
Cash	$ 4,733,090.24		
U. S. Government Bonds	2,500,000.00		
U. S. Treasury Certificates	3,000,000.00	$10,233,090.24	
Receivables: (Less Reserve)			
Bills Receivable	$ 264,567.90		
Accounts Receivable	6,680,773.89	6,945,341.79	
Inventories:			
Crude and Oil Products	$26,242,595.22		
Materials and Supplies	4,587,747.22	30,830,342.44	48,008,774.47
DEFERRED CHARGES:			
Taxes and Insurance in Advance		$ 310,972.85	
Other Charges		347,660.35	658,633.20
			$155,213,405.07

* Oil Lands, Rights and Leases does not include $28,951,145.01 representing appreciation of new discovery areas brought in as producing territory subsequent to March 1, 1913, less depletion accrued to December 31, 1924, the values of which properties have not been agreed upon with the Natural Resources Division of the Internal Revenue Department.

FORM 8

OF CALIFORNIA

COMPANIES

December 31, 1924

LIABILITIES

CAPITAL STOCK:		
Authorized	$125,000,000.00	
Less: Unissued	30,500,000.00	$ 94,500,000.00
MORTGAGE DEBT:		
First Mortgage 5% Bonds	$ 6,173,000.00	
20 Year 6% Gold Bonds, Series "A"	8,937,500.00	
6% Serial Gold Bonds, Series "B"†	5,000,000.00	
Purchase Money Obligations	962,401.60	21,072,901.60
CURRENT LIABILITIES:		
Accounts Payable	$ 5,973,855.38	
Reserve for Taxes and Other Contingencies	2,976,992.85	
Interest Accrued	305,684.36	9,256,532.59
SURPLUS:		
Balance as per Summary attached hereto	$ 12,652,720.70	
Balance of Marine and Workmen's Compensation Insurance Reserves	589,797.93	
Appreciation of new discovery areas brought in as producing territory, subsequent to March 1, 1913—less depletion accrued to December 31, 1924—the values of such properties for the purposes of depletion having been agreed upon with the Natural Resources Division of the Internal Revenue Department	17,141,452.25	30,383,970.88
		$155,213,405.07

† Installment of $2,500,000 payable April 1, 1925.

FORM 9

UNITED STATES

Consolidated General Balance

ASSETS

PROPERTY ACCOUNTS:			
Properties Owned and Operated by the Several Companies			
Balance of this account as of December 31, 1925, less Depletion, Depreciation and Amortization Reserves per table			$1,692,197,704.27
MINING ROYALTIES:			
Mining Royalties on unmined ore, in respect of part of which notes of subsidiary companies are outstanding in amount of $27,910,868.35, as see contra		$ 65,194,784.36	
Less, Reserved from Surplus to cover possible failure to realize all of the foregoing		7,000,000.00	58,194,784.36
DEFERRED CHARGES (Applying to future operations of the properties)			
Advanced Mining and other operating expenses and charges		$ 1,899,952.71	
Discount on subsidiary companies' bonds sold (Net)		996,349.07	2,896,301.78
INVESTMENTS:			
Outside Real Estate and Investments in sundry securities, including Real Estate Mortgages		$ 8,950,601.00	
Land Sales Installment Contracts and Mortgages under Employes' Home-owning Plan		12,296,413.29	21,247,014.29
SINKING AND RESERVE FUND ASSETS:			
Cash resources held by Trustees account of Bond Sinking Funds		$ 1,480,586.15	
(Trustees also hold $199,601,000 of redeemed bonds, not included as liabilities in this balance sheet.)			
Contingent Fund and Miscellaneous Assets		3,874,860.41	
Insurance and Depreciation Fund Assets (includes bonds available for future sinking fund requirements):			
Securities*	$110,937,198.77		
Cash	1,809,676.07	112,746,874.84	118,102,321.40
CURRENT ASSETS:			
Inventories, less credit for Reserve and for amount of inventory values representing Profits earned by subsidiary companies on Inter-Company sales of products on hand in Inventories December 31, 1925 (see note opposite)		$285,677,394.96	
Accounts Receivable		77,366,679.41	
Bills Receivable		6,047,705.00	
Agents' Balances		1,315,348.47	
Sundry Marketable Securities (including part of U. S. Gov't Securities owned)		50,612,197.15	
Time and other special Bank Deposits		6,456,840.04	
Cash (in hand and on deposit with Banks, Bankers and Trust Companies, subject to cheque)		125,529,039.74	553,005,204.77
			$2,445,643,330.87

* There are not included in this item capital obligations of subsidiary companies amounting to $38,795,365.54 held in these funds, as such obligations are excluded from liabilities in this consolidated balance sheet. Such securities were acquired direct by United States Steel Corporation from the Subsidiaries.

FORM 9

STEEL CORPORATION

Sheet, December 31, 1925

LIABILITIES

CAPITAL STOCK OF UNITED STATES STEEL CORPORATION:		
Common	$508,302,500.00	
Preferred	360,281,100.00	$ 868,583,600.00
CAPITAL STOCKS OF SUBSIDIARY COMPANIES NOT HELD BY UNITED STATES STEEL CORPORATION (Book value of same)		573,719.28
BONDED, MORTGAGE AND DEBENTURE DEBT OUTSTANDING:		
United States Steel Corporation 50 Year 5% Bonds	$188,073,000.00	
United States Steel Corporation 10-60 Year 5% Bonds	162,853,000.00	
	$350,926,000.00	
Subsidiary Companies' Bonds, guaranteed by U. S. Steel Corporation	102,856,000.00	
Subsidiary Companies' Bonds, not guaranteed by U. S. Steel Corporation	55,039,900.00	
Subsidiary Companies' Real Estate Mortgages and Purchase Money Obligations	657,677.99	509,479,577.99
SUBSIDIARY COMPANIES' MINING ROYALTY NOTES—Maturing over a period of 33 years, substituted for previously existing mining royalty obligations —Guaranteed by United States Steel Corporation. (Of the total $538,639.22 are interest bearing notes; balance non-interest bearing)		27,910,868.35
CURRENT LIABILITIES:		
Current Accounts Payable and Pay Rolls	$ 54,686,451.01	
Accrued Taxes, not yet due, including reserve for Federal Income Tax	39,980,757.29	
Accrued Interest, Unpresented Coupons and Unclaimed Dividends	7,050,741.87	
Preferred Stock Dividend No. 99, payable February 27, 1926	6,304,919.25	
Common Stock Dividend No. 86, payable March 30, 1926	8,895,293.75	116,918,163.17
Total Capital and Current Liabilities		$1,523,465,928.79
SUNDRY RESERVES:		
Contingent, Miscellaneous Operating and other Reserves	$123,326,346.69	
Insurance Reserves	36,987,946.36	160,314,293.05
APPROPRIATED SURPLUS TO COVER CAPITAL EXPENDITURES:		
Invested in Property Account—Additions and Construction		240,000,000.00
UNDIVIDED SURPLUS OF UNITED STATES STEEL CORPORATION AND SUBSIDIARY COMPANIES:		
Capital Surplus provided in organization	$ 25,000,000.00	
Balance of Surplus accumulated by all companies from April 1, 1901, to December 31, 1925, per table	496,863,109.03	
Total, exclusive of Profits earned by Subsidiary Companies on Inter-Company sales of products on hand in Inventories December 31, 1925 (see note below)		521,863,109.03
		$2,445,643,330.87

NOTE: That part of the Surplus of Subsidiary Companies representing Profits on sales of materials and products to other subsidiary companies and on hand in latters' Inventories is, in this Balance Sheet, deducted from the amount of Inventories included under Current Assets.

FORM 10

THE WILLYS-OVERLAND COMPANY, TOLEDO,

Consolidated Balance Sheet, at

ASSETS

CURRENT:				
Cash			$ 7,248,321.34	
Notes Receivable	$ 856,739.79			
Accounts Receivable	3,654,123.87	$ 4,510,863.66		
Less: Allowance for Doubtful Accounts		166,280.92	4,344,582.74	
Merchandise Inventories (Est.)			26,430,165.28	$38,023,069.36
OTHER ASSETS:				
Due from Affiliated Companies			$ 260,770.73	
Investments in Affiliated and Other Companies			1,230,071.68	
Miscellaneous Notes and Accounts Receivable			124,703.05	1,615,545.46
TRUST FUND:				
On Deposit with Union Trust Company				264,253.25
PERMANENT:				
Land			$ 1,959,393.08	
Buildings	$19,737,314.29			
Machinery, Equipment, etc.	19,157,048.37	$38,894,362.66		
Less: Allowance for Depreciation	$12,767,359.71			
Less: Allowance for Loss	1,383,497.13	14,150,856.84	24,743,505.82	26,702,898.90
GOOD WILL, PATENTS, ETC.:				
Less: Reserve provided to reduce value of these items to				1.00
DEFERRED:				
Prepaid Insurance, Taxes, Etc.				149,963.33
				$66,755,731.30

NOTE: The Company was reported contingently liable as endorsers on notes, acceptances, etc., at June 30, 1923, in the amount of $2,356,078.96.

This Balance Sheet is subject to any adjustment that may be necessary upon final determination by the Government of the Company's Federal Tax Liability.

Dividends on the 7% Cumulative Preferred Stock of the Company have been paid to Oct. 1, 1920; the accumulated Dividends amounted to $4,244,528.75 at June 30, 1923.

FORM 10

OHIO, AND SUBSIDIARY COMPANIES

the Close of Business June 30, 1923

LIABILITIES

CURRENT:			
Accounts Payable:			
For Purchases, Expenses, etc....	$ 8,216,812.04		
Dealers' Initial Payments.......	535,440.33		
Price Adjustments, Allowances, etc..........................	66,431.58		
Unpaid Payroll	716,029.57		
Excise Taxes	661,687.28		
Refund Certificates	362,145.00		
Land Contract and Interest....	30,330.00		
Earned Discounts	270,383.08	$10,859,358.88	
Accrued Taxes, Interest, etc.....................		431,323.33	$11,290,582.21
FIRST MORTGAGE AND COLLATERAL TRUST 7% GOLD NOTES:			
Due December 1, 1923			6,943,000.00
DEFERRED:			
Stock Purchase Contract—Payable $153,140.00 annually beginning 1924		$ 1,069,380.00	
Other items		8,873.75	1,078,253.75
RESERVES:			
For Contingencies, etc..........................		$ 3,604,413.80	
For Inventory Shrinkage		2,883,249.47	6,487,663.27
NOMINAL:			
Capital Stock of Subsidiary Company Outstanding			
Capitol and Michigan Realty Company Preferred 7% Cumulative		$ 219,400.00	
Capital Stock:			
Preferred 7% Cumulative:			
Authorized	$25,000,000.00		
Less: Unissued and Redeemed	2,950,500.00	22,049,500.00	
Common:			
Authorized	$75,000,000.00		
Less: Unissued and Treasury.	21,006,075.00		
	$53,993,925.00		
DEFICIT—June 30, 1923 (Est.).....	35,306,592.93	18,687,332.07	40,956,232.07
			$66,755,731.30

FORM 11

BALANCE

ASSETS

Current Assets:			
1. Cash in Banks and on Hand		$ 75,056.00	
2. Accounts Receivable:			
Trade Debtors	$366,415.00		
Less: Reserve for Doubtful Accounts	7,214.00		
	$359,201.00		
3. Other Accounts Receivable	6,840.00	366,041.00	
4. Notes Receivable		16,813.00	
5. Interest Accrued on Notes Receivable		210.00	
6. Interest Accrued on Mortgages Receivable		940.00	
7. Merchandise on Hand (cost)	$916,440.00		
Less: Reserve for Shrinkage in Inventory value	22,618.00	893,822.00	$1,352,882.00
Outside Investments:			
8. Permanent Holdings:			
Majority Ownership in the Capital Stock of three allied Corporations (cost)			460,000.00
9. Other Investments:			
Income-producing Real Estate (cost)		$262,000.00	
First Mortgages on Improved Real Estate		66,400.00	328,400.00
Sinking Fund Investments:			
10. Securities and Cash in hand of Trustee—representing the accumulated cash installments transferred to the Bond Sinking Fund			138,262.00
Fixed Assets:			
Land, Buildings, and Equipment:			
11. Land (cost)		$140,260.00	
12. Buildings (cost)	$665,745.00		
Less: Reserve for Depreciation	151,218.00	514,527.00	
13. Store Equipment (cost)	$ 85,362.00		
Less: Reserve for Depreciation	37,195.00	48,167.00	
14. Warehouse Equipment (cost)	$ 11,440.00		
Less: Reserve for Depreciation	5,118.00	6,322.00	
15. Office Equipment (cost)	$ 6,284.00		
Less: Reserve for Depreciation	2,312.00	3,972.00	
16. Stable Equipment (cost)	$ 26,311.00		
Less: Reserve for Depreciation	9,240.00	17,071.00	730,319.00
17. Good Will			250,000.00
Expense Items Paid in Advance:			
18. Insurance Premiums Unexpired		$ 2,715.00	
19. Advertising Prepaid: Catalogues, etc., on Hand		9,216.00	
20. Warehouse Supplies on Hand		2,798.00	
21. Office Supplies on Hand		239.00	
22. Stable Supplies on Hand		278.00	
23. Interest Prepaid on Notes Payable Discounted		1,141.00	16,477.00
			$3,276,340.00

FORM 11

SHEET

LIABILITIES AND NET WORTH

	CURRENT LIABILITIES:				
	Accounts Payable:				
24.	Trade Creditors		$124,000.00		
25.	Other Accounts Payable.		352.00	$124,352.00	
	Notes Payable:				
26.	Collateral Demand Notes (4½%) (Secured by the assignment of $50,000 of 5% Mortgages Receivable included in the item of $60,000 per contra)		$ 35,000.00		
27.	Notes Discounted at Bank		40,000.00		
28.	Notes Issued for Merchandise		21,645.00	96,645.00	
	Accrued Items:				
29.	Salaries and Wages Accrued		$ 2,485.00		
30.	Interest Accrued on Bonds		18,000.00		
31.	Interest Accrued on Mortgages		1,700.00		
32.	Interest Accrued on Notes		816.00		
33.	Taxes Accrued (estimated)		3,100.00	26,101.00	
34.	Semiannual Dividend of 3%—Declared on December 30, 1911—Payable February 15, 1912			52,500.00	$ 299,598.00
	FIXED LIABILITIES:				
35.	Bonds Outstanding: First Mortgage 6% Coupon Bonds—due July 1, 1924 (Interest payable January and July 1)			600,000.00	
36.	Mortgages Payable: Mortgage Liens (5%) on Income-producing Real Estate			56,000.00	656,000.00
	TOTAL LIABILITIES				$ 955,598.00
	CAPITAL STOCK AND SURPLUS:				
37.	Capital Stock: Authorized Issue—25,000 Shares at the par value of $100. Issued and Outstanding—17,500 Shares			$1,750,000.00	
38.	Appropriated Surplus: Bond Sinking Fund Reserve from Surplus Earnings (see contra)			138,262.00	
39.	Undivided Surplus:				
	Balance December 31, 1910		$320,344.00		
	Net Profit—For the Year ended December 30, 1911 (see Exhibit B) ..		239,754.00		
			$560,098.00		
	Deduct:				
	Dividends—				
	Declared June 30, 1911	$52,500.00			
	Declared December 31, 1911	52,500.00			
	Reserve for Shrinkage in Inventory Values.	22,618.00	127,618.00	432,480.00	2,320,742.00
					$3,276,340.00

From Bentley, in *Journal of Accountancy,* XIII, p. 318.

FORM 12

BALANCE SHEET RECOMMENDED

Assets

Cash:			
1a. Cash on hand—currency and coin		....	
1b. Cash in bank		....	
			....
Notes and Accounts Receivable:			
3. Notes receivable of customers on hand (not past due)		....	
5. Notes receivable discounted or sold with indorsement or guaranty		....	
7. Accounts receivable, customers (not past due)..		....	
9. Notes receivable, customers, past due (cash value, $......)		....	
11. Accounts receivable, customers, past due (cash value, $......)		....	
Less:			
13. Provisions for bad debts	....		
15. Provisions for discounts, freights, allowances, etc.....	....		
		....	
			....
Inventories:			
17. Raw material on hand		....	
19. Goods in process		....	
21. Uncompleted contracts ..	....		
Less payments on account thereof..	....		
		....	
23. Finished goods on hand		....	
			....
Other Quick Assets (describe fully):			
....		....	
....		....	
			....
Total Quick Assets (excluding all investments)....		....	....
Securities:			
25. Securities readily marketable and salable without impairing the business		....	
27. Notes given by officers, stockholders, or employees		....	
29. Accounts due from officers, stockholders, or employees		....	
			....
TOTAL CURRENT ASSETS		....	....
Fixed Assets:			
31. Land used for plant		....	
33. Buildings used for plant		....	
35. Machinery		....	
37. Tools and plant equipment		....	
39. Patterns and drawings		....	
41. Office furniture and fixtures		....	
43. Other fixed assets, if any (describe fully)		....	
....		....	
Less:			
45. Reserves for depreciation		....	
			....
TOTAL FIXED ASSETS		....	
Deferred Charges:			
47. Prepaid expenses, interest, insurance, taxes, etc.		....	....
Other Assets (49)		....	....
TOTAL ASSETS		....	....

FORM 12

BY THE FEDERAL RESERVE BOARD

LIABILITIES

BILLS, NOTES, AND ACCOUNTS PAYABLE:			
Unsecured bills and notes—			
2. Acceptances made for merchandise or raw material purchased		....	
4. Notes given for merchandise or raw material purchased		....	
6. Notes given to banks for money borrowed		....	
8. Notes sold through brokers		....	
10. Notes given for machinery, additions to plant, etc.		....	
12. Notes due to stockholders, officers, or employees		....	
			....
Unsecured accounts—			
14. Accounts payable for purchase (not yet due)		....	
16. Accounts payable for purchases (past due)		....	
18. Accounts payable to stockholders, officers, or employees		....	
			....
Secured liabilities—			
20a. Notes receivable discounted or sold with endorsement or guaranty (contra)		....	
20b. Customers' accounts discounted or assigned (contra)		....	
20c. Obligations secured by liens on inventories		....	
20d. Obligations secured by securities deposited as collateral		....	
			....
22. Accrued liabilities (interest, taxes, wages, etc.)		....	....
OTHER CURRENT LIABILITIES (describe fully):			
....		....	
....		....	
			....
TOTAL CURRENT LIABILITIES		....	....
FIXED LIABILITIES:			
24. Mortgage on plant (due date........)		....	
26. Mortgage on other real estate (due date......)		....	
28. Chattel mortgage on machinery or equipment (due date......)		....	
30. Bonded debt (due date......)		....	
			....
32. Other fixed liabilities (describe fully):			
....		....	
....		....	
			....
TOTAL LIABILITIES		....	....
NET WORTH:			
34. If a corporation—			
(*a*) Preferred stock (less stock in treasury)		....	
(*b*) Common stock (less stock in treasury)		....	
(*c*) Surplus and undivided profits		....	
Less—			
(*d*) Book value of good will	....		
(*e*) Deficit	....		
		....	
			....
36. If an individual or partnership—			
(*a*) Capital		....	
(*b*) Undistributed profits or deficit		....	
TOTAL		....	....

FORM 13

FORM OF BALANCE SHEET PRESCRIBED

ASSET SIDE

INVESTMENTS:

701. Investment in road and equipment.
702. Improvements on leased railway property.
703. Sinking funds.
    Total book assets at date. (*In short column.*)
    Carrier's own issues at date. (*In short column.*)
    Other assets at date. (*In long column.*)
704. Deposits in lieu of mortgaged property sold.
    Total book assets at date. (*In short column.*)
    Carrier's own issues at date. (*In short column.*)
    Other assets at date. (*In long column.*)
705. Miscellaneous physical property.
706. Investments in affiliated companies—
    (*a*) Stocks.
    (*b*) Bonds.
    (*c*) Notes.
    (*d*) Advances.
707. Other investments—
    (*a*) Stocks.
    (*b*) Bonds.
    (*c*) Notes.
    (*d*) Advances.
    (*e*) Miscellaneous.

TOTAL

CURRENT ASSETS:

708. Cash.
709. Demand loans and deposits.
710. Time drafts and deposits.
711. Special deposits.
    Total book assets at date. (*In short column.*)
    Carrier's own issues at date. (*In short column.*)
    Other assets at date. (*In long column.*)
712. Loans and bills receivable.
713. Traffic and car-service balances receivable.
714. Net balance receivable from agents and conductors.
715. Miscellaneous accounts receivable.
716. Material and supplies.
717. Interest and dividends receivable.
718. Rents receivable.
719. Other current assets.

TOTAL.

DEFERRED ASSETS:

720. Working fund advances.
721. Insurance and other funds.
    Total book assets at date. (*In short column.*)
    Carrier's own issues at date. (*In short column.*)
    Other assets at date. (*In long column.*)
722. Other deferred assets.

TOTAL

UNADJUSTED DEBITS:

723. Rents and insurance premiums paid in advance.
724. Discount on capital stock.
725. Discount on funded debt.
726. Property abandoned chargeable to operating expenses.
727. Other unadjusted debits.
728. Securities issued or assumed—Unpledged. (*In short column only.*)
729. Securities issued or assumed—Pledged. (*In short column only.*)

TOTAL.

FORM 13

BY INTERSTATE COMMERCE COMMISSION

LIABILITY SIDE

STOCK:

751. Capital stock—
    Book liability at date. *(In short column.)*
    Held by or for carrier at date. *(In short column.)*
    Actually outstanding at date. *(In long column.)*
752. Stock liability for conversion
753. Premium on capital stock.
    TOTAL.

GOVERNMENTAL GRANTS:

754. Grants in aid of construction.

LONG TERM DEBT:

755. Funded debt unmatured—
    Book liability at date. *(In short column.)*
    Held by or for carrier at date. *(In short column.)*
    Actually outstanding at date. *(In long column.)*
756. Receivers' certificates.
757. Nonnegotiable debt to affiliated companies—
    (*a*) Notes.
    (*b*) Open accounts.
    TOTAL.

CURRENT LIABILITIES:

758. Loans and bills payable.
759. Traffic and car-service balances payable.
760. Audited accounts and wages payable.
761. Miscellaneous accounts payable.
762. Interest matured unpaid.
763. Dividends matured unpaid.
764. Funded debt matured unpaid.
765. Unmatured dividends declared.
766. Unmatured interest accrued.
767. Unmatured rents accrued.
768. Other current liabilities.
    TOTAL.

DEFERRED LIABILITIES:

769. Liability for provident funds.
770. Other deferred liabilities.
    TOTAL.

UNADJUSTED CREDITS:

771. Tax liability.
772. Premium on funded debt.
773. Insurance and casualty reserves.
774. Operating reserves.
775. Accrued depreciation—Road.
776. Accrued depreciation—Equipment.
777. Accrued depreciation—Miscellaneous physical property.
778. Other unadjusted credits.
    TOTAL.

CORPORATE SURPLUS:

779. Additions to property through income and surplus.
780. Funded debt retired through income and surplus.
781. Sinking fund reserves.
782. Miscellaneous fund reserves.
783. Appropriated surplus not specifically invested.
    TOTAL APPROPRIATED SURPLUS.
784. Profit and loss—Balance.
    TOTAL CORPORATE SURPLUS.

FORM 14

FORM OF BALANCE SHEET RECOMMENDED BY R. H. MONTGOMERY*

Assets			
Current Assets:			
Cash	$1,000		
Notes and accounts receivable	2,000		
Inventories	3,000		
Prepaid insurance, etc.	4,000	$10,000	
Deferred Charges:			
Bond discount, etc.	$5,000	5,000	
Plant Assets:			
Real estate	6,000		
Machinery, fixtures, etc.	7,000	13,000	
Goodwill, patents, etc.		14,000	$42,000
Liabilities			
Notes payable	$1,000		
Accounts payable	2,000		
Accrued wages	3,000		
Reserves (not deductible from assets)	4,000	$10,000	
Bonded debt		5,000	$15,000
Excess of Assets (or Net Worth)			
Capital stock		$16,000	
Surplus (or deficit)		11,000	$27,000

* *Auditing, Theory and Practice,* 3d ed., II, pp. 367-8. The *pro forma* figures, here introduced, are not in the original.

FORM 15

BALANCE SHEET PRESCRIBED IN TABLE A, COMPANIES ACT, 1862

Balance Sheet of the Co., Made Up to 19——

Capital and Liabilities		£. s. d.	Property and Assets		£. s. d.
I. Capital	Showing: 1. The number of shares. 2. The amount paid per share. 3. If any arrears of calls, the nature of the arrear, and the names of the defaulters. 4. The particulars of any forfeited shares.		III. Property held by the company	Showing: 7. Immovable property, distinguishing: (*a*) freehold land; (*b*) freehold buildings; (*c*) leasehold buildings. 8. Movable property, distinguishing: (*d*) stock in trade; (*e*) plant. The cost to be stated with deductions for deterioration in value as charged to the reserve fund or profit and loss.	
II. Debts and Liabilities of the company	Showing: 5. The amount of loans on mortgages or debenture bonds. 6. The amount of debts owing by the company, distinguishing— (*a*) Debts for which acceptances have been given; (*b*) debts to tradesmen for supplies of stock in trade or other articles; (*c*) debts for law expenses; (*d*) debts for interest on debentures or other loans; (*c*) unclaimed dividends; (*f*) debts not enumerated above.		IV. Debts owing to the company	Showing: 9. Debts considered good for which the company hold bills or other securities. 10. Debts considered good for which the company hold no security. 11. Debts considered doubtful and bad. Any debt due from a director or other officer of the company to be separately stated.	
VI. Reserve Fund	Showing: The amount set aside from profits to meet contingencies.		V. Cash and Investments	Showing: 12. The nature of investment and rate of interest. 13. The amount of cash, where lodged, and if bearing interest.	
VII. Profit and Loss	Showing: The disposable balance for payment of dividend, etc.				

Contingent Liabilities	Claims against the company not acknowledged as debts. Moneys for which the company is contingently liable.

Attention is called to the following points in the several balance sheets printed above:

FORM 1. *American Agricultural Chemical Company.*—Current assets placed first. Marketable securities and inventories both included in current assets. Deductions for bad debts and for depreciation both shown as subtractions. Current prepaid expenses included among deferred charges. Goodwill included among capital assets. Deficit shown on asset side of balance sheet rather than as subtraction from proprietorship. Deferred credits treated as a liability, but without explanation. Unissued stock shown as subtraction in short column.

FORM 2. *Bethlehem Steel Corporation.*—Deferred charges to operations as a separate item. Stock held by corporation deducted in short column. Funded debt included in total with capital stock.

FORM 3. *General Motors Corporation.*—Assets divided into only two groups. Distinction made between prepaid expenses (current and working assets) and deferred expenses (fixed assets). A threefold division on the credit side of the balance sheet; that is, liabilities, reserves, and capital stock and surplus. Reserves includes valuation accounts (depreciation), true surplus (Reserve for Completion of Office Building), and an item which may be a liability (Reserve for Bonus to Employees). Capital includes no-par stock, which is listed at the nominal value of $10 per share. Surplus over and above this amount shown as separate item without indication as to how much of this surplus represents earnings and how much contributed surplus.

FORM 4. *J. I. Case Threshing Machine Company.*—Investment in affiliated company and real estate acquired by foreclosure included among current assets.

FORM 5. *Pacific Gas and Electric Company.*—Discount and expenses on capital stock issued shown as a separate item among the assets. Reserve for Bad Debts shown as subtraction, but Reserve for Depreciation grouped with other reserves.

FORM 6. *Packard Motor Car Company.*—Exhibit of property account showing recent additions as well as depreciation. Rights, privileges, franchises, and inventions included in Property Investment, but at nominal figure of $1.00. Property listed at depreciated value but without indication as to the amount allowed. The balance sheet includes brief summary of profit and loss statement, in that it shows balance of surplus at beginning of the fiscal period, profits added during the period, and reductions because of dividends.

FORM 7. *Sears, Roebuck, and Company.*—Arranged in report form. List of assets begins with fixed assets, in which Goodwill, Patents, etc., are included. Liabilities precede proprietorship items, all of which are included in a single sum. Stock held in treasury shown as subtraction from total authorized.

FORM 8. *Union Oil Company of California.*—Depletion as well as depreciation subtracted from book value of property. Investment in control of affiliated companies shown in separate group, investments, but marketable securities included in current assets. Reserve for Bad Debts subtracted from receivables, but without any indication of the amount so subtracted. Surplus account includes abstract of Profit and Loss. The property marked up above its cost to correspond with appraisal as of March 1, 1913, but this increase shown as an addition to Surplus. Unissued Stock shown as subtraction from authorized.

FORM 9. *United States Steel Corporation.*—This balance sheet is noticeable because of the large number of subdivisions on both sides of the balance sheet. Other features are the treatment of deferred charges, of sinking and reserve fund assets including redeemed bonds, the listing of the outstanding stock of subsidiary companies at its book value, the grouping together in a single total of capital stock and liabilities, with the peculiar definition of the terms there used, and the showing of Appropriated Surplus as a separate item.

FORM 10. *Willys-Overland Company.*—Both assets and liabilities list current items first. Goodwill not grouped with permanent assets but listed separately and reduced through reserves to $1.00. Deferred liabilities signifying a purchase contract. The use of the title Allowance for Depreciation instead of Reserve for Depreciation. Allowance for Doubtful Debts and for Depreciation, and for losses on permanent assets subtracted in the balance sheet, but Reserve for Inventory Shrinkage shown on the opposite side. Unissued and Treasury Stock shown as subtraction from the amount authorized. Deficit shown as subtraction from outstanding common stock. Dividends on cumulative preferred stock, which have not been paid, and contingent liabilities as endorsers shown in note.

FORM 11. *H. C. Bentley.*—A highly differentiated form, with admirable arrangement of items. The clear showing of total liabilities and total proprietorship is to be commended.

FORM 12. *Federal Reserve Board.*—Many subdivisions in both assets and liabilities. Classification of receivables and payables in accordance with the nature of loan, maturity of loan, and to whom payable. Allowances for Bad Debts, Depreciation, etc., subtracted from the asset. Use of the term quick assets as a subdivision of current assets. Deferred charges includes prepaid expenses. Rediscounted notes shown both as asset and liability. Book value of Goodwill subtracted from net worth, Deficits subtracted from net worth. Total liabilities shown.

FORM 13. *Interstate Commerce Commission.*—The division of assets into four classes with peculiar use of the terms deferred assets and unadjusted debits. Investments in marketable securities listed with fixed rather than with current assets. Governmental Grants, a peculiar item, analogous to capital but with some of the characteristics of surplus. Securities of the company held in the treasury shown as a subtraction. The peculiar use of terms deferred liabilities and unadjusted credits. Allowance for depreciation listed under unadjusted credits, although in actual balance sheets ordinarily shown as a subtraction from the investment in road and equipment.

FORM 14. *R. H. Montgomery's Ideal Form.*—The list of assets begins with current assets. Deferred charges placed between current and plant assets, and differentiated from prepaid expenses included among current assets. Goodwill shown as separate item.

FORM 15. *Prescribed in Table A, Companies Act, 1862.*—This form has doubtless had a great effect on English practice as its use was for many years obligatory for all companies which did not specifically adopt other articles. Under the modification of Table A made in 1906 the use of this particular form is, however, no longer prescribed. The British custom of placing the assets on the right-hand side has been due largely to this form. Other points of interest are: the minute details regarding the issue and payment of shares, the addition of contingent liabilities as a supplement to the balance sheet proper, and the classification of items in seven heads.

BIBLIOGRAPHICAL NOTE

CHARPENTIER, J.—*Étude juridique sur le bilan dans les sociétés par actions* (Paris, 1906). A good presentation of French law and custom, containing also a bibliography.

COLE, W. M.—*Accounts, Their Construction and Interpretation* (Revised ed., Boston, 1915), chap. ix.

COUCHMAN, C. B.—*The Balance Sheet* (New York, 1924). The latest and most satisfactory treatise.

DICKINSON, A. L.—*Accounting Practice and Procedure* (New York, 1914), chap. ii.

DICKSEE, L. R.—*Auditing* (13th ed., London, 1924), chap. vii.

ESQUERRÉ, P.-J.—*Applied Theory of Accounts* (New York, 1915), chaps. xxxv, xxxvi.

KESTER, R. B.—*Accounting, Theory and Practice* (2d ed., New York, 1922), II, chap. iv.

MCKINSEY, J. O.—*Managerial Accounting* (Chicago, 1924), chap. ix.

MONTGOMERY, R. H.—*Auditing, Theory and Practice* (3d ed., New York, 1922), I, chap. xix.

PATON, W. A.—*Accounting* (New York, 1924), chap. xxiii.

PIXLEY, F. W.—*Auditors, Their Duties and Responsibilities* (11th ed., London, 1918), chaps. xi, xii.

SIMON, H. V.—*Die Bilanzen der Aktiengellschaften* (3te Auflage, Berlin, 1899). While dealing with German law the discussion of theoretical matters is of general interest.

SPRAGUE, C. E.—*The Philosophy of Accounts* (5th ed., New York, 1922), chap. v.

Tovey, P.—*Balance Sheets, How to Read and Understand Them; a Guide for Investors, Business Men, Commercial Students, etc.* (London, 1921).

United States Federal Reserve Board—*Approved Methods for the Preparation of Balance Sheet Statements* (Washington, 1918).

An interesting collection of various forms of balance sheets with critical comments is found in *Encyclopædia of Accounting*, VIII, pp. 249-326.

CHAPTER II

ASSETS AND THEIR VALUATION

Separation of Assets from Other Debits

A trial balance of a ledger shows a list of debit items whose sum equals that of a similar list of credit items. The sum shown as the total of the debit items is meaningless, for it is a sum of altogether dissimilar items. Some of the items such as cash and accounts receivable represent assets, but others, such as wages and interest expense, are charges against current earnings and to that extent represent not an asset but a reduction of proprietorship. Still other items, although these are relatively few in number, represent valuation or offset accounts, which are neither assets nor expenses but merely a technical correction of some figure appearing among the credits.

In the process of closing the ledger which leads up to the preparation of a formal balance sheet, an attempt is made to separate the assets from the items which represent reductions of proprietorship. The latter are ordinarily carried to the Income or Profit and Loss account and unless there remains a net deficit, will no longer appear as debit balances in the ledger. After the ledger has been closed, the accounts showing debit balances, with few exceptions, are assets, and as such will appear in the balance sheet.

Not all published balance sheets, however, are in an ideal form. In many of them, items are listed along with the assets which should either appear as subtractions on the other side of the balance sheet or should not appear in the balance sheet at all, having been eliminated by charging to Income. Such a practice is extremely misleading and causes many of the misunderstandings of corporation accounts. This is particularly true where the item included in the list of assets bears a title which does not clearly indicate its nature. If an item entitled Operating Deficit or Loss from Fire, instead of being subtracted from Capital appears on the left-hand side of the balance sheet, it is somewhat confusing, but not necessarily misleading. It is so obvious that a deficit cannot be an asset that one who reads anything more than the footing of the column at once sees that this sum is not represented, to its full amount, by assets. But oftentimes items which really represent an impairment of the proprietor's capital are carried in the balance sheet with some colorless or misleading title and a gross misconception of the actual status of the concern is the result. Thus, a manufacturing concern carried on its balance sheet the following items: Moving account, Fair Machines account, Material and Labor Expended on Self-binder; and another carried as an asset the expenses of an exhibit at a world's fair. If these had been actual assets, as some of them might well have been, so far as the title indicates, the footing of the left-hand column correctly represented the gross assets with which the concern secured its creditors and indemnified its stockholders. But in both of these instances, the court decided that the items represented expenses and not assets and the confusion amounted to a positive fraud on the creditors.[1]

To one interpreting a balance sheet, or to one charged with the duty of preparing it, the first task is to distinguish properly between assets on the one hand, and the other debit items which appear in the ledger, and which if not correctly treated will appear on the debit side of the balance sheet in the goodly company of the assets. The better rule is to eliminate such altogether from the asset side of the balance sheet, but where for some reason this is not done, it is indispensable that they be so labeled and distinguished that there may be no uncertainty as to their real nature.

The difficulty in making proper discrimination is greater because the ledger itself, of which the balance sheet is an

---

[1] Hubbard *v.* Weare, 44 N. W. 915 (Ia. 1890); Davenport *v.* Lines, 44 Atl. 17 (Conn. 1899).

abstract and epitome, does not immediately serve as a guide. The original transaction was a payment of cash for services rendered or material supplied. Cash being diminished, the Cash account was properly credited and some other special account, Fair Machines, in the instance cited, was debited. But exactly the same booking might legitimately be made whether the payment was a loss transaction, or an exchange; whether the amount standing to the debit of Fair Machines represents an expense or an asset. Nor can the proper determination be based on the crude fact of whether or not there was an actual purchase of some commodity. For convenience in accounting it is customary to treat some purchases, such as stationery, railroad ties, or tools to replace those worn out, as an immediate expense; and on the other hand certain payments, *e.g.*, attorneys' fees and interest, for which nothing tangible is received in return, are at times legitimately treated as representing the cost price of some tangible or intangible asset. Whether a given payment is an expense or whether it is the means of securing an equivalent asset is a fundamental problem, but one sometimes difficult of determination. In either case it first appears upon the books as a debit entry in some account, and may, therefore, ultimately be found among the items which appear on the debit side of the balance sheet. Confusion may result either from purposeful deception, or from the misunderstanding of ambiguous or doubtful titles.

Capital Expenditures and Charges against Revenue

The difficulty of distinguishing between these two classes of transactions has been made prominent in railway accounting. To use the technical terms, it is an ever-recurring problem whether a given expenditure is a charge against revenue or a capital expenditure, whether it is an operating expense or an increase in the cost of road and equipment. If the former it reduces net profits, if a capital expenditure the account representing the cost of the road is debited and the equivalent of the money expended is therefore carried among the assets in the balance sheet.

Three Criteria for Capital Expenditures

No less than three theories exist as to the criterion for the proper division of expenditures between capital expenditures and charges against revenue.

1. The most commonly accepted is that in so far as the transaction results in an addition of substantial and permanent character which increases the value of the plant such increase should be shown as an asset.[2] Or as it is clearly expressed in Hubbard *v.* Weare:

> Money paid out is not on hand, and should not be reckoned as an asset. If paid for property, that is on hand, the property is an asset. If expended in a way that has enhanced the value of the general assets it is included in its valuation. If so expended as to have brought no property, and no enhancement of that on hand then it is a loss, and should not be counted as an asset. (44 N. W. 918.)

2. Another view, extreme in its conservatism, is held by many accountants, and is well expressed, for instance, by T. F. Woodlock:

> An addition which does not increase revenue or diminish expenditure is not a proper capital charge according to the best modern practice in railroads. That which simply tends to *hold* business and not to *increase* business is a proper charge against *operating expenses.*[3]

3. At the other extreme is the view, presented in the decision by Lord Kyllachy in Cox *v.* Edinburgh and District Tramways Company, Limited (6 S. L. T. 63 [1898]) that where an improvement is made in the plant, even though it be in the nature of the substitution of new plant for old, the entire cost of the new plant, and not merely the excess in value of the new over the old may be considered a capital expenditure.

Of these three views the first is not only the most generally accepted but seems to comport best with accounting principles.

---

[2] Mackintosh *v.* Flint & Pere Marquette Ry., 34 Fed. 609 (1888).

[3] *Engineering Magazine,* XI, p. 241. See also, T. L. Greene in *Accountant,* XXXIII, p. 287.

It has furthermore been authoritatively adopted for railway accounting by the Interstate Commerce Commission.[4] The second view, while praised for its conservatism, seems to imply that there must be a constant rate of normal interest or profits, a condition denied by economic history. If a general decline in profits occurs, an improvement which, in a given enterprise, prevents the fall and maintains the old rate of profits is clearly a source of additional value, and would be capitalized in determining its market value.

This may be illustrated by assuming an investment of $100,000 made at a time when 6 per cent was the normal rate of return. If later the normal rate of return fell to 5 per cent the investment would still be worth $100,000 even though it yielded only $5,000. A further expenditure which served not to increase the return above $6,000 but merely to maintain it at that figure, would be a real addition to the value of the investment. If it could be assumed that the return of $6,000 would be perpetual the capitalized value would be $120,000, due to the fact that the amount of earnings was maintained despite the fall in the normal rate of return in industry as a whole.

The third view is rarely justified by accountants.[5] In some cases, however, there may be some logical ground for such a procedure. If one is to construct a concrete building, it is necessary first to erect a complete set of molds into which the concrete is to be poured. This is in a way equivalent to erecting an entire wooden structure which is displaced as soon as the concrete building is formed. No one would deny, however, that the cost of erecting the wooden molds and the cost of tearing them down, should both be represented in the cost value of the completed concrete building. It may be argued in the case of the tramway that a condition precedent to the final construction of the electric road was the construction of a line for horse cars. It was impossible to construct the electric road at first, both because of the undeveloped state of

---

[4] *Classification of Investment in Road and Equipment of Steam Roads, 1914*, p. 10.

[5] *Cf.* Adams, *American Railway Accounting*, pp. 80-1.

electrical invention and also because the city was not sufficiently developed to justify the more expensive construction. The argument would, therefore, be that the first construction was in a way a preliminary to the final erection of the electrical plant and that there is an analogy to the preliminary erection of the wooden framework. The application of this theory is, however, difficult and is likely to lead to entirely unwarranted overvaluation of assets. Recognizing that in certain cases, it may be justified, it should always be looked at askance and in general condemned.[6]

Problems of the Inventory

Assuming (*a*) that it has been possible to differentiate all expense items and (*b*) that all expense accounts have been closed into Profit and Loss, and further (*c*) that all valuation accounts are deducted from the appropriate account, the balance sheet, in its best form, contains on the debit side a list of all the assets belonging to the concern and nothing else. In other words it is a complete inventory, and in its preparation enter all the problems connected with taking an inventory of goods on hand.

The problems of the inventory are three: (1) What items are to be included in it? (2) What expenditures are to be considered as entering into their cost price? (3) In subsequent revaluations are the assets to be continued at the original valuation or are their values to be estimated on some new basis?

These three problems are not entirely distinct. They may all be implied in the last one, that of the current revaluation of assets; for it matters little whether an object, say a worn-out machine, be excluded from the list of assets or be valued at zero; it matters not what was the original value of an asset if at each new inventory it must be independently revalued. But in practical accounting the questions are likely to arise somewhat in the form and order given above.

---

[6] For discussion of this problem as it relates to depreciation see below, p. 167.

1. *Items to Be Included in the Inventory*

The underlying principle is that all valuable goods are to be included. Goods is here used in the proper most inclusive sense of all desirable things and does not in any sense imply a discrediting of immaterial or intangible property. Whether the property be material, consisting of land, or permanent plant, or of merchandise; whether it be less tangible credits such as securities, customers' notes, or merely non-negotiable book accounts; or whether it be that most elusive form of property, goodwill—in any event, all goods are alike to be included in the inventory.

There is, nevertheless, a well-founded prejudice against goodwill, as an item in the balance sheet, based upon the fact that in many cases the value placed upon it is wildly extravagant and incorrect. Thus Bell says: "A goodwill account is usually regarded with more or less suspicion,"[7] and Pixley, whose opinion is always worthy of respect, states: "Goodwill is always a blot on the balance sheet."[8] The same attitude is emphasized in the form of balance sheet recommended by the Federal Reserve Board where goodwill is shown as a subtraction from proprietorship, while if it be an asset at all it must be a representative of proprietorship rather than an offset to it. But the objection is not to the inclusion of goodwill, but to its overvaluation. To include among the assets a nonexisting building is as objectionable as to include nonexisting goodwill; to overstate the value of cash on hand is even more heinous than to overstate the value of goodwill.

While goodwill and the allied immaterial goods such as patent rights, and trade names are forms of property to which legal rights adhere, it may even be correct to include among assets items representing the cost of some good to one who has no real property right therein. For instance, additions and betterments to leased property, the expenses incurred by a railroad company to improve a street giving access to its station, or the contribution which it has made to the cost of a

---

[7] *Accounting*, p. 325.
[8] *Accountancy*, p. 242.

tunnel are cited as items which may legitimately be reckoned among the assets of a company although it has acquired no legal property.

2. *What Is Cost Price?*

At the time of acquiring an asset it is an almost, but not quite, unbroken rule to list it at the cost price. But this clearly rests upon an assumption and is not an expression of a fundamental principle. It obviously does not apply where the asset is found or received as a gift. The marked preference for entering acquired assets at cost is by some thought to rest upon a desire to show the sacrifice involved in acquiring the asset; by some it is supposed to be an expression of a dislike to show "unrealized" profit; by some it is exalted into a "principle of accounting" to the effect that there can be no gain nor loss on a purchase—an assumption clearly contrary to fact and hence at best a poor kind of principle.

Probably the soundest explanation is that, of many possible values, cost is in most cases the easiest of objective verification.[9] The handling of cash is, more than anything else in business, carefully safeguarded. Its outgoings are meticulously recorded, and the vouchers therefor diligently safeguarded. There is less guesswork about the cost of an asset than about almost any other feature of accounting. Its certainty, rather than its exactness as a measure of value, has led to the rule of generally entering a newly acquired asset at its cost, rather than at its supposed value.

Organization Expenses.—Even the matter of cost, however, is not always free from uncertainty, and it is, at times, not easy to determine just which expenditures entered into the cost of a particular asset. This may be illustrated by the case of a railroad whose principal asset is its roadway. The cost of the right of way, the purchase price of rails and ties, the salaries of superintendents, and the wages of laborers, are all clearly part of the cost of acquiring the road and are to be

[9] See Couchman, *The Balance Sheet*, p. 45. But this is not always so. It is not true in the case of stock-exchange securities.

charged to Investment in Road and Equipment. But a more debatable question arises concerning payments not made in the form of a direct purchase of property or payment for productive labor but which may perhaps be construed as the cost price of acquiring the property. In this class come what are known as organization expenses. For instance, a corporation is started with $100,000 capital, all of which is paid in cash. In the process of organizing the corporation, expenses must be incurred for stationery and printing, for engraving certificates of stock, for fees paid to the state, and to attorneys. These may amount, say, to $2,500. Is this sum merely an expense, or does it represent part of the cost? If an expense, the corporation is in the position of having encroached on its capital, for with a capital stock of $100,000 it has no assets whatever except cash, and of that it has only $97,500.

From the foregoing it is seen that it is by no means easy to lay down a rule by which to determine whether certain charges are to be treated as expense or whether they are to be held in the balance sheet as representing the cost of assets. From a purely theoretical viewpoint it seems that any expenses necessarily involved in organizing a going concern are properly assets of that concern, as much as are the real estate, the machinery, or the stock in trade. To the stockholder or proprietor it is part of the investment from which profit is to come and is hence capital expenditure. Being necessary to the establishment of such a concern rivals cannot spring up, unless they too provide capital for such a payment, and actuarially figured a concern fully established is worth to new operators a premium equal to the cost of organization. Furthermore, as was most clearly brought out by Justice North in Abstainers and General Insurance Company ([1891] 2 Ch. 125), any other treatment of such payments would have the result, already alluded to, of making necessary an initial inroad into capital except where a company started with a nominal surplus.

The effect is similar whether the payment of organization and other similar expenses is charged directly to the Property account or is carried along as an independent item. The significant fact is that both in theory and practice the sums so paid are held to represent assets. Whether it is better to show them in increased cost of plant or as an independent item is debatable. German legislation allows only the former, the idea being that it is dangerous to allow the appearance of "fictitious" accounts among the assets. It also attempts to discriminate between the preliminary costs of construction which are to be charged to the plant, and the costs of organizing the corporation itself, which are not to be counted as an asset at all. In order to provide for these latter it is customary in Germany to issue the original capital at a premium sufficient to cover the preliminary expenses. But in America the preferred practice seems rather to favor listing organization expenses and similar charges as separate items, for attention is thus called to their intangible character.[10] This custom also furthers the conservative practice of annually charging off a considerable portion of such items, so that in a few years they disappear from the assets altogether. The Interstate Commerce Commission, however, provides that organization expenses shall be charged to the Construction or Equipment account.[11]

Interest during Construction.—Interest charges are normally an unquestioned charge against revenue, but even interest may at times be construed as capital expenditure. Thus a railroad borrows money with which to construct the road, an undertaking which will require several years. During the period of construction interest must be paid while no revenue is accruing. It is not unreasonable to say that the asset which the company is acquiring is a finished road ready for operation. To secure such a plant there must be paid not merely the cost of material and equipment, the salary of engineers and the wages of laborers, but equally essential is the payment of interest to the bondholders. Without this latter payment the finished road could not be acquired. To include it among

[10] *Cf.* Paton, *Accounting Theory,* p. 337. Kester, *Accounting,* 2d ed., II, p. 365.

[11] *Classification of Investment in Road and Equipment,* Primary Account 71.

the costs of construction is, therefore, not illogical, and the custom of so doing is gaining increasing sanction. It is approved by almost all accountants, so far, as the amount actually paid on borrowed funds, in contradistinction to estimated interest on the entire cost. In valuation cases, however, interest during the construction period on the entire investment, including the contribution of stockholders as well as borrowed funds, is generally admitted as an element of cost [12] and is authoritatively provided by the Interstate Commerce Commission.[13] Great Britain provides that dividends in lieu of interest may with certain restriction be paid during construction, and that such payments as well as interest on borrowed funds are to be charged to the cost of constructing the plant.[14] Where this is done, it permits the stockholder in a public utility, as is shown in the keen analysis by J. H. Bickley, to receive double return; "He enjoys his return before operations; and after operations are commenced and profits realized, he receives a return on this return. This happens because interest paid during construction is added to the fixed capital on which the utility is permitted to earn a certain sum." [15]

The accepted custom of treating as a capital expenditure only so much of the interest as was actually paid on borrowed funds is supported by curiously illogical arguments. By many writers it is justified as representing the value of the completed structure, as a price which would have to be paid to a contractor. But this would compel an addition of estimated interest upon the entire cost, and not merely of interest actually paid on so much of the cost as is represented by borrowed funds. The other argument adduced is that it is necessary to add interest paid during construction in order to

---

[12] Whitten, *Valuation of Public Service Corporations*, sec. 291. An adverse opinion by an eminent accountant is found in the testimony of Sir William Barclay Peat in the National Telephone Co. case. See *Accountant*, XLVIII, p. 351, and discussion *ibid.*, p. 105.

[13] *Classification of Investment in Road and Equipment of Steam Roads*, p. 38.

[14] Companies (Consolidation) Act, 1908, sec. 91.

[15] "Interest During Construction," *Journal of Land and Public Utility Economics*, I, p. 417.

avoid showing initial loss,[16] but this is begging the question as to whether there may not be an initial loss, as to whether an initial loss should or should not be shown, and as to whether there is an increase in the value of the property at all parallel with the payment of interest.

There is disagreement as to the proper account to be credited when imputed interest upon the corporation's own funds during the period of construction is considered part of the cost of construction. According to the rules of the Interstate Commerce Commission the accompanying credit is to account 515, Income from Unfunded Securities and Accounts. This includes such imputed interest in the ordinary net income of the year.[17] Montgomery, however, objects to such an item being included in the current income and states that it should be credited to Surplus.[18]

The taxes accruing upon property during the course of construction is analogous to interest. It is considered proper to include them in the cost of the property.

Discount on Bonds.—It formerly was the custom of American railroads to charge discount on bonds issued to cost of construction, and there are, even now, some who justify this procedure on the ground that discount represents a cost of procuring funds and hence of securing the plant. But so far as the bonds run longer than the period of construction, the justification of such a practice rests on an illogical distinction between discount paid in advance and current interest installments. As is shown in the chapter on liabilities, discount on bonds is prepaid interest for the entire life of the loan, and it is only interest during construction, not for the later period that can legitimately be construed as part of the cost of construction. Somewhat similarly American railroads, and to some extent other corporations, have at times charged discount upon stock as a part of the cost of construction on securing the plant. There is even less justification for this than for including the discount on bonds, for the discount

---

[16] Couchman, *The Balance Sheet*, p. 145.
[17] See *Accounting Bulletin 15*, Case 177.
[18] *Auditing, Theory and Practice*, 3d ed., I, p. 589.

on bonds represents a payment which in time will have to be made, but the discount on stock is merely a subtraction from the purely nominal figure of the par value. The Interstate Commerce Commission has ruled that discount on securities is not properly included in the cost of property.[19]

Expenses of Securing Funds.—By some accountants, the expenses incurred in securing the initial capital are considered as entering into the cost of the completed plant. This would include such items as fees connected with executing the mortgage, cost of engraving and printing, commissions paid for services in marketing securities, and similar items. These were allowed in the English telephone case.[20] But the Interstate Commerce Commission treats these items the same as discount, debiting them to a separate ledger account which is to be amortized during the life of the securities.

Cost of Experiments.—A similar problem arises in connection with the expenses incurred in making experiments in search of new inventions, now a recognized part of many industrial plants. This may be treated as a part of general expense but there is colorable argument on the other side. An improvement might be secured by purchasing a patent right from an outside inventor. The alternative plan is to hire the inventor to work for the company, in which case the salary and other expenses incurred seem to be the cost of the secured invention just as truly as the price paid for the patent right. If this is so, may not expenses be counted as part of the prospective cost even though the goal has not been quite reached?

The difficulty is that while the experiments are still being carried on it is impossible to determine whether the expenditure will fructify into a valuable asset or whether, being unsuccessful, it represents merely an unproductive expense.

---

[19] *Classification of Income, Profit and Loss and General Balance Sheet Accounts for Steam Roads,* Issue of 1914, pp. 39-40. But it should be noted that such portion of the discount on bonds as may properly be apportioned to the period of construction may, as representing interest during construction, be charged to the cost of the road. See Primary Account 76.

[20] See editorial discussion in *Accountant,* XLVIII, p. 108.

There is also a difficulty in determining whether the successful invention is to be charged with the expenses of previous unsuccessful experiments, or only of those leading directly to the valuable discovery. With so many uncertainties involved, accountants are generally inclined toward a conservative policy, preferring an understatement to an overstatement of the value of assets. The legitimacy of including as an asset the expenses of experimentation which have already resulted in securing a more valuable process, is established in Lincoln Chemical Company *v.* Edwards (272 Fed. 145 [1921]).

Property Purchased with Stock.—In the problems thus far discussed the question has been whether a payment of a definite sum should be considered the cost of an equivalent asset, or merely the payment of an expense. Another problem arises in connection with the purchase of property with stock instead of with cash. Here the difficulty turns not on whether an asset has been acquired, but on the uncertain value of that which has been given in exchange therefor. In actual practice it is all too customary to treat the cost of such property as being equal to the par of the stock issued therefor. Even accountants of the highest standing justify such a procedure. Evidently this is but one aspect of the much-debated question of stock watering. To assume that the value of the property acquired equals the face of the stock issued is to assume that stock never is, and never can be issued in excess; that there can be no stock watering. It argues in a vicious circle, for it makes the value of the property dependent upon the amount of stock issued, while capital is to the accountant properly an expression of the value of the net assets owned—a sum representing the net wealth of the proprietary interests. If carried to the logical extreme, this principle would require that where stock is sold at a discount the cash received should be treated as equal to the full face value of the stock, though it is in fact only a fraction of that sum.

It is true that there are difficulties in determining the real value of the property purchased with stock, and statutes and courts have doubtless been wise in refusing to interfere with valuations placed upon property, except where there has clearly been fraud as well as overvaluation. But there has been a marked improvement along this line in the last fifteen years. The action of the Interstate Commerce Commission has been wholesome and influential; this has been followed by most of the state commissions dealing with public utilities; and the various blue-sky laws have in general tended toward the correct principles of valuation. Accountants, in practice, have not rigorously insisted upon the same correct principles in the published accounts of private corporations, but progress along even this line, if not startling, is at least encouraging. The subject is discussed more fully in Chapter VIII.

3. *Basis for Revaluation*

Having accepted the principle that the original valuation of assets is normally their cost price, and having noticed the practical and theoretical difficulty in determining the exact cost price, there remains the more important question as to subsequent revaluations of assets.

There are many values, which might be attached to assets. Shall the accountant base revaluation on (1) the original cost, modified by such factors as depletion and depreciation; (2) on the estimated present cost of acquiring a similar asset (reproduction cost); or (3) on what the asset might be expected to bring if thrown upon the market in the process of liquidation? [21]

---

[21] The extent to which accountants disagree on this point is illustrated by the following quotations: An editorial in the *Journal of Accountancy*, XXXII, p. 50, says: "Logically considered books of account should be kept so as to reflect cost and not value and this is the theory at the basis of accounting structure." Esquerré agrees that the inventory should be valued at cost (*Applied Theory of Accounts*, p. 171), but Montgomery commenting on this says that it is "inaccurate and its application leads to self-deception and the deception of others," and states that the balance sheet should always reflect value rather than cost. He also criticizes the rule of cost or market whichever is lower as injecting "into the balance sheet a false and misleading element and losing much if not all of the virtue of conservatism." (*Auditing, Theory and Practice*, 3d ed., I, pp. 145-6, 126.) But in his *Auditing Principles* it is stated that "cost or market whichever is lower" is still the basic principle and he adds, "The departures observed in published balance sheets during the post-war period of deflation from the principle of cost or market, whichever is lower, do not seem to have been the results of conviction as to any unsoundness of the principle but appear rather to have been

The first method implies, to some extent, the conception of the balance sheet as a history of what has taken place. It would present a statement more nearly accurate, so far as its purposes are concerned than either of the other two. For cost is a recorded fact, capable of verification, objectively established, while present cost and liquidation value are often matters of estimate. The replacement value, if more of an estimate, does in a way present a more significant picture, at least to the owners of the business. Cost has little to do with present conditions. The present, and still more the future, is what really interests the investor; the past is dead, and the investment made therein is, in ordinary competitive enterprises, of little effect in determining present values or future earnings. The liquidation value is of significance to the creditor. He makes a loan looking to the assets as security. Hence there is some tendency, noticeable though not dominant, to insist that assets should be revalued at what they would bring. It is the attitude which "clearly realizes the possibility of forced sales with the factory door closed."[22]

Value to the Going Concern

It is unfortunate that here, as elsewhere in accounting matters, it is difficult, if not impossible, to find any guiding rule, imperative in its authority, universal in its acceptance. Perhaps the nearest approach to such a general rule is that "everything in accounting is based upon the assumption that the undertaking is a going concern."[23] This rule, or assumption, even though it may at times be difficult of application, has a wide significance. It is of service in deciding how to treat certain expenditures, such as organization

---

due to motives of expediency" (p. 153). Kester states in one place that inventory should be valued at cost or market, whichever is lower, but on a subsequent page of the same book states that from every viewpoint the most desirable practice is to value the inventory at cost with supplementary information as to market value. In a later edition of the same work he states that valuation based on selling price is theoretically the proper basis (*Cf.* his *Accounting, Theory and Practice,* II, 1st ed., pp. 226 and 229, 2d ed., p. 156).

[22] Arnold, *The Complete Cost-Keeper,* p. 358.

[23] Dicksee and Tillyard, *Goodwill and Its Treatment in Accounts,* p. 78.

expenses; it gives some indication as to the basis for discriminating between various kinds of assets; it helps materially in selecting a somewhat general principle for valuation of assets.

The proper value of assets is that which they have to the holding concern, and not that which they might have to other persons, whether these persons are ordinary customers, or those who might bid in the assets at a liquidation sale. The value is that which they have to the company as then existing and not to a company in the hands of a receiver, or one closing up its accounts and going out of business. It is true that in the case of a corporation this represents the interests of the stockholders rather than those of the creditors. Yet it is little exaggeration to say that if all assets were listed at the value which they would realize at forced liquidation, no balance sheet would show solvency. Valuation on such a basis would, therefore, be absurd, and the general principle must be adopted that the basis of inventory values is the present value of the asset to the holders as a "going concern."[24] To this rule there may be exceptions or modifications, mostly introduced for the sake of preventing a self-deceiving exaggeration of values.

Fixed and Circulating Assets

The acceptance of the going-concern basis for revaluing assets leads to a differentiation between fixed and circulating or current assets. It is impossible to draw a rigid line between these two classes, but in general the differentiation is easily made. By fixed assets are meant those acquired for permanent or long continued use with the expectation that by such use revenue will be produced. The essential feature of

---

[24] This phrase, "value to the going concern," is used by accountants somewhat differently from the use of "going-concern value" as found in the discussion of the value of public utilities for rate-making purposes. In these, going-concern value represents a specific value represented by the cost to the public utility of getting its plant into full operation. It costs much for a new gas company to secure the consent of the householders to avail themselves of the new luxury. The expenses of one kind or another involved in securing this result are spoken of as the going-concern value.

current assets (other than cash) is that "the whole aim of the undertaking is to convert them into cash at the earliest possible opportunity,"[25] or they are of such a character that they may readily be converted into cash without impairing the business. There is coming to be recognized a difference in the basis of valuation of these two classes of assets, which permits much greater latitude in regard to fixed assets than is allowed concerning circulating assets. In general it is considered legitimate to continue fixed assets at their cost despite a subsequent decline in their value. But in valuing circulating assets regard must be had to current values, although there is some question as to whether the market value, even of circulating assets, can be accepted where that exceeds the original cost. This is clearly an application of the principle of the going concern. A piece of land, for instance, is purchased at a fair price for the purpose of erecting a factory. Its services are presumably perpetual and undiminishing; the value to the company was, in the first instance, represented by its full cost price; its services, and hence its value to the going concern, are the same as before. It is therefore proper to continue in the inventory the cost price of the land quite irrespective of changes in its market value whether that be greater or less than the cost. The market price, evidently, can never be realized so long as the land is still used as a factory site, the abandonment of the factory means ordinarily that the enterprise ceases to be a going concern. To be sure, the factory site might conceivably be sold and a less expensive one be bought in its stead, but this implies recognition of a double set of unrealized conditions and is too vague for embodiment in formal accounts. Changes in the market value of an absolutely fixed asset are generally ignored on the ground that such changes do not affect the value to the going concern. This is most common in the case of land used as a building site, but it is also applied to any form of fixed asset provided, of course, that allowance is made for accruing depreciation.

---

[25] Dicksee, *Auditing,* 13th ed., p. 198.

Somewhat similarly it may be argued that the going-concern value of machinery is not at all affected by changes in the market price of such machinery. It has been bought to serve as an instrument of production and its entire cost represents eventually an expense of producing the manufactured goods. Its cost and the service which it renders are not affected by later changes in the market value of similar machinery. Hence it is considered proper tò base its inventory value upon its cost, with proper allowance for the depreciation which has taken place, or as Leake expresses it, allowing for the "expired outlay."

Recognition of Changed Values of Fixed Assets

While the consensus of opinion is against recognizing changes in the value of fixed assets in the accounts, there are some few dissenting voices. The most outspoken statement is found in Paton and Stevenson, who take the ground that in all cases, the book value of all assets should be the present value, irrespective of whether this is higher or lower than the cost.[26] Dickinson, with some apparent hesitation, admits that in some cases it may be proper to show an increase in the value of fixed assets, though admitting the difficulties in carrying out such a policy.[27] In recent years, because of the provisions of the law regarding the tax on excess profits, there has been a noticeable tendency to mark up the value of the plant, to correspond to the estimated value on March 1, 1913.[28] But it remains true that accountants are, in general, strongly opposed to marking up the value of fixed assets, and do not insist that they must be marked down to correspond to current value.

Appreciation as Related to Income

The objections to marking up the value of fixed assets is, however, to a large extent, an objection to showing a profit

---

[26] *Principles of Accounting*, chap. xx. In his latest book, *Accounting*, Professor Paton, while he does not reject this view, is more guarded in his statement. See pp. 367-8.

[27] *Accounting Practice and Procedure*, pp. 81-2.

[28] See, *e. g.*, the balance sheets of General Petroleum Co., 1923, and Union Oil Co., of California, 1923.

due to such appreciation. When do profits arise? When are profits realized? When are profits available for dividends? These are all questions of infinite intricacy. The subject is discussed at some length in Chapter XII. Here it suffices to say that much of the objection to showing appreciation of fixed assets is removed if such a showing is freed from the evil ordinarily accompanying it, that is a showing of a corresponding profit. It would be little objectionable to indicate the increment in the value of land, if the balance sheet shows as the offsetting item, not Profit and Loss, nor Surplus, but a separate account distinctly labeled, say, Reserve for Appreciation in Value of Lands, or Surplus from Land Appreciation. Such treatment is found in the balance sheet of the Union Oil Company referred to above, where oil lands have been marked up with the approval of the Internal Revenue Bureau.

Price Fluctuations Ignored

A corollary of the foregoing is that mere fluctuations in the market value, even in the case of circulating assets, may be ignored. This is theoretically correct, for fluctuations so transitory as to be included within the period during which the company holds the given asset are analogous to changes in the value of a fixed asset. If raw material is bought in July and the finished goods are to be marketed during the following June, the oscillations of price within that period need have no effect on the value of the material in the manufacturer's hands. To take account of a temporary rise or fall in a December inventory in such a case would perhaps be erroneous, certainly so if it were known that the normal price would again appear before the year's end. But in practice the principle is difficult of application, because of the impossibility of determining which changes in price are mere temporary fluctuations and which are more permanent alterations in value. It is, however, of importance in application to the fluctuation in the market price of investments, although here, as is shown in Chapter III, conservative practice justifies a less logical treatment.

Depreciation Must Be Recognized

Another corollary needs mentioning. If changes in the market value of an unchanging asset need not be reckoned the converse is true. Actual changes in the use value of a fixed asset, a machine for instance, must be reckoned, even though to the eye the machine remains unchanged. In technical terms, while fluctuations in fixed assets may be ignored, depreciation must always be considered. This is true whether there is actual physical deterioration or, as in the case of a patent right or a terminable leasehold, the decline is due to the approach of the time when the present asset will cease to have value.

The three rules of appraisal of general application are, therefore: (1) The value to be taken in the inventory is not the liquidation value, but that to a going concern; (2) Changes in market value of fixed assets may be ignored; (3) Depreciation must always be taken into account.

Undervaluation of Assets

In all the foregoing discussion it has been assumed that the purpose of accounting is to present the facts fully and without reservation; but argument is sometimes made that the statement set forth in the balance sheet does not even profess to be true; indeed, that a variation from the truth, provided only that it understates the wealth of the concern, is really a merit rather than a fault. This view has formally been set forth in an English case where the court stated that "the purpose of the balance sheet is primarily to show that the financial position of the company is at least as good as there stated, not to show that it is not or may not be better." [29]

This view is frequently supported by theoretical writers and has the further sanction which comes from the precedent set by conservative corporations in all lands. Thus it has been argued that an undervaluation improves the economic position of the corporation, that it prevents the danger of fictitious dividends, and that "absolute truth in the balance

[29] Newton *v.* Birmingham Small Arms Co., [1906] 2 Ch. 378.

sheet is not only not demanded by law but is in itself undesirable." For precedents may be cited the Bank of England which omits from its statement its land and building, which are certainly worth many millions; the practice common among German companies of listing their real estate and sometimes their other fixed plant at the nominal sum of one mark; and the tendency at one time so noticeable in American railways, to mark down the valuation placed on the road whenever large earnings made that convenient.

In so far as the undervaluation of certain assets is merely an attempt to secure a more truthful conspectus of the entire situation, the action may be justified. An argument that however truthful his intentions may be, one is almost sure to overestimate the value of his own possessions, and therefore after having determined what he really thinks they are worth, his results will be more accurate if he arbitrarily writes off certain sums, is not without force. But to state that an absolute understatement is praiseworthy neglects the fact that fraud may surely be perpetrated in that manner; and while the reaction against overvaluation is but natural and in general healthful, it seems a mistake to overlook the value of accuracy and to cease to hold it up as the goal of accounting. Time was, and that not long since, when even the Supreme Court of the United States stated that there is but little danger that any board of directors will ever understate the value of the assets, thereby also underestimating the profit, the temptation being in the opposite direction.[30] But certain notorious bear operations in the stock exchanges show that the unforeseen has frequently happened, and the undervaluation of assets, with its accompanying understatement of profits and establishment of a secret reserve, if the lesser of two evils, nevertheless falls far short of the ideal standard of accounting.

---

[30] Union Pacific R. R. Co. *v.* U. S., 99 U. S. 402 (1878).

Bibliographical Note

Cole, W. M.—*Accounts, Their Construction and Interpretation* (Revised ed., New York, 1915), chap. xiii.

Couchman, C. B.—*The Balance Sheet* (New York, 1924), pp. 39-48.

Dickinson, A. L.—*Accounting Practice and Procedure* (New York, 1918), chap. v.

Herr, J. P.—"The Appreciation of Assets, When Is It Legitimate?" *Journal of Accountancy,* III, p. 1.

Kester, R. B.—*Accounting, Theory and Practice* (2d ed., New York, 1925), II, chaps. vi, viii.

Montgomery, R. H.—*Auditing, Theory and Practice* (3d ed., New York, 1922), I, chap. viii.

Paton, W. A.—*Accounting Theory* (New York, 1922), chaps. xiv, xv, xviii, xx.

Paton, W. A., and Stevenson, R. A.—*Principles of Accounting* (New York, 1918), chap. xx.

Pixley, F. W.—*Auditors, Their Duties and Responsibilities* (11th ed., London, 1918), chap. xii.

Rehm, H.—*Die Bilanzen der Aktiengesellschaften* (Munich, 1903), pp. 693-790.

Wildman, J. R.—*Principles of Accounting* (New York, 1922), chap. xii.

CHAPTER III

THE VALUATION OF PARTICULAR ASSETS

In the light of the norms laid down in the preceding chapter the problem of the proper valuation of various kinds of assets may be considered. These may conveniently be grouped into certain classes: land, buildings, machinery, investments, mercantile credits, and merchandise.

Land

Permanent Holdings Valued at Cost

What has been previously said in regard to fixed assets generally, applies preëminently to land where that is held for the uses of the company. The rule here is that land for permanent holding may be held at its cost despite a decline or rise in its market value. Legal authority for this view is given in Bolton *v.* Natal Land and Colonization Company, Limited ([1892] 2 Ch. 124) where the court held not only that a company need not bring into its accounts the increase or decrease in the value of its lands but that, at least so far as it affects the showing of profits, it is not right so to do.

Occasionally, however, a question may arise as to what is the cost of the land. Difference of opinion arises as to the treatment of legal fees connected with the examination and recording of title. Practice seems to favor adding these to the price paid in determining the cost, but the high authority of Pixley is against such a practice.[1] The arguments previously given regarding organization expenses support the current practice. The cost of options upon lands may also be considered as entering into the cost price where the land is subsequently purchased.

[1] *Duties of Auditors,* 11th ed., p. 526.

Where a purchase mortgage has been given in partial payment of land it is sometimes the custom to add interest paid on the mortgage to the value of the land; but this is unjustifiable for the interest is not a part of the cost of acquisition nor does it represent any additional value acquired, and even though it were parallel to an accretion in value (an assumption far from true), appreciation of a fixed asset is not to be booked.

Real Estate as Merchandise

Property acquired not for permanent use but for resale is analogous to merchandise bought by a trader. Where the land requires improvement—as where a large tract is purchased to be provided with sewers, streets, gas and water pipes, sidewalks, and other improvements, with the expectation of subdividing and selling it in small parcels—it is in almost the same category as raw material bought by a manufacturer to be used in producing his finished commodity. In such cases the principles applying to the valuation of merchandise and of partly finished manufactures respectively are to be applied to the valuation of the land. The expenditures actually incurred in acquiring the land, including those incident to bringing it into the desired form for sale, may properly be considered as entering into the value at any time during the process; but it is objectionable to add a sum representing an estimated appreciation. By some authorities interest actually paid on a purchase mortgage during the improvement period may be added to the value of the land, but interest at a rate which it is estimated would normally have accrued on a similar sum loaned out, may not be added. This makes the treatment of interest payments on land where the land is being worked up into a marketable commodity similar to that of interest paid during construction of a railroad. But the better practice is against such a marking up of the value of land designed for sale. That there is no absolute criterion universally adopted is shown by the fact that in Germany the laws permit interest paid to be added to the value of real estate held by a company with limited liability

(*Gesellschaft m. b. H.*) but does not allow this to be done where the owner is an ordinary corporation. (*Aktiengesellschaft.*)

Development of New Resources

Property held for exploitation of natural resources is in a somewhat similar position. Where as a result of exploration and development new or greater resources are discovered, there is an undoubted increase in the value of the land. It is accepted that the costs of such development may, without question, be added to the book value of the property [2] and it is frequently urged that the entire increase in value may properly be shown. An important, far-reaching and perhaps unfortunate English decision was rendered in regard to an unexpected deposit of rock salt which was brought to light in the course of explorations designed for another purpose. The court justified marking up the value of the property to correspond to the new value, even allowing this increase to be made the basis of dividends.[3] To show a reasonable valuation of such a treasure trove seems no more out of place than to enter in one's books the real value of a discovered hoard of coin. That this should be treated as the basis of dividends is not a necessary implication, and the discussion of the latter point is deferred to the chapter on profits.

Valuation of Parcels of Real Estate

While the improvement of a tract of land is analogous to the manufacture of commodities, the fact that the various small parcels of land differ widely in value makes the estimation of the value of the unsold portion of a tract of land a little more difficult than the appraisal of the unsold portion of the stock of identical commodities. A tract may have been purchased and divided into say one hundred lots, half of which are sold. The presumption is, however, not at all that the remaining half represents one half of the original cost.

---

[2] La Belle Union Iron Works *v.* U. S., 256 U. S. 377 (1921).
[3] Ammonia Soda Company, Ltd. *v.* Chamberlain, [1918] 1 Ch. 266.

The proper basis is to appraise the value of each separate parcel at the market price, and to assign to it, as the inventory value, that proportion of the total cost which its appraised value bears to the total appraisal. Thus, if a block of land is bought and divided into one hundred lots at a cost including improvements of $150,000 the sum of the appraised value of the one hundred lots after improvements have been completed may be $200,000, the appraised value of lot A because of its superior location, being $4,000. The value to be assigned to A in the inventory (some of the lots having been sold) is not $1,500, nor $4,000, but $\frac{4,000}{200,000} \times \$150,000$ or $3,000.

Buildings

The principle here is not different from that applicable to land although there are differences in detail. These arise from the difference in the cost of maintenance, and the certainty that in most cases even after liberal renewals the buildings will some time be worn out or antiquated. To continue the original cost it must be certain that all necessary repairs have been charged to expense. This is more difficult because during a course of years it is likely that additions and improvements, as well as normal repairs, will be made. Where an improvement, say the introduction of an electric lighting plant, or an addition to the building has been made, it is difficult to determine how much of the money thus expended is to be considered as the cost of an additional amount of building and how much is a mere repair or restoration of part of the old building. The ever difficult task of distinguishing between so-called capital expenditures and charges against revenue must be accomplished; and, after all that is done, allowance must be made for the inevitable progress toward the time when the building will no longer be serviceable for the purposes of the company.

The cost of the building may include the necessary incidental costs, including the removal of a previous building occupying the building site. In harmony with the custom in railroad accounting, some accountants include interest on borrowed money, during the period of constructing the building, as part of the cost of the building. This is true even of some who object strongly to treating interest paid as part of the cost of goods manufactured in the regular course of business.[4]

Machinery, Tools, etc.

Machinery Valued at Cost Less Depreciation

Valuation at cost price, with proper allowance for depreciation, is evidently the correct basis. But it should be borne in mind that much of the equipment of the factory is of very temporary use, and a valuation near the cost would be far from correct. Such articles as patterns, in a short time may have practically no value. Lasts in a shoe factory are a very large item and accumulate with changes in fashion at an appalling rate. Much care must be exercised if the balance sheet is to escape being overloaded with what represents a real cost but is no longer a real asset. Where the machinery used is not purchased but made within the factory itself, as is very often the case, the value is not the price which that machinery would bring in the open market but the actual manufacturing cost.

The inventory value of machinery may properly include its cost of installation in the factory.[5] This is in harmony with the general principle that the inventory has to do with the value to the going concern. When a machine which is still serviceable is discarded in order to substitute an improved model, some accountants consider that the book value of the discarded machine should be considered as an added cost of installing the new machine. This subject on which opinion is by no means unanimous is discussed below, pages 167-169.

---

[4] Montgomery, *Auditing*, 3d ed., I, p. 589.
[5] Whittaker *v.* Amwell Nat. Bank, 29 Atl. 203 (N. J. 1894).

Investments

Permanent Investments Valued on Basis of Cost

In the foregoing pages there has been only one objective criterion of value, cost price, and that is confessedly faulty for it refers to an earlier and not to the present-day valuation. But for investments that are quoted in a stock exchange there is conclusive evidence of to-day's value. The objection to making an independent valuation of one's lands or houses is that there may be an unconscious overvaluation, or that an intentional, and perhaps fraudulent, overvaluation cannot easily be detected. But where there is a definitely ascertainable market price, known to the public and fixed by outside interests, the objections just urged do not apply and it would seem that it might be safe and justifiable to ignore altogether the cost price, and alter the book value with every fluctuation in the market price.

But if the securities are real investments, and not the stock in trade of a banker, the objection at once arises that there can be no availing of the market price so long as the securities are thus held. Thus when a national bank was required to buy and hold a minimum amount of government bonds as a condition for obtaining a charter, subsequent changes in the market value of such bonds might well be ignored. To list the bonds at more or less than cost price, including commissions paid to brokers and similar expenditures, would, for the ordinary purposes of the bank, be futile. It is true that if the bank went into liquidation the variation would be realized, but to take account of that possibility is counter to the generally accepted rule that assets are to be inventoried at their value to the going concern.

The bank may furthermore buy other bonds to serve as the basis for additional circulation. These bonds may be sold, but only where the covered circulation is withdrawn. The impossibility of realizing an appreciation of these additional bonds is less absolute than in the case of the required minimum holding, but here again the principle of the going concern applies. The bank could not continue the note-issuing function and at the same time realize on the bond premium. So here too the variation in market price seems to be of little import. The same conditions exist in regard to holdings of stock acquired by a railroad to give it control in the management of another road or of some allied enterprise. The market price of this stock may vary, but such changes in value cannot be realized by the purchasing company while it still continues to exercise the function for which it acquired the stock—that is, to control the other road.

In many cases, however, there is no such indissoluble connection between holding some given security and the maintenance of the business. Securities are held not because required by some provision of law, not for the sake of controlling business nor even for the sake of income alone. It is desirable to hold some funds as an available reserve against emergencies, and a low-rate marketable security is somewhat less expensive and almost as serviceable a reserve as the bare cash. The sale of such securities at the market price would not at all interfere with the business of the concern; and the appreciation, as shown by the market price, indicates merely that the reserve to-day really contains more than the sum that was originally invested. May not the inventory here rely solely on the market quotation? Strict consistency would seem to give an affirmative answer. On the other hand, the present price is only one point in a fluctuating scale of market prices and there is no ground for assuming that it will be realized. If it has risen there is at least a possibility that it will fall. The emergency that will call for the sale of the securities is likely to be at the time of a monetary stringency and hence of low prices, so that a high valuation would be purely illusory. The attitude of statute law and of the courts on this point is that where the securities are permanent holdings, disregard of market prices is proper whether these prices are above or below cost. This is clearly set forth by the English courts in Verner *v.* The General and Commercial Investment Trust, Limited ([1894] 2 Ch. 239) where the distinction is made between securities held as investments for the sake of the income, and those carried as the stock in trade of a dealer in investments. In France, too, the Bank of France holds all government securities which were bought for permanent holding at cost price irrespective of market quotations.[6] In Germany, however, the law provides that the market price is to be taken except where it is higher than cost price, which is equivalent to saying that of the two prices, cost and quoted market price, the lower is always to be taken as the basis of the inventory. This provision of the Commercial Code leads therefore toward conservatism at the expense of logical consistency. In Austrian law the quoted market price is always to be taken whether higher or lower than the cost. The general practice of conservative American accountants, especially in banks, insurance companies, and other fiduciary institutions, is in line with German law, and favors marking down the investments when the market price is below the cost price, but opposes taking recognition, except in an explanatory footnote to the balance sheet, of the appreciation due to a rising market. Under the New York banking law, however, bonds are listed at their market value, although a change to the adoption of the cost value, properly amortized, has been strongly urged by the state superintendent of banks.[7]

Occasionally in America both practice and law, as for instance the Maine Savings Bank Law,[8] adopt an even less logical rule that securities may not be listed above par even though they cost a considerable premium, but if costing less than par they are to be listed at cost.

Amortization of Premium

In the justification of listing permanent holdings at cost it has been assumed that the lapse of time has, in itself, worked no change in the serviceability of the security. This is true only in case of permanent securities such as corporation stock

---

[6] Simon, *Die Bilanzen der Aktiengesellschaften,* p. 332.

[7] *Annual Report of the Superintendent of Banks of the State of New York,* 1907, xlvii *ff.*

[8] R. S. chap. 48, sec. 23.

in this country, or the perpetual annuities issued by some foreign governments. Time differences may be ignored also in certain bonds which while due at a definite time have so long a duration as to be practically perpetual, the bonds of the West Shore Railroad running 475 years being an illustration. But wherever an ordinary bond is bought at a premium it is to be recognized that the purpose of this premium is to make the nominal rate of interest conform to the market rate for a loan of that particular type, and is a payment in lump sum to offset the receipts from future interest payments whose rate is higher than the market rate. If the current market rate is 5 per cent, a 6 per cent bond running five years will not be worth so much as a bond bearing the same rate of interest but running twenty years. In one instance there is, in addition to the normal rate of 5 per cent, an annuity of 1 per cent running for five years, in the other case the annuity runs twenty years. To continue to list the bond in successive annual inventories at its cost price is incorrect. At the time of purchase an estimate is made of the rate which the bond nets the investor, the three factors of time, rate, and price being considered. Thus if $112.46 is paid for a $100 bond running twenty years and paying annually 6 per cent interest, it nets the investor 5 per cent. In each successive inventory the bond should be listed not at $112.46 but at the price at which the bond with its shortened duration would net 5 per cent, that is, at $112.08, $111.69, and so on until the nineteenth year when its value is $100.95. Looking at it in another way the investor pays a premium of $12.46 because he will receive, over and above the normal 5 per cent on $100, a series of twenty successive annual payments of $1.00 each. If twenty such payments are worth $12.46 it is obvious that the value of nineteen such payments must be less than $12.46. A calculation of the value of such an annuity, again assuming a normal rate of 5 per cent interest, gives a value of $12.08. Figures for the valuation of bonds of different rates and maturities are easily obtained from tables of bond values, many of which are in the market.

Formula for Bond Values

The formula by which these values are obtained is derived as follows:

Letting:

V_n = the present value of a bond running for n interest periods.

I = the amount of interest paid on each \$100 at each interest payment.

i = the rate of interest to be yielded the holder for each interest period.

It is clear that the present value of the bond is made up of a series of values composed of each coupon maturing at successive periods and of the principal, assumed to be \$100, due at the end of the n periods. But the first coupon due in one period (for convenience the period will be assumed to be a year) has for its present value $\frac{I}{1+i}$, the coupon due in two years is worth at present $\frac{I}{(1+i)^2}$ that in three years $\frac{I}{(1+i)^3}$ and so on until the last coupon which is worth $\frac{I}{(1+i)^n}$ Adopting the conventional symbol $v = \frac{1}{1+i}$ then the entire series of coupons is worth at present $I\ (v + v^2 + v^3 + v^4 \ldots + v^n)$ or $I\,\frac{1 - v^n}{i}$. The principal of \$100, also due in n years, is worth $100\ v^n$ so that the equation reads: $V_n = I\,\frac{1 - v^n}{i} + 100\ v^n$. This, for the bond used as illustration in the text, would be:

$$V_{20} = 6.\,\frac{1 - \frac{1}{(1.05)^{20}}}{.05} + \frac{100}{(1.05)^{20}}$$

In other words the present value of the bonds represents two sums: one the present value of an annuity (I) furnished by the series of coupons, running for n years, the other the present value of the principal due in n years.

The same result is gained by considering, in the formula, only the excess of interest (over the market rate) which the bond pays. A bond bearing 5 per cent interest would, of course, sell at par when the market rate is also 5 per cent. A bond paying a higher rate of interest will be worth a premium equal to the present value of an annuity whose annual installment is the difference between the nominal rate of interest and that taken as the basis of calculation.

The formula, derived in a manner similar to that given above, is:

$$P = (I - 100\,i).\frac{1 - v^n}{i}$$

or, substituting the values used above:

$$P = (6 - 5)\,\frac{1 - \dfrac{1}{(1.05)^{20}}}{.05}$$

or the value at 5 per cent of a twenty-year terminable annuity of $1.00. Where the nominal rate of interest is less than that taken as the basis the result will, of course, show a discount instead of a premium.

The value of the bond at the time of each successive inventory is obtained by merely changing the value of n so that it equals the number of interest periods still remaining before maturity.

Interest is more customarily paid semiannually. Where that is the case the same formula is used but n represents the number of half-year periods, and i of course, the rate to be obtained not for the year but for the half-year. Thus for a twenty-year 6 per cent bond with interest payable semiannually n would be 40, i would be .025 and I would be 3. Tables are published for bonds with annual, semiannual and quarterly interest and also to show the price at which a bond bearing interest annually would be as remunerative as one bearing interest semiannually, etc.

Accounting for Amortization

In the technic of double entry bookkeeping it is not necessary to apply a series of formulas in order to record the changing values of an investment purchased at a premium, provided the net rate which the investment yields is known at the time of purchase. This may be illustrated by the following entries, assuming that $10,000 bonds bearing 6 per cent interest are bought at 112.4622, yielding the investor 5 per cent. At the time of purchase the entry would be:

Bonds	$11,246.22	
Cash		$11,246.22

or:

Bonds	$10,000.00	
Premium on Bonds	1,246.22	
Cash		$11,246.22

Either of the above forms is entirely satisfactory; but investments are generally listed at their par value with the premium or discount shown in a separate account. This facilitates somewhat the checking up of securities held by the concern.

A year later when $600 interest is collected the entry should be:

Cash	$600.00	
Interest		$562.31
Premium on Bonds (or Bonds)		37.69

The entry is arrived at in the following manner. It is known that the investment yields 5 per cent. The amount actually invested was $11,246.22, therefore Interest should be credited with 5 per cent of that amount, or $562.31, and the difference between that sum and the $600 received is a repayment of part of the original investment. This is credited to Premium as indicated above, or to Bonds if the original entry had debited Bonds with the entire amount paid for them. The value of the bonds, including both par and premium, is by this entry reduced to $11,208.53. Accordingly when $600 is collected on the coupons at the end of the second year the entry will be:

Cash	$600.00	
Interest		$560.43
Premium on Bonds		39.57

and so on with each payment of interest. The book value of the bonds at the end of the first and second years, $11,208.53

and $11,168.96, respectively, corresponds to the values which would be obtained through the use of the formula given above, or by referring to a bond-values table; but the more complicated calculation is only necessary to obtain the net yield, at the time that the bonds are first purchased.

Discount on Bonds

Logically bonds bought at a discount should similarly be treated by being marked up in value with each annual approach toward maturity. If a 6 per cent bond is worth 112.46, that is it nets 5 per cent, a 4 per cent bond would have an actuarial value (its market value would probably vary somewhat from this) of 87.54. That is, the bond bearing a nominal rate 1 per cent above the net rate of 5 per cent is worth a premium of 12.46 per cent; one whose nominal rate is 1 per cent below the normal should sell at a discount of 12.46 per cent. To continue to list the latter bond at the purchase price is mathematically incorrect, for at maturity the holder will receive not only the regular payment of interest and his invested principal of 87.54 but an additional sum of 12.46, the full face of the bond being then payable. The value of a promise to pay this sum of 12.46 increases as the date for its payment draws near, and a correct valuation would therefore demand that each year the bond purchased at a discount should be marked up just as the bond purchased at a premium should annually be marked down.

The journal entries at the time the bond was bought would be:

Bonds	$100.00	
Discount on Bonds		$12.46
Cash		87.54

and a year later, when the first coupon was collected:

Cash	$4.00	
Discount	.38	
Interest		$4.38

But accounting practice has not fully accepted this principle. In many cases the annual writing off of premium paid is justified, but there is hesitation at writing up the bond bought at a discount. This is largely an evidence of the conservative tendency which looks askance at anything which tends to swell the value of assets, but encourages undervaluation. Moreover the courts in apportioning the receipts of estates between the one with a life interest and the remainderman, generally hold that premiums given and received are a part of the corpus of the estate and do not enter into revenue, so that where a bond is bought at a discount the tenant for life receives only the nominal rate of interest. But the rulings of the courts in probate matters do not necessarily apply to ordinary commercial accounting[9] and the better practice is to adjust both premium and discount on the correct actuarial basis given above.

Interest Accrued on Investments

Interest accrued on investments should be estimated and shown on the balance sheet. This is not analogous to taking recognition of an appreciation in market value, for the interest is earned and is as much an asset as the face of the bond itself. Whether interest accrued but not yet due, or interest due but not yet paid, may be used as a basis of dividends is a question discussed in Chapter XII. But accounting practice uniformly estimates interest, whether due to or by the company, even though the law may object to a dividend in anticipation of its receipt.

Mercantile Credits

Accounting for Notes Receivable

The holding of mercantile credits—book accounts, acceptances, promissory notes, etc.—being an essential part of ordinary commercial life they must be treated somewhat differently from investments. They are so clearly a part of the circulating assets (are "circulating capital," to use the term employed by the courts) that there can never be any justification for allowing them to appear at more than their real value. The argument frequently made that shrinkage in the

[9] *Cf.* Merchants Loan and Trust Co. *v.* Smietanka, 255 U. S. 521 (1920).

real value of fixed assets, inasmuch as it works no change in the conduct of the business, may be ignored is not without some plausibility. But a loss in any of the circulating assets cannot be disregarded. It immediately manifests itself in reducing profits and must appear in some form in the balance sheet.

For convenience mercantile credits are entered and carried on the books at their face rather than at their present actual value. Thus a thousand-dollar note due without interest in sixty days appears in the Notes Receivable account at $1,000 not at $990, leaving the adjustment to be made through an interest or discount account.[10] This is much more convenient in checking over the contents of the bill portfolio, and, unless a daily revaluation of the notes is made, it is also as accurate as to list the note at the discounted value on the day when it is acquired. But when a new inventory is to be made it is necessary to take full account of interest adjustments.

Bad Debts

The adjustment of interest is, however, a mere matter of arithmetic and offers no problem in accounting. The estimate of probable loss due to insolvency of debtors, being an estimate merely, is a debatable and interesting problem. A company may hold a thousand notes of customers aggregating $100,000, its books showing:

Balance Sheet

Merchandise	$140,000	Capital	$220,000
Notes Receivable	100,000	Profit and Loss	30,000
Cash	10,000		
	$250,000		$250,000

[10] Banks, whose dealings are so largely in discounted notes, generally make such adjustment when the note is discounted, debiting, for instance, Notes Receivable $1,000 and crediting Discount on Notes Receivable $40. Properly speaking the amount here credited is a valuation account, necessary to show the real value of the note, but it is more commonly looked upon as an element of profit representing interest paid in advance to the bank. In the less meticulous accounting of commercial concerns the common procedure is to make no immediate adjustment for the discounted value, but to show the note as if it were actually worth its face value.

If some of these notes are clearly worthless they should at once be stricken from the list of assets, without waiting even for the annual inventory. No justification can be found for retaining on the books the note of A for one hundred dollars if it is known to be worthless. As soon as that fact is manifest the note must be eliminated by charging it at once to Profit and Loss, or pending the annual balance of the books to some subsidiary account indicating a loss.[11] The accounts would then furnish the following:

Balance Sheet

Merchandise	$140,000	Capital	$220,000
Notes Receivable	99,900	Profit and Loss	29,900
Cash	10,000		
	$249,900		$249,900

Where there remains a slight chance that the debt may some time be paid and yet one on which it is not safe to count, it may be desirable to keep a remainder of the debt on the books without appreciably swelling the assets by including doubtful debts. This is conveniently done by charging off the bulk of the note, but leaving a purely nominal sum, perhaps one dollar, or even a smaller sum, as a reminder that there is still an unsettled claim outstanding.

Allowance for Doubtful Accounts

A more delicate question arises in connection with probable losses which have not been made known. Of the remaining 999 notes in the assumed case no one of the makers has as yet failed, and yet past experience shows that it is a certainty that some of the notes will not be paid in full, and the probabilities are that at least one of them will ultimately prove worthless. Each note must be kept on the books at the face value, the estimated shrinkage appearing in a separate valuation account. The journal entry would be:

Bad Debts	$100	
Allowance for Doubtful Accounts		$100

[11] The deduction of bad debts from sales has the same effect on net profits as charging them to Profit and Loss.

At the end of the fiscal period, the balance in Bad Debts would be carried to Sales or to Profit and Loss. In the formal publication of the balance sheet this would appear as:

Balance Sheet

Merchandise		$140,000	Capital	$220,000
Notes Receivable	$99,900		Profit and Loss	29,800
Less Allowance for Doubtful Accounts	100			
		99,800		
Cash		10,000		
		$249,800		$249,800

That such allowance should be made is not only dictated by business prudence and accounting practice but is as well commanded by the courts in England and the United States, and, since 1921, permitted in determining income for the Federal tax.[12] The amount to be allowed is to be decided in each individual case but it certainly should not be much below what has been generally accepted in the specific business concerned. The basis of figuring is also subject to individual preference; some preferring to take a percentage of gross sales, some a percentage of debts outstanding, still others a percentage of credits given. With business of a constant character correct results could be reached as well with one method as another. But a change in the character of the business done would necessitate a change in the rate adopted. Thus if 2 per cent on total sales was correct with a business which was 50 per cent cash it would probably be insufficient if the change in business methods gave 80 per cent of the sales for credit and only 20 per cent for cash. Similarly an increase in term of credit granted would invalidate an allowance based on debts outstanding. And any rates would need to be changed if there arose a general panic or other commercial disturbance.

It is incorrect to list in the balance sheet merely the excess

[12] Providence Rubber Co. *v.* Goodyear, 9 Wall. 788 (1869); *in re* Oxford Benefit Building and Investment Society, 35 Ch. Div. 502 (1886); Regulations 62, art. 151; 65, art. 155.

of debts due to the concern over the amounts due from it. The canceling of one against the other does not exhibit the true condition, for the failure of debtors to pay does not at all affect the necessity of providing for the claims of creditors.

Merchandise

Cost or Market Whichever Is Lower

Current practice in regard to the valuation of merchandise, including raw material and partly finished goods, is curiously inconsistent and illogical. If one were to adhere to the oft-extolled principle that the value to the going concern is the fundamental viewpoint, merchandise, being designed and destined for sale, should be valued at its selling value, making such allowances as might be appropriate for expenses of selling, fluctuations, and sundry contingencies. Those who say that the selling price of fixed assets, being of no significance to a going concern, should be disregarded in revaluations, should, by that same token, maintain that to a concern engaged in selling merchandise the price at which it can be sold is the significant one.

This basis, however, is by no means accepted. The traditional view has been that merchandise should normally be valued at its cost, but that, when the market price is less than the cost, the latter should be substituted. Confessedly illogical, this practice became rather general in the United States, being approved of by most accountants as having the merit of conservatism. Conservatism, as used in accounting, ordinarily means any action which tends to keep down the value of assets, which understates rather than exaggerates the showing of profits. Undoubtedly a rule which calls for the lower of two possible figures is conservative to that extent. If the cost were $1.10 and the market price is $1.00 it is more conservative to list at the latter than at the former figure. But one can easily see that in many cases the crude rule, cost or market whichever is lower, is in no sense *truly* conservative. This may be illustrated by two merchants who each bought a commodity, but at different times and prices. A bought on

January 1, at $1.00. The market steadily rose until, on December 1, it reached the price of $2.10, when B bought a similar quantity at the latter price. On December 31 the price had fallen to $2.00. According to the rule, A must value his commodity still at $1.00, and B his at $2.00. Of course it is more conservative for A to value at $1.00 than at any higher price. But a logical conservatism would say that A might value at considerably more than cost, say at $1.50 and still be more conservative in his valuation than B who must value at $2.00. For A to value at $1.50, even though this is an advance of 50 per cent over cost, still leaves a margin of safety, for he still undervalues to the extent of 25 per cent. But B while valuing below cost allows for no margin. If the market, which has already apparently passed the peak, continues on the downward course there will immediately appear an overvaluation, which would not be true in the case of A, valuing his at $1.50. Bankers would presumably be willing to lend to the full extent of A's valuation, but assuredly would not lend to the full extent of the value set by B.

Valuation for Income Tax

In income-tax matters, the government, more intent upon administrative simplicity than on accounting principles, at first prescribed that all merchandise inventories should be valued at cost.[13] This in the course of years would not affect the total income, for any additional profit shown in one year, because of a higher closing inventory, would be offset in the following year because of the excessive value placed upon the opening inventory. While the income would amount to the same in the long run, the attributing of income to one year or another is not a matter of indifference to the taxpayer, because of variations in the normal tax rate and because of the surtax levied upon higher income in any given year.

The provision requiring inventory to be invariably at cost was so much objected to by accountants and taxpayers that the rule was soon changed and the taxpayer was given the

---

[13] *Income Tax Primer,* December 17, 1917, Question 31.

privilege of valuing inventories either at cost or at cost or market, whichever is lower.[14]

Despite its inconsistencies the rule mentioned above has become well established. Indeed the concession made by the government was largly due to the fact that such a procedure was in accordance with good accounting practice.

Recent Opinion Regarding Valuation of Merchandise

This rule would probably have been little questioned, save by some few accountants with a strongly developed love of consistency, in a period of relatively stable market prices. But in recent years price fluctuations have been enormous, almost unprecedented. Accountants and taxpayers were alike disturbed at the idea of valuing in accordance with any rule, designed for normal times. In the mighty upswing of prices incident to the war, cost seemed utterly inadequate to portray the financial condition of a concern which had bought at earlier prices. On the other hand when the peak had been reached, it was far from conservative to value at the cost or even at the market value, if by market value was meant the only quotations obtainable, when sellers were unwilling to quote low, and buyers would not pay high, prices.

It is difficult to state satisfactorily the present attitude of accountants. Montgomery [15] argues against the universal acceptance of the cost or market whichever is lower. But at the same time he argues that he does not advocate a new rule, but only a new interpretation. This seems merely that the alternative would be between cost and market value in a strict sense, not between cost and a set of misleading quotations. On the other hand, Couchman [16] and Esquerré say that costs should always be used, the latter stating: "Accounting is not interested in what would have happened if, but in what actually happened." [17] Kester favors the single standard of

---

[14] Regulations 45, art. 1582. But this rule must be applied to each item separately and does not allow that the whole inventory is to be valued at cost, and again at market and the lower of these two totals taken.

[15] *Auditing, Theory and Practice,* 3d ed., I, p. 119.

[16] *The Balance Sheet,* p. 45.

[17] *Applied Theory of Accounts,* p. 171.

cost with the present market value "carried parenthetically in an inner column on the face of the balance sheet or in a footnote to it."[18] Paton, who at one time argued strongly for taking the present value rather than the cost, in his latest work states that the "actual cost furnishes the most satisfactory basis or starting point for the pricing of inventory in the trading field."[19]

Valuing at Market in Relation to Current Operations

An argument in favor of inventorying merchandise at its market value is that only by so doing can the operations of each year be properly judged. The selling organization, if efficient, should be able to sell its goods at an advance over the price at which it purchases them. Thus for illustration, if goods are purchased from the manufacturers at $1.00 per unit, the selling organization would be expected to dispose of them at $1.20. If in an advancing market, goods which at the beginning of the year are worth $1.00, but which had been previously bought at 90 cents, are disposed of at $1.10, the relative inefficiency of the selling organization would be obscured if the profits on the sale were shown as 20 cents instead of 10 cents. More clearly to exhibit the operations of each year, the merchandise on hand may be inventoried at its market value, thus bringing out the profits made as a result of the selling organization in contradistinction to gains previously brought about by fluctuations in the market.

Recommended Accounting Procedure

It will probably continue to be the custom to value, in ordinary cases, at cost or market whichever is lower, but in cases of marked variation from cost, to value at market (using the best obtainable evidence of what present market value is), clearly indicating, by subsidiary accounts, the amount of such variation. Thus where there has been a disastrous decline in value, the Inventory account can still remain at cost, but with

---

[18] *Accounting, Theory and Practice*, 2d ed., II, p. 153.

[19] *Cf.* Paton and Stevenson, *Principles of Accounting*, p. 468; and Paton, *Accounting*, p. 373.

an account, Allowance for Decline in Inventory Value. This would be created by charging Profit and Loss, and in the balance sheet would preferably be shown as a subtraction from the listed value of the inventory. In case of a marked appreciation the increment should appear as a credit to Reserve Due to Marking up Inventory, the inventory appearing among the assets either simply at present value, or as made up of two items, cost price, and estimated appreciation, the sum of these being extended into the outer column. When the goods are sold, so much of the credit to Reserve Due to Marking up Inventory as is properly allocated to the goods sold should be transferred from this reserve to the general Profit and Loss account or to Surplus. Where the value of the goods declined the allowance is an offset correcting the exaggeration of value due to continuing to list the assets at cost price. Where there has been an appreciation the reserve is a surplus account showing an actual increase in proprietorship though one not as yet converted into cash or receivables.

Exceptional Rules for Inventories

It may be of some significance to note exceptions to the ordinary rules for valuing inventories. The crystalizing of accounting rules in definite legislation is, of course, not binding outside the special jurisdiction or sphere concerned, but the rules do, at least, indicate decisions, presumably reached after careful consideration, and as such are entitled to some respect. In Germany [20] the universal rule is to value at cost, but an exception is made, which applies only to securities or commodities which have an officially quoted price in some public stock or produce exchange. In such cases the rule is that the inventory shall be at cost or market whichever is lower. But this rule does not apply to the inventorying of unquoted commodities, which must be listed at cost. In Austria,[21] on the contrary, all the assets "are to be listed at their actual value at the time of taking the inventory" without modification when this exceeds the cost. In the United

[20] *D. H. G. B.*, secs. 261 and 40.
[21] *Regulativ für Aktiengesellschaften*, sec. 49.

States,[22] so far as calculations for income-tax purposes are concerned, the taxpayer has in general the option of selecting either cost or cost or market, whichever is lower, but a narrowly restricted exception is made in regard to the valuation of securities, by dealers. To these is given a third choice, that is of taking the market price, whether higher or lower. This regulation differs materially from either of the two preceding. It is permissive not obligatory; it relates to the valuation of securities not of other commodities; it applies only to securities in the hands of dealers; and the valuation of securities at more than cost applies to unlisted and unquoted securities as well as to those sold on a stock exchange.

Determination of Cost Price

In the case of merchandise purchased for sale the cost price ordinarily can be easily obtained. There may, however, be some room for question even here as to what items, if any, may be added to the quoted cost price for inventory purposes. It is apparent that if two consignments be purchased one at $1,000 c. i. f. and the other for $990 f. o. b., the freight and other charges on the second consignment being just $10, it would be illogical to list the two lots at different figures. In other words the familiar principle of valuing the goods to a going concern applies here as well as in other cases. The retailer needs the goods in his own store and the expenses of getting them there, whether paid by the manufacturer and included in the cost price or paid by the retailer in addition to the cost price, are legitimately included in the inventory value.

Until recently it has been customary where merchandise is inventoried at the cost price to consider that the cost is represented by the price at which the goods were invoiced, even though the purchaser took advantage of an offered discount and actually paid less for the goods. This involved the idea that the discount was in the nature of a profit and was so shown in the income sheet. The custom is happily growing, however, of considering the cost price as the net price paid

[22] Regulations 65, art. 1615.

for the goods.[23] Some accountants claim not only that the merchandise should not be valued at more than the price actually paid but that it should not be valued at more than the price at which it might have been purchased if advantage had been taken of an offered discount. This, however, has not gained such wide acceptance. During the Great War, however, the government insisted in its payments upon the cost-plus system, that the cost must be calculated upon the basis of net cash price whether the purchaser did or did not take advantage of the discount offered. While this was not a ruling regarding a method of taking an inventory, the principle is the same. The treatment of discounts offered but not taken where goods are valued at the net cash price, is discussed in Chapter XVII.

Valuation of Merchandise Bought at Different Prices

Where merchandise is bought at different times and at different prices it is difficult to determine just which of the various prices should be assigned to the remaining stock. If the various invoices are kept physically separate, made up of easily distinguishable units, as, for instance, automobiles identical but each bearing a separate number, or where the units are individually not distinguishable but are kept in separate bins or storerooms, the cost to be taken for inventory is the actual cost of the particular units still on hand. But where the several invoices are indistinguishably blended, as for instance grain placed in a common bin, some arbitrary rule must be adopted.

Recent Purchases Method

Alternative procedures are recognized. The goods inventoried may be considered as those most recently purchased and hence valued at the actual cost of an amount of the more recent purchases equaling the quantity on hand; or they may be valued at the weighted average cost of all the goods han-

---

[23] See results of questionnaire on this subject in *Journal of Accountancy,* XVIII, p. 461.

dled during the year, including the inventory price of the goods on hand at the beginning of the year. Either of these methods is an attempt to list at cost, not at present value. Thus if there appear on the books the following items:

Opening inventory	200	units	at	$1.10
Purchase	100	"	"	1.25
Purchase	50	"	"	1.50

and there are on hand at the close of the year 200 units, these would not all be valued at the latest price, although that presumably most nearly represents the present value. In accordance with the first method they would be valued as follows:

50	units	at	$1.50	$ 75.00
100	"	"	1.25	125.00
50	"	"	1.10	55.00
				$255.00

This assumes that all of the latest consignment and all of the second consignment are still unsold, and that the remaining 50 bushels was part of the inventory carried over from the preceding period. This corresponds, probably, although not necessarily, somewhat closely to the facts, because presumably the stock of goods on hand is more likely first drawn upon for deliveries, and furthermore the prices taken are more recent and therefore presumably nearer the present values, as well as actual costs. This method seems to be preferred by the Treasury in its income-tax regulations.[24]

Weighted Average Method

By the second method, the 200 units on hand would be valued at $240. The entire amount of goods handled (including the opening inventory) amounted to 350 units and cost $420 giving as the weighted average price $1.20.

By taking the average price, the goods on hand are charged with part of the burden of earlier purchases with which they in fact have no connection. It is a current delusion frequently

[24] Regulations 65, art. 1612. While the other method is permissible, it may be employed only where book inventories have been kept in accordance with good accounting practice.

held by dabblers in speculative activities that a later purchase at a lower price brings down the cost of the earlier purchase. This is obviously incorrect. The first purchase cost what it cost, as did the later purchases. The loss on an earlier purchase may be offset by a later gain, but the two transactions are distinct. The acceptance of an average cost in inventories may be desirable, because of the ease of administration, avoiding numerous examinations as to dates of purchase, but it is unsound even though justified on the score of convenience; or the average price may be accepted because it is thought impossible to determine which goods were sold first, and it is used not because it is correct but because there is no way of ascertaining a more nearly correct price.

Moving Weighted Average Method

Other methods of valuing in similar circumstances are discussed by accountants. Thus selling prices may be used as a base from which to work back to cost, by making proper allowances for the mark-up. This is evidently an effort to ascertain cost, and varies more in technic than in principle. Similarly a moving weighted average may be used which assumes as the cost of each sale the weighted average cost price of the goods then on hand. Thus, in the illustration given above, it might be that 100 units were sold after the first purchase, the other 50 units after the second purchase. Using the moving weighted average, the calculations would be as follows:

	Units	Price per Unit	Total
Opening inventory	200	$1.10	$220.00
1st purchase	100	1.25	125.00
Total	300	(average) 1.15	$345.00
1st sale	100	1.15	115.00
On hand	200	(average) 1.15	$230.00
2d purchase	50	1.50	75.00
Total	250	(average) 1.22	$305.00
2d sale	50	1.22	61.00
Closing inventory	200	(average) 1.22	$244.00

Comparison of Different Bases for Valuation

The inventories would accordingly vary as follows:

Basis of Valuation	Value per Unit	Total Value
Cost of most recently acquired units	$1.275	$255.00
Weighted average	1.200	240.00
Moving weighted average	1.220	244.00

The moving weighted average has whatever theoretical defects apply to the ordinary weighted average, but it differs in the degree to which later prices affect the result. The estimated cost of goods sold at any time is not affected by any subsequent purchases, but is affected by all previous purchases.[25] The moving weighted average method requires more frequent calculations, and virtually consists in a series of intermediate valuations, made after each sale, such valuations being each made on the basis of a weighted average.[26]

Valuation of Self-Manufactured Goods

When the merchandise to be inventoried has not been purchased but has been manufactured the determination of cost price is much more difficult and the general question of manufacturing cost will receive further consideration. The principle is clear enough. All the costs which are immediately necessary to secure the goods may be included in the inventory price. But difficulties arise in applying this simple rule, because of the doubt whether certain payments such as partners' salaries should be included in cost of goods or treated either as part of the general expenses of the business or as a distribution of profits. Attempts have even been made to include a certain percentage, representing normal profits, in

[25] Assuming that the goods first bought were first sold, the actual cost of the goods sold in the above example was $1.10; by the moving weighted average the goods sold are treated as having cost $1.17⅓ per unit, by the simple weighted average $1.20.

[26] The moving weighted average method is admirably discussed and illustrated in Finney, *Principles of Accounting,* chap. xxviii, pp. 11 *ff*.

the cost price, a procedure which not only opposes accounting practice but which has been prohibited by the courts.[27]

Goods in the process of manufacture for the general market should not be inventoried at more than the cost price; but when they are manufactured on a specific contract it is correct to take into account the selling price, making due allowance for the unfinished work still to be done, the risks intervening, and interest charges involved. Where the contract period extends beyond the current fiscal period such inventorying is not only permissible but is the only correct method. Otherwise the profits on the contract work would all appear in the year when goods are delivered, although the labor involved belonged almost entirely to a preceding year.

Bibliographical Note

COLE, W. M.—*The Fundamentals of Accounting* (Boston, 1921), chap. xxi.

DICKINSON, A. L.—*Accounting Practice and Procedure* (New York, 1918), chaps. iv, v.

FINNEY, H. A.—*Principles of Accounting* (New York, 1923), chap. xxviii.

GREELEY, H. D.—*Business Accounting* (New York, 1920), pp. 132-8.

HURD, R. M.—*Principles of City Land Values* (4th ed., New York, 1924).

KESTER, R. B.—*Accounting, Theory and Practice* (2d ed., New York, 1925), II, chaps. vi, viii, xviii, xix.

LITTLE, A. S.—"The Tyranny of the Engraver," *Journal of Accountancy,* XX, pp. 186-202.

MAY, G. O.—"The Proper Treatment of Premiums and Discounts on Bonds," *Journal of Accountancy,* II, p. 174.

MONTGOMERY, R. H.—*Auditing, Theory and Practice* (3d ed., New York, 1922), I, chaps. viii-xi.

NEYMARK, A.—"Du meilleur mode à indiquer au point de vue statistique international pour la confection des bilans des sociétés anonymes," *Bulletin de l'Institut international de statistique,* Tome XIV, livraison 2, pp. 143-99. Contains answers to a series of questions propounded to various members of the Institute.

PATON, W. A.—*Accounting* (New York, 1924), chap. xviii.

[27] Providence Rubber Co. *v.* Goodyear, 9 Wall. 788 (1869).

PIXLEY, F. W.—*Auditors, Their Duties and Responsibilities* (11th ed., London, 1918), I, chap. xii.

SIMON, H. V.—*Die Bilanzen der Aktiengesellschaften* (3te Auflage, Berlin, 1899), pp. 326-444.

SPRAGUE, C. E.—*The Accountancy of Investment* (New York, 1910).

——— "Premiums and Discounts," *Journal of Accountancy,* II, p. 294. A criticism of the article by May.

See also the references to Chapters VI and XII.

CHAPTER IV

INTANGIBLE ASSETS

Definition

Intangible assets are defined as meaning patents, copyrights, secret processes and formulas, goodwill, trade-marks, trade brands, franchises, and other like property.[1] The phrase is not particularly appropriate and, except by enumeration, the separation between tangible and intangible assets is not easily made. Accounts receivable are considered tangible assets, although literally there is nothing tangible about them. Real estate is considered typically tangible, a franchise intangible. But there is no real difference between them as regards tangibility, materiality, or realness. Real estate represents a right, tracing ultimately back to the sovereign power which permits an individual to make use of a portion of the earth's surface. The uses to which it may be put are many, but not unlimited. The owner may not, for instance, erect a glue factory in a residential district nor, even before 1921, locate a saloon within a given distance of church or school. A franchise is similarly a right granted by the sovereign power permitting an individual to make certain restricted uses of a portion of the earth's surface. It is an important but not an essential difference that the uses are even more restricted than in the instances cited above. It is certainly not an essential difference that the portion of land is a long narrow strip rather than a square forty-acre tract. While the term intangible assets is without etymological significance, it is still of use as a collective term, in general embracing the items given in the definition just quoted.

---

[1] "Report of Committee on Terminology, A.I.A.," *Journal of Accountancy*, XXXV, p. 466.

Goodwill

Nature of Goodwill

Goodwill, which may be taken as the typical form of intangible assets, represents the value of business connections, the value of the probability that present customers will continue to buy in spite of the allurements of competing dealers.

While the inclusion of intangible assets in the inventory of corporations is not infrequently the object of popular criticism the legitimacy of goodwill has long been recognized both by the courts and by accountants. A clear statement of the principle is given in the case of Washburn *v.* National Wall Paper Company, where the court said:

> When an individual or a firm or a corporation has gone on for an unbroken series of years conducting a particular business, and has been so scrupulous in fulfilling every obligation, so careful in maintaining the standard of the goods dealt in, so absolutely fair and honest in all business dealings that customers of the concern have become convinced that their experience in the future will be as satisfactory as it has been in the past, while such customers' good report of their own experience tends continually to bring new customers to the same concern there has been produced an element of value quite as important—in some cases, perhaps, far more important—than the plant or machinery with which the business is carried on. That it is property is abundantly settled by authority, and, indeed, is not disputed. That in some cases it may be very valuable property is manifest. The individual who has created it by years of hard work and fair business dealing usually experiences no difficulty in finding men willing to pay him for it if he be willing to sell it to them.[2]

Similarly accountants have recognized that the purchase of goodwill of an established firm may be a most valuable transaction, for it may save, as Guthrie has neatly put it, "the period of perilous probation."[3] Indeed even the goodwill of a bankrupt house is at times legitimately sold at a high price, and where so purchased it is as true an asset as factory, machine, or stock of merchandise.

---

[2] 81 Fed. 20 (1897).
[3] *Accountant*, XXIV, p. 425.

Value of Goodwill Limited to Cost

But in valuing goodwill for the inventory the limitation of its value to its cost is rigorously observed. It has been seen that the restriction of inventory value to cost price is of rather general application, but its force is much greater when the assets to be valued are intangible. No one would object to the inclusion in the inventory of treasure trove even though it cost the finder nothing, but goodwill is rigorously excluded unless it has been secured at a cost. Hence it is recognized as legitimate for the purchaser of goodwill to include it among his assets, but accounting practice prudently, though perhaps illogically, forbids the firm which created the goodwill to place in the balance sheet any value on the clientele which it has built up and which it could at any moment sell for a large sum.

This conservative restriction is doubtless necessary to prevent a harmful exaggeration. Human nature is so incurably optimistic, especially when it comes to estimating one's own possessions. The boy's jackknife, the citizen's fatherland, the man's children, are in normal cases a little better than similar possessions of any one else. The same phenomenon appears in the valuation of one's business assets, where the natural instinct to overvalue one's own possessions is augmented by the fact that such overvaluation may be the means of overreaching some one else in a business deal. In proportion as it is difficult to verify values it is therefore customary to limit the amount at which they are estimated. Cash being of definite value may be listed though it cost nothing; quoted securities or commodities may, according to some authorities, be listed at the market value even though that exceed the cost; but goodwill, because of its vague nature and the difficulty of verifying its appraisal, is to be excluded unless it has been purchased.[4]

[4] For a possible exception to this see the decision in the English case *in re* Barrow Hæmatite Steel Co. ([1900] 2 Ch. 855), where it was held that a decline in the value of part of the assets should be offset by the introduction of goodwill before it could be claimed that capital had been impaired.

Goodwill Purchased with Stock

But it is not always easy to determine whether there has been an actual purchase of goodwill, or what price, if any, has been paid. Most frequently where a corporation buys out the business of a partnership or of another corporation, the purchase is made with stock, not with cash. When, as is generally the case, the par value of the stock given is in excess of the value of the tangible assets it is at times difficult to determine whether the difference in these values represents goodwill purchased or a mere discount of the stock issued. In ordinary American practice the accountants have assumed the existence of goodwill wherever the tangible property purchased is less than the par value of the stock issued therefor. For instance, in the capitalization of a large catalogue house, whose total assets were less than $20,000,000, there was added at the time of reorganization the item of goodwill valued at $30,000,000. The exaggeration in this figure was clearly established by the quoted prices of the stock immediately following its issue.

Advertising as Cost of Goodwill

An argument is frequently made that while goodwill should not appear in the balance sheet except at its cost price, it is legitimate to consider that advertising, in the early years, is a cost of obtaining goodwill, as truly as the price paid in purchasing the goodwill of some established concern. A distinction is made between what may be considered a normal amount of advertising necessary to maintain a given volume of trade (which would always be considered an operating expense) and the presumably greater amount of advertising necessary to increase the amount of sales, especially that necessary to establish a market for a new product. This argument is ably set forth by E. W. Sells[5] and meets with the approval of many accountants. But if accepted at all, it must be done conservatively. Like the expense of experimentation, adver-

---

[5] *Journal of Accountancy,* XXI, p. 424. *Cf.* Kester, *Accounting,* 2d ed., II, p. 359.

tising may fail to bring forth fruit and instead of creating goodwill it may cause only a deficit. A better way is to show such unusual cost of advertising, not as goodwill, but as a special item, with a title clearly indicating its nature, and listed among deferred charges rather than as an intangible asset.

Initial Deficits as Cost of Goodwill

Somewhat similarly it is argued that it is quite proper to regard deficits in the first few years of a new enterprise as being a capital expenditure made in the acquirement of goodwill.[6] A practically identical procedure has had considerable recognition in the case of public utilities, although in such cases early deficits, though capitalized, are apt to appear on the balance sheet under some title other than goodwill. But the justification of this capitalizing of deficits is greater in the case of public utilities than in ordinary commercial enterprises. The arbitrary fixing of rates, based to some extent upon the amount invested, justifies a public utility in capitalizing items which can hardly be considered a cost of goodwill. In ordinary circumstances the carrying of a deficit as an asset, either tangible or intangible, does not meet with the approval of accountants.

Improper Recognition of Goodwill

What has been said in support of the legitimacy of including goodwill and similar intangible assets in the inventory in no way justifies the practice, all too common, of listing a nonexistent or a greatly overvalued goodwill. Such an item is not merely intangible but also imaginary. From the viewpoint of accounting, there is no more justification for such a procedure than there is for placing in the list of assets a brick building which has no existence, or for stating in the balance sheet the money in bank at twice the sum actually on deposit. Goodwill is a legitimate asset if, as was said by the United States Supreme Court, it be "substantial and not of

---

[6] See article, "Value of Goodwill," 145 *Law Times*, 452 (1918).

so shadowy a nature as to be incapable of pecuniary estimation."[7]

In general the earlier organizations of the so-called trusts included a high valuation for goodwill, ordinarily roughly corresponding to the amount of common stock issued, as, for instance, in the National Steel Company, where each was stated as $32,000,000. In most cases the value of goodwill was grossly overstated, and openly and notoriously incorrect. This is shown for instance by the experience of the Asphalt Company whose earnings estimated at 10 per cent of the capitalization proved to be less than 1 per cent, or by that of the American Malting Company where the $2,100,000 earnings estimated in the prospectus dwindled to a negative quantity in the first year of operation.

The assumption that the difference between the value of the tangible assets purchased and the par value of the stock given in purchase is represented by goodwill, is altogether unwarranted. The frequency of this error does not lessen its incorrectness. It is therefore necessary to examine the conditions in which goodwill exists, and to consider the principles governing its valuation.

The Bases of Goodwill

The value of goodwill, or the other similar categories, such as franchise, patent rights, trade-marks, trade names, depends on the existence of some legal right or trade custom which will bring to the owner of the business profits in excess of that to be obtained in other ordinary channels of trade. If the firm's name and its past reputation for good dealing will bring to its doors a flow of customers without the expense of profuse advertising or despite the lower prices of less favorably known rivals, there is a source of profits in excess of what could be obtained by establishing a new house. If the right to use a particular location to the exclusion of others, whether that location be of a newspaper stand on a crowded corner, or a street railway with an exclusive franchise to the streets,

---

[7] Camden *v.* Stuart, 144 U. S. 115 (1892).

there is at least a possibility that it opens the doors to the receipt of profits which could not be gained in any line of business not thus specially favored. If any business is protected by a monopoly, whether the legal monopoly of a patent right or a partial business monopoly resting on the combination of all present competitors in a trust, there is a possibility of maintaining prices at a level which will yield profits in excess of the current normal rate, and hence a legitimate basis for the valuation of goodwill.

The one justification for including goodwill among the assets is the existence of some transferable right which will secure to the purchaser profits in addition to the normal returns on the amount of capital invested in the business. Such a surplus over the normal income to be derived from investment is practically an uncertain annuity and its value depends (1) on the annual amount, (2) on the degree to which it can be transferred, and (3) on the length of time during which it will continue.

Amount of Excess Profits

The determination of the amount of excess profits is generally based on the records of the past experience of the firm or corporation selling its goodwill. How long a period should be taken into survey is a delicate problem. A single year is not a sufficient period, for the high profits of that year may be altogether due to exceptional temporary conditions. Nor should too long a period be considered lest the conditions of the remoter years be so different from those prevailing at the time of valuation as to make an average of little significance. Especially if the business is declining, the inclusion of the operations of the earlier years in the estimate is objectionable, as tending to exaggerate the showing of profits. Yet in recent capitalizations the National Wall Paper Company based the estimate of the valuation of goodwill on the earnings of only eleven months; the Rubber Goods Manufacturing Company took the earnings of a single year; the National Salt Company averaged the earnings of two years, and the National Cordage Company those of three to five years. In English corporation finance the figures of the latter period seem to be most generally used.

Transferability of Excess Profits

When a lawyer, physician, or other professional man sells his goodwill it is always a question as to how far the clientele which he has had is a purely personal matter. On the other hand, the surplus derived from an exclusive franchise of a street railway is clearly transferable. Between these two limits there is room for variation, depending largely on the degree to which the personal element of the proprietor has been a determining factor in creating the profits. It is not uncommon where goodwill is bought by a corporation to specify that the former proprietors, managers, or officers shall agree to continue their services for a given time after the purchase, as was done, for instance, in the case of the Cordage Trust.

Duration of Excess Profits

The duration of the annual excess depends on two factors: those having to do with competition, and those relating to general trade conditions. Error has been committed in the calculations of many of the large combinations both in this country and in England in assuming the continuance of large profits, where that is conditioned on the absence of competition. A notable instance was in the case of the Columbia Straw Paper Company, where large profits were perhaps honestly estimated on the basis of the high prices to be obtained by a practical monopoly. But as soon as prices were raised old mills were reopened, new mills were immediately constructed, and, in addition, new competition arose through the introduction of wood-pulp as the basic material of wrapping paper such as was previously manufactured exclusively from straw. As a result the company was insolvent in less than two years.[8]

Almost equal error has arisen from neglecting the possi-

---

[8] See *v.* Heppenheimer, 61 Atl. 843 (N. J. 1905).

bility of change of general trade conditions. Thus in the consolidation of English factories for making bicycles a large valuation was placed on the goodwill based on the continuance of previous demand; but almost immediately after the shares of the combination were floated the fad for bicycle riding ceased, and with it the value of the shares so eagerly purchased by the public. Similarly the goodwill of a distillery, or of a saloon, might cease because of the emergence of a sentiment in favor of abstinence or the enactment of a prohibition law.

Methods of Calculating Value of Goodwill

In determining the capitalized value of surplus profits, two distinct methods are used. One is to capitalize the entire net profits, of course being sure that the profits are really net profits (due allowance having been made for depreciation and other charges), and from this capitalization to deduct the value of the tangible assets. This was done in the organization of the National Wall Paper Company.

The second way is to deduct from the net profits the assumed normal rate of profits on the capital invested in tangible assets (in the case of a partnership estimated salaries of the partners would also be subtracted) and then to capitalize the remaining surplus earnings. This method is more commonly used in floating English companies. This method has been recognized by the American courts in valuation for inheritance matters as is illustrated in the following decision:

> The value of the decedent's interest in the ex-partnership should be determined in the following manner: From the average net profits of $400,990.70 for the three complete fiscal years preceding the death of decedent should be deducted 6 per cent on the average net capital of $1,050,333 employed for the same period, amounting to $63,019.98 and $100,000 for the salaries of the two partners. The difference, or $237,970.72, multiplied by 5, is $1,189,853.60 the value of the good-will.[9]

---

[9] Matter of Flurscheim quoted in Conyngton, *Financing an Enterprise*, II, p. 350.

An illustration of the application of this method in estimating the goodwill of a corporation is given by Charles S. Fairchild as follows:

In some cases the value of the goodwill acquired has been very carefully estimated. For example, the promoters of one company made a special point of the conservative methods employed in arriving at the value of the goodwill of the companies which were consolidated. According to their statement, the new company was virtually buying the real estate, plants, stock, etc., on the basis of appraised cash value. In addition an allowance was made for goodwill, calculated upon this basis; from the net profits of each company deduct 7 per cent upon the capital actually employed, 1½ per cent upon sales, which were about three times the capital, 2 per cent for depreciation on brick buildings, 4 per cent on frame buildings, and 8 per cent on machinery. If the average net earnings were in excess of all this, and in this case it appeared from the promoter's statement that they usually were, the excess was capitalized as "goodwill" on the basis of 20 per cent per annum—*i.e.*, the value of the goodwill was estimated to be five times the amount of such earnings in excess of 7 per cent on capital and allowance for depreciation.[10]

The multiplier to be applied to the profits would vary according to which of the two methods of valuing goodwill is used. This may be illustrated by assuming the case where a concern with an investment in tangible assets of $100,000 has annual net earnings of $12,000. Calculation according to the first method might be as follows:

Net earnings of $12,000 capitalized at 12½ years' purchase..	$150,000
Less value of tangible assets	100,000
Value of goodwill	$ 50,000

The calculation according to the second method:

Net earnings	$12,000
Less 7% on investment	7,000
Surplus earnings	$ 5,000
Value of goodwill (10 years' purchase)....................	50,000

In the above calculations, the net earnings are multiplied by 12½ in the first case, while the surplus earnings are multiplied

[10] *Publications of the American Economic Association*, 3d Series, I, p. 156.

by 10 in the second place. The same multiplier could be used only where excess earnings are capitalized at the same rate as tangible assets are assumed to yield. With these assumptions, the second calculations would be as follows:

Net earnings	$12,000
Less 8% interest on investment	8,000
Surplus earnings	$ 4,000
Value of goodwill (12½ years' purchase)	50,000

American Practice in Capitalizing Goodwill

In the American courts a multiplier from 2 to 6 has been common in valuing goodwill for inheritance although the goodwill of Tiffany and Company was valued by multiplying the excess average profits by 10.[11]

In determining the value of goodwill of the trusts already referred to the profits were multiplied by 5 for the Salt Trust, by 10 for the Cordage Trust, by 14²⁄₇ for the Rubber Goods Manufacturing Company, and by 16 for the National Wall Paper Company, but in these cases the entire net earnings were taken (not the net earnings minus estimated interest on invested capital), and from the figures thus obtained the invested capital was subtracted to obtain the value of goodwill. The exaggeration of value is, therefore, not so great as if the same figures had been used in the second method described above. But even with this admission, the multiplier was so large in some of the reorganizations that highly erroneous results were obtained. To apply so large a multiplier as 16 to the total net earnings implies that the excess profits are almost as permanent as the normal income on investment in tangible property. In some of these cases the element of monopoly was erroneously supposed to exist. On the other hand, payment in these cases was generally made in stock worth far less than its par value.

[11] Matter of Moore, 161 N. Y. S. 142 (1916). Decisions in which low multipliers were used are: Matter of Silkman, 105 N. Y. S. 872 (1907); Page *v.* Ratliffe, 75 L. T. R. N. S. 371 (1896); and Mellersh *v.* Keen, 28 Beav. 453 (1860). A discussion of legal decisions regarding the valuation of goodwill is found in *Bench and Bar,* XII, p. 51. See also H. C. Freeman, "Some Considerations Involved in the Valuation of Goodwill," *Journal of Accountancy,* XXXII, p. 247.

Capitalizing on a Sliding Scale

As has been shown by Francis More [12] it is correct to have a different rate for capitalizing different portions of the surplus earnings. Thus, to use the illustration given by him, if it is assumed that 8 per cent is the normal rate of profits, a concern having assets worth $100,000 and earning $8,000 affords no basis for goodwill, the earnings showing no excess over the normal rate. If earning $13,000 the excess of $5,000 might be capitalized, say at 7 years' purchase making a valuation of $35,000. But if the earnings were $18,000 it would be unwise again to add $35,000, but the additional surplus of $5,000 might perhaps be multiplied by 5. And so each additional portion of surplus should be multiplied by a smaller figure, or to express the idea more generally, the larger the surplus earnings are relative to normal profits, the lower should the multiplier be. This is reasonable since a small excess is more likely to continue than a large one, affording a smaller field for competition, and probably being less subject to other fluctuations.

Latent Goodwill

It should be borne in mind that the calculation of goodwill rests upon an estimate of excess earnings in the future, not in the past. The earnings in the past may be a valuable indication of what may be expected in the future, but they are of course imperfect and often erroneous indications. Thus, the goodwill of a bankrupt concern was at one time sold for a million dollars, it being considered that the clientele which had been built up and the reputation for fair dealing would be valuable to the successors even though the firm through bad financial management had been unable to make any profits. Kester speaks of this as dormant or latent goodwill which he defines as the "excess earning power that would exist if it were not for poor management . . . which the new management will remove." [13] The same idea has been rec-

[12] *Accountant,* XVII, p. 285.
[13] *Accounting, Theory and Practice,* 2d ed., II, p. 357.

ognized in the legal valuation of the intangible assets of a public utility.[14]

Writing off Goodwill

The question has arisen as to whether goodwill having once been properly entered in the books at its cost price should continue at that figure, or whether it should be subject to periodical revaluation or regularly written off, as machinery is marked down to allow for depreciation. In this, as in other questions of accounting theory, opinions differ.

Among accountants favoring the writing off of goodwill are Bell, Leake, Pixley, Webner, and Wildman, while Cole, Couchman, Dicksee, Finney, Kester, and Montgomery hold that it is unnecessary or even improper.[15] Even among those advocating writing off of goodwill there is a strange difference as to the circumstances in which this should be done. The more general opinion is that, if done at all, it should be done when the company has enjoyed unusual profits which can be appropriated for that purpose. But some, on the contrary, say that it is when profits are below the expected amount that goodwill has declined, and hence it is then that it should be marked down.[16] As Couchman has cleverly expressed it, "to put it briefly, if you can write it down, you need not; if you can not, you should!"

The English courts have decided in Wilmer *v.* McNamara ([1895] 2 Ch. 245) that even where the goodwill has actually declined in value it is not necessary to charge the shrinkage against profits. The decision was based on the conception that goodwill is fixed capital, and the application of a previous decision [17] that a decline in the value of fixed capital (or per-

---

[14] People *ex rel.* Hudson & M. R. Co. *v.* State Board of Tax Commissioners, 125 N. Y. S. 895 (1910).

[15] Bell, *Theory and Practice of Accounting,* II, 325; Pixley, *Duties of Auditors,* 11th ed., p. 535; Leake, *Commercial Goodwill,* p. 77; Webner, *Factory Costs,* p. 188; Wildman, *Principles of Accounting,* p. 102; Cole, *Fundamentals of Accounting,* p. 368; Couchman, *The Balance Sheet,* p. 138; Dicksee, *Auditing,* 13th ed., p. 221; Finney, *Principles of Accounting,* chap. xli, p. 12; Kester, *Accounting,* 2d ed., II, p. 363; Montgomery, *Auditing,* 3d ed., I, p. 195.

[16] See Welton in *Accountant,* XVI, p. 680.

[17] See below, p. 269.

manent assets) need not be taken into account in determining profits.

From one point of view it is true that goodwill is the most permanent of assets. Anything else, even the factory site, may conceivably be sold without necessarily terminating the business. But goodwill cannot be disposed of without selling the business itself. Furthermore the very indefiniteness of goodwill renders its overvaluation less harmful than that of other assets. Every one knows that the price paid for goodwill gives no indication of its present value, and that at any time a new valuation needs to be taken. Hence there is little danger of deception by continuing it among the assets at the cost price. But this doctrine of the permanence of goodwill seems inconsistent with the theory of valuing it as the purchase of a temporary, terminating annuity. Strict logic requires, at least where the price paid for goodwill is calculated as representing the present value of a series of excess annual profits, that it should be written off, as is any other terminable annuity, with reference to the duration of the annuity.[18]

To require the writing off only when the expected returns are not realized appears unnecessarily hard on the stockholders for they are doubly burdened: first, by the decline in expected earnings, and then by a further charge against the diminished earnings to cover decline in goodwill. To mark down goodwill when profits are unusually high is clearly illogical, though it is not thereby necessarily discredited in accounting practice, for it reduces the valuation of excess earnings at the very time and in direct ratio to the increase of

[18] Students should be on guard against misinterpreting phrases used in this connection, especially by British authors. To capitalize an annual income at 5 per cent means simply to multiply it by 20. It does not mean that at that price it yields 5 per cent to the purchaser. That is true only when the annuity is perpetual. Again, to value an annuity at so many years' purchase, means merely to multiply the amount of the annuity by the number mentioned. This does not mean that, if a given annuity is valued at 5 years' purchase, it is expected to continue 5 years; that would be true only in case the current rate of interest is taken at 0 per cent. Thus, assuming interest at 5 per cent, to value an annuity at 12 years' purchase implies that it will run 19 years; to value it at 16 years' purchase implies that it will run 33 years.

such earnings. Probably the most satisfactory solution is ordinarily to write off goodwill during the period of its calculated duration. In any event it is an uncertain asset, and a depreciation of even fixed assets (in which class it is somewhat forced to include goodwill), while it legally need not be made, is justified on the plea of conservatism. And where it is clear that the valuation of the goodwill was erroneous, that it is not worth its book value, the best method of adjustment is that advocated by Dicksee,[19] to offset the decline in its value by a reduction of capital, not by a charge against profits.

It is also sometimes argued that both in the case of goodwill and of patents or trade-marks, while the advantage acquired by purchase expires with time, there is coincident with such decline a new goodwill being built up. It is argued that while ordinarily goodwill, which is being gradually acquired through conducting a satisfactory business, is not to be entered upon the books, yet such an acquisition of goodwill may be considered as offsetting the decline in the value of goodwill or patent rights originally purchased. There is strength in this argument, but accountants in this matter, as in others, are inclined to recommend conservatism.[20]

Goodwill in American Balance Sheets

In American corporation finance goodwill frequently is not openly shown on the balance sheet. Oftentimes it is included with the tangible property under the title "Property, etc.," or it may be combined with other items of an intangible nature under headings such as "Goodwill, Patents, Leases, Trade-marks, etc." While such property rights as patents, trade-marks, etc., are quite different in their legal nature from goodwill, yet economically they are very similar, both

---

[19] *Goodwill,* pp. 82-3.

[20] This view is to a certain extent supported by a decision of the Supreme Court to the effect that a mortgage upon purchased goodwill of a newspaper did not give to the mortgagee a lien upon the goodwill some years later, it being held that the goodwill at the later date was not necessarily the same as that originally purchased. Metropolitan Bank *v.* St. Louis Dispatch Co., 149 U. S. 446 (1892). See also Couchman, *The Balance Sheet,* pp. 128-9.

representing a transferable right from which exceptional profits may be derived. Those which are distinctly terminable, as patents, copyrights, etc., differ from goodwill in that the value must some day disappear, and hence the necessity of marking down their value is apparent.

To include goodwill in the same category with tangible assets, listing them under a single caption such as Plant, Machinery, and Goodwill is not good accounting practice, any more than it would be considered proper to list accounts payable and long-time bonds in a single account, Debts Payable. Indeed under English law it was held to be illegal to group goodwill with fixed tangible assets.[21]

While American corporations in years past have very generally not set forth goodwill as a distinct item in the balance sheet but have combined it with other capital assets, there is an indication of improvement in this direction in recent years. A large number of the more important corporations have in recent years adopted the policy of showing it as a separate item.[22]

Deferred Charges

Definition

This class of items appearing in the balance sheet has been defined by the Committee on Terminology of the American Institute of Public Accountants as "that portion of expense items which is applicable to the period subsequent to the closing date." [23]

Attention has been called to the discussion as to whether certain expenditures, especially those made at the beginning of a company's operations, should be considered as expenses or as part of the cost of the plant. The items listed as deferred charges hold to some extent an intermediate position, for they are not conceived of as representing part of the cost of permanent assets, nor are they charged at once to the

[21] Galloway *v.* Schill Seebohm & Co., Ltd., [1912] 2 K. B. 354.
[22] *Journal of Accountancy*, XXII, p. 123.
[23] *Ibid.*, XXXV, p. 465.

expenses of the year. Being clearly expenses, they are yet regarded as offsets of future, not of past earnings.

Charging off Deferred Items

If the prepayment, whether listed among current assets or as a deferred charge, represents an expense of the following month (as rent paid in advance), it should be charged against the income of that month. If as in the case of prepaid insurance, it provides protection for two years in advance, its cost should similarly be apportioned as an expense of those two years. If, as in the case of the cost of surface stripping, the expense covers mining operations of twenty years, the charge should be distributed over that period of time. In all cases it is strictly necessary that the total amount should be charged off within the period to which it applies.

In some cases the deferred charges really represent payments covering permanent advantages, as where organization expenses are included under this general head. Here it is not strictly necessary that the charge should be written off, but it may be carried indefinitely, just as it might legitimately have been added to the value of the plant. But conservative companies are apt to charge these items off more rapidly than strict necessity demands. Thus one company charges off annually one-sixth of the discount on bonds, although the bonds run for twenty years. In another case one-eighth of a similar discount on bonds was written off in the first year, but in the following year the entire remainder disappeared.

According to the definition given above, such items as interest paid in advance, as well as organization expense, cost of stripping mines, and discount on bonds issued, are considered deferred charges. But there is some tendency to distinguish between prepayment of expenses belonging to the immediate future and other items often found in the group of deferred charges. It is thought by many that when the prepayment relates to an expense of the near future, it should be listed among current or among working assets.[24]

---

[24] *E.g.*, Dickinson, *Accounting*, pp. 34-5; Finney, *Principles of Accounting*, chap. iii, p. 11. For a different basis of differentiating de-

Deficits as Deferred Charges

At times there appear among the assets items which represent not anticipated expenses but unusual losses which the corporation does not see fit to charge at once to Profit and Loss, nor to make manifest in a reduction of capital. In such cases the charges which are deferred are not the costs of future earnings, but losses which it is expected future profits will cover. A striking instance of such an item is found in the balance sheet of the United Railways Investment Company for December 31, 1906, where there appears "Earthquake, Fire, and Strike, $859,983." Openly to show such an item is a vast improvement over carrying it concealed among the charges to plant and other material assets. Of course, it is in no sense an asset, properly speaking not even a deferred charge. But by treating it as shown above the loss does not necessarily interfere with current profits. The legitimacy of so doing is discussed at length in Chapter XII.

Trade-mark, Patents, Franchises, etc.

The above items are customarily considered as intangible assets. They are closely allied to goodwill in that their possession presumably enables a business concern to gain profits in excess of that which might be expected without such privileges; indeed a trade-mark has been legally spoken of as a protection to goodwill, the legal form by which it is maintained when dealing with customers at a distance.[25]

What has been said regarding goodwill in general applies to these other intangible assets. The argument in favor of gradually writing off their value is, however, perhaps a little stronger as each has a definite legal life. The Interstate Commerce Commission provides that the cost of franchise shall be written off by equal annual charges during the life of the

---

ferred charges from prepaid expenses, see Couchman, *The Balance Sheet*, p. 31.

[25] Liedersdorf *v.* Flint, 15 Fed. Cas. 219; Esquerré, *Applied Theory of Accounts*, p. 253.

franchise.[26] It is sometimes argued that there is no necessity for writing off the value of a patent even though it legally expires at a definite date. It is urged that goodwill of at least equal value will have grown up during the life of the patent and that the cost of the patent may therefore be considered as the cost of the goodwill gradually acquired during the life of the patent. While there is some force in this argument, conservative accountants generally approve of writing off the patent during its lifetime.[27]

Bibliographical Note

Cole, W. M.—*Accounts, Their Construction and Interpretation* (Revised ed., Boston, 1915), pp. 346-51.

Couchman, C. B.—*The Balance Sheet* (New York. 1924), chaps. xi, xii.

Dawson, S. S.—"Goodwill," Article in *Encyclopædia of Accounting*, III, p. 196.

Dawson, S. S., and de Zouche, R. C.—*Accounting* (London, n. d.), chap. xx.

Dicksee, L., and Tillyard, F.—*Goodwill, and Its Treatment in Accounts* (4th ed., London, 1920).

Esquerré, P.-J.—*Applied Theory of Accounts* (New York, 1915), chaps. xx, xxv.

Finney, H. A.—*Principles of Accounting* (New York, 1923), chaps. xli, xlii.

Guthrie, E.—"Goodwill," *Accountant*, XXIV, p. 425.

Kester, R. B.—*Accounting, Theory and Practice* (2d ed., New York, 1925), II, chap. xviii.

Leake, P. D.—*Commercial Goodwill, Its History, Value and Treatment in Accounts* (London, 1921). The most complete treatment of the subject.

Montgomery, R. H.—*Auditing, Theory and Practice* (3d ed., New York, 1922), pp. 195-200.

More, F.—"Goodwill," *Accountant*, XVII, p. 282.

Paton, W. A.—*Accounting Theory* (New York, 1922), chap. xiii.

---

[26] *Accounting Bulletin 15*, Case 99.

[27] Dickinson, *Accounting Practice and Procedure*, p. 79; Couchman, *The Balance Sheet*, p. 128. The propriety of amortizing patents is affirmed in Bagot Pneumatic Tyre Co. *v.* Clipper P. T. Co., [1902] 1 Ch. 159.

CHAPTER V

DEPRECIATION: GENERAL CONSIDERATIONS

Nature of Depreciation

Destruction is the law of nature. Fixed capital, using the term here in its economic rather than in its accounting sense, despite its name, is not exempt from this law. Even so-called permanent improvements, such as buildings, are all subject to the ravages of time, which Alfred Marshall aptly defines as "the complex of destructive agencies." All machinery is on an irresistible march to the junk heap, and its progress, while it may be delayed, cannot be prevented by repairs.

This obvious economic fact is of momentous import to accounting, although full recognition has not been given to it in general practice. It is one phase of the question of the inventory discussed in the preceding chapters. It implies that, in valuing all fixed assets, account must be taken of the lapse of time, and even in the case of machinery giving no evidence either of use or misuse, the bare fact that it is a year nearer its inevitable goal is an item of which technical account must be taken.[1]

In the language of accounting this inevitable decline in value is called depreciation. "Depreciation has been defined by the Interstate Commerce Commission as the lessening in cost value due to the smaller number of service units in the property as found than in the same property new."[2] The typical case is the decline in value due to ordinary wear and tear, but the term is also used by some writers to include the

---

[1] Even land which is ordinarily spoken of as not subject to depreciation may be subject to the same law when the fertility of agricultural land is being steadily exhausted by overcropping. See Montgomery, *Auditing, Theory and Practice*, 3d ed., I, p. 638.

[2] Valuation Docket, No. 2.

decline in the value of a machine because it becomes inadequate for the growing needs of the business or because of the fact that new inventions have made that particular type of machine obsolete. Usage in this point is not uniform, as some accountants, while recognizing that possible obsolescence should be taken into account, prefer to provide for it under some other title than depreciation.[3] Depreciation is not ordinarily used to cover the decline in value of wasting assets, such as mining property or standing timber, due to the normal processes of exploitation. This is described as depletion rather than depreciation, and depreciation is not used to cover changes in value due to fluctuations in market price.

In estimating the cost of production there must be considered not merely wages, material, fuel, and repairs, but in addition some allowance must be made for the diminished value of the fixed assets due to gradual loss of serviceability. Consequently profits are not determined until after allowance has been made for depreciation. Depreciation is not a disposition of part of the profits, but an expense without which profits can never be earned. The principle is clear. Materials consumed in manufacturing a commodity, as for instance fuel or oil, are, of course, an element of expense. This is so because an item of wealth disappears and its effect can only be to diminish *pro tanto* the expression indicating the net wealth. Its loss is in other words an expense. In the case of fuel the loss is immediate, and is, therefore, charged at once to expense. Exactly similar is it with the productive instruments whose use extends over a longer period. The article consumed in a single use must be considered an expense of the current production, the temporary structure or the tools lasting only a year are a charge against the production occurring during that year. The cost of more permanent assets, serving for productive use during a period of years, should be spread as an expense during the period of use, whether that be five or fifty years.

---

[3] See "Report of Committee on Terminology, A.I.A.," *Journal of Accountancy,* XXXIV, p. 232.

Depreciation and Efficiency

Considerable confusion has arisen as to the relation between depreciation and efficiency. This has been particularly true in the discussions of engineers who are inclined to discredit the accountant's view of depreciation as being purely theoretical. In many of these discussions, sometimes illustrated by formal diagrams, the idea is presented that in a machine having only twenty years of possible life, there is almost no depreciation until almost the end of its period of serviceability.[4]

This is due to the fact that for many years the machine may run with the same apparent efficiency; that is, if it is an engine it may furnish the same number of horsepower with practically no increase in the consumption of fuel or in the amount of repairs. But this is a misunderstanding of what is involved. Efficiency from the viewpoint of accounting involves the duration of the service as well as its quantity. To take a homely illustration: the "one-hoss shay" ran just as well in the last year of its life as it did in the first. The argument of the engineers would imply that no depreciation took place until the memorable moment when it utterly collapsed, but the account is correct in stating that there was a continuous decrease in value; that the purchaser paid for a hundred years of service, and one year after purchasing, because he had then an instrument which could possibly furnish only ninety-nine, instead of one hundred years' service, depreciation had taken place. It may even be said that at the end of the first year the "shay" was not so efficient for it had in it the possibility of only ninety-nine years' service instead of one hundred. This point may be made somewhat clearer by taking the analogy of the annuity. A twenty-year annuity yielding $100 a year furnishes just as much of an income in the twentieth year as it did in the first. If the engineers' crude conception of efficiency is accepted that

[4] See, *e.g.*, Floy, *Valuation of Public Utility Properties*, pp. 170-1. The correct view is, however, set forth in the admirable report of the Special Committee on Valuation of Public Utilities in *Proceedings of of American Society of Civil Engineers,* XLII, p. 1852.

remains unchanged through its entire life, but it is obvious that the value has steadily declined. Whether one has to deal with an annuity yielding each year a sum of money or a machine yielding each year a given amount of service is immaterial in regard to the principle involved. The calculation of the decline in the value of the annuity may be more accurate or more easily made than in the case of a machine, but there is no essential difference between the two.

In this connection, Couchman says that depreciation as used by accountants does not imply decreased intrinsic worth,[5] but here he too seems to be making the mistake of treating the efficiency of operation at a given moment as being an index of the worth of an article. The productive instrument which has only a fraction of its useful life before it has decreased in worth.

Purpose of Apportioning Depreciation

If, instead of considering the year as the fiscal unit of time, the entire economic period of production is regarded as the unit, the purchase of a machine is an expense—an expense, if the worn-out machine has no residual or junk value, to the full amount of the cost. If a manufacturer, renting his plant, produces a thousand engines in a year, it is clear that the annual rental is a part of the expense of producing the thousand engines. But, if the fiscal period is extended, it is equally correct to say that the production of ten thousand engines includes the total payment of rent for ten years. Exactly similar is it with machinery and patent rights. Assuming the life of each to be ten years, the expense of producing ten thousand engines includes not only rental for ten years, but as well the total cost of the machinery used and the cost of the patent rights. A purely artificial division of the productive process into fiscal years is made. It is, therefore, necessary to make an artificial and at best merely approximate division of these total expenses into the shares to be allotted to the operations of the several years.

---

[5] *The Balance Sheet*, p. 49.

Where rent, interest, or other time payments are made in advance, it is customary, when any such sum is outstanding at the time the annual balance is taken, to show the prepaid rent, interest, or insurance as an asset. Thus on December 1, a company may have paid $300 being six months' interest in advance on $10,000, $1,500 as a quarter's rental in advance and $1,200 one year's insurance. A balance sheet made December 31 would show among the assets: Interest Prepaid $250, Rent in Advance $1,000, Unexpired Insurance $1,100, making the apportionment, as is customary in the case of short-time items, proportionate to the time elapsed. The accounting procedure here is practically identical with the treatment of depreciation of machinery. Considering the entire productive process, the total cost of machinery and patent rights, is, as already stated, simply an expense of production. But at the end of each year part of this expense is conceived as pertaining to future, not to past operations, and therefore a portion of the cost of these so-called permanent, but really temporary assets, is treated just as prepaid rent, interest, and insurance. In other words, the asset item representing the value of the destructible or otherwise terminable instruments of production is logically similar to any of the deferred charges or prepaid expenses which also appear among the assets.

The immediate effect of allowing for depreciation is properly to apportion the annual expenses of operation over the different years during which the asset subject to depreciation is used. Otherwise the total cost of the machine must appear as an expense of the year when it finally proves unserviceable. At that time, its value ceasing, it can no longer appear in the inventory. The amount of assets on hand being thus diminished, there must needs be a subtraction from the Profit and Loss, or other proprietorship account. But if the original value of the discarded machine, say $20,000, was continued on the books throughout its entire life of twenty years it may roughly be said that the proprietors in the last year showed an excessive loss of $19,000, while the proprietors during the preceding nineteen years overestimated their profits by the same amount. Such a procedure is improvident where there is no change in proprietors or stockholders; it is inequitable where the personnel has changed; in all cases it is dangerous to the creditors who, up to the last year, have not been shown the true condition of the company's assets.

Depreciation and the Law

The earliest writers on accounting did not provide for regular depreciation charges, and the recognition that they were necessary has been a matter of slow growth. This is particularly true in the United States. Germany, Belgium, Switzerland, Austria all prescribe in their statutes that depreciation must be recognized before showing profits, but in the United States, and to a somewhat less degree in England,[6] there is no such regulation of accounting practice as is found on the continent.

In the absence of statutory provisions, the courts too were slow in recognizing the logical necessity of providing for depreciation. England was somewhat in advance of the United States in this respect, for as early as 1879 it was recognized that at least so far as material wear and tear is concerned, depreciation must be taken into account before profits can be ascertained.[7]

A clear expression of the same view was given in the later case of Bond *v.* Barrow Hæmatite Steel Company, Limited ([1902] 1 Ch. 353), but the earlier decisions of the American courts were exceedingly unsatisfactory. In this respect, however, there has been a great improvement in the last twenty years. Both Federal and state courts have to a considerable extent reversed their former attitude. This is well illustrated by the changed attitude of the Supreme Court of the United States. In an early decision it was stated that depreciation was not a proper charge, but more recently the

---

[6] But so early as 1878 an allowance for wear and tear was authorized for income-tax purposes. See *Report Royal Commission on Income Tax*, 1920, p. 48.

[7] Davison *v.* Gillies, 16 Ch. Div. 347 n.

court has frankly admitted that it should be taken into account.[8] While it stated in 1876 that the public "rarely ever took into account the depreciation of the buildings in which the business is carried on," the same court stated in 1917: "It is common knowledge that business concerns usually keep a depreciation account in which is charged off the annual losses for wear and tear and obsolescence of structures, machinery, and personalty in use in the business."[9] The changed opinion probably reflects a better understanding of accounting principles by the court as well as improved practice in business circles.

A similar most gratifying improvement is shown in the decisions of the state courts. In California, the idea that depreciation should be allowed was, in 1897, made the subject of ridicule and said by one of the judges to be "all wrong" and "not to be tolerated for a moment;"[10] but the more recent decisions in many of the states fully recognize the propriety of a charge for depreciation.[11]

In this progress, the Interstate Commerce Commission has been a most important factor. In its accounting rules which went into effect in 1907 it was, for the first time, definitely prescribed that a regular allowance estimated monthly must be made for the depreciation of seven named classes of equipment. These provisions have since been extended to cover other property of railroads and other classes of public utilities. The example set by the Interstate Commerce Commission has to a considerable extent been followed by the public utility commissions of the several states. Another factor in establishing the propriety of depreciation charges has been the regulations regarding the Federal income tax.

---

[8] U. S. *v.* Kansas Pacific R. R. Co., 99 U. S. 459 (1878); Knoxville *v.* Knoxville Water Co., 212 U. S. 1 (1909).

[9] Eyster *v.* Centennial Board of Finance, 94 U. S. 503 (1876); Von Baumbach *v.* Sargent Land Co., 242 U. S. 503, 524 (1917).

[10] San Diego Water Co. *v.* San Diego, 50 Pac. 633 (Cal. 1897).

[11] Cedar Rapids Gas Light Co. *v.* Cedar Rapids, 120 N. W. 966 (Ia. 1909); People *ex rel.* Jamaica Water Co. *v.* State Board of Tax Commissioners, 89 N. E. 581 (N. Y. 1909); Boothe *v.* Summit Coal Mining Co., 104 Pac. 207 (Wash. 1909); Contra Costa Water Co. *v.* Oakland, 113 Pac. 668 (Cal. 1911).

In these regulations depreciation was at first disallowed, then permitted, but still later recognized as necessary. An examination of the published accounts of American corporations shows a marked increase in the number of corporations making allowance for depreciation.

Despite the progress which has been made in recent years in accounting for depreciation, as shown both in the decisions of courts and in the practice of corporations, there is still considerable misunderstanding as to just what is involved in an allowance for depreciation.

Two Uses of the Term Depreciation

It is not uncommon to find depreciation defined as "a sum of money set aside out of profits to provide for the replacement of an asset." This statement contains so many grievous misconceptions that it deserves careful analysis. In the first place, it is necessary to discriminate between depreciation as a fact and depreciation as a term used in accounting. As a fact, depreciation is the decline in value of an asset due to wear and tear and similar causes. This fact largely physical, though it may be in part financial, has of course nothing to do with any of the characteristics given in the definition quoted above. Considering depreciation, however, as a term used in accounting, the definition is equally unsatisfactory. In accounting, the term depreciation is used in two senses. One of these is as the title of an account to which is charged a sum representing the periodical decline in value of the depreciating asset. The meaning of a debit to that account is exactly similar to a debit to any other subdivision of the Income or Profit and Loss account. It signifies that for some reason proprietorship has suffered a reduction to the extent named. It means and means only that proprietorship is less and the specific title to the account differentiates it from other similar subdivisions of the Income account in that it specifies that the decline in proprietorship is due to the fact of depreciation and not to the burden of rent, interest, fire losses, or any other specified cause. The other use in accounting of the term depreciation is that found in the title of an account ordinarily showing a credit balance and entitled in full Allowance for Depreciation or less satisfactorily Reserve for Depreciation. Presumably, it is this latter use of the term that the above definition attempts to describe.

Misconceptions Regarding Depreciation

The specific objections to the definition under consideration are as follows:

1. It does not represent a sum of money. It represents not an asset, but as Professor Cole has picturesquely described it, a hole in the assets. Money might conceivably be set aside corresponding to the estimated amount of depreciation, but that is another matter in a sense entirely independent of booking an allowance for depreciation. It is obvious that the depreciation exists whether cash is set aside or not and therefore the statement that it represents money set aside is obviously incorrect.

2. The allowance for depreciation has no reference to profits. The debit item already mentioned ultimately gets into the Income account, but the debit to Depreciation and the credit to Allowance for Depreciation are entirely distinct, although correlated conceptions. The definition of depreciation as something set aside from profits or as taken out of profits is not only misleading but dangerous. It carries with it an implication that if there are no profits there can be no allowance for depreciation. It implies that profits can be ascertained before calculating depreciation, and that the recognition of depreciation is to some extent a disposition of profits rather than a condition precedent to the ascertainment of profits. This may be conclusively illustrated by assuming the case of the owner of a steamship valued at $2,000,000 upon which the estimated annual depreciation is $100,000. For some cause the ship is not employed during the entire year. During that period there has been no income and of course no profit. But depreciation has, nevertheless, taken place. Proprietorship has been reduced at least $100,000 because of the fact of depreciation. In the case given this creates a deficit or an encroachment upon the original capital

but cannot in any sense be said to be something set aside out of profits.

3. The allowance for depreciation is not inherently a provision for the replacement of an asset. It shows that the asset is worth less than it was at the beginning of the year. Whether the asset is to be replaced or not depends upon the policy of the proprietor. The owners of a single ship might well carry on business without necessarily planning to replace the ship when it becomes no longer usable. Having already made the investment, it might be advisable to continue to make use of it, without implying that it would be desirable to reinvest in a similar enterprise.

This may be further illustrated by assuming that a railroad has laid in a supply of coal sufficient to last for many months. No railroad manager would for a moment think that the value of the coal taken from the stock in hand and consumed in the locomotives could be ignored in estimating the income of that particular month. No railroad accountant would think of contending that the credit to the Fuel on Hand account represented a part of the profits set aside for replacement of fuel nor that it in any technical sense represented a reserve for the maintenance of capital nor that in any sense whatever did it constitute any part of profits.

There is no logical distinction between the consumption of part of a stack of coal used in running the locomotives and the consumption of part of the value of a locomotive called depreciation. It would be a great improvement if all concerned in accounting understood that a credit to the Allowance for Depreciation of Locomotives is exactly similar in its effect to a credit to the Fuel on Hand account. It may be that the estimated depreciation is less accurate than the estimate of how much coal has been consumed, but errors may exist in either case and the difficulty in ascertaining the exact amount which should be credited to an account does not mean that there is any difference in the significance of the amount which is credited as representing the most accurate estimate possible.

Depreciation in American Practice

The present practice unfortunately does not always correspond to the correct principle. Corporations are still apt to look upon the charge for depreciation as being an act of grace rather than of necessity and the allowance is frequently less in the lean than in the prosperous years. But the improvement since the first edition of this book in 1908 has been very marked. At that time any recognition of depreciation was relatively uncommon in the accounts of American corporations and the relatively few companies which showed depreciation in prosperous years grew faint-hearted when business was poor. But an examination of the balance sheets of corporations during the trying period following the Great War shows that many of them made charges for depreciation even though that resulted in a net deficit. This closer adherence to correct accounting principles was doubtless stimulated by the provisions of the income-tax law.

The "50 Per Cent Theory"

Depreciation is ordinarily regarded as an annual expense in addition to repairs and regularly recurring annual replacements. This is because it is thought that despite such minor renewals as are involved in what is ordinarily termed repairs, the time will come when the plant as a whole or some major unit thereof will have to be discarded. In certain circumstances, however, annual repairs and renewals would theoretically make unnecessary any further allowances for depreciation. The conditions in which this would apply are as follows: (1) the plant is made up of a number of similar units; (2) which have been gradually added; (3) the units so added equal the number of years of anticipated life of each unit. This may be illustrated as follows:

A cab driver purchases for $1,000 a cab which will last five years. At the end of one year, his business expanding, he adds a second cab, also at the cost of $1,000. This continues until the end of five years, after which there is no further expansion of business. At the end of the fifth year, the first cab will, by hypothesis, be worn out, and if the business is to continue it must needs be replaced at a cost of $1,000. The same circumstances will exist at the end of the sixth and of each following year. There will therefore be regularly recurring annual replacements of $1,000; but the plant as a whole consisting of the five cabs will, with such annual renewals, be perpetual. It is to be noted that this annual replacement equals in value the annual depreciation upon the five cabs as each of these cost $1,000 and, lasting five years, depreciate $200 each year, a total for the five cabs of $1,000.

The conditions described above constitute what is spoken of as the 50 per cent basis. This means that after the organization has reached its normal growth, its estimated value fluctuates around 50 per cent of the total original cost. In the illustration used above this is shown as follows:

VALUE AT THE END OF FIVE YEARS

CAB NUMBER	Just before purchasing new cab	Just after purchasing new cab
1	$ 0	
2	200	$ 200
3	400	400
4	600	600
5	800	800
6		1,000
Total	$2,000	$3,000

The value of the plant as shown above fluctuates from 40 per cent to 60 per cent, or an average of 50 per cent. If the plant had consisted of ten cabs, each one with a life of ten years, the average value would also be 50 per cent of the original cost, but fluctuating only between 45 per cent and 55 per cent.

The above somewhat fanciful illustration brings out clearly the theory of the 50 per cent basis. It can of course never be fully realized. It is, however, frequently argued that an approximation is reached in any very widely spread plant consisting of a great many units which from time to time are being replaced. It is therefore urged that the underlying theory applies to the case of a railroad which, in almost every case, has been gradually constructed and extended. The units annually replaced are not uniform, but it is argued that there are so many different units that their differences are wiped out in a general average.[12] Therefore railroad accountants have been inclined to argue that after a road has become well established its annual value is approximately 50 per cent of the cost of all of the units and that the annual replacements, which are necessarily made, if the road is to continue in operation, render unnecessary the calculation of annual depreciation.[13]

Excessive Depreciation

Depreciation should cover all decline in value due to the use of productive assets. No less than this is required by accounting prudence. But while this standard is frequently not reached, some corporations charge to depreciation sums far in excess of the actual decline in value. Yet such excessive depreciation offends the very principles of accounting. To charge too much to depreciation is no less a deviation from accuracy than to charge too little. Yet the two trans-

---

[12] An interesting problem arises in case depreciation charges have been made prior to a company's reaching the so-called normal conditions described above. In this case, the allowance for depreciation should amount to 50 per cent of the cost of the plant and other presumably current assets would be held by the company to this extent. But these assets are, by hypothesis, not needed for extension of the plant nor will they be needed for replacements as the gradual replacements occurring year by year will be charged to operation expense. In this case it would seem as if the logical procedure would be to distribute these funds to the stockholders as a reduction of capital stock. The propriety of such a return has, however, not generally been admitted.

[13] This view has the support of E. Waterhouse (*Accountant,* XIX, p. 395) and of C. W. Haskins (*Accountant,* XXIX, p. 814). It has also a somewhat qualified support in the case of Pioneer Telephone and Telegraph Co. *v.* State, 167 Pac. 995 (Okla. 1917), in which the court states: "We have reached the conclusion that in plants of considerable size that have attained their gait, to which class the plant herein is conceded to belong, there is both theoretically and actually a normal condition in which the replacements come along with comparative evenness, and where there can be no possible use for a so-called depreciation fund of any considerable amount."

The distinction between maintenance and the allowance for depreciation is however clearly drawn in San Joaquin & Kings County Canal *v.* Stanislaus Co., 191 Fed. 875 (1911).

actions are very differently regarded by the public and by the profession. To charge too little is considered dishonorable, to charge more than enough is considered a sign of conservatism and is not only done by the most reputable corporations, but where this occurs the action is very frequently praised by financial writers.

The effect of excessive depreciation is to conceal the amount of profits, to create what is known as a secret reserve. Depreciation is normally charged to Expense, or at least to Profit and Loss. If, in fact, there has been no actual decline in value, the result is that the balance sheet shows an understatement of both assets and profits. The questions involved are, therefore, those of undervaluation of assets and secret reserves, both of which are elsewhere discussed. Here it suffices to call attention to the fact that an excessive depreciation, while generally condoned, is still a divergence from an ideal accounting, and its effect is the establishment of a secret reserve.

Depreciation and Replacement

The question is frequently raised as to whether depreciation provides for the replacement of the wasting article. The question itself, although sometimes propounded by accountants, involves a misapprehension. Depreciation in itself merely means that there has been a decline in the value of certain assets. If this results in a net loss, evidently there is nothing with which to replace a destroyed asset. For instance, a company with plant $100,000, capital $50,000, and debt $50,000 suffers a depreciation of 2 per cent. If other expenses just balance income, this means a net loss of $2,000. The balance sheet then would read:

Balance Sheet

Plant	$100,000		Capital	$ 50,000
Less Depreciation	2,000		Debt	50,000
		$ 98,000		
Loss		2,000		
		$100,000		$100,000

The plant is the only possession of the company, and there are no other free assets with which the loss can be made good. But where, after the deduction for depreciation, there is a net profit, the case is different. Assuming that the expenses other than the depreciation were $10,000 and the income $12,001, the balance sheet shows:

Balance Sheet

Plant	$100,000		Capital	$ 50,000
Less Deprecia-tion	2,000		Debt	50,000
		$ 98,000	Profit and Loss	1
Other Assets		2,001		
		$100,001		$100,001

In such a case the Allowance for Depreciation account signifies that other assets are now held equal to the depreciation. Part of the original plant has disappeared, but its value is represented by other assets. Evidently so, for if a decline in the value of one asset has not resulted in a net loss, there must, by the most fundamental principle of double entry bookkeeping, be an equivalent increase in the value of another asset.

The presence of an Allowance for Depreciation account signifies, then, the substitution of some new, presumably some floating asset in place of part of the value of one of the fixed assets. Whether this implies the presence of means to replace the old asset, or not, depends on the interpretation of the terms used. If the new asset consists of cash, evidently there are means on hand for replacement; if the assets exist in the form of some new fixed asset, that in itself does not directly give ready money. Constructively there is power to replace because of the equivalence of assets. Practically that power may be hindered by inability to realize on the asset. But a similar difficulty would exist under any circumstances; for the existence of a special replacement fund, composed, say, of stock-exchange securities might not always prevent difficulty in raising funds in a pressing emergency. The existence of an Allowance for Depreciation account implies, except in a balance sheet showing a net loss, the presence of new assets, that is of assets acquired since the purchase of the plant, of equivalent value. Whether these new assets furnish means of replacement depends on their nature and the conditions of the general market.

An apparent exception occurs where the new wealth is used to pay off a debt, when the balance sheet becomes:

Balance Sheet

Plant	$100,000		Capital	$ 50,000
Less Deprecia-tion	2,000		Debt	48,000
		$ 98,000	Profit and Loss	1
Other Assets		1		
		$ 98,001		$ 98,001

Here the cancellation, presumably, gives an equivalent borrowing power, and the presence of additional assets or the lessening of debts (that is the cancellation of negative assets) are practically identical.

Depreciation in Reference to Replacement Value

Considerable discussion has been held as to whether the charge for depreciation should provide for the cost of the asset (less any salvage value) or whether it should, during the life of the asset, amount to a sum sufficient to replace the asset. This discussion is of particular significance during a period of rising prices when it might easily be that a machine costing $10,000 would be replaced by a similar machine at twice that sum. The Interstate Commerce Commission definitely states that the depreciation is to be based solely upon cost, and this in general is favored by accountants.[14]

A similar question is often raised during the life of a machine whose market value has materially increased. Thus a machine with an estimated life of twenty years may have

[14] See *e.g.*, Couchman, *The Balance Sheet*, p. 202.

been purchased for $10,000. Five years later a similar machine is added but at a cost of $20,000. The question is raised as to whether during the remaining fifteen years of life of the first machine, depreciation should be estimated at $500 a year or at $1,000 a year. The depreciation upon the identical machine added to the equipment is at the higher rate. A somewhat specious argument is made to the effect that the real expense of running the plant includes the use and wearing out of machines worth $20,000 each. This view is in general not accepted by accountants who look upon depreciation as a distribution of actual cost. Under other circumstances the use of the machine would cost $1,000 a year, but in the peculiarly favorable circumstances, due to having purchased at an earlier date, the actual cost is only $500 and it is this which depreciation attempts to show.

Functional Depreciation

In addition to the loss from wear and tear even material goods are subject to further depreciation from economic changes. This includes changes in the residual value due to outside conditions, and, if it can be reckoned, the likelihood that the machine will be displaced by new models long before it is worn out. Experience may show that on the average a given class of machinery will be serviceable for twenty years, but that invention is so active that it is more profitable to displace the machines and buy new models as often as once in ten years. This is confessedly vague and indefinite, and implies the ability to calculate the future activities of inventive genius. The process is, of course, constantly taking place. Indeed, the success of American iron masters has sometimes been attributed to the readiness with which they discard serviceable machines in order to install new inventions. If an airship as now made would certainly run with undiminished mechanical efficiency for thirty years, probably no one would object to the statement that long before that time the present models will be displaced by some new and greatly improved type, and that a calculation to that purport should wisely be made. A more practical illustration is found in the lasts owned by manufacturers of shoes. Materially, these will serve for an indefinite number of years without destruction. Practically, it is a matter of certainty that the present models will be displaced by fashion long before they are worn out, and, as a matter of fact, the accumulated stock of out-of-date lasts is one of the serious burdens of shoe factories. The same principle applies to patterns used in foundries, sets of cards for Jacquard looms, and other assets whose continued serviceability is limited by the dictates of fashion rather than by wear and tear.

The propriety of making a definite allowance for obsolescence was recognized later than in the case of depreciation for wear and tear. In normal times such an allowance might be questioned, but the rapid and catastrophic changes which took place during and after the Great War, coupled with the fact that the taxpayer was vitally interested in showing all possible expenses, has secured general recognition of the fact that provision should be made for obsolescence. This has definitely been allowed by the Internal Revenue Bureau.[15]

Depreciation in all such instances is scarcely to be distinguished from a reserve created to provide against contingencies. If the loss of value is certain enough to be calculable it approximates closely to ordinary depreciation; if less certain and yet not to be neglected it resembles rather a reserve discussed in Chapter XIII.

Amortization of Nonmaterial Assets

The depreciation, or more properly speaking, the amortization of nonmaterial assets is, of course, not due to wear

[15] Regulations 65, art. 161. For further details of these provisions see, Salier, *Depreciation*, pp. 257 *ff*. The propriety of providing in advance for anticipated obsolescence is also recognized in: People *ex rel.* Brooklyn Heights Co. *v.* State Board of Tax Commissioners, 127 N.Y.S. 825 (1910); Pioneer Telephone and Telegraph Co. *v.* Westenhaver, 118 Pac. 354 (Okl. 1911); Thomas *v.* Crabtree, 106 L.T.R. 49 (1912). See also I. C. C. Valuation Docket, No. 2, p. 127.

and tear, but is no less inevitable. Where there is a time limit, as, for instance, in the case of a ten years' mining concession, the depreciation must be accomplished within that period. In many cases it is legitimate to charge off the value even more rapidly. Thus a copyright is likely to become of little value before its legal termination. One general rule is here applicable, namely: The more indefinite or uncertain the value of the asset the more rigid and rapid should be its depreciation.

Rate of Depreciation

The application of these general principles governing depreciation to the various classes of assets, and the determination of the proper rate to be allowed in each case are matters of the greatest difficulty. Material goods are subject to depreciation for both physical and economic causes. Physical loss or deterioration is a question whose ultimate decision is in each case to be based on the opinion of technical experts. Only thus can an estimate, even approximating correctness, be made of the probable life of the asset and its residual value. The nature of the machine, the intensity of work, the amount of repairs, the character of the operations, and many other technical matters enter into the calculation for machinery. Equally is each building to be considered by itself, for the nature of its construction, the use to which it is put, the climate to which it is exposed, the expenditures to be made in repairs, and other items are effective in determining its duration. Evidently in so complicated a problem, with so many uncertain, if not unknown quantities, no one even attempts minute accuracy. All the more need for making the calculation as carefully as possible.

It is impossible to lay down specific rates of depreciation which have any absolute value. Even the Interstate Commerce Commission, while requiring depreciation, has as yet not prescribed specific rates; but when asked to specify the rates replied:

Conditions under which equipment is used vary so greatly that no uniform rate of depreciation for all roads could be reasonably determined. The proper rate will, of course, vary inversely with the life of the property to which it pertains, and its determination must take into consideration whatever affects the life of the property. Each reporting officer should determine the rate to be used according to such experience tables as he may be able to construct from equipment records.[16]

However, the Commission is at present engaged in investigations with a view to establishing rates for depreciation as authorized in the amended Interstate Commerce Act. Many tables of rates have been prepared by various authorities covering different classes of assets, and extended detailed abstracts of these rates have been prepared by the American Institute of Accountants.[17]

For bibliography see note to Chapter VI.

---

[16] *Accounting Series, Circular No. 12a,* p. 2, Case 109.
[17] *Accountants Index, 1920,* pp. 353-677. ***Accountants Index Supplement,*** **pp. 145-232.**

CHAPTER VI

DEPRECIATION: METHODS OF CALCULATION

Annual Apportionment of Depreciation

Admitting the necessity of allowing for depreciation, the question arises as to the basis on which it is to be estimated. It is not possible to determine by inspection the present value of a machine or plant. Appraisers may make the attempt, but in doing so one element which they consider is the age of the machine and the depreciation which time itself has wrought in its value. Some basis must be adopted which, even if not strictly accurate, can be conveniently applied. So far as depreciation by wear and tear is concerned three factors are to be considered: original cost, tenure of use, and residual value. The last-named is of importance, for a machine is often displaced before it becomes entirely worthless. Its residual value as junk is exceeded by its value as a second-hand machine, for the progressive establishment often discards machinery still capable of considerable use.

With these factors it is clear that the problem is how to divide the difference between the initial value and the residual value among the years intervening between the purchase and the discarding of the asset. Various systems are in actual use, among which the most prominent are given below.

Straight-Line Depreciation

The simplest method is to divide the total depreciation by the number of years' use, and charge the quotient as annual depreciation, or in other words to charge each year a fixed per cent of the original cost. Thus a machine costing $600, expected to last five years, at which time it will have a residual value of $100, should each year have a charge of $100 or 16⅔ per cent of its cost to depreciation. Expressed algebraically,

$$D = \frac{V_1 - V_2}{n}$$

in which D represents the amount of annual depreciation, V_1 equals the cost price, V_2 the residual value, and n the number of years.

The advantage of this method is the extreme simplicity and the ease with which it can be estimated. For short-lived assets it is doubtless to be preferred. Objection is sometimes made that it requires constant reference to the original cost price. If depreciation is directly subtracted from the book value of the asset by crediting the amount to the ledger account in which the asset appears, this defect is of some significance, necessitating repeated reference to a value no longer exhibited by the accounts. But where a separate depreciation account is established and the original cost remains an integral part of the accounts, the criticism fails.

Depreciation as Percentage of Diminishing Value

A second method is to charge a fixed percentage of the decreasing net value. This gives not a constant, but a diminishing annual charge for depreciation. In the instance given above the depreciation instead of being 16⅔ per cent of the original cost, would be 30.12 per cent of the diminishing net value. The annual charges would, therefore, be:

Year	Value at beginning of year	Depreciation at 30.12% of diminishing value
1	$600.00	$180.72
2	419.28	126.29
3	292.99	88.25
4	204.74	61.67
5	143.07	43.10
Residual value	99.97	

Expressed algebraically the formula is:

$$V_1\ (1-r)\ (1-r)\ (1-r)\ (1-r)\ (1-r) = V_2$$

in which r represents the percentage of the diminishing value to be annually deducted for depreciation, and V_1 and V_2 represent, as before, the initial and the residual value of the asset. Hence is derived as a working formula:

$$r = 1 - \sqrt[n]{\frac{V_2}{V_1}}$$

which is easily solved by the use of logarithmic tables. It should be noted that this formula cannot strictly be applied where the asset has no residual value, that is where $V_2 = 0$, as for instance, in a terminable leasehold, or an expiring patent right. Practically it is applied even in such cases by assuming a nominal sum, say one dollar, or one cent, as the residual value. It will further be noted that because of the elimination of fractions the balance worked out generally will not exactly correspond with the assumed residual value of the asset, but as, at best, depreciation is a matter of estimate such small divergencies are of no significance.

The advantage of this method, in addition to its easy application to accounts showing the depreciated value of the asset, is that it makes the charge for depreciation less with each additional year. The argument in favor of this course is that in the earlier years the charges for repairs will be slight, but these will increase as the machine becomes older. As both repairs and depreciation are a charge to expenses of production, the increasing repairs and the decreasing depreciation make a uniform charge to expense, and thus profits are more equally apportioned between the several years during which the machinery is used. Furthermore a declining depreciation is thought to correspond better with the economic facts. The difference in value between a new machine and one that is one year old is probably much greater than the difference in value of a machine which has been used nineteen years and the same machine a year later. Thus Tiffany estimates that machinery in a flour mill depreciates 12½ per cent of its cost the first year, 8 in the second, 5 in the third, 2½ in the fourth, and only 2 per cent each year thereafter. This decreasing rate of depreciation is preserved by figuring depreciation as a percentage of the diminishing value. The objections to this method are obvious. It involves a complicated mathematical calculation, and the annual rate of depreciation gives little indication to the ordinary man of the period required to write off the asset. Furthermore it increases the depreciation charge in the earlier years, and in the case of a new concern this may be distasteful as being an additional charge against profits at a time when business has not come into full swing and profits are low.

Sum-of-the-Year-Digits Method

This method resembles the fixed percentage of the diminishing value in that the amount charged declines with each successive year. It is used because the calculation of the amount is a matter of simple arithmetic and does not employ the complicated algebraic formula above given. The calculation is as follows: The amount of depreciation for any given year is obtained by multiplying the total depreciation by a fraction obtained as follows: The denominator is the sum of a series of numbers representing the years which the machine will last. Thus, if its life is five years the denominator will be the sum of 1+2+3+4+5 or 15. The numerator of the fraction for the first year is the highest in this series, that is the number of years of life. In each successive year, the numerator is reduced by one. Applying this to the illustration previously used the depreciation for the first year is taken as 5/15 of \$500; for the second year as 4/15 of \$500, and for the fifth year as 1/15 of \$500.[1]

The calculation of depreciation by a constant percentage of diminishing value is generally justified on the ground that

[1] As neither the rate nor the amount of depreciation is the same in any two years no general algebraical formula is applicable; but the amount of depreciation to be written off in any given year may be expressed as follows:

$$\frac{2\,(n - n_1)}{n\,(n + 1)}\left(V_1 - V_2\right)$$

in which n_1 represents the number of years of elapsed life preceding the given year for which depreciation is to be calculated, the other symbols being the same as previously used. Thus, if it is desired to calculate the amount of depreciation for the third year the substitutions in the formula would show:

$$\frac{2\,(5 - 2)}{5\,(5 + 1)}\,(600 - 100) = 100$$

the declining charge to depreciation offsets the increasing charge for repairs. But this argument is merely an argument for a method which calls for decreasing depreciation charges and has nothing whatever to say in favor of the particular series of decreasing charges secured by this particular formula. The-sum-of-the-year-digits method is equally a system of decreasing charges and an infinite number of similar formulas could be derived, all of which would have a decreasing annual charge. Thus, for instance, the apportionment might be made so that the charge in each succeeding year should be $10, or any other stated sum, less than the amount in the preceding year.

Annuity Method

A fourth method, known as the annuity method, is even more complicated. It rests upon the assumption that the cost of production includes not only repairs and the depreciation of machinery, but as well interest on the amount of capital invested in the machine. Depreciation on this theory should be a sum figured as a constant annual charge sufficient not only to write off the decline in value, but also to write off annual interest charges on its diminishing value. Assuming the rate of interest to be 6 per cent, the reckoning should show:

Machinery Account

Cost price	$600.00	Depreciation	$124.70
Interest at 6%	36.00	Balance	511.30
	$636.00		$636.00
Balance	$511.30	Depreciation	$124.70
Interest	30.68	Balance	417.28
	$541.98		$541.98
Balance	$417.28	Depreciation	$124.70
Interest	25.04	Balance	317.62
	$442.32		$442.32
Balance	$317.62	Depreciation	$124.70
Interest	19.06	Balance	211.98
	$336.68		$336.68
Balance	$211.98	Depreciation	$124.70
Interest	12.72	Balance	$100.00
	$224.70		$224.70
Balance	$100.00		

Algebraically the formula is derived as follows:

$$[\{[(V_1 R-D) R-D] R-D\} R-D] R-D = V_2$$

in which R equals $1 +$ (the rate of interest), or in this case 1.06, and D the annual charge for depreciation.

Hence

$$V_1R^5-D(R^4+R^3+R^2+R+1) = V_2$$

or in simpler form:

$$D\frac{R^5-1}{R-1} = V_1R^5 - V_2$$

and

$$D = (V_1R^5 - V_2) \div \frac{R^5-1}{R-1}$$

or generally:

$$D = (V_1R^n - V_2) \div \frac{R^n-1}{R-1}$$

These values are obtained easily by the use of logarithms, or still more simply by the use of actuarial tables prepared for the use of insurance companies; for evidently V_1R^n is the accumulated value of V_1 at 6 per cent compound interest for n years, and the expression $\frac{R^n-1}{R-1}$ represents the accumulated value at 6 per cent interest of an annuity of one dollar paid at the end of each of n years. Such values are given in ordinary actuarial tables.

The use of this system implies that at the time interest is charged to the plant there is a corresponding credit to interest account. Consequently the net result to Profit and Loss account taken as a whole is that there is an equal annual charge of depreciation, and a diminishing annual credit for interest.

An objection to the last-named method is that it introduces the custom of marking up the value of assets by an allowance for assumed interest. In this particular case no inflation of profits results because there is an increased charge against profits for depreciation. But it is questionable whether it is not so dangerous a practice as to make objectionable anything which seems to justify it. Where depreciation is charged to the manufacturing account, the element of interest included in depreciation is reflected in the higher valuation of unsold products, a procedure to which many accountants would object. Furthermore, unless interest is charged on all capital invested, not merely on that subject to depreciation, there is a logical inconsistency in reckoning it in depreciation. It has, however, the advantage of separating the profits of manufacturing, or other business operations, in which depreciating capital assets are used, from the profits derived from the use of capital. This is so because the large depreciation charge goes into the Trading account,[2] while the countervailing credit to interest goes into the Profit and Loss account proper.

Sinking Fund Method

A variation of the annuity method is that called the sinking fund method. It consists in charging each year such a sum which if invested at a stipulated rate of interest, would amount to the total depreciation when the machine is outworn. It really implies an actual investment of the annual appropriations. The amount so set aside each year is less than the amount set aside under the annuity method by exactly the interest upon the original cost of the machine. The effect upon accounts is identical. In both cases the actual net charge for depreciation increases from year to year as illustrated in the following table. A larger sum than this is charged to depreciation under the annuity method but is offset by a decreasing credit to income representing the assumed interest upon the unexpired capital outlay. In the sinking fund method, the accumulations of interest upon sinking fund installment which is really income to the proprietor, is not credited to the income account. The interest

---

[2] See Chapter XVI.

actually received but not credited in one case exactly offsets the interest credited but not actually received in the other case.

Comparison of Methods

The four methods of figuring depreciation have this marked difference. The annual charge against profits decreases where depreciation is a fixed percentage of the diminishing value of the asset and in the sum-of-the-year-digits method. It is constant where depreciation is a fixed percentage of the cost; it increases where the annuity method is used. A comparison of the amount annually charged to depreciation under each of the methods described is shown by the following table:

DEPRECIATION OF ASSET COSTING $600 WITH ESTIMATED RESIDUAL VALUE AT END OF FIVE YEARS, OF $100

Year	16⅔% on Cost	30.12% on Diminishing Value	Sum of the Year-Digits	Annuity System, 6% Interest	
				Gross Charge	Gross Less Interest
1........	$100	$180.72	$166.67	$124.70	$ 88.70
2........	100	126.29	133.33	124.70	94.02
3........	100	88.25	100.00	124.70	99.66
4........	100	61.67	66.67	124.70	105.64
5........	100	43.10	33.33	124.70	111.98
Total....	$500	$500.03	$500.00	$623.50	$500.00

Authorities differ as to the desirability of one or other of the four methods. Where the courts prescribe depreciation they have generally allowed the basis and, indeed, the period to be left to the discretion of the company authorities. Even in Germany where statute law is most precise, demanding that depreciation be reckoned, and in certain cases even prescribing the period, there is no legal preference given to one or other of the methods of calculation.

In practice the straight-line method seems at present to be preferred. It has generally been used in rate-fixing cases in this country. It seems to bear the approval of the Interstate

Commerce Commission.[3] It was officially adopted in England in the valuation of the National Telephone Company[4] following the recommendations of such eminent authorities as P. D. Leake and Sir William Barclay Peat. This method has also the general approval of Sir Arthur Lowes Dickinson.[5] To many its simplicity is a strong recommendation.

The method of writing off a constant percentage of the diminishing value is favored because of its simplicity of application when the rate is once established and the fact that it can be applied directly to the book value even though that book value represents many different similar units of various ages. This method was approved by Sir Josiah Stamp[6] and by Dicksee[7] for machinery and short-lived assets. The annuity method, according to Leake,[8] is almost never used in commercial undertakings, but is used by municipalities. Bauer states that it is the correct basis on fundamental economic grounds but too complicated for practical use.[9] Dicksee recommends it only in the case of long-time leaseholds.[10] It has, however, the most hearty approval of the Special Committee on Valuation of Utilities of the American Society of Civil Engineers who in their admirable report state that it is the complete and logical method.[11]

---

[3] The rules of the Commission prescribe that a uniform monthly charge shall be made, but it has not made any ruling as to a choice between the annuity method and the straight-line method, both of which provide for a uniform charge. However, the Depreciation Section of the Commission very strongly recommends the straight-line method and makes the somewhat questionable statement that the annuity method "involves accounting that is misleading and such a procedure is really a manipulation of accounts and should not be permitted." See: Interstate Commerce Commission, Bureau of Accounts, Depreciation Section, *Report on the Problems and Investigations of Depreciation Charges . . .*, p. 23.

[4] 29 T.L.R. 190 (1913).

[5] *Accounting Practice and Procedure*, p. 169.

[6] See testimony in *Report of the Royal Commission on the Income Tax*, London, 1920, sec. 9757.

[7] *Auditing*, 13th ed., pp. 224, 238.

[8] *Report of the Royal Commission on the Income Tax*, London, 1920, sec. 3661.

[9] *Effective Regulation of Public Utilities*, p. 143.

[10] *Auditing*, 13th ed., p. 223.

[11] *Proceedings of the American Society of Civil Engineers*, XLII, p. 1868.

Depreciation on Basis of Service

The above methods all take elapsed time as the basis for distributing depreciation. In the second and third method this is very materially modified on the theoretical ground that the probable increasing cost of repairs should be offset by a diminishing charge for depreciation, but in some cases depreciation is not treated at all as a function of elapsed time. This is generally the case where a close estimate can be made of the amount of service which a machine will probably render. Thus if it is calculated that an automobile will run fifty thousand miles, half of the depreciation might be charged off after it had run twenty-five thousand miles whether that mileage was distributed over a greater or less number of years. In iron foundries it is usual to charge depreciation in accordance with the tonnage of output rather than in proportion to estimated life. Such a distribution is permitted by the Bureau of Internal Revenue.[12]

Controversy over Curved-Line Depreciation

The subject of depreciation in recent years has been principally discussed in connection with the regulation of rates for public utilities. In these discussions the method of spreading depreciation has been discussed as if there were an alternative between only two methods, generally spoken of as the straight-line method and the curved-line method. This terminology originated in this country, but has more lately been introduced into England.[13]

By the straight-line method is meant the division of the total depreciation equally between the number of years of use as described above. By the curved line is ordinarily meant a method which involves compounding interest. Mathematically speaking, the method of figuring a constant percentage on the diminishing value would also be represented by a curved line on a graph, but in most of the discussions, curved line is used as applying only to methods

[12] Regulations 65, art. 165.
[13] *Accountant,* XLVIII, p. 107.

involving the calculation of interest. The discussion of the propriety of including interest, as in the annuity method, has been well-nigh interminable and the problem seems insoluble. References to arguments on either side are found in the bibliographical note at the end of this chapter. It will suffice here to call attention to one or two matters involved in the controversy. Advocates of the straight-line method are apt to speak of it as being the obvious one. Thus a learned engineer says that if he pays ten cents for ten firecrackers, the value remaining after one has been exploded is obviously nine cents. But this, if obvious, is nevertheless specious in that it implies that what is true at a given moment is also true in a problem which necessarily involves the lapse of time. The assumption made by the engineer is that the value of each of the ten units is just one-tenth of the cost of all the units. This is true of present goods, but not of a series of future goods. This may be illustrated as follows:

A tenant rents a building on a ten years' lease for $1,000 per annum, payable annually in advance. The landlord makes a proposition to him that instead of paying merely one year's rent in advance, he make a payment for the entire ten years. It is inconceivable, unless a loan of capital commands no interest whatever, that the tenant would pay the entire $10,000, but it would be quite reasonable that he should pay in advance the actuarial value of the annuity covering the ten years. The amount that he would pay depends upon the rate of interest used in the calculation. If 5 per cent were taken, he would pay $8,107.82, and conversely if he pays $10,000 that represents an annual rental not of $1,000, but of $1,233.37. It follows: (1) that the value of the annual rental is not one-tenth of the total amount paid; and (2) the depreciation during the first year is not, in the case first given $810.78 (1/10 of $8,107.82) but a smaller sum $644.61.

Depreciation in Relation to Total Cost

In discussing the relative merits of the differing systems of depreciation, it must be borne in mind that allowance for depreciation is only part of a broader scheme whose purpose is to apportion expenses of operation over different years. It has been shown that the real cost of manufacturing includes both repairs and depreciation of plant. The total amount paid on both these accounts is properly a charge to the total cost of production during the period that the plant lasts. But the accidental fact that actual payments are not made uniformly is not proof that the annual charge should vary. One does not consider the semiannual installment of rent or interest as an expense peculiar to the month in which it is paid. Neither should the fact, if it be one, that a machine declines in value more in the first year than in the last year of its life justify making a greater charge to costs in the former year. The complete and scientifically correct method of figuring depreciation compels that there should be at the same time a recognition of the necessity of repairs and a simultaneous apportioning of both repairs and depreciation between the years irrespective of the time when the expense is actually incurred. There should, therefore, be two estimates made, one of the total shrinkage of value during the life of the machine, the other of the total cost of repairs during the same period. This being done there should be an equitable apportionment of the sum of these two between the several years. In other words, there should be an equal annual charge to expense and a credit to Allowance for Depreciation account and to Allowance for Repairs account. Replacement of outworn machines or repairs made can then be charged to these accounts. If the estimates are made with approximate accuracy there will result a proper distribution of expense between the several fiscal periods. But where no such uniform annual charge is made to cover repairs, and where expense is annually charged with the repairs actually made, sometimes more and sometimes less, a more correct final showing will be secured by making a sliding charge to depreciation, as is done where it is based on a fixed percentage of the diminishing value. This does not mean that the allocation of depreciation in this manner is in itself more correct, but that this error in apportionment offsets and neutralizes the increasing charges for repairs. But this is at best a rather awkward rule of thumb. The fuller, more scientific treatment of both repairs and depreciation, as being properly a uniform annual charge, is gaining recognition although rarely used in accounting.

Depreciation as a Percentage of Profits

From a purely theoretical viewpoint, there might be a justification of making the annual depreciation charge proportionate to profits. Ordinarily the charge is made in some way proportionate to time. Thus if the machine lasts five years, it is assumed that the depreciation in the first year has some relation to the total of five years. But in many cases, as for instance, an automobile, it is apparent that a time basis is illogical. A machine is not bought for the purpose of having it last a given number of years, but that it may render a given amount of service, mileage in the case of an automobile, output in the case of a stamping machine. This argument may be extended a step further. The ultimate purpose of a machine may be said to be, not so many years of life nor even so many units of service, but the yielding of so many dollars profit. The manufacturer pays $1,000 for a machine with the expectation that during its life it will yield $2,000 profit. Logically, therefore, it would be appropriate to charge the cost of the machine in proportion to the profits realized.

This may be made somewhat clearer by taking the case of an annuity. An annuity regularly yields the same amount each year so that its amortization is ordinarily a function of the elapsed time including, of course, a calculation of the effect of compounding interest, but it is conceivable that one might buy an annuity which would yield $100 the first year, $200 the second, $300 the third, $200 the fourth, and $100 the fifth. The amortization of such an annuity would not be at a uniform rate and a larger amount would be written off in the third year than in any other year simply because in the third year it yielded a larger income.

If one could with similar accuracy estimate the varying

amount of profits which would be derived from the use of a machine, it would be proper to base the annual charge for depreciation upon the annual profits. The objection to a depreciation charge varying with profits is therefore not one resting upon theoretical grounds. It is due to the practical difficulty that the calculation of the total profits to be derived from the use of a given machine is probably even more inaccurate than the calculation of the number of miles which an automobile will run, or the number of years that a building will last.

Irregular Charges to Depreciation

Whatever uncertainty there may be as to the choice between the methods of depreciation described, and despite the theoretical arguments that depreciation might be considered a function of profits, accountants agree that it is improper to make the amount annually written off for depreciation vary irregularly, charging off more in the prosperous years and less when profits are less. The natural inference from this practice is that in the absence of profits no depreciation is to be reckoned; while the fundamental fact involved is that depreciation is something inexorable, inevitable, an expense to be reckoned before it is possible to determine profits. This view is accepted not only by accountants but in Germany at least has been given legal authority by judicial decisions. The correct attitude has been taken in this country, too, by the Interstate Commerce Commission which has adopted as its rule the statement made by P. D. Leake:

> One of the most vital matters connected with productive industries and trading concerns is the regular assessment with substantial accuracy of the annual net profit or loss which has resulted from the operations of each year; and unless a near approximation to the outlay on productive plant which has expired within each year is made and fully provided for out of gross revenue, no correct statement of profit or loss can be obtained. . . . No profit can exist until expired outlay on productive plant has been provided out of gross revenue.[14]

---

[14] Interstate Commerce Commission, *Accounting Series, Circular No. 13.*

Depreciation in the Balance Sheet

Two methods are used for booking depreciation. For instance in a company whose balance sheet, before taking account of depreciation, is:

Balance Sheet

Plant	$100,000	Capital	$100,000
Cash	10,000	Profit and Loss	10,000
	$110,000		$110,000

an allowance of $2,500 for depreciation can be shown either by crediting that amount to the Plant account, reducing it to $97,500 or by crediting it to a separate account called Allowance for Depreciation, or some similar title, in either case the corresponding debit being to Profit and Loss. In the latter case the balance sheet should be in the form below:

Balance Sheet

Plant at Cost	$100,000		Capital	$100,000
Less Depreciation	2,500		Profit and Loss	7,500
		$ 97,500		
Cash		10,000		
		$107,500		$107,500

It is much more satisfactory thus to exhibit the original cost of the plant and not to show only the present depreciated value. Two companies might each show a plant valued at $50,000. It is not a matter of indifference that in one case this represents the total original cost of the plant, while in the other it gives the residual value of what was once worth $100,000. It has often been claimed that to credit the depreciation to a separate account, instead of to the account showing the asset, may lead to deception. This is rendered more likely because the terms used to indicate depreciation are frequently ill defined, and there is danger that a recognition of depreciation may be misunderstood as indicating a reserve of profits. Indeed this fear of deception is so strong that German law, at least according to the interpretation of Rehm, makes it illegal to book depreciation by crediting a separate account and requires that it be shown by writing down the value of the asset. But any danger from this score is fully obviated by a correct arrangement of the balance sheet. In the ledger the decline in the value of the asset is shown by an appropriate credit to Allowance for Depreciation, but in preparing the balance sheet this item should not appear with the other credit balances but, as explained on an earlier page, as a subtraction in an inner column from the appropriate asset.

Usage varies as to the title given to the valuation account. Probably in the majority of cases, it is entitled Reserve for Depreciation rather than Allowance for Depreciation. This is somewhat objectionable as the term reserve ordinarily indicates a portion of the profits, or surplus.[15] The Interstate Commerce Commission gives to the valuation account the titles "Accrued Depreciation—Road," "Accrued Depreciation—Equipment," and "Accrued Depreciation—Miscellaneous Physical Property." The exact title used is a matter of relative unimportance provided the item is shown as a subtraction from the asset account instead of being grouped with the entirely dissimilar surplus reserves.

Journal Entries for Depreciation

The technical procedure for booking depreciation is as follows. Assuming the case where a machine costing $600 has a life of five years with a residual value of $100, the journal entry, if the straight-line method is used, to be made at the close of each year would be:

Depreciation	$100	
Allowance for Depreciation		$100[16]

Accordingly, at the end of the fifth year the balance stand-

---

[15] See correspondence in *Journal of Accountancy,* XXXV, p. 63.

[16] In closing the books the charge to depreciation would be carried to Profit and Loss or to an account indicating the cost of manufacturing goods.

ing to the credit of Allowance for Depreciation would be $500. If then (after closing the books) the machine is sold for $100 as was originally anticipated, the following adjustments would be made:

Cash	$100	
Machinery		$100
Allowance for Depreciation	500	
Machinery		500

or more simply:

Cash	$100	
Allowance for Depreciation	500	
Machinery		$600

Adjustment of Inaccurate Estimates

It would, however, be an almost impossible coincidence if the calculations proved to be exact. The machine might have to be discarded before or after the anticipated five years and the residual value might also vary in either direction. We may assume the case that the machine was abandoned at the end of the fifth year at which time the credit to Allowance for Depreciation was $500, but the amount received for the discarded machine was only $50. Adjustment might be made as follows:

Allowance for Depreciation	$500	
Machinery		$500
Cash	50	
Machinery		50
Surplus	50	
Machinery		50

or more simply by a compound entry:

Allowance for Depreciation	$500	
Cash	50	
Surplus	50	
Machinery		$600

If the estimate had erred in regard to the life of the machine and in fact it was abandoned at the end of the fourth year and sold for $100 (the sale taking place subsequent to the closing of the books for the fourth year) the journal entry would be as follows:

Allowance for Depreciation	$400	
Surplus	100	
Cash	100	
Machinery		$600

The shrinkage in value not provided for through previous charges to Depreciation is by the above entries debited to Surplus rather than to the current Profit and Loss account. An error has been made in the preceding years which it is not altogether possible to correct. The result of these successive errors has been to show an excessive amount to the credit of Surplus. The adjustment therefore should be made through that account rather than through Profit and Loss, the loss being one of preceding years rather than one of the current year. If the abandonment, however, were made during, rather than after the closing of a fiscal period, the Depreciation account of the current year should be altered so that the proper proportion of the entire depreciation will be charged against the earnings of the current year.[17]

In the illustrations given above the calculation of depreciation has been made only once each year at the time of closing the books. Frequently, however, depreciation is estimated monthly and as in the case of any other expense account, closed into Profit and Loss (or into Manufacturing account) at the close of the year. The accumulating amount standing to the credit of Allowance for Depreciation remains upon the books until the depreciating asset is discarded.

Accounting for Discarded Machinery

A perplexing problem arises when machinery is abandoned before its anticipated life has expired in order to replace

[17] Thus, if the sale in the illustration just given were made just before closing the books at the end of the fourth year, the entry should be:

Depreciation	$125	
Allowance for Depreciation		$125
Allowance for Depreciation	425	
Cash	100	
Surplus	75	
Machinery		600

The actual annual depreciation being $125, the current year should be charged with that amount and the surplus should be reduced by only $75 representing a deficient charge of $25 for each of the three preceding years.

it with more efficient machinery. This may be illustrated by assuming a machine bought for $10,000 with an anticipated life of ten years at which time there would be no residual value. For eight years the machine has been used and each year $1,000 charged to depreciation. At that time it is decided to abandon the machine and buy a new one at a cost of $20,000. There are three different methods of handling the book value of the machine which at the time of abandonment is $2,000:

1. It may be charged against Surplus. This rests upon the interpretation that during the preceding eight years the charges to depreciation have been insufficient, being based upon an anticipated life of ten years, rather than on an actual working life of eight years. The annual charges have been $1,000 when they should have been, assuming a life of eight years, $1,250. The surplus for these years is overstated to the extent of $2,000 and this is corrected by charging off the book value of the abandoned machine to Surplus.

2. The $2,000 may be considered a deferred charge to be gradually written off against the earnings of future years. In extreme cases it might even be charged against the earnings of the single year during which the abandonment took place. Interpretation here is that in order to secure the advantages of using the improved machine, the company is willing to undergo the expense incident upon abandoning property worth $2,000. The earnings of the future will be larger because of the change made. It is therefore argued that it is appropriate that they should also bear the expense incident upon making such a change.[18]

3. The book value of the abandoned property may be considered as an additional cost of the new machine. This does not materially differ from the treatment described above, although the booking would be somewhat different. It definitely distributes the expense of $2,000 during the entire life of the new machine rather than having it possibly written off during a somewhat shorter period. The provision for

---

[13] See Cole, *Fundamentals of Accounting,* p. 322.

depreciating the new machine would of course cover that part of the attributed cost representing the abandoned property, and so the income of each of the years during which the new machine is used would be burdened by an appropriate portion of the $2,000.

Between these two views regarding the book value of the abandoned machine, that it represents an additional cost of past operations or on the other hand that it is an item to be charged against future operations, it is difficult to make a choice that would be binding in all cases. In cases of doubt, accountants are unfortunately apt to decide upon the basis of convenience, rather than on any scientific principle. If the concern has a large surplus already accumulated, the convenience of charging the book value of the abandoned machine against such surplus is obvious. If the surplus is insufficient, accountants and their clients would probably hesitate to make an entry which would result in a deficit appearing in the balance sheet and in such circumstances the book value of the abandoned machine would probably be spread over future earnings by entering it either as a deferred charge or as an additional cost of the new machine. If one desires to treat the transaction in a manner which is theoretically correct and not merely convenient, the weight of the argument seems in favor of considering it in all cases an additional expense of past operations. The arguments opposing this view are, however, worthy of respectful consideration.

Bibliographical Note

Allison, J. E.—"Depreciation," *Annals of the American Academy of Political and Social Science,* LIII, pp. 198-213.

Cole, W. M.—*Fundamentals of Accounting* (Boston, 1921), pp. 295-328.

Delano, F. A.—"The Application of a Depreciation Charge in Railway Accounting," *Journal of Political Economy,* XVI, p. 585. A criticism of the rules of the Interstate Commerce Commission.

Dicksee, L. R.—*Depreciation, Reserves and Reserve Funds* (3d ed., London, 1912). An important work.

GRINLING, C. H.—"The Need of a Depreciation Fund in Railway Accounts," *Bankers' Magazine* (London), LXXV, p. 692.

INTERSTATE COMMERCE COMMISSION, BUREAU OF ACCOUNTS, DEPRECIATION SECTION—"Report of the Preliminary Investigation of Depreciation Charges in Connection with Steam Railroads, etc.," August 23, 1923.

JACKSON, J. H.—"Some Problems in Depreciation," *Journal of Accountancy,* XXXI, pp. 81-102.

KESTER, R. B.—*Accounting, Theory and Practice* (2d ed., New York, 1925), II, chaps. xi-xvii.

LEAKE, P. D.—*Depreciation and Wasting Assets and Their Treatment in Computing Annual Profit and Loss* (London, 1917).

MAY, G. O.—"Problem of Depreciation," *Journal of Accountancy,* XIX, pp. 1-13.

MONTGOMERY, R. H.—*Auditing, Theory and Practice* (3d ed., New York, 1922), I, chap. xxviii.

PATON, W. A.—*Accounting Theory* (New York, 1922), chap. xviii.

SALIERS, E. A.—*Depreciation, Principles and Applications* (New York, 1922).

TURNER, S. H.—"Depreciation and Sinking Funds in Municipal Undertakings," *Economic Journal,* XIV, p. 47. Discusses the duplication of charges under English law.

CHAPTER VII

CAPITAL STOCK I

The Capital Account of Individuals

The Capital account, in the initial bookkeeping equation, represents the net wealth of the proprietor. It shows in a single item the net value of all the items listed in the accounts showing assets and liabilities. If the proprietor is an individual, a single Capital account represents the net wealth with which he starts his business; if it is a partnership, separate Capital accounts are established to show the amount contributed by each of the partners.

The keeping of the Capital account of individuals or partnerships is extremely simple. The original contribution made by each of the proprietors is definitely known, and there is ordinarily no doubt as to its value. This original contribution is accordingly credited to the account representing the capital. This is frequently headed with the name of the proprietor, with perhaps a further statement that it represents a capital contribution, and is not a loan, thus: John Smith, Capital account. The actual proprietorship interest in the business, however, necessarily changes from day to day, with each transaction, with the incurring of each expense, the suffering of any loss, or the taking of a profit. While each of these changes might logically be entered at once in the proprietor's Capital account, there is good reason for the bookkeeping practice of entering these daily changes in temporary subdivisions of the proprietorship account, which at stated periods, customarily at the end of the year, are all gathered into the Profit and Loss account. The balance of this account shows the net change in the proprietor's wealth which has occurred during the course of the year through business operations, or the misfortunes incident thereto. When the net change has been thus ascertained, it is transferred to the proprietor's Capital account, so that at the end of each year, as at the beginning of the business enterprise, that account shows, as accurately as may be, the net wealth of the proprietor. There is nothing fixed, arbitrary or conventional regarding the Capital account of the private trader. If he starts with an investment of $10,000 that amount appears as the initial entry to the credit of his Capital account. If he gains $2,000 profits during the year and withdraws from the business $1,500 for outside use, the Capital account is credited with the former sum and charged with the latter, so that at the beginning of the new year his Capital account again starts out with a balance, $10,500, which in a single sum represents the net wealth of which he is for the moment possessed. If in the second year the results show a loss of $1,500 this, at the end of the year, is in turn charged to the Capital account, which starts out the new year with a balance showing that the net wealth has been reduced to $9,000. From year to year, then, the account shows the actual net wealth, making no discrimination between the original capital contribution, the surplus or deficit due to business operation, or the alterations due to withdrawals or additions of capital by the proprietor.

Capital Account of Corporations

In corporations, however, the treatment of capital is not so simple. The original entry does not necessarily represent the amount of wealth which has been contributed by the stockholders; and increments to the net wealth are not annually added to the original sum, which remains constant at the par value. The Capital account of a corporation represents a nominal sum, the par value of the capital stock. The actual present net wealth is obtained only by combining with this item one or more other accounts, kept separate in the ledger and on the balance sheet, which show variations from this nominal capital and alterations in it due to business operations and other changes.[1]

---

[1] The phrase capital stock is frequently used in statutes as meaning "not the shares of which the nominal capital is composed but the

The accounting problems having to do with the Capital account are therefore, mainly, those connected with the capital of corporations. They arise generally from a divergence between the nominal or par value of the capital stock issued and the actual net wealth of the corporation. But even these problems would, in most cases, cause no difficulty were it not for the further fact that in many cases the corporation is unwilling to show clearly its exact condition. It may have done some financing which is prohibited by law, and it then becomes a problem how to present the accounts in such a way as to conceal this illegal action. Or it may be that not law, but business prudence, has been violated and again it becomes a problem how to conceal this fact in the company's balance sheet. The accountant should have no interest in solving such problems, nor is he, as an accountant, primarily interested in the exact legal status of certain financial transactions. For instance, in some states a corporation may legally purchase its own stock in the market, in others this is prohibited. In either case, the accountant, as such, is concerned only in showing that the purchase has been made, not troubling himself as to the legal problem, and still less attempting to find a way in which to conceal the fact that such a purchase has been made. If it is kept clearly in mind that the only legitimate purpose of accounts is to show the truth, and if accounts are kept strictly to this rigid standard, the problems of the accountant will be materially lessened.

Opening Entries

When a new corporation is started, the first step, normally, is to secure subscriptions for the capital stock authorized by the charter. If such subscriptions are obtained for the full authorized capital of the company the initial condition is then that the company begins with an authorized capital of a given amount, the net wealth which it represents being

---

actual capital, that is the assets with which the corporation carries on its corporate business.'' Schulte *v.* Blv'd Gardens Land Co., 129 Pac. 582 (Cal. 1913). This corresponds to the economic, not to the accounting definition of capital.

composed entirely of promises made by the subscribers to pay that amount. In this initial stage, then, the balance sheet is:

Balance Sheet

Subscriptions	$100,000	Capital Stock	$100,000

This may be assumed to be the normal opening balance sheet for a corporation where the stock is fully subscribed. It is perfectly correct, for while no wealth has been paid into the treasury of the company, the signing of the subscription list creates an obligation on the part of the subscriber which is legally collectible by the company. It is as truly an asset, as the accounts receivable or the notes receivable held by a merchant.[2]

As the subscriptions are called and paid, the treatment is identical with that of any other form of account receivable when it is paid to the proprietor. The cash received is debited, the Subscription account is credited, and gradually the item subscriptions disappears from among the assets, and there is substituted therefor cash or some other form of property.

Unsubscribed Stock

But not infrequently the incorporators desire to begin business without securing subscriptions for the entire authorized capital stock. At the beginning of operations the entire sum, here $100,000, is not needed, and it is thought better not to receive subscriptions until later when it can be profitably used, and when the evidence of successful operation will perhaps make it easier to secure the desired subscriptions. Assuming that, of the $100,000 authorized capital stock, subscriptions are obtained for only one half, or $50,000, the booking of the transaction is variously made, the more common forms being given below.

Balance Sheet

Cash	$50,000	Capital Paid In	$50,000

[2] Coleman *v.* Booth, 186 S.W. 102 (Mo. 1916).

Balance Sheet

Cash	$50,000	Capital Stock		$100,000
Unissued Stock	50,000			
	$100,000			$100,000

Balance Sheet

Cash	$50,000	Capital Stock		
Unissued Stock	50,000	Outstanding	$50,000	
		In treasury	50,000	
				$100,000
	$100,000			$100,000

Balance Sheet

Cash	$50,000	Capital Authorized	$100,000	
		Less amount held in treasury	50,000	
				$50,000
	$50,000			$50,000

Many accountants argue in favor of the first form given above, saying that $50,000 is all that the company has received, that it is all that serves as a guarantee to creditors; and that the unsubscribed and unissued stock is virtually nonexistent. The same idea is embodied in some laws.[3] Despite these authoritative statements there is some ground for holding that the treatment is not altogether sufficient.

The argument that unsubscribed and unissued stock must not appear at all in the accounts of the company because it is nonexistent is somewhat specious. The amount of depreciation of machinery or plant is no less nonexistent. Indeed, unsubscribed stock has a certain reality, for it does constitute a means by which directors can, at least in times of prosperity, raise funds, while the depreciation of property represents an

[3] *E.g.*, Austria, Germany, and Quebec.

absolutely nonexistent quantity. Yet the appearance of depreciation under Allowance for Depreciation, is a recognized and legitimate convention of accounting.

While unsubscribed stock is not an asset so far as the creditor is concerned, yet the existence of such stock, subject to issue at the discretion of the directors, is a matter of which the stockholder should be informed. Perhaps the desired information is sufficiently given in a footnote, or other memorandum attached to the balance sheet, which is the form used by British companies. But to many accountants it seems desirable to show the total authorized capital stock as an item entering into the accounts proper, with the unissued stock as an item appearing elsewhere in the balance sheet. This may be accomplished in various ways. In the second balance sheet given above the authorized capital stock appears among the proprietorship items with unissued stock as an asset. The objection to this is that the balance sheet gives an exaggerated and perhaps misleading statement of the actual capital of the corporation. In the third form the total authorized capital stock also appears as the significant item in the extended column of the balance sheet but in an interior column this is divided into two items: outstanding stock and stock in treasury. While the unissued stock is listed among the assets, attention is in this way called to the fact that not all of the capital stock has been issued. A much better method, however, is not to include unissued stock among the assets but to show it in the balance sheet as the subtraction from the amount of authorized capital. This is the form prescribed for railroads by the Interstate Commerce Commission. It should be noted that while there may be little difference in the balance sheet where unissued stock is treated as just described and one where unissued stock has been left entirely out of the accounts, there is a real difference in the ledger accounts. In the latter case there is no account showing unissued stock to be found in the ledger and the Capital Stock account in the ledger shows a credit for the amount of outstanding stock only. But the other balance sheets, while differing in arrangement, represent identical ledger entries.

In each instance, an Unissued Stock account is found in the ledger showing a debit balance and the Capital Stock account proper shows a credit for the entire amount authorized.[4]

Journal Entries I

There is considerable divergence in the detail of booking capital stock where this is not paid up in full at the time of organization. One method which should be recommended for simplicity and directness is represented by the following journal entries:[5]

Unsubscribed Capital Stock	$100,000	
Authorized Capital Stock		$100,000
Subscriptions	60,000	
Unsubscribed Capital Stock		60,000
Cash	40,000	
Subscriptions		40,000
Cash	20,000	
Subscriptions		20,000

The first of these entries is a formal, technical entry to record upon the books the total amount of authorized capital stock. Attention has already been called to the objection made by some accountants that both the debit and credit are fictitious in that the unissued stock is not an asset nor does the mere authorization mean that the corporation actually has a proprietary interest of the amount authorized. But the objections are minimized if in the balance sheet the unsubscribed stock is shown (as in Form 2) as a subtraction from the amount authorized, just as the allowance for depreciation is subtracted from the book value of the machine. The fact that the debit balance of an account may not properly appear among the assets in the balance sheet is in no sense an argument against having in the ledger an account showing such a debit balance. The second entry above records the subscription. This properly shows an asset consisting of contractual rights against the subscribers and by lessening the

[4] These different methods of handling capital stock in the balance sheet are all exhibited in the model forms on p. 175.

[5] This method is set forth in Anderson, *Complete Accounting Course,* I, 17, pp. 6-7; Esquerré, *Applied Theory of Accounts,* p. 325.

amount of unsubscribed stock shows that the proprietorship of the corporation actually amounts to $60,000. The subsequent entries are entirely analogous to the payment of any other receivable and are in no sense peculiar to corporation accounting.

Journal Entries II

In the above method the amount of outstanding stock is obtained only by taking the difference between the Authorized Capital Stock and Unissued Capital Stock as shown in the ledger accounts. The second method differs primarily in establishing an account which will specifically show the amount of stock outstanding. According to this method the sequence of the journal entries is:[6]

Unissued Capital Stock	$100,000	
Authorized Capital Stock		$100,000
Subscriptions	60,000	
Capital Stock Subscribed		60,000
Cash	40,000	
Subscriptions		40,000
Cash	20,000	
Subscriptions		20,000
Capital Stock Subscribed	60,000	
Unissued Capital Stock		60,000
Authorized Capital Stock	60,000	
Capital Stock Outstanding		60,000

In this procedure it is not recognized that there is any actual capital until the certificates of stock are issued. Many accountants assume that this does not take place until the subscriptions are paid in full and that the issue of certificates must inevitably follow promptly upon such payment. Both of these assumptions are, however, questionable. The last two entries are for the purpose of showing, respectively, that the unissued capital stock has now been issued and not merely subscribed for and that that which was previously merely authorized is now actually outstanding stock.[7]

---

[6] Recommended by Conyngton, *et al.*, *Corporation Procedure*, p. 1076.

[7] The Interstate Commerce Commission (*Classification of Income, Profit and Loss, and General Balance Sheet Accounts for Steam Roads*, p. 50) makes a fourfold division of capital stock as follows:

A variation in the second method omits the initial entry, which necessitates a corresponding modification of the journal entries made when the stock is issued; the sequence of the entries would be as follows: [8]

Subscriptions	$60,000	
Capital Stock Subscribed		$60,000
Cash	40,000	
Subscriptions		40,000
Cash	20,000	
Subscriptions		20,000
Capital Stock Subscribed	60,000	
Capital Stock Outstanding		60,000

Forfeited Stock

It is customary to provide that in the case a subscriber to capital stock fails to make the required payments the stock for which he has subscribed may be forfeited. In some cases, whatever the subscriber may have paid is lost to him, in other cases part or all may be returned to him, depending upon the terms at which the corporation later disposes of the forfeited stock. This may be illustrated by assuming a subscription for $10,000 stock at par, on which the first call for 20 per cent of the subscription has been paid, but a second call for 25 per cent is defaulted. Appropriate entries in this case would be:

Forfeited Stock	$10,000	
Subscriptions		$8,000
Surplus from Forfeited Stock		2,000

If another subscriber were secured who agreed to take over the rights of the defaulting subscriber the surplus from forfeited stock would be canceled and the corporation would be

Nominally issued, when certificates are prepared and made ready for sale;
Actually issued, when sold to a bona fide purchaser for a valuable consideration and such purchaser holds it free from all control by the accounting company;
Actually outstanding, when actually issued and not reacquired; and
Nominally outstanding when stock actually issued has been reacquired.

[8] New York Public Service Commission, *Uniform System of Accounts for Electrical Corporations*, p. 20; Couchman, *The Balance Sheet*, p. 183; Paton, *Accounting*, p. 699. Alternative forms differing slightly in detail are given in Finney, *Principles of Accounting*, I, chap. viii; Kester, *Accounting, Theory and Practice*, 2d ed., I, pp. 341 *ff*.

in the same position as if the original subscriber had met his obligation. The journal entries would accordingly be:

Subscriptions	$8,000	
Surplus from Forfeited Stock	2,000	
Forfeited Stock		$10,000

If the new subscriber were willing to take the stock at par, paying as much for the stock as the other subscribers, the surplus from donated stock would not be affected and would represent a real gain to the corporation because of the default of the first subscriber. It is more likely that the stock will be disposed of at some intermediate figure; perhaps some one being found who would be willing to pay $8,500; the entry then would be:

Subscriptions	$8,500	
Surplus from Forfeited Stock	1,500	
Forfeited Stock		$10,000

The above entries assume that at the time the subscription is forfeited the corporation plans, if possible, to dispose of the defaulting subscriber's right and to substitute a new subscriber in his place, and this accords with ordinary procedure. If, however, the company makes no effort to place the stock but merely considers the transaction as canceled it would be undesirable to debit the Forfeited Stock account; a proper entry would be:

Capital Stock Subscribed	$10,000	
Subscriptions		$8,000
Surplus from Forfeited Stock		2,000

This places the company in the same position as it would have been if the subscription for this $10,000 of stock had never been made with the exception that it has $2,000 additional in the treasury.

If at the time the subscriptions were received the credit had been to Unsubscribed Capital Stock rather than to Capital Stock Subscribed (that is, if the first method of recording subscriptions given on p. 177 had been followed) the journal entries at the time of the forfeiting of the stock would be correspondingly modified; thus, instead of journal entries just given, there would appear:

Unsubscribed Capital Stock	$10,000	
Subscriptions		$8,000
Surplus from Forfeited Stock		2,000

The surplus derived from forfeiture should not be credited to the current Profit and Loss account nor to the general Surplus account. In some jurisdictions it might perhaps be legally distributable, but in any event it is especially important that its source should be clearly indicated.

Repurchase of Stock

Very similar is the problem of the treatment of the capital stock which after issue has been reacquired by the company. Aside from the question of the legality of this action, which is not an accounting question at all, the discussion turns on whether stock so acquired is a real asset, and, if so, how it is to be represented in the accounts. The argument against the legitimacy of showing unissued stock is also used though with less cogency, regarding repurchased stock.[9] In a certain sense any return of capital stock to the issuing company may be considered as a virtual cancelation of that amount of the previously issued stock. A distinction may be made according to the purpose for which the stock is acquired. If it is done with the intention of reducing the capital stock, certainly the stock so acquired and canceled should be deducted from the amount of outstanding stock, and should appear as below:

Balance Sheet

Plant and other assets	$120,000	Capital Stock		
Investments	15,000	Authorized	$100,000	
Cash	5,000	Less Canceled Stock	10,000	
				$ 90,000
		Bonds		50,000
	$140,000			$140,000

But if there is no intention of reducing the capital and the acquired stock is not canceled, accounting practice occasion-

[9] Dickinson states that the practice of showing treasury stock as an asset is "erroneous and misleading." *Accounting Practice and Procedure,* p. 130.

ally shows the stock listed among the assets, under the title Treasury Stock or Reacquired Stock.[10] An illustration of such treatment is found in the balance sheet of the Chicago and Northwestern Railway Company. Where this is the case it is better to call attention to the fact also on the credit side of the balance sheet as is shown below:

Balance Sheet

Plant, etc.	$120,000	Capital Stock:		
Investments	15,000	Outstanding	$90,000	
Treasury Stock	10,000	Held in treasury	10,000	
Cash	5,000			$100,000
		Bonds		50,000
	$150,000			$150,000

The preferable way is not to list the treasury stock among the assets but to show it as a deduction from the total capital stock on the credit side of the balance sheet as in Form 5. A slight modification is found in the rule of the Interstate Commerce Commission which, indeed, lists the stock held in the treasury on the asset side of the balance sheet but only in an interior or short column not extending it into the outer column, the footing of which shows the total assets.[11] The amount of such treasury stock is, of course, also deducted on the credit side of the balance sheet.

It is, however, misleading, and hence incorrect, to allow the stock held in the treasury to be included in some general designation which does not clearly show that it is the company's own stock. In the statement above, to include both Investments and Treasury Stock under the single title Investments would be thus misleading. This decidedly objectionable form is not infrequently used, and occasionally, it may be, to the deception of creditors.

If the reacquired stock is purchased at less than par the difference should be credited to a special account clearly indi-

[10] Treasury stock is occasionally used to describe unissued stock. It is, however, preferable to restrict the use of this term to stock which has once been issued by the corporation and subsequently reacquired.

[11] See form of general balance sheet statement, Form 13.

cating the origin of the surplus thus derived. This account might be entitled Discount on Treasury Stock or Surplus Arising from the Purchase of Stock. The Interstate Commerce Commission, however, authorizes its credit to Profit and Loss through an account called Miscellaneous Credits.[12] But Profit and Loss as used by the Commission is not the account in which current profits are shown but one in which adjustments of accumulated profits are made. For income-tax purposes, however, the proceeds of the sale of treasury stock do not constitute income of the corporation.[13]

Sale of Treasury Stock

When fully paid stock has been reacquired by the corporation and held as treasury stock, it is generally assumed that it may be sold by the corporation at any price, without any obligation on the part of the purchaser for any discount allowed to him. This, however, is probably incorrect except where the stock has been donated to the corporation. Thus, if stock issued at par was reacquired by the corporation at 90 to sell it at less than 90 would work an actual reduction of the contributed capital. If sold at 90 or above the protection which the creditors of the company have a right to assume will be fully maintained. Where reacquired stock is sold at an advance over the purchase price, the excess should be credited to some account clearly showing the nature of the item. A descriptive title such as Premium on the Sale of Treasury Stock would be satisfactory. It should not be credited to current Profit and Loss or ordinary Surplus.[14]

Donated Stock

Occasionally a company reacquires some of its stock, not by purchase but by gift. So far as booking is concerned, this is

---

[12] Account 607.

[13] Regulations 65, art. 543.

[14] But Montgomery distinguishes between the buying and selling of the stock of the company in the open market and the sale of donated stock. He considers that gain arising in the former case is income, in the latter case an increase in capital. *Auditing, Theory and Practice,* 3rd ed., I, p. 292.

practically equivalent to purchasing it at a price of zero, or otherwise expressed as a purchase at a discount of 100 per cent. Where stock is donated it is ordinarily that which has been issued in exchange for property rather than for cash. The more extended discussion of this rather unusual and peculiar transaction is accordingly deferred to the following chapter.

Uncalled Subscriptions

In the case of some corporations, subscriptions are received for all the capital stock but without any intention of having the entire amount paid up in the near future. An extreme instance is found in the British Joint Stock Banks which continued for many years with only a small portion of its capital paid up. Thus the Bank of Liverpool and Martins Limited has only one-eighth of its subscribed capital paid in. The actual capital needed in business is supplied by the cash paid in; the total security to creditors is eight times that amount. Such uncalled subscriptions differ materially from capital stock authorized but unissued. If, for example, $80,000 were subscribed for and only $10,000 paid in, it would be really incorrect to present the capital as only $10,000 and to make no reference to the uncalled subscriptions. Yet practice is not uniform on this point, and to what extent the uncalled subscriptions are to be included in the accounts proper, and how far they are only to be referred to as an explanatory item is not uniformly agreed upon. In England the standard form for balance sheets which obtained vogue from being included as a model form in Table A of the Companies Act (shown in Form 15) excludes the uncalled subscriptions from the accounts proper, the form used being:

LIABILITIES

Nominal capital (10,000 shares of £10 each)	£100,000	
Capital called up (£5 per share)	£ 50,000	
Less calls in arrears	100	
Capital paid in		£ 49,900

In this the nominal capital is no part of the balance sheet proper, and a further distinction is made between uncalled subscriptions and those called but in arrears. Only the paid-in capital shows in the extended column.

In France, however, the uncalled subscriptions appear generally as an asset; and in Germany, while not always shown, the omission is said by Rehm to be contrary to both law and principle.[15] In this country it is less common to issue stock not fully paid up, but the propriety of showing the uncalled subscriptions as assets is backed by the authority of the frequently cited case of See *v.* Heppenheimer [16] stating explicitly that it is a "rule of the common law that the unpaid subscriptions to the capital stock of a corporation form an asset for the payment of the debts thereof." Where the calls are in arrears it may be better to indicate that fact clearly, as is done in the English form above, on the principle that a call in arrears, at best, is of doubtful value. Either of the forms given below is satisfactory.

Balance Sheet

Cash	$50,000	Capital Fully Subscribed	
Uncalled Subscriptions	50,000	Paid In	$50,000
		Subscriptions Uncalled	50,000
	$100,000		$100,000

Balance Sheet

Cash	$50,000	Capital Fully Subscribed	$100,000
		Less Subscriptions Uncalled	50,000
		Capital Paid In	$50,000
	$50,000		$50,000

It is sometimes stated that it is illogical to include the contingent asset of uncalled subscriptions in the balance sheet,

[15] Dicksee, *Auditing,* 13th ed., p. 274; Rehm, *Die Bilanzen,* p. 380.

[16] 61 Atl. 859. See also Coleman *v.* Booth, 186 S.W. 1021, 1027 (Mo. 1916).

since, as a rule, both contingent assets and contingent liabilities are omitted. Thus, in the case of a national bank, where the stockholder who has paid up his subscription in full is liable to a further assessment of 100 per cent if that is needed to pay off creditors, this additional contingent asset is never included in the balance sheet. But there is a marked difference; the additional liability of the shareholders of a bank is only available in case of insolvency, while the subscriptions are an asset on which the directors can call, and are therefore more evidently an item to appear in the balance sheet.

Stock Issued at a Premium

Subscriptions to capital stock are not infrequently made at a premium. This is particularly common in the case of banks, where for one or another reason the institution prefers to start in with assets in excess of the nominal capital. It is also common where an established company increases its capital stock in circumstances which make investors glad to pay a premium for a share in an enterprise which is already eminently successful. In all such cases the premium is economically a capital contribution and nothing else; but the requirement that the capital appear at its par value makes it necessary to enter the sum thus paid under some other head. The customary title is Surplus which is the term always used by national banks. It is, however, preferable to use a more distinctive title, such as Premium on Capital Stock, so as clearly to indicate that it in no respect represents profits arising from the business. To credit it to Profit and Loss, whether legally permissible as in England, or prohibited as in Germany, is a procedure condemned by business prudence in all countries. The subject is discussed more fully in Chapter XII.

Determination of Premium

At times the accountant meets difficulty in determining whether or not a premium has been paid on the stock, and this unavoidable uncertainty is sometimes used as a means of showing an apparent surplus when none exists. To take a familiar illustration, a company is organized with capital stock of $100,000. A contract is made whereby an owner of a plant agrees to turn over his property valued nominally at $90,000, and $9,000 cash in return for $90,000 stock. The interpretation of this transaction frequently made is that the cash contributed is a premium on the stock. A more conservative interpretation is that the real value of both plant and cash is only $90,000, so that no surplus exists. Sometimes an attempt is made to base the interpretation of the transaction on the terms on which the other stock is placed. If this is subscribed for, the subscription to be paid in cash at the rate of 110, the presumption is evident that the stock given in exchange for the plant and cash was also really taken at a premium of practically that percentage, and that the surplus really exists. But even this criterion is faulty. The company might be capitalized say, at $90,100, of which $90,000 is given in exchange for the plant and $9,000 cash. It would be a simple matter for the promoters to subscribe for the remaining $100, at 110, or at any other exorbitant rate, if by so doing they could establish the surplus which is claimed in the purchase of the property. The reality of a claimed surplus is, therefore, not to be established by any such simple rule of thumb, but can be determined only by a careful estimate of the real value of that which is given in payment of the subscription.

Reduction of Capital Stock: by Purchase

The reduction in the amount of capital stock, at least when performed directly, offers no problem of accounting. If it is decided to reduce the capital, assuming that the legal requirements are complied with, the booking is identical with that in case of the payment and cancellation of any other credit balance, the amount debited to Capital Stock and that credited to Cash offsetting each other. Or, if the stock retired is redeemed not with cash but with bonds, as was the case in the refunding operations of the United States Steel Corporation, the bonds paid out offset the capital stock retired, just as in a merchant's books the Notes Payable given to a creditor offset the amount previously standing as an account payable. But at times the retirement of the stock is made dependent on the existence of surplus profits, and the payment to the stockholders is treated as if it were actually a charge against profits. Provision for the retirement of stock may be made in precisely the same manner as is the payment of bonds by a sinking fund, as described fully in Chapter XV. Evidently the same difficulty arises in either case. If the retirement of capital, not being a loss transaction, is yet charged against profits, there must be created a corresponding credit, sometimes called Retired Stock, sometimes, more correctly, "Reserve created by the retirement of capital out of profits." In any event when the stock has been purchased for the purpose of reducing the amount, it is misleading to carry the canceled stock among the assets. The Capital Stock account should itself be debited, for whatever argument there may be in favor of carrying live treasury stock as an asset, there can be none in favor of retaining stock which has actually been canceled. Such stock is certainly nonexistent.

Reduction of Capital Stock: by Surrender

Where the stock is reduced not by purchase but by surrender of part of their holdings on part of the stockholders, sometimes the case where the company has met with losses and desires to remove the deficit from the balance sheet, the reduction of the capital acts to create a corresponding surplus.[17] This may be used as a fund to which the existing deficit, if such there be, is charged. To illustrate: a company with the following:

Balance Sheet

Assets	$140,000	Capital Stock	$150,000
Deficit	10,000		
	$150,000		$150,000

[17] For discussion as to whether such a surplus is available for dividends see below, p. 293.

arranges with the stockholders to surrender 20 per cent of their holdings to cover the deficit and provide a surplus. After the reduction of the capital stock the books would show:

Balance Sheet

Assets	$140,000	Capital Stock	$120,000
		Surplus	20,000
	$140,000		$140,000

No-Par Stock

In almost all corporations a share of capital stock is expressed in terms of nominal or par value, which, in the United States, is ordinarily $100 for each share. The legal assumption implied or clearly expressed in the statutes of most of the states is that a share of stock is a certificate representing that the nominal value of the share has been contributed by the stockholder. But in many cases, this assumption is confessedly false. For some years agitation has taken place attempting to remedy the condition of having stock bear upon its face a statement that it represents a share of $100 when its actual value is greatly below that figure. To many interested in this reform, it seemed hopeless to attempt to secure the equality between the par and the actual value of the stock by compelling in all cases a bona fide contribution of the par value. Furthermore, it was urged that even if this requirement could be enforced, the statement on the face of the certificate that it represented $100 would immediately become meaningless as the ordinary incidents of business would tend to cause variations in its value. As it seemed impossible therefore to secure an actual equivalent between par and market value, it was thought that the desired end could be secured by abolishing altogether the par value so that the certificate would not in any place state that it represented so many dollars, but merely one out of a total number of shares of stock in the corporation. It was thought that the engraving of $100 upon a share of stock oftentimes led the investor to pay, if not the full $100, at least a larger sum than he would have paid if freed from the hypnotic effect of the $100 emblazoned upon the certificate.

Since 1912 when a law was enacted in New York authorizing the issue of shares of stock without par value, the use of such no-par stock has been increasing. This process has been furthered by certain technical peculiarities of the income-tax law. The issue of such stock is authorized in almost all of the states with varying conditions which it is not necessary to consider here. While the stock is declared to be without par value, there are in most of the states restrictions which are almost of the nature of a nominal value. The most common of these is a provision that the stock may not be issued for less than a stated minimum per share. This minimum in several states is $5.00.

Opening Entries

When the stock is issued, three methods of recording the transaction are found. These are: to credit Capital Stock with the exact amount received; to credit Capital Stock with the legal minimum and if more than that is received to credit Capital Surplus; to credit Capital Stock with the exact amount received for the first sales, but in subsequent sales to credit any excess above the price paid by the original subscribers to Capital Surplus.

The first method is probably more generally used and is distinctly recommended by Montgomery, Couchman, Finney, Kester, and Paton.[18]

The second method is sanctioned by the New York Corporation Law [19] which recognizes it as an alternative to the first method. An interesting example of its use is found in the balance sheet of the Kennecutt Copper Corporation where the credit to Capital Surplus is ten times as large as the legal minimum credited to Capital Stock. The third form seems illogical.

[18] Couchman, *The Balance Sheet*, p. 191; Finney, *Principles of Accounting*, chap. ix, p. 5; Kester, *Accounting*, 2d ed., II, p. 20; Montgomery, *Auditing, Theory and Practice*, 3d ed., I, p. 275; Paton, *Accounting*, p. 695.

[19] Laws, 1923, chap. 787, art. 3, par. 12.

As to whether any part of the capital surplus may be returned to the stockholders is a matter which has not been legally determined. The question involved is not materially different in the case of no-par stock from that where ordinary stock is subscribed for at premium. This question is discussed in the chapter dealing with profits. In whatever manner the issue of no-par capital stock is recorded, it is important that later balance sheets should clearly distinguish between the amount originally contributed and subsequent cash additions through earnings. This has not always been done and some writers even seem to assume that it is unnecessary or undesirable so to do, but restrictions upon the payment of dividends save out of profits are just as important for the protection of the creditors of a corporation organized with no-par stock as in any other case. The balance sheet of Montgomery, Ward and Company, which shows only a single item representing the total proprietorship interest, is therefore unsatisfactory. This of course enables one easily to calculate the book value of the shares of stock as the number of such shares is indicated, but it gives no information whatever upon the important point as to how much of this proprietorship is due to operating profits and hence available for dividends.

No-Par Stock in Treasury

There seems no adequate reason for handling no-par stock in accounts in a manner different from that for stock with nominal value except in so far as a different treatment is necessitated by this difference in form. But accountants have at times recommended that no-par stock reacquired by the company should be treated in a peculiar manner. Three methods have been suggested for its booking, providing respectively that such stock should be valued: (*a*) at the amount which was credited when the shares were issued; (*b*) at the average value per share credited when stock was issued; (*c*) at the cost at which it is reacquired. If the principle involved in the booking of reacquired stock with a nominal value, as explained above, is also followed when no-par stock is reacquired, the first method, that is, entering it at the value per share at which the stock was credited when issued, is the consistent one. Where stock with nominal value is issued, Capital Stock is credited with this nominal value; if it is reacquired, Treasury Stock is debited for the same amount as was credited to Capital Stock at the time of its issue. There seems no adequate reason for varying this merely because of the variation in the work of the engraver. While this is the ideal procedure it may not always be practical to carry it out. When stock with a nominal value is issued Capital Stock is always credited with the same amount, that is, par value; where stock with no par value is issued at different times Capital Stock may be credited with different amounts per share. If it is possible to ascertain just how much was credited to Capital Stock when the particular shares which have been reacquired were issued, that sum should be debited to Treasury Stock, but these particular shares may have been commingled with others and it is not possible to ascertain at the time when the stock is repurchased just how much was credited at the time of issue. Where this is the case it may be necessary to enter the treasury stock at the average value per share credited when stock was issued, not that this is theoretically correct but it is the nearest approximation to correctness that can be made. There seems no valid reason for entering it at its cost merely because it bears no nominal value. Where the reacquired stock is donated the same rule should apply although accountants have not been agreed on this matter. Some recommend that there should be only a memorandum without any money value attached. Somewhat better than this is the suggestion that it should be listed at a nominal figure say $1.00, which assures that the memorandum actually gets into the accounts in such a way that it will not escape attention. Either of these procedures is practically adopting the idea of entering the reacquired stock at its cost which in the case of donated stock is zero, rather than entering it at the amount that was credited to Capital Stock at the time of issue. It is true that the donation of stock does not reduce the amount of contributed capital; it does, however, reduce the amount that was contributed by the outstanding shares. This is a fact which may seem worthy of presentation in the accounts and this would be secured by the debiting of Treasury Stock with the amount credited when issued. If objection is made to this procedure it should equally be made where the donated stock has par value.[20]

For bibliography see note to Chapter VIII.

[20] Views in part or altogether opposing those set forth in the text may be found in Montgomery, *Auditing, Theory and Practice,* 3d ed., I, p. 208; Haskins & Sells, *Bulletin,* IV, p. 87; Gundelfinger, "The Principles Which Should Govern the Determination of Capital and the Amounts Available for Distribution of Dividends in the Case of Corporations, with Special Reference to the System of Capital Stocks without a Par Value," *Journal of Accountancy,* XXXVIII, p. 36.

CHAPTER VIII

CAPITAL STOCK II

Sale of Capital Stock below Par

In the discussion in the preceding chapters, it has been assumed that all subscriptions for capital stock are to be paid in full at some time. This is the well established principle which has been accepted by all courts. Indeed, it corresponds with the historical and common law conception of capital stock that it is a representation of value contributed to the corporation either in the form of cash or in valid promises to pay. But in some instances a distinction has been made between stock subscribed for, and stock sold in the market. A subscription not paid in full carries with it a corresponding liability to pay the unpaid portion, which from the point of view of the corporation constitutes an asset. Yet in some circumstances the courts have allowed the sale of stock for less than par, the stock to appear as full paid. The most important case on the subject is that of Handley *v.* Stutz, (139 U. S. 417 [1891]). In this case an embarrassed company sold some of its stock for less than par in order to raise funds to enable it to carry on its business. The court, while upholding the general principle that creditors have a right to rely on the subscribers having paid par for their stock, nevertheless, in the exceptional case of a going concern which cannot place its stock at par, sanctions selling it at the best price obtainable. It should be noted that this decision applied only to exceptional conditions; that Chief Justice Fuller gave a very able dissenting opinion; that Justice Brown, who himself rendered the decision, declared in the later case of Camden *v.* Stuart (144 U. S. 104 [1892]), that it must not be used to evade the obligation of subscribers to pay for stock which obligation "cannot be defeated by a simulated payment of such subscription, nor by any device short of an actual payment in good faith''; and that an able legal critic has declared that ''the reason and conscience of the profession have been shocked at the doctrine'' enunciated in Handley *v.* Stutz.[1]

In the state courts, moreover, it has been held that ''one who receives stock as full paid without paying for it occupies the position of a subscriber who has not paid his subscription.''[2] In England, too, the highest court has given a most drastic decision in Ooregum Gold Mining Company of India *v.* Roper ([1892] A. C. 133) where the House of Lords held that when a corporation sells its new stock below par—even though at double what the old stock commands in the market—the purchasers are liable for the discount to the corporation as well as to the creditors of the company. In this decision the Lord Chancellor said:

> It may be that such limitations on the power of the company to manage its own affairs may occasionally be inconvenient, and prevent its obtaining money for the purposes of its trading on terms so favorable as it could do if it were more free to act. But, speaking for myself, I recognize the wisdom of enforcing on a company the disclosure of what its real capital is and not permitting a statement of its affairs to be such as may mislead and deceive those who are either about to become its shareholders or about to give it credit.

Recent Legislation

There has been of recent years, however, some tendency to weaken through legislation, the provision that stock must be paid in full. In England an amendment, generally authorizing the issue of shares of an established company below par, was passed in the House of Lords. While this was rejected by the Commons and later withdrawn by the Lords, the revised law as passed makes it lawful for a company, with certain restrictions, to pay a commission to any person for subscribing to the shares of a company.[3] The difference be-

---

[1] E. W. Huffcut, 26 *Am. Law Rev.* 865. See also Fogg *v.* Blair, 139 U. S. 118 (1891); and discussion in 14 *Corpus Juris,* p. 959.

[2] See *v.* Heppenheimer, 61 Atl. 843 (N. J. 1905).

[3] Companies (Consolidation) Act, 1908, sec. 89. See also Great Britain, Board of Trade, *Report of the Company Law Amendment Committee* (1906), p. 10.

tween allowing a commission for subscribing and issue of stock at a discount is, of course, merely nominal. Ten years later a parliamentary committee declared that Lord Macnaghten's statement quoted above, had been so much infringed that it cannot be said to exist as a principle. The committee recommended that issue of stock at a discount should be made legal, at the same time making the stock assessable.[4] While this did not result in immediate legislation the matter is still under discussion and in the hearings of a later committee (1925) strong pleas were made that: "it is desirable to permit a company to do openly and directly what it can in effect achieve indirectly at the present time."[5] In this country, too, several of the states rather openly permit the issue of stock at a discount. Thus, in California, despite the fact that the Constitution prescribes: "No corporation shall issue stock or bonds except for money paid, labor done or property actually received and all fictitious increase of stock or indebtedness shall be void,"[6] public utilities may, with the permission of the Railroad Commission, issue stock at a discount.[7]

Stock Issued for Property

There is, however, comparatively little difficulty regarding the issue of capital stock for cash to an amount less than the full par value of the stock. Save in certain exceptional circumstances already described the rule that capital stock is to be paid in full is generally accepted. Where cash is received for the stock, there is little room for doubt as to the amount actually paid in and evasion is in such cases rarely attempted. The real difficulty comes where stock is issued in exchange for property. Here, too, the general assumption is that full value is given. As has been clearly stated in New Jersey, "the distinction between the contemplated issue of corporate stock for property and its issue for money lies not in the rule for

[4] Great Britain, Board of Trade, *Report of the Company Law Amendment Committee* (1918), secs. 41-9.

[5] *Accountant*, LXIII, p. 421.

[6] Art. XII, sec. II.

[7] See, *e.g.*, the balance sheet of the Pacific Gas and Electric Co., shown in Form 5 above.

valuation but in the fact that different estimates may be formed of the value of property."[8] Such undoubtedly should be the case from the accounting viewpoint, as well as in law. The accountant recognizes no difference between things of the same value, for it is the money value of goods and of capital in which he deals.

This is clearly provided for in the rule of the Interstate Commerce Commission that the excess of the par value of stocks issued over the actual money value of the consideration received for such stocks shall be shown as discount.[9]

Unfortunately, in practice, very different principles prevail. Not only is stock time and again issued for property, which in the mind of every one concerned is worth much less than the par value of the stock with which it is purchased, but the very terms of the sale give conclusive evidence to the general public that there has been gross overvaluation. The reason that this is so is that there is lacking any satisfactory criterion as to the real value of the property purchased with stock. Such purchases are frequently large plants, as, for instance, the manufacturing establishments bought by any of the "trusts." Including, as it may, land, buildings, machinery, raw materials, finished goods, mercantile credits, goodwill, perhaps also mines and quarries, railroads and steamers, and any other forms of assets, it is clearly impossible to form an authoritative estimate of the value of the plant. For such a complicated property there can, of course, be no publicly quoted price, nor can any reliance be placed on its cost to the vendor, for he may have acquired it either at an exorbitant price, or at a bargain sale far below its real value. The courts, therefore, are inclined to be liberal, and to leave the determination of value in all such cases to the discretion of the officers of the company. An illustration of the extent to which this deference to the directors' discretion may go is found in a decision of one of the Federal courts to the effect

---

[8] Donald *v.* American Smelting and Refining Co., 48 Atl. 772 (N. J. 1901).

[9] *Classification of Income, Profit and Loss and General Balance Sheet Accounts for Steam Roads,* p. 39.

that the purchase by a corporation, for $200,000 bonds and $3,600,000 stock, of a railroad bed, the construction of which cost $2,000 and for which the vendor had paid $15,000, was not, on the face, a fraudulent transaction.[10] On the other hand, it has been held "that the taking of property at a valuation forty times greater than its actual worth" was not a bona fide exercise of judgment and discretion.[11]

Where the purchased property is worth the par value of the stock there is no difficulty whatever. The exchange of stock for an equal value of any kind of property, is, to the accountant, no whit different in principle from the purchase of merchandise by means of a promissory note.

Journal Entries

Ordinarily where the company exchanges stock for plant the transaction is looked upon as a purchase by the company paid for in stock, and not as a payment in property of a subscription for stock. In the first interpretation the entries would accordingly be:

Unissued Stock	$100,000	
Authorized Capital Stock		$100,000
Plant (in detail)	100,000	
Unissued Stock		100,000

This entry may be varied by omitting any reference to unissued capital stock and booking the transaction with a single journal entry:

Plant (in detail)	$100,000	
Capital Stock Outstanding		$100,000

If, however, the transaction were looked upon as the payment of a subscription, any of the forms given above on pages 177-179 could be used, substituting Plant in place of Cash.

Distinction between Par and Market Value

In some instances the courts have sanctioned the issue of stock for property where that is confessedly worth less than the par value of the stock, on the ground that although issued

---

[10] Stewart *v.* St. Louis, etc., R. R., 41 Fed. 736 (1887).
[11] Elyton Land Co. *v.* Birmingham Co., 9 So. 129 (Ala. 1891).

below par, the stock has been issued at its full market value. It is argued that the stock of an embarrassed company is clearly worth less than its par value. To prevent its issue at less than par would be a hardship since no one would be willing to take it on that basis.

Is Issue below Par Necessary?

The above argument, however, involves an economic fallacy, for it assumes that the only way in which an embarrassed corporation can acquire, say, $10,000 worth of property is by issuing stock of a greater par value. This assumption is unfounded in logic or experience, save as reliance is placed on the meager experience of American corporations in recent years. To illustrate, there may be taken the case of a corporation with $60,000 capital stock and earning $3,000 yearly. Considering the nature of the business this profit may be insufficient, and the stock may sell below par. But the directors see that by acquiring certain additional property worth only $30,000 the net profits may be raised to $6,000. But the owner of the property is unwilling to sell his property for $30,000 of the stock of the company. Is there, therefore, no other way to acquire the property than by increasing the amount of the capital stock to be issued, making it $40,000? This is the position taken by the courts. But the owner's unwillingness to take $30,000 stock for his property is due to the fact that this would entitle him merely to a 3/9 interest in the earnings of the company, and the prospect of getting $2,000 is not sufficient to induce him to take the risk. The reason why he would sell the property for $40,000 stock is that such a deal would give him a right to 4/10 of the earnings, and a chance of receiving $2,400 is a sufficient inducement to him. But it does not therefore follow that the company need issue $40,000 stock for the property worth only $30,000. Two other methods of securing the end are open to the company. The stockholders might agree to contribute 4/10 of their holdings and to give this $24,000 of stock in purchase of the property, which should be a satisfactory inducement to the vendor, as that would give him exactly the same relative rights as though he had received a new issue of $40,000. Or if that were not possible, a simpler method is open of issuing new preferred stock of $30,000 bearing cumulative dividends of say, 8 per cent. This again would bring the same returns to the holder as would $40,000 new common stock. It might even be issued with a smaller preferred dividend, possibly 7½ per cent as the greater security would allow some reduction in the returns. Thus it is quite easy to issue stock in such a form as to make a smaller amount equally as attractive as an excessive amount of a less favored issue. Nor is this a method which is merely theoretically possible. It is currently followed in Germany where the issue of stock in excessive amounts is rendered difficult by legal prescriptions, but where corporations do occasionally become embarrassed and need to obtain funds on unfavorable terms. The provisions of Massachusetts law looking toward the issue of "special-preferred" stock are of similar purport.

Objections to Issue below Par

But aside from the faulty economic assumption implied in the legal doctrine here discussed, the accountant objects seriously to the theory that to the corporation itself the new stock can have a value below par. Stock perhaps should not be said to have a "nominal" value, but to have a par value, of $100. That is to say that the value of the stock should be *equal* to 100 cents on the dollar. The balance sheet should show the real condition and with certain technical forms understood, the statement that a company has $100,000 capital stock should mean, and mean only, that $100,000 net assets have been contributed to the corporation. To speak of a corporation issuing stock at its market value, but at less than par should be considered self-contradictory. The expression "capital stock" means proprietorship of the amount stated, and to say that the receipt of less assets is still payment in full is surely misleading.

Indeed this peculiar doctrine of distinguishing between the real value and the par value of newly issued stock is criticized even from the legal point of view, as, for instance, the *Corpus*

Juris states that the Supreme Court of the United States, in sanctioning the gratuitous issue of stock because it "was without value" refused to "follow the decisions of the highest courts in the states construing their own statutes,"[12] and the *Cyclopedia of Law and Procedure* says that the opinion in Handley *v.* Stutz, already cited, "is a departure from the general current of authority as it stood at the time."[13]

Despite the fact that the courts properly hesitate to pass upon the value of property purchased with stock and despite the fact that they have occasionally, in exceptional circumstances, sanctioned the issue of stock for less than its par value, the decisions are in the main opposed to the issue of stock for property worth less than the full par value. Especially in New Jersey, which has had a perhaps unmerited reputation for looseness in corporation finance, has there been a clear enunciation of the correct principles both in the pages of the statutes and in the interpretation of the judges. A series of the decisions of the highest court of that state illustrates this. In Wetherbee *v.* Baker (35 N. J. Eq. 513 [1882]) it was said that "the courts have inflexibly enforced the rule that payment of stock subscriptions is good as against creditors only where payment has been made in money, or in what may fairly be considered as money's worth." Ten years later it held that: "to justify a corporation in issuing stock under our act for property purchased there should be an approximation at least in true value of the thing purchased to the amount of the stock which it is supposed it represents."[14] Again, after nearly a decade, it was held in Donald *v.* American Smelting and Refining Company (48 Atl. 772 [1901]) that where the overissue is based on a false estimate on the part of the directors,

> their honest judgment, if reached without due examination into the elements of value, or if based in part upon an estimate of matters which really are not property, or if plainly warped by self-interest

---

[12] XIV, p. 959, n. 65.
[13] X, p. 543.
[14] Edgerton *v.* Electric Improvement, etc., Co., 24 Atl. 540 (N. J. 1892).

may lead to a violation of this statutory rule as surely as would corrupt motive.

And in See *v.* Heppenheimer (61 Atl. 849 [1905]), it was stated that

> although this practice [issuing stock in excess] has been frequently indulged in and has brought obloquy upon our state and its legislation . . . such practice is entirely unwarranted by anything either in our statutes or in the decisions of our courts; and whenever it has been indulged in it has involved a clear infringement of, if not a fraud upon the plain letter and spirit of our legislation.

In England, too, there is the very interesting dictum of Vaughan William, L. J.:

> I hope that the day may come when it will be gravely considered by the legislature whether it is not for the advantage of the community that an act should be passed that in all cases the full nominal value of the shares shall be paid in cash and nothing else.[15]

Accounting for Issue below Par

To the accountant, however, the problem is simpler than to the jurist. He needs to know the facts and knowing these, the method of entering the transaction is easily determined.

Where the property is not worth the full par value of the stock issued therefor, the accountant should ascertain as accurately as possible its actual value. The deficiency must appear upon the books if the accounts are to be correct as discount on the issue of the capital stock. In some cases the amount of the discount may constitute a legal claim against the holder of the stock.[16] It might even legitimately appear in the balance sheet as an asset similar to subscriptions. But even if the company has no claim against the stockholders, and that is the turning point in the decisions cited in this chapter, the discount must be shown if the accounts are to present the facts. Any other treatment involves an exaggera-

---

[15] Moseley *v.* Koffyfontein Mines, Ltd., [1904] 2 Ch. 117.

[16] Permission to issue stock for property worth less than par value of the stock does not necessarily imply that the stock is to be considered full paid or nonassessable. (Peters *v.* United States Mortgage Co., 114 Atl. 598, 602 [Del. 1921]).

tion of the value of the assets and thereby violates the cardinal principle that accounts should be accurate. In preparing the balance sheet the discount should be shown as a subtraction from the par value of stock just as an allowance for depreciation is in the balance sheet shown as a subtraction from the cost price of machinery.

In the balance sheet of the Pacific Gas and Electric Company, printed above, such a discount is shown, listed as a separate item along with the assets. In this case the company was specifically authorized by the Railroad Commission to issue the stock below par. The Interstate Commerce Commission provides also for listing discount on stock on the asset side of the balance sheet, but under the somewhat invidious group heading, unadjusted debits. In this the Commission is inconsistent. Discount and premium are antithetical terms. The Commission adds premium to Capital Stock in the balance sheet; it should therefore subtract discount. The balance sheet recommended by the Federal Reserve Board preferably and consistently shows discount as a subtraction from the nominal capital.

Discount and Premium

While it is altogether wrong to conceal in the accounts the fact that stock has been issued at a discount, there is nevertheless some uncertainty as to whether discount upon part of an issue of stock may be offset by premium received on other shares of the same issue. The rules of the Interstate Commerce Commission require these to be offset, one against the other, only the net balance appearing in the balance sheet either as surplus or discount, as the case may be.[17] The propriety of this procedure may be questioned. If $100,000 capital stock is issued at 110, all agree that the premium of $10,000 must appear on the balance sheet. It is difficult to see why a subsequent issue of the same amount at 90 should not be clearly set forth to show that the later stockholders had

---

[17] For opinions opposing that set forth here and supporting that of the Interstate Commerce Commission see Couchman, *The Balance Sheet*, p. 195; Paton, *Accounting*, p. 747.

not all paid the full par value of the stock. If there is a liability upon the part of each individual stockholder for the full par value of the stock, it is difficult to see how this is obviated by the fact that some years previously other stockholders had paid more than par.

Amortization of Discount

Discount on capital stock is in no sense a loss nor, granting that the discount is legal, is there any reason why it should be amortized against earnings. The debit balance appearing in the account, Discount on Capital Stock, is merely an offset to the exaggerated figure appearing to the credit of Capital Stock Outstanding. It represents that the proprietorship is less than the nominal amount of capital stock issued. If the corporation feels that additional capital is desirable it may, of course, as in any other similar case, retain earnings in order to increase the capital. If it is thought desirable to indicate an irrevocableness to such retention of profits the accumulated surplus may in part be used to cancel out the discount on stock. Such booking is similar to the capitalization of surplus such as takes place when additional stock is issued as a dividend. But there is no theoretical requirement that discount on capital stock and accumulated surplus must cancel one against the other. It is perfectly regular and perhaps, in some respects, more illuminating, to exhibit the fact that the original capital stock was issued, say at a discount of 10 per cent and that since the organization of the company profits, equal or exceeding the amount of discount, have been earned and are being held as a permanent surplus.

Bonus Stock

At times stock is issued as a bonus to induce investors to purchase bonds of a company. Thus in one instance, each purchaser of a $1,000 bond was given a bonus of ten shares of stock. Such a transaction is somewhat difficult to interpret. It is not correct to assume that if the purchaser paid $1,000, this entire sum was for the bond and that nothing was paid for the stock. The proper procedure in booking such a transaction is to ascertain as accurately as possible the market price of the bonds without any accompanying stock. If the bonds are judged to be worth 85, the transaction would be booked as follows:

Cash	$1,000	
Discount on Bonds	150	
Discount on Stock	850	
Bonds		$1,000
Treasury Stock		1,000

Concealing Discount in Accounts

To those at all familiar with corporation accounts it is clear that unfortunately the discount allowed on stock is seldom shown. This is generally because of unwillingness to show clearly the exact nature of a transaction which is of doubtful legitimacy. While the transaction itself is not altered by the method in which it is treated in the accounts, its legal status may be greatly improved by withholding from the accounts any evidence that the discount has been allowed. It is so difficult to determine accurately the value of any piece of property, that the courts hesitate to pass upon its equivalence to the stock issued therefor. If the accounts make a showing that full value has been received for the stock, the court may not attempt to disprove the statement. But the circumstance that a misleading statement hoodwinks the court, and thus allows the transaction to stand free from legal interference, by no means indicates that the failure to show discount on stock issued for less than its full face value is in accord with the correct principles of accounting.

In actual practice two subterfuges are resorted to. Assuming again a corporation acquiring a plant worth, all things included, $50,000 and issuing therefor $100,000 stock, instead of showing:

Balance Sheet

Plant	$50,000	Capital Stock	$100,000
Discount on Stock	50,000		
	$100,000		$100,000

the first method of concealing this status presents the following statement:

Balance Sheet

Plant	$100,000	Capital Stock	$100,000

In this form there is attributed to the plant a value equaling the par value of the capital stock.

Another method of concealing the discount on stock issued for property is to present a balance sheet, as follows:

Balance Sheet

Plant	$50,000	Capital Stock	$100,000
Goodwill (Franchise)	50,000		
	$100,000		$100,000

In the latter form the plant is correctly listed at $50,000, but there appears a new asset, *ex nihilo fit*, which is sometimes called goodwill or sometimes franchise. Surprising as it may seem both of these procedures have been tolerated and at times distinctly approved by reputable accountants. There seems little room for argument as to the impropriety of stating that the plant is worth $100,000 when in reality all concerned know it is worth only half that sum. As concerns the second form, there is no objection to including goodwill or franchise among the assets if such has been purchased, but the discussion is here limited to a case where the entire property with all its rights and appurtenances is confessedly worth only $50,000 and where the addition of the item goodwill is clearly a subterfuge. The insertion of a nonexistent goodwill, which was the method used by the promoters of the Columbia Straw Paper Company, as well as the exaggeration of the value of existing assets—the method pursued, for instance, by the United States Shipbuilding Company—is entirely opposed to the fundamental principle of truthfulness in accounting.

An illustration will emphasize this obvious statement. Had the stock been issued to subscribers who contributed $50,000 gold, no one would for a moment justify a balance sheet which either multiplied the amount of gold received by two, or calmly added to its list of assets an utterly imaginary $50,000 in silver, in order to make the assets equal the nominal capital. But the "rule for the valuation of property is not different from that of money," and there is no reason for a different standard of integrity where stock is issued in one way from that required in another.

It is not argued here that equal exactness can be secured in the two cases. All that is discussed is the booking where the deficiency in value is recognized by those preparing the accounts. No plea is made for a fanciful or impossibly high degree of accuracy. It is only argued that conscious misstatement, which exists all too often in corporation finance, which, indeed, has been characteristic of American higher finance, is an outrage to the principles of accounting.

Argument Favoring Present Practice

Justice to the reader, however, requires the statement that the standard here urged is not in accord with current custom, and is subject to one line of reasonable criticism. While it cannot be denied that the listing of an asset at an overvaluation is technically untruthful it may be claimed, with a good show of reason, that it is not necessarily misleading. It may even be urged that truthfulness can never be obtained by any system of valuation of such a property as a manufacturing plant, and that any attempt to make a valuation is more likely to be misleading than is the bare statement that it cost, not so much money, but so much capital stock. This leaves the creditor or investor to guide himself, so that, if he goes astray, it is due to his own wandering and not to his being misled. There is much force in this argument which, indeed, is not altogether contradictory to what has been stated in these pages. Such a scheme of valuation is even approved by Sir Arthur Lowes Dickinson [18] to oppose whose opinion on

[18] "If stocks or bonds are issued for the purchase of any definite property, it may be presumed that the property is worth the par value thereof." *Proceedings of the International Congress of Public Accountants*, 1904, p. 185. *Cf.* Rehm, *op. cit.*, p. 706.

accounting matters, the layman must, indeed, be daring. On this principle all property purchased by stock is listed at the par value of that stock, but with an explanatory statement, clearly shown in the balance sheet, that the assets thus listed were obtained, not for cash but in exchange for stock. This principle is furthermore embodied in the Massachusetts Business Corporation Act and in the English Companies Acts.

But despite the high authority opposed to the views set forth in this treatise, the claim is still made that to reject the standard of attempted accuracy is a confession of impotence, which, while it exhibits a commendable modesty on the part of professional accountants, seems, to the layman, to do scant justice to the ability of that profession.

Stock Watering

It is interesting to see how this problem in accounting bears on the much discussed question of stock watering. The view generally expressed is that "stock watering"—a term vague and as yet ill-defined—is in itself a fraud upon investors and a crime against the public. From the viewpoint of accounting the misdeed is more definitely located. The amount of stock issued is relatively unimportant. Such a transaction, as Vice-Chancellor Pitney has said,

> does not at all or in any manner increase its intrinsic or practical value or in the least degree promote the real prosperity of the enterprise. . . . Its rental value will be practically the same. . . . The division of profits . . . among the stockholders will be on the same basis, and the amount received by each stockholder will be the same . . . and the market values will finally settle down to the gauge of the dividends earned and declared.[19]

The issue of excessive stock may be bad business policy, indeed T. L. Greene takes the ground that in the future it will come to be recognized as such, but the watering of the stock, in itself, aside from accompanying complications is the merest peccadillo. The wrong consists in the positive misstatement, that among the assets is a plant worth $100,000 when every

[19] See *v.* Heppenheimer, 61 Atl. 850 (N. J. 1905).

one concerned in the transactions knows it is worth only $50,000, or the untruth that the company has acquired good-will worth $50,000 when it is absolutely innocent of any such possession. If the other accounts in the balance sheet are correct little concern need be felt over stock watering. Its evil will be slight, its correction automatic. The onus of stock watering is that it leads to a misstatement of the value of assets and the rigid insistence on absolute integrity in accounts both prevents and cures any harm from large issues of stock. It must not then be granted for a moment that it makes no difference at what figure a given asset, speculative or otherwise, is listed. It makes all the difference in the world, the difference between truth and falsehood.

Stock Dividends

The principles of accounting throw light also on the question of stock dividends. Assuming the following:

Balance Sheet

Plant, etc.	$45,000	Capital Stock	$100,000
Merchandise	30,000	Undivided Profits	25,000
Treasury Stock	20,000		
Cash	30,000		
	$125,000		$125,000

the company has accumulated profits of $25,000 and is in position legally to pay a 25 per cent dividend. If this is paid in cash the balance sheet becomes:

Balance Sheet

Plant, etc.	$45,000	Capital Stock	$100,000
Merchandise	30,000	Undivided Profits	5,000
Treasury Stock	20,000		
Cash	10,000		
	$105,000		$105,000

If the directors, however, think it unwise to distribute so much of the cash on hand, they may declare a dividend payable, not in cash, but in stock, as indeed they might declare one payable in merchandise. If a stock dividend is declared and paid there results the following:

Balance Sheet

Plant, etc.	$45,000	Capital Stock	$100,000
Merchandise	30,000	Undivided Profits	5,000
Treasury Stock	0		
Cash	30,000		
	$105,000		$105,000

Not at all different in principle is it where there is no stock in the treasury, for if the condition had been:

Balance Sheet

Plant, etc.	$45,000	Capital Stock	$100,000
Merchandise	50,000	Undivided Profits	25,000
Cash	30,000		
	$125,000		$125,000

new stock could have been issued (provided the company had power to increase its capital stock) with which to pay the dividend. In the latter case the final balance sheet would show:

Balance Sheet

Plant, etc.	$45,000	Capital Stock	$120,000
Merchandise	50,000	Undivided Profits	5,000
Cash	30,000		
	$125,000		$125,000

The only difference in the two cases is that in one stock already held in the treasury is decreased, in the other Capital Stock outstanding is increased.

However objectionable such a transaction may be considered in its effect on the public, or however much it may be prohibited by particular statutes of individual states, it is, to the accountant a perfectly simple and, indeed, from his viewpoint a perfectly legitimate transaction. New stock is indeed issued without the receipt of additional wealth, but the wealth has previously been received by the corporation, as is shown by the credit to Undivided Profits. The cancelation of $20,000 undivided profits against $20,000 stock is a full payment therefor, so far as accounting is concerned.

This is clearly brought out in Williams *v.* Western Union Telegraph Company (93 N. Y. 190 [1883]) where the point at issue was whether a stock dividend was legitimate when the company had a large accumulated surplus. The court said:

> We know of no law that is violated and no public policy that is invaded by issuing to the stockholders stock to represent that amount of property rather than in any mode to divide it up and distribute it among them. If it can issue stock in payment of property to be obtained by it as part of its capital for its legitimate uses, why may it not issue stock in payment for property in effect purchased of them and added to its permanent capital and which they relinquish the right to have divided? So long as every dollar of stock issued by a corporation is represented by a dollar of property, no harm can result to individuals or the public from distributing the stock to the stockholders.

The difficulty which the accountant cannot overcome is when he is asked to book a stock dividend where no profits have been earned, a transaction which unfortunately sometimes occurs. Had the balance sheet given above shown no undivided profits, the payment of a dividend of any sort, whether in stock, or cash, would be equally objectionable, for a dividend implies profits to be divided. Were either cash or stock to be distributed as a dividend, in the absence of accumulated profits, a correct accounting would require the showing of a deficit due to the payment of the dividend. But this, showing at once the illegality of the dividend, is not satisfactory to the directors guilty of such action. The only way to hide the unlawful act is to introduce into the accounts some fictitious asset, creating thereby a correspondingly unreal profit, which, once created, can in turn be canceled against either cash or stock paid out in dividends. It is to be noted, however, that the wrong accounting here consists in the preliminary creation of fictitious profits, by falsely marking up the value of the assets, and not in the stock dividend as such. A dividend, whether in cash, merchandise, real estate, or stock is, in the absence of statutory prohibition, legitimate whenever real profits exist, and only when they so exist. But such profits failing, a cash dividend is just as objectionable as one in stock; in fact it is more so, as the paying out of cash may damage existing creditors, the issuing of stock cannot.

Stock Dividends Not Income

There has been considerable discussion, particularly in connection with the income tax, as to whether a stock dividend is income to the receiver. The Supreme Court has decided that it is not income, and states:

"Far from being a realization of profits to the stockholder, it tends rather to postpone such realization." [20]

The decision in general meets with the approval of accountants, for a stockholder is neither richer nor poorer after a stock dividend has been made. It is however of interest to note that somewhat the same thing may be said in the case of the payment of a cash dividend. Just before such payment the stockholder as a proprietor had a claim upon the assets representing not merely his original contribution but also the profits accumulated to date. If a cash dividend representing part of these profits is made, the stockholder increases the amount of cash which he has in hand, but at the same time his claim against the assets of the corporation is decreased by a similar amount.

Donated Stock

A transaction, unusual in character but not infrequently occurring, is where some of the outstanding stock is donated to the company by its original holders. The stock thus received is ordinarily sold for the purpose of raising cash for

---

[20] Eisner *v.* Macomber, 252 U. S. 189 (1920).

the use of the company, the selling price generally being below par, as the stock, having previously been issued as full paid stock, carries with it no liability to subsequent purchasers at a lower price.

Thus, to cite as illustration an actual case, a company gave its entire capital stock, $300,000, in purchase of property, the vendors agreeing to donate $40,000 of the stock to the company. Assuming that the property purchased was actually worth $300,000—in this particular case a false supposition—the accounts should show:

Balance Sheet

Property	$300,000	Capital Stock	$300,000
Treasury Stock	40,000	Surplus from Donated Stock	40,000
	$340,000		$340,000

In the above balance sheet the account credited is given the descriptive title Surplus from Donated Stock. This is incontrovertibly correct, although it may be that a less cumbersome term would serve in its place, such as Capital Surplus. It is highly desirable, however, that the receipt of donated stock should not result in a credit to the general Surplus account and of course still less to any account showing profits of the current year.

A surplus is truly created when the donation is received by the corporation and is not dependent upon a subsequent sale. If the stock were never sold and were canceled, the books would necessarily show a surplus of $40,000 for the property is valued at $300,000 but is represented by capital stock outstanding of only $260,000. A modification of the above statement may, however, be made; while it is true that technically there is a surplus because the net assets exceed the amount of outstanding capital stock there is not actually any increase of assets over the amount originally contributed. In so far as the creditors are concerned they have a right to look upon the originally contributed capital as a protection against loss. Obviously the donation of capital stock has not added anything to the real capital of the corporation. To distribute any of the surplus created by the mere donation of capital stock would clearly be such a return of capital to the stockholders as would be unwarranted unless the legal requirements for reduction of capital stock had been fulfilled.

If the treasury stock received by donation is sold at less than par, the discount should be charged against the surplus. The journal entries if the stock is sold at 60 being:

Cash	$24,000	
Surplus from Donated Stock	16,000	
Treasury Stock		$40,000

This would show a balance in Surplus from Donated Stock of $24,000. The correct interpretation of the entire transaction, assuming again that the plant was not overvalued, is that a surplus of $40,000 was gained through the donation, but this has been reduced by $16,000 through the unfortunate sale of the treasury stock at only 60 per cent of its par value.[21]

Accounting for Donated Stock

The above treatment rests upon an implied assumption that the plant was worth the par value originally issued for it, $300,000. The subsequent transactions make this assumption doubtful and various methods of expressing that doubt have been made by accountants. Four methods varying in conservatism are as follows:

1. The book value of the plant is marked down by the net amount received on the sale of the donated stock.

2. The plant is marked down to the full amount of stock donated.

3. The plant is marked down to the market value (60 per cent) of the stock given in exchange.

4. The plant is marked down to the market value (60 per cent) of the amount of stock retained by the vendors.

---

[21] Kester, *Accounting, Theory and Practice,* 2d ed., II, p. 15.

Journal Entries I

In the illustration given above, the journal entries at the time of the sale of the treasury stock, if the first interpretation is adopted, would be:

Cash	$24,000	
Surplus from Donated Stock	16,000	
Treasury Stock		$40,000
Surplus from Donated Stock	24,000	
Plant		24,000

After these entries the balance sheet would be as follows:

Balance Sheet

Plant	$276,000	Capital Stock	$300,000
Cash	24,000		
	$300,000		$300,000

While this procedure may have the advantage which attaches to any conservative writing down of overvalued property, it is clearly illogical and inconsistent. The marking down of the property is less the lower the market price of the stock; but the lower the price of the stock, the greater the presumable inflation in the book value of the property.[22]

Journal Entries II

According to the second method, the journal entries at the time of the sale of the treasury stock would be:

Cash	$24,000	
Discount on Treasury Stock	16,000	
Treasury Stock		$40,000
Surplus from Donated Stock	40,000	
Plant		40,000

with the resulting balance sheet:

Balance Sheet

Plant	$260,000	Capital Stock	$300,000	
Cash	24,000	Less Discount	16,000	
	$284,000			$284,000

[22] Bentley, *Journal of Accountancy*, XIII, p. 337.

This is somewhat more logical, as the larger the amount of stock donated the lower will be the book value of the plant. Furthermore, it shows distinctly the actual discount suffered on the sale of the treasury stock. It is somewhat illogical in that it assumes that $40,000 of the stock was worth 60; while the larger amount $260,000 was worth par.[23]

Journal Entries III

The third method assumes that because $40,000 of the stock was sold at 60, it is to be inferred that all of the stock must have been issued on similar terms. If this interpretation were adopted, the proper journal entries at the time the stock was sold would be:

Cash	$ 24,000	
Surplus from Donated Stock	16,000	
Treasury Stock		$ 40,000
Discount on Stock	120,000	
Plant		120,000

which would result in the following balance sheet:

Balance Sheet

Plant	$180,000	Capital Stock	$300,000	
Cash	24,000	Less Discount	120,000	
				$180,000
		Surplus from Donated Stock		24,000
	$204,000			$204,000

Journal Entries IV

The fourth method is even more drastic in its conservatism.[24] Its interpretation of the transactions is that the plant was purchased from the vendors for $260,000 of stock which was worth only 60. This would give the value of the plant as $156,000. Otherwise expressed, the company actually issued $300,000 stock, which valued at 60 represents a net value of the assets of $180,000, of which $24,000 is represented by cash. The net value to be attributed to the plant is the

[23] See Krebs, *Outlines of Accounting*, p. 426; and Paton, *Accounting*, p. 714.

[24] Paton, *Ibid.*, p. 715.

difference between these two sums or $156,000. This situation might be brought on to the books by the following journal entries:

Cash	$ 24,000	
Surplus from Donated Stock	16,000	
Treasury Stock		$ 40,000
Discount on Stock	120,000	
Surplus from Donated Stock	24,000	
Plant		144,000

with the corresponding balance sheet as follows:

Balance Sheet

Plant	$156,000	Capital Stock	$300,000	
Cash	24,000	Less Discount	120,000	
	$180,000			$180,000

The last method probably most accurately represents the situation and has the advantage of being logically consistent, although it is a little rigid in assuming that the vendors may not actually make a contribution of value. The difficulty in all these cases is that an effort is made to record two contradictory concepts of the situation. The accountant is at once asked to assume that stock is represented by assets to its full par value and at the same time to make entries recognizing the overissue of stock and the inflation of values. This is indeed a difficult task.

Objections to Stock Donations

The donation of wealth is so unusual a business transaction that by some critics it is always considered tainted. But it is at least conceivable that it may be perfectly legitimate. Granting that the property is really worth $300,000, it may nevertheless be difficult to persuade outside capitalists of that fact, and the organizers of the corporation have no ready money with which to exploit the property. In order to secure the success of the enterprise the vendors, confident of the ultimate success, may be willing to make the sacrifice in order to get it started, just as an inventor may sell a half interest in a patent at a price which he is perfectly confident is far below the capitalized value of the anticipated earnings.

While it is possible to conceive of such a transaction as being just what it pretends to be, it is perhaps not extravagant to claim with Schuster that "generous benefactors, who give away their savings to trading companies are freaks of nature who need not trouble the legislator's [or the accountant's] mind."[25] In many cases, probably in the great majority of cases, the transaction thus described is the barest subterfuge to enable the company to sell its stock below par free from liability. In the case cited the vendors were really selling their property for $260,000 in stock, and the company was placing $40,000 of its stock on the market to raise working capital. But to have sold such stock below par would have involved obligation on the part of the purchaser to make up the difference, and so there was a resort to a subterfuge both stupid and palpable. Here again the error from the accounting view goes back to the first entry, namely, the statement that the property acquired was worth $300,000, when in fact it was clearly worth not over $260,000. Like all other cases of overissue of stock the culpable element, at least from the accountant's viewpoint, is in the misstatement of facts regarding the valuation of the assets acquired. That being correctly given no real problem can arise. For if the balance sheet had correctly shown the status as follows:

Balance Sheet

Property	$260,000	Capital Stock	$300,000
Discount on Stock	40,000		
	$300,000		$300,000

even though the discount were treated as something which could not be collected, there need be no misleading of the public, and the donation of the stock could not hide the fact of the discount on the later sale.

[25] In *Economic Journal*, X, p. 14.

By some rigid accountants, the donation of part of the stock by vendors is to be construed inevitably as a deduction to be made from the nominal purchase price of the property. But no such severe standard has been set by the courts. It is true that in an early New York case it was held that such a contribution was at least corroborative evidence of overvaluation. But a more recent English case takes a different view; and in Colorado the court distinctly stated that such a transaction is not evidence of issue below par.[26] But whether the presumption is in favor of valuing the property at the amount of stock originally given the vendors, or at the net amount retained by them, if it is established that the former figure would be an actual overvaluation, there is no excuse for such an incorrect representation in the accounts. The accountant should transcend the limitations under which the courts labor.

Donations to Cover Original Expenses

The donation of stock has a further purpose, one which might be otherwise obtained, of providing a fund which can be used in covering the organization expenses, or those which may be incurred during the early years of the corporation. The securing of such a fund is a perfectly legitimate, indeed a praiseworthy, procedure. The contribution of stock is no more unreasonable, and has exactly the same effect as the sale of the stock at a premium for the same purpose of providing a fund for initial expenses. As these are incurred they can be charged against the Surplus, which thus gradually disappears. The process is identical whether the Surplus is raised by the contribution of stock, or by the practical contribution of cash under the name of premium on stock.

BIBLIOGRAPHICAL NOTE

On the technical bookkeeping entries to be made:

FINNEY, H. A.—*Principles of Accounting* (New York, 1923), chap. viii.

---

[26] Douglass *v.* Ireland, 73 N. Y. 100 (1878); *in re* Innes & Co., [1903] 2 Ch. 254; Speer *v.* Bordeleau, 79 Pac. 332 (Col. 1905).

KESTER, R. B.—*Accounting, Theory and Practice* (2d ed., New York, 1923), I, chap. xxxix.

PATON, W. A.—*Accounting* (New York, 1924), chap. xxx.

For discussion of the principles involved:

CHARPENTIER, J.—*Étude juridique sur le bilan dans les sociétés par actions* (Paris, 1906), pp. 42-81.

COLE, W. M.—*The Fundamentals of Accounting* (Boston, 1921), chap. xvi.

CONYNGTON, T., BENNETT, R. J., and PINKERTON, P. W.—*Corporation Procedure* (New York, 1922), pp. 595-611, 1065-112.

DICKSEE, L. R.—*Advanced Accounting* (6th ed., London, 1921), chap. ix.

KESTER, R. B.—*Accounting, Theory and Practice* (2d ed., New York, 1925), II, chap. xxiii.

PATON, W. A.—*Accounting Theory* (New York, 1922), chap. xvi.

REHM, H.—*Die Bilanzen* (Munich, 1903), pp. 342-477.

SIMON, H. V.—*Die Bilanzen der Aktiengesellschaften* (3te Auflage, Berlin, 1899), pp. 201-27.

For a discussion of the laws relating to issue of capital stock:

COOK, W. W.—*The Principles of Corporation Law* (Ann Arbor, 1925), chap. iv, "Watered Stock."

HUFFCUT, E. W.—"Selling New Shares at Less than Par," *American Law Review,* XXVI, p. 861. Discusses Handley *v.* Stutz, and Ooregum Co. *v.* Roper.

PALMER, F. B.—*Company Law* (11th ed., London, 1921).

On no-par stock:

BERLE, A. A., JR.—"Problems of Non Par Stock," *Columbia Law Review,* XXV, pp. 43-63.

BONBRIGHT, J. C.—*Railroad Capitalization* (New York, 1920), pp. 100-30.

CONYNGTON, T., BENNETT, R. J., and PINKERTON, P. W.—*Corporation Procedure* (New York, 1922), chaps. xi, xii.

MITCHELL, W. D.—"Capitalization of Corporations Issuing Shares without Par Value," *Journal of the American Bar Association,* XI, pp. 377-80. Contains bibliography of legal articles.

WICKERSHAM, G.—"The Capital of a Corporation," *Harvard Law Review,* XXII, pp. 319-38.

CHAPTER IX

LIABILITIES

Liabilities in the Balance Sheet

As was shown in Chapter I, the right-hand side of the balance sheet has conventionally been headed liabilities. A more exact title is gradually coming into more common use, the phrase capital and liabilities being found in many balance sheets. This is a sufficiently comprehensive title for in the improved form of the balance sheet, valuation, or offset accounts (such as Allowance for Depreciation) being subtracted from the book value of the assets, there remains on the right-hand side only capital including all unrepresented capital (such as surplus, reserves, and undivided profits), and the outside liabilities of the concern.

Liabilities as Negative Assets

In a strict sense, liabilities as well as valuation accounts are a subtrahend from the assets, for a debt is really a negative asset. It would therefore be logical to prepare a balance sheet in which the total liabilities were subtracted from the total assets, leaving upon the right-hand side of the balance sheet merely the items representing proprietorship. If this were done the balance would be one between net assets and proprietorship. Both of these sums are of significance and each of them represents a fact which the business man often desires to present. But a total which represents the sum of proprietorship and liabilities has no particular importance. This more logical presentation is, however, rarely found when the balance sheet is in account form,[1] but it is frequently

[1] For an illustration of this form with an argument in its favor see Rehm, *Die Bilanzen,* p. 10.

found in the report form of the balance sheet. Thus Gilman [2] suggests the following arrangement:

Total assets		$100,000
Total liabilities		60,000
Net worth		$ 40,000
Represented by:		
Capital Stock	$30,000	
Surplus	10,000	$ 40,000

and a similar arrangement is presented by Montgomery, Dickinson, and Kester.[3] Montgomery's discussion of the ideal balance sheet would imply that the liabilities should thus be subtracted even though the balance sheet is arranged in account form, but he does not present any model form showing such an arrangement.

Subtraction of Liabilities in the Balance Sheet

In the account form, liabilities are occasionally subtracted, not as a total from the sum of all of the assets, but certain liabilities or groups of liabilities being subtracted from corresponding assets. Thus a mortgage upon real estate is occasionally shown in the balance sheet as a subtraction from the asset upon which it rests.[4] Similarly Couchman approves of an organization which has a number of bank accounts, showing an overdraft in one of its bank accounts, as a subtraction from the asset balances in other banks. But a net overdraft should appear among the first in the list of current liabilities.[5]

In the balance sheet of the Sperry Flour Company, the current liabilities are subtracted from the current assets and the bonds are subtracted from the book value of property. Such an arrangement while unusual is not objectionable so long as both assets and liabilities are clearly shown. To present merely a net equity in the real estate or the net

[2] *Principles of Accounting,* p. 146.

[3] *Auditing, Theory and Practice,* I, p. 367; *Accounting Practice and Procedure,* p. 51; *Accounting,* 2d ed., II, p. 84.

[4] See balance sheet of the California Delta Farms Company for 1922, and Greeley, *Theory of Accounting,* p. 125.

[5] *The Balance Sheet,* p. 160.

current assets in excess of current liabilities would however be misleading and highly objectionable.

Separation of Liabilities from Proprietorship

While from a theoretical viewpoint, debts are negative assets and differ radically from proprietorship, the well-nigh universal custom of listing capital and liabilities on the same side of the balance sheet is not to be criticized. It is however necessary clearly to differentiate the two. The present tendency is to list all of the liabilities at the head of the right-hand side of the balance sheet and to give distinctly a footing showing the total liabilities. Occasionally capital stock is grouped with funded debt forming a subtotal entitled capital liability.[6] Still less frequently appropriated surplus is also included in total liabilities, excluding from that total only the items representing current profits.

Problems Concerning Liabilities

The accounting problems having to do with liabilities are extremely simple as compared with those relating to assets. This is principally due to the fact that the question of valuation, so perplexing in regard to assets, practically disappears when liabilities are concerned. One may suffer, indeed one must expect, some diminishment in the value of assets, but debts, so long as the principle of the going concern is recognized, must be shown at their full amount. The only problems which arise in the booking of liabilities are those which group around the classification of liabilities, the calculation of interest, the treatment of unissued, repurchased, and canceled debts, and a few questions in which there may arise a doubt whether there is an existing liability or not. These will be considered in order.

Classification of Liabilities

The clearness and consequent value of the balance sheet is increased if some classification is made of the various kinds

---

[6] As in the balance sheet of the Bethlehem Steel Corporation, Form 2, above.

of debt. Thus a showing of the funded or long-time debt separate from the short-time or floating debt is of great importance, indicating, as it does, the immediate financial strength of the concern, and whether or not it is likely to suffer loss because subject to a sudden demand from its creditors.

There can be no clear line of demarcation between long-time debts and short-time debts. A commonly drawn line is however to classify as long-time debts all those which run more than one year. The distinction between debts for which notes or acceptances have been given and open book accounts is also important. The extent to which such classification is to be carried, as in the corresponding classification of assets, is a matter of discretion, governed by individual circumstances. The statements rendered by the national banks to the Comptroller five times yearly contain seven different subdivisions of liabilities to depositors. One of these same banks will give, in the condensed balance sheet published for advertising purposes, only the single item Deposits. Both of these statements are correct; each, for its purpose, is full as well as fair. But whatever subdivisions are made, the classification adopted must be strictly observed. It may be perfectly correct to include all liabilities to depositors under the one head Due to Depositors. But where a subdivision is made it is incorrect and fraudulent to list under the title Accounts Payable items which really are Notes Payable or to include either of these items under the title Funded Debt.

In some balance sheets, accrued liabilities are separately listed as if they were not current. This is of course incorrect. Occasionally a group is found entitled deferred liabilities. This is an unfortunate and somewhat meaningless term. All liabilities are deferred in the sense that payment is not to be made until some time in the future. The Interstate Commerce Commission uses the term deferred liabilities to cover a "liability for provident funds," representing the amount of assets in the hands of its officers for administering pension and other funds. It also includes percentages due contractors to be paid on completion of contracts and similar items. The term deferred liabilities has arisen as an antonym to deferred assets. The better terms are, however, deferred credits and deferred charges respectively. In this sense, the deferred credits should represent items of income which properly pertain to operations yet to be performed rather than to those already rendered. In this sense, the deferred credit representing for instance rent received in advance implies at least a quasi-liability to furnish to the tenant the use of the building without further payment. In that sense it may properly be included among current liabilities where the period is a short one. If the payment should cover a long period extending over several years, the deferred credit is more nearly akin to a fixed liability. The use of the term deferred liabilities to describe some obligation maturing in the distant future is unsatisfactory.

The Federal Reserve Board, as shown in Form 12, goes further in the classification of liabilities than is customary. There is not merely the ordinary differentiation between current and fixed liabilities but the current liabilities are divided into three subheads: unsecured notes, unsecured accounts, and secured liabilities; and each of these subdivisions is again minutely segregated so as to classify the liabilities in accordance with the transactions in which they arose, the person to whom the debt is owed, the date of maturity, and the nature of security.

Interest on Notes

The questions which relate to the calculation of interest on debts are the most interesting which arise in regard to the accounting for liabilities. As a matter of convenience, debts, whether receivable or payable, are ordinarily listed in books at their face value rather than at their real value. Where the note is discounted, it follows that there must be a counter entry to a Discount account. Where the note, or other obligation, is not discounted, but bears interest from date, the adjustment is not made until some later date. When a formal balance sheet is prepared it is accordingly necessary, in order to make a correct showing of the liabilities of the concern, to make an exact reckoning of interest on outstanding liabilities. If the note draws interest the adjustment is made through an item, Accrued Interest, appearing among the current liabilities. If the note does not draw interest but has been discounted so much of the discount as pertains to the unexpired life of the note appears either as discount on notes payable or sometimes as interest paid in advance. This item most often appears in the balance sheet as a deferred charge. Logically, however, it represents an offset to the face value of the notes payable.[7]

Discount on Notes

Discount on notes not bearing interest is generally spoken of, both in banking circles and by accountants, as interest paid in advance. But in reality, interest is not prepaid where a note is discounted. It is immaterial to the borrower whether he discounts a sixty-day note of $1,000 at 6 per cent (true discount) or whether he issues a note for $990.10 maturing in sixty days at 6 per cent interest. In either case, the borrower receives $990.10. In either case, he pays to the lender sixty days later $1,000. It seems obvious that only when he pays the agio of $9.90 has interest been paid, but according to ordinary bookkeeping technic, the liability appears upon the books in one case as $1,000 with an offsetting current asset—Interest Paid in Advance, $9.90. In the other, the liability appears as $990.10 without any recognition in the books of the amount to be paid at maturity. If it is proper to list the interest-bearing note at its face without booking the interest which sometime will be paid, it would seem as if it would be logically consistent to treat the discounted note in a similar manner. This would mean that the discount, or so-called interest paid in advance, is logically to be deducted from the face value of the discounted note. At the time the

[7] But the Interstate Commerce Commission gives to the carrier the option of charging to the current income account the entire discount on short-term notes and not merely that part which properly belongs to the current period. This logically unsound procedure may perhaps be justified on the ground of convenience. *Accounting Bulletin 15*, Case 178.

money is borrowed, the then value of the obligation is the face less the discount. It is true that the borrower might not be able to cancel the debt immediately for that sum but it is equally true that the borrower would have no right to pay off the interest-bearing note before maturity and escape paying interest for the period covered by the contract. The actuarial value of a liability is that which should appear upon the books even though the debt may not be canceled at that figure.

Premium on Bonds Issued

The calculation of interest is very simply made in case of short-time obligations. When bonds are emitted the calculation is more complicated, and the treatment in the accounts is not uniform. The estimation of simple interest accrued on the bonds since the time the last interest payment was made is of course identical with the calculation of interest on a short note, and no divergence of practice occurs in that regard. The main point of difficulty is in regard to the premium or discount allowed on the bonds at the time of issue. As shown in discussing investments, the premium paid on a bond is virtually the price paid for the privilege of receiving nominal interest at a rate higher than the market rate. Viewing the transaction from the borrower's point of view, the premium received is, therefore, a lump payment made in return for the obligation to pay an excessive rate of interest during the life of the bond. If the credit of the company and the conditions of the market would have enabled the company to issue a 5 per cent twenty-year bond at par, its 6 per cent bond, running the same time, should sell at approximately 112.46. This premium of 12.46 is, therefore, the present value of the annuity, of 1 per cent which the company must pay for twenty years. The issuer of the bonds actually borrows not $100 but $112.46. Of this sum $100 is payable in twenty years. The remainder $12.46 is repaid by an annuity so adjusted that the borrower actually pays 5 per cent on the loan. The correct entry at the time of issuing the bonds is therefore:

Cash	$112.46	
Bonds		$100.00
Premium on Bonds		12.46

At the time of the payment of the first coupon one year later the entry would be:

Interest	$5.62	
Premium on Bonds	.38	
Cash		$6.00

The amount here debited to interest is just 5 per cent upon the total sum borrowed. At the end of the second year interest is properly chargeable only on $112.08, for $.38 has been repaid. The journal entry would accordingly be:

Interest	$5.60	
Premium on Bonds	.40	
Cash		$6.00

In the ordinary routine, payments in the guise of interest are ordinarily debited immediately to the interest account. If in this case the entire $6.00 paid when the coupon is cashed, were charged to interest it would be necessary to make an adjusting entry:

Premium on Bonds	$ .38	
Interest		$ .38

The result thus obtained would be correct so far as showing the net expense of interest. It is, however, somewhat less desirable than the method first given in that it charges as an interest expense a sum larger than that actually incurred and offsets this by crediting to the interest account that which is in no sense income. Another treatment sometimes found in accounts of crediting the entire premium at once to profit and loss is manifestly incorrect for the premium is in no sense profit and least of all profit of the single year in which it is received. According to Pixley,[8] however, unless the articles of the company prohibit, a premium may be used for dividend purposes, but even though this may be legally permissible, it should be objected to by accountants.[9]

---

[8] *Accountancy,* p. 225.

[9] Premium is frequently written off in equal annual sums and this practice is approved by some accountants and utility commissions. It is, however, scientifically incorrect and can be justified only on the grounds that the error is in some sense offset by the ease of calculation.

Expenses of Issuing Bonds

It is considered proper when bonds are sold at a premium to charge against the reserve thus established miscellaneous expenses incurred in issuing the bonds. This is logically justifiable as the premium represents an offset to the interest payments made during the life of the bond and hence is in reality a reduction of the expense normally incurred in borrowing the money. On the other hand, the expenses incurred in issuing the bonds pertain to the entire period during which the money is borrowed and should be properly allocated to the profit and loss accounts of each year. Offsetting the premium received as against the expenses incurred merely means one adjustment to be made each year instead of two. However, in calculating the rate of interest which is actually paid the expense as well as the premium received should be considered. Thus, for instance, if $100,000 ten-year 6 per cent bonds are sold for $107.79 the yield at that rate is 5 per cent, but if the expenses of issuing the bonds amount to $2,020 the bonds should be treated as if they had sold at $105.77 at which price instead of yielding 5 they would yield 5¼. The adjustment to be made at the time of the payment of the first interest coupons should therefore be made upon the basis of 5¼ per cent interest, and journal entries should be as follows:

Interest	$2,776.46	
Premium on Bonds	223.54	
Cash		$3,000.00

Discount on Bonds Issued

Exactly the same principle applies to bonds issued at a discount. A 4 per cent twenty-year bond issued at $87.54 would also yield 5 per cent. The entry at the time of issue would be:

Cash	$87.54	
Discount on Bonds	12.46	
Bonds		$100.00

The discount would be written off similarly to the writing off of the premium, the entry at the end of the first year being:

Interest	$4.38	
Discount on Bonds		$ .38
Cash		4.00

The amount charged to interest is 5 per cent on $87.54, the amount actually received by the borrower. In each successive year, similar treatment would take place, the amount of interest being charged increasing each year, for it must cover not merely interest on the amount originally borrowed, but also interest upon that portion of interest due but not covered by the amount paid when the coupon is cashed. Thus the entry at the end of the second year should be:

Interest	**$4.40**	
Discount on Bonds		**$ .40**
Cash		**4.00**

In most balance sheets the discount appears among deferred charges. Some accountants [10] who include in that group only prepayments applicable to the next fiscal period place discount on bonds in another group called Other Assets. The Interstate Commerce Commission places it among unadjusted debits. Logically however, it is an offset to the liability shown by the face value of the outstanding bonds and might therefore, be appropriately subtracted in an interior column of the balance sheet.[11] In any event, however, the discount should gradually be written off as the years pass, thus making the annual charge to interest correspond to the real rather than to the nominal rate paid. The only theoretically correct method is to write off the discount in accordance with the change, actuarially estimated, in the value of the annuity which it represents. But many accountants, for the sake of simplicity, merely divide the discount into equal annual charges. Others, still less scientifically, but even more conservatively, charge it off much more rapidly, within a few years or even charge all in the first year.

It was formerly almost universally the custom among the American railroads to charge discount on bonds to the Construction account. The temptation to do this is great as in the early years of a railway's life, the burdening of the Income account with any additional charges is always unpleasant.

---

[10] *E.g.*, Kester, *Accounting, Theory and Practice,* 2d ed., II, p. 364.
[11] Paton, *Accounting,* p. 500.

The practice has even been justified by so distinguished an authority as T. L. Greene.[12] In railroad accounting, however, the practice has been definitely abandoned because of the rule of the Interstate Commerce Commission which specifically provides "no discount or expense on funded debt shall be charged to or be included in any account as a part of the cost of acquiring any property tangible or intangible."[13] But an exception is made in so far as part of the expense and discount is properly attributable to the period of construction.

Bonds Repayable at a Premium

Occasionally bonds are issued repayable at a premium. Where such repayment is optional on the part of the borrower the provision for the premium is in the nature of a special reserve. If, however, the repayment at the premium is accepted as part of the financial policy of the concern, the premium as well as the par value of the bonds becomes an obligation and should appear in the balance sheet. The two elements may, however, be kept separate. Where bonds thus redeemable at a premium are sold at a price other than the redemption figure, the difference between the two should be treated just as premium or discount on bonds redeemable at par are treated.

The calculation of the net yield and the corresponding provision for amortization of bonds repayable at a premium is relatively simple. All that is necessary is to ignore for the purpose of calculation the nominal par and the nominal rate of interest. Thus a bond for $1,000 bearing 6 per cent interest and redeemable at 120 at the end of ten years is sold at 108. This is in reality a promise to pay $1,200 with $60 a year interest. The interest accordingly amounts to 5 per cent on the principal and, as it is sold for $1,080, its price, based upon the redemption value not on its par, is 90. The net yield of such a bond as shown by tables is not 4.97 per cent, which

[12] *Political Science Quarterly,* VII, p. 601.
[13] *Classification of Income, Profit and Loss, and General Balance Sheet Accounts for Steam Roads,* pp. 40-1.

would be the yield of a ten-year 6 per cent bond at 108, but 6.37 per cent.

Journal Entries for Premium Bonds

Two ways of booking such bonds are possible. For the sake of brevity these may be illustrated by taking a two-year 6 per cent bond interest payable annually, redeemable at 110. If this bond were sold at 105, it would yield approximately 8 per cent upon the investment. The journal entries at the time the bond was sold and when interest and principal are paid would be as follows:

Jan. 1, 1920		
Cash	$1,050.00	
Bonds		$1,000.00
Premium		50.00
Jan. 1, 1921		
Interest	84.00	
Cash		60.00
Premium		24.00
Jan. 1, 1922		
Interest	85.92	
Cash		60.00
Premium		25.92
Bonds	1,000.00	
Premium	100.00	
Cash		1,100.00

This leaves a discrepancy of eight cents due to neglected fractions, the actual rate of interest being, not 8 per cent, but 8.004.

By this method the entry at the time the bonds are issued shows the then value of the bonds rather than the amount which is to be paid when the bonds mature. If it were desirable to show the full amount to be paid it would be necessary not only to show the premium to be paid on redemption but also a discount to bring this sum down to the present value. The entry at the time of issue would therefore be:

Jan. 1, 1920		
Cash	$1,050.00	
Discount on Bonds	50.00	
Bonds (par value)		$1,000.00
Bonds (premium on redemption)		100.00

The later entries would therefore be:

Jan. 1, 1921

Interest	$ 84.00	
Cash		$ 60.00
Discount on Bonds		24.00

Jan. 1, 1922

Interest	85.92	
Discount		25.92
Cash		60.00
Bonds (par value)	1,000.00	
Bonds (premium on redemption)	100.00	
Cash		1,100.00

The former of these two methods has the advantage of somewhat greater simplicity but does not exhibit the entire amount of the absolute obligation. It is, however, practically the form recommended by Sir Arthur Lowes Dickinson.[14]

Unissued Bonds

The treatment of bonds authorized but not yet issued is not different in principle from that of unissued stock already discussed. Where the unissued bonds are secured by a lien on specific property, there is, perhaps, somewhat greater justification in including them among the assets rather than in merely deducting them from the outstanding debts. The property pledged to secure the bonds gives them a somewhat independent value and makes them, perhaps, an available asset even where the company is in a poor financial condition. Furthermore bonds, unlike stock, may in the absence of special legislation be freely issued below par. Hence, it is not so important to distinguish in the case of bonds, as it is in the case of stock, between those which are unissued and those which have been reacquired.

But while any one of the alternatives given on page 174 may be used for unissued bonds the most satisfactory way is to show them as a subtraction from the authorized debt. This is the form prescribed by the Interstate Commerce Commission. A slight variation of this form is found in the balance sheet of the Pacific Gas and Electric Company shown

[14] *Accounting Practice and Procedure*, p. 135.

in Form 5. In this case bonds in the treasury are listed only in the short column on the asset side, with the statement that they are not included in assets or liabilities.

Treasury Bonds

The treatment of bonds purchased in the market is similar to that of stock thus purchased and held in the treasury. The purchased bonds may, however, at any time be canceled and the outstanding debt thus reduced without any further formality, while the purchase of its own stock by a company does not in itself work a reduction of the nominal capital, to accomplish which, certain legal procedures must be followed. Reacquired bonds as well as unissued bonds are nevertheless preferably shown as a subtraction from the liabilities,[15] thus:

Bonded Debt Issued	$100,000
Less Held in Treasury	50,000
Bonds Outstanding	$ 50,000

A distinction should be made between a bond redeemed, especially where it is formally canceled, and one merely bought on the open market and held in the treasury as a live bond. Where the former takes place it must disappear entirely from the balance sheet.

Contingent Liabilities

The showing of contingent liabilities, that is of liabilities for which the proprietor may be held under certain contingencies but which he never expects to have to meet, is a perplexing problem. These include such items as endorsements, guarantees, unfulfilled contracts, etc. Where the liability is in the nature of an endorsement or guarantee of another's liability, whether given as an accommodation to trade associates or as a means of rediscounting notes receivable the treatment is simple. These constitute a definite liability to the holder of the endorsed note, but one which the endorser does

[15] "To argue otherwise is equivalent to saying that a payment to a creditor should not be deducted from the liability because one might borrow from him again." Couchman, *The Balance Sheet*, p. 166.

not expect to be called upon to pay as he relies upon the original maker protecting his note. But even if he does not expect to have to provide funds his obligation should be shown among the liabilities offset by a claim against the original maker. This has not always been observed. Thus, in case the holder of a note receivable rediscounts it at the bank, the more customary procedure has been to debit Cash and Discount and credit Notes Receivable. In this way the note receivable disappears entirely from the books of the former owner and there is no indication that he is under any liability to the bank at which the note has been discounted. This is in contrast to usage in transactions which at heart are identical, that is, where funds are obtained on the promisor's own note, secured by trade paper as collateral. Where this is done the custom is to show the trade paper still among the assets and the collateral note itself as a liability. But whether the funds are secured by endorsing the trade paper and rediscounting it, or by hypothecating it as collateral does not affect the real position of the borrower. But national banks have for long been required to show the transaction properly and instead of crediting Notes Receivable a new account, Notes and Bills Rediscounted, is credited. In this way the note receivable is still included among the assets of the former even though it is now technically the property of the bank at which it has been rediscounted. Somewhat greater clearness would be secured by segregating the note which has been rediscounted from those still held as is shown in the balance sheet recommended by the Federal Reserve Board. In this notes receivable are subdivided into Notes Receivable of Customers on Hand, and Notes Receivable Discounted or Sold with Endorsement or Guarantee, the latter subgroup, of course, appearing also among the secured liabilities.

Another classification of contingent liabilities is more difficult to handle. This may be illustrated by the guarantee of quality or of service which may be given by a manufacturer. Here, there is no definitely stated liability as there is in the case of a rediscounted note. In some cases experience enables the manufacturer to estimate approximately how much he will have to pay under such guarantees. This amount may be shown in an account entitled Reserve to Cover Guarantees, or better and more frankly, Liability under Guarantees. This is in essence a current liability and should be included with other current liabilities in the balance sheet. But where the amount of the liability cannot be obtained through statistical methods with a fair degree of accuracy there is a rather general agreement among accountants that the contingent liability is not to be shown in the balance sheet but should be explained in a footnote or appendix thereto.

The Interstate Commerce Commission provides that contingent liabilities shall not be included in the body of the balance sheet statement but it defines contingent liabilities as items which may, under certain conditions, become obligations of the company but are neither direct nor assumed obligations on the date of the balance sheet.[16] The distinction here may be a real one but it is difficult to define. A guarantee involving the obligation to make a payment in case a machine fails to satisfy certain specifications doubtless is a contingent liability under the definition of the Commission, but the endorsement upon a customer's note sold to a commercial paper dealer is similarly an item which will become an obligation of the company only under the condition that the maker of the note fails to pay it at maturity. The prescribed form of balance sheet does not specifically provide for the treatment of such a liability.

The Commission does not specifically mention rediscounted notes; but as it requires a railroad to show among its liabilities the total par value of securities jointly issued by it and others with offset deferred assets representing the portion of the liability which it is expected will be liquidated by the other party, presumably discounted notes are to be shown among the liabilities and are not to be treated under the rules for contingent liabilities. The Federal Reserve Board[17] recognizes endorsements as contingent liabilities and provides that

---

[16] *Op. cit.*, p. 41.
[17] *Uniform Accounting*, p. 18.

contingent liabilities other than those arising from the special hypothecation of current assets should appear as a footnote and not as part of the balance sheet proper. Pixley [18] apparently recommends that all contingent liabilities be thus shown in a note attached to the balance sheet, a form made familiar in Table A of the English Companies Act, 1862, and illustrated in the balance sheet of the Willys-Overland Company printed as Form 10 above.

Liability for Dividends

A dividend which has been declared becomes at once a liability of the company and must accordingly be shown in the balance sheet. This corresponds with the legal position, for while undivided profits are not a liability of the corporation, and the individual stockholders have no right to compel their distribution, the declared dividend is an obligation, for which, in case of bankruptcy, the stockholder has the same rights that any other creditor has against the company. Undeclared dividends do not appear at all on the books, unless in the case where there are cumulative preferred dividends in arrears. The position of such dividends is somewhat unique. So far as the company and the preferred stockholders are concerned there is no obligation to pay, indeed the company cannot pay unless profits are earned. But from the viewpoint of the common, or deferred stockholder delinquent cumulative dividends on preferred stock are a liability which must be met before anything can be paid to him. Consequently there is a good argument for making an exhibit of the amount in arrears. Practice is, however, not uniform on this point. Perhaps the best treatment is to show them in a note to the balance sheet rather than in that statement itself.[19]

Liability for Pensions

The provision for pensioning employees raises a question as to whether there exists a liability which should appear in

---

[18] *Accountancy,* p. 236.

[19] Pixley, *Duties of Auditors,* 11th ed., p. 513. See also Form 10, above.

the balance sheet. An agreement definitely made to pay pensions is nothing more than one way of paying wages. In order to apportion charges properly between years, the amount necessary to provide for future pensions must be counted among the expenses of each year; and the corresponding sum is a real obligation payable to employees some time in the future. Evidently in such a case to omit such a liability from the balance sheet is incorrect. But if the provision for the pensions is not a definite matter of bargain, but is rather an optional beneficence of the proprietors, the accumulated fund is of the nature of a reserve rather than a liability. In some cases, where the pension system is well established, the annual appropriations thereto are paid to trustees who hold them, and the accumulations thereon, in trust for the beneficiaries. In such cases both the assets and the liability entry may properly be left entirely out of the accounts of the company. Here the payment of wages consists of two parts, one paid currently to the workman, the other paid to his trustees. After such payment the company need, in neither case, make further accounting. The treatment of pensions therefore depends on the exact legal nature of the pension agreement, and on the financial policy adopted in its administration.

Accrued Taxes

Occasionally there appears in the balance sheet an item Reserve for Taxes. This phraseology is unfortunate as it represents an actual liability and should be included with other liabilities not with other reserves. It ordinarily represents the estimate of the amount of accrued taxes. The fact that it is an estimate rather than an exact figure does not materially affect its character. Many of the items in a balance sheet are estimates. The point to be borne in mind is that this is an estimate of a liability rather than an estimate of reserve profits. The more direct phraseology Accrued Taxes is decidedly preferable. This subject is discussed further in Chapter XIII.

BIBLIOGRAPHICAL NOTE

DICKINSON, A. L.—*Accounting Practice and Procedure* (New York, 1914), chap. vi.

ESQUERRÉ, P.-J.—*Applied Theory of Accounts* (New York, 1915), chaps. xxviii, xxxi.

KESTER, R. B.—*Accounting, Theory and Practice* (2d ed., New York, 1925), II, chaps. xx, xxi.

PATON, W. A., and STEVENSON, R. A.—*Principles of Accounting* (New York, 1918), chap. xiv.

REHM, H.—*Die Bilanzen* (Munich, 1903), pp. 342-477.

SIMON, H. V.—*Die Bilanzen der Aktiengesellschaften* (3te Auflage, Berlin, 1899), pp. 201-27. The last two authors present opposing views of the nature of discount on bonds.

CHAPTER X

THE PROBLEM OF PROFITS

Two Phases of Accounting

Accounting is essentially of a twofold character. It seeks to disclose the facts regarding the amount and kind of assets and of liabilities. In addition to this and of equal if not superior importance, is the information which it gives in regard to proprietorship, the extent to which it has been increased, and the various causes which have contributed to this result. The showing of assets and liabilities is the main function of the balance sheet and it is this phase of accounting which has thus far been discussed. The exhibit of the changes in proprietorship is embodied in an income or profit and loss statement. Each of these statements has its own value and use.

If a differentiation is to be made, it might perhaps be said that the balance sheet is primarily of interest to the creditor of a concern. It is the statement demanded by a bank before it will lend to a depositor; it is demanded by the wholesaler before extending credit to a customer; it is what a depositor requires before he entrusts his cash to the keeping of a bank. The profit and loss statement is primarily of interest to the owner in contradistinction to the creditor. The proprietor has more than a mere curious interest in learning how much profits he has made through his business operations. It determines the direction of future business and which line of activity should be extended because it is relatively more profitable, and which should be reduced or cut off entirely. It furnishes the information which the investor should have when considering the desirability of entering into a partnership or purchasing shares of stock in a corporation. But while it is true that the two statements appeal primarily to two different interests, both are of importance alike to creditor and proprietor. A bank hesitates to lend to a concern which is doing a losing business even though at the present time its assets far exceed the liabilities, and the investor properly refuses to engage in an undertaking which is yielding large profits if the balance sheet shows that the relations of assets and liabilities is such that there is great danger of bankruptcy being brought about by the action of creditors.

These two documents are therefore both of paramount importance. The outstanding merit of double entry bookkeeping is that it not only provides for the preparation of both of these statements but does it in such a way that there is a reciprocal check between them and notice is ordinarily given if an error in either is made. This connection between the two statements is found in the fact that the balance of the Profit and Loss account is one item in the balance sheet.

Accountants generally present the information regarding proprietorship in an annual statement setting forth the changes which have occurred during the fiscal period. In a very general way the record of such changes is known as the Income account, and its balance is, in most instances, presumed to set forth the net results of all factors affecting the amount of proprietorship. Its goal is to show the annual profits.

Definitions of Profit

It is a peculiar fact that while all business is carried on for the purpose of securing profits, while the distribution of profits is continually the subject of controversy in the courts, while the ascertainment of profits enters into the sum and substance of accounting and the nature of profits enters largely into the discussions of every economist, the term is still vaguely and loosely used and without satisfactory definition by either economist, man of affairs, jurist, or accountant.

The income or profit [1] of a given period may be defined

[1] The author has vainly tried to find any accepted differentiation between these two terms. The committee on terminology defines profit as

as the increase in proprietorship which has taken place during that period, making due allowance for any part of such increment as may have been distributed. This is the broadest use of the terms, but is one which is occasionally employed by both accountants and economists. Thus Sir Arthur Lowes Dickinson says:

> In the widest possible view, profits may be stated as the realized increment in value of the whole amount invested in an undertaking; and, conversely, loss is the realized decrement in such value. Inasmuch, however, as the ultimate realization of the original investment is from the nature of things deferred for a long period of years, during which partial realizations are continually taking place, it becomes necessary to fall back on estimates of value at certain definite periods, and to consider as profit or loss the estimated increase or decrease between any two such periods.[2]

And Alfred Marshall says:

> When a man is engaged in business, his profits for the year are the excess of his receipts from his business during the year over his outlay for his business; the difference between the value of his stock and plant at the end and at the beginning of the year being taken as part of his receipts or as part of his outlay, according as there has been an increase or a decrease of value.[3]

But profits is often used in a more restricted sense. It regards not all the changes which have taken place during the period but only some of them. Sometimes the concept is limited to those changes which have come about through the operations of the business, excluding extraneous gains to pro-

---

"the gain resulting from employment of capital in any undertaking" while income is "the gain resulting from the use of capital or the rendering of personal service as distinguished from the return of capital. It includes earnings, gains, or profits from any source." (*Journal of Accountancy,* XXXIV, pp. 68-9.) Other accountants use income as applying to the current increases in proprietorship, and profits as a residuum or reservoir of accumulated income. In this sense profit is practically synonymous with surplus as used by other writers. This differentiation is observed by Sir Arthur Lowes Dickinson and in the accounts prepared by the Interstate Commerce Commission. Other writers either make no discrimination or differ so much from other accountants that no standard use of the terms can be found. In this treatise, therefore, the words are used indiscriminately.

[2] *Accounting Practice and Procedure,* p. 67.

[3] *Principles of Economics,* 8th ed., p. 74.

prietorship; sometimes the items excluded are those which do not seem to have a recurring character and a change which is exceptional in amount may perhaps be excluded even though it arises in connection with the conduct of the business; sometimes the basis of discrimination rests upon arbitrary legal provisions, and gains in proprietorship which may not be made the basis of dividends by a corporation are excluded from the showing of the profits of the year.

Profits Related to Other Accounting Problems

Because of the reciprocal relations of the two phases of accounting, the problem of profits is not one set off by itself but is involved in all other accounting problems. The proper valuation of assets (the problem of the inventory) is clearly a question of profit, for changes in the book value of assets mean corresponding changes in the net wealth. The question as to whether organization expenses belong in the inventory is just as much a question as to whether they should be kept out of the Profit and Loss account. Depreciation if established must be booked by a charge to Profit and Loss, and the adoption of one or another method for distributing depreciation over the life of the asset thereby determines a corresponding distribution of profit as between one or another year. A discussion of profits is, therefore, merely another view of the general problems of accounting which, while pertinent to the consideration of profits, have already been discussed and need not be repeated in this chapter.

Problem I. Has Proprietorship Decreased?

Most of the entries made in the Profit and Loss account are unequivocal and undisputed. An expense is, in most cases, easily recognized and the necessity for charging expenses to Profit and Loss is generally not questioned. But there are two problems of general significance in connection with the ascertainment of profit which are the source of illimitable dispute.

One of these has already been discussed in connection with the valuation of assets. It is generally spoken of as the distinction between capital expenditures and charges against revenue. It relates to the situation where some asset, ordinarily cash, has been decreased, and the problem to be faced is whether, when recognizing the decrease of cash, the counter entry is one indicating that proprietorship is thereby decreased, or one showing that there has been an exchange and that some other asset, presumably part of the plant, has replaced the cash so that proprietorship is by that transaction left unchanged. This problem, though relating to the ascertainment of profits, has been sufficiently discussed above and the arguments need not be repeated.

Problem II. How Is the Change in Proprietorship to Be Shown?

The second problem arises in a different set of circumstances. Here there is no question as to the decline in one asset being offset by the acquisition of an equivalent. The net assets are reduced in value, perhaps by some great cyclic swing in price levels, perhaps by some catastrophic event such as the Great War, perhaps through some conditions peculiar to the business but unusual in nature. The land, because of the discovery of new mineral deposits, is admittedly vastly more valuable than when purchased; the investments were unwisely and disastrously made and even the most optimistic can see no countervailing appreciation; the company has less net assets; it is indisputably poorer than at the beginning of the year; the proprietorship has changed in value.

Changes in Proprietorship Sometimes Disregarded

In many cases, there is no dispute as to the effect which the events have had upon the current income, no doubt as to how the effect should be portrayed in the accounts. Occasionally, however, there is a problem or a series of problems which the accountant must face. According to some authorities certain changes in the net value of assets, instead of being clearly shown in the accounts, are to be altogether ignored, and the accounts are to continue as though the event had not taken place. What was said above in regard to the customary failure to record changes in the value of the land used as the factory site is a case in point. Every one knows that the land which cost $100,000 is now worth only $10,000 or is worth $1,000,000. But it is still allowed to stand upon the books at its original cost, and that remaining unchanged, there is, of course, no corresponding change in the proprietorship, no credit to Profit and Loss. Or a new concern has by good management built up goodwill, which it could easily sell for a large sum. The tendency among accountants is nevertheless to ignore this new asset and to continue proprietorship and assets unchanged by the event. This phase of the problem has, also, in part been discussed in connection with the valuation of assets, and further discussion is deferred to the next chapter.

Various Methods of Booking Changes in Proprietorship

Another aspect remains for consideration. A change has taken place in the value of the net assets, and the change is one which is properly recorded by debiting or crediting the asset account affected. The list of assets shows an increase or a decrease in value and some counter entry must be made to maintain the validity of the accounting equation. The dilemma here faced is not, as in the case of the alternative of capital expenditure and charge against revenue, whether proprietorship has been affected; it is not as in the circumstances mentioned above, a question as to whether a change shall be altogether ignored or be recorded in the accounts. The question now to be decided is whether an admitted change in proprietorship is to be shown in the Income account, that is as something affecting the current income, or is it to be recognized by some other bookkeeping device.

Various answers may be given. Instead of entering the item in the current Income account, one of the following may be adopted as the counter entry offsetting the admitted decline in the value of net assets.

1. The item may be charged to capital. This is not in the sense that a capital expenditure is often spoken of as a capital charge, meaning merely that the item is added to the book

value of the fixed assets, but in the literal sense of being debited to the Capital account, so as to show that the net capital has actually suffered a diminution.

2. It may be charged against some account showing the accumulations of past profits, such as the general Surplus account.

3. It may be handled in such a way as to cause it to be deducted from future earnings, rather than from the earnings of the current fiscal period. This would be accomplished by establishing some special account, of the nature of a deferred charge, which would be gradually amortized out of the earnings of future years. In this way the change which has actually taken place in the present year does not, at least to its full extent, affect the profits of the year in which the event occurred, but is regarded as affecting future profits.

4. It may be entered in an account which admittedly shows a profit, but excluded from the general Profit and Loss account. This is more likely to be done in the case of an increase than a decrease. Its purpose is often to show that there has been an actual increase made in proprietorship, during the current year, but one which is not to be considered as available for dividends.

Alternative between Change of Capital and Income

The idea that a change in proprietorship may alternatively be either an element of profit or a change directly affecting capital is familiar, in an unimportant way, to every student of elementary bookkeeping. Ordinarily a decrease in the net assets causes a debit to the Profit and Loss account. But where the decrease is due to the proprietor's taking either cash or merchandise for his own use, the charge is universally to the proprietor's Capital account and not to Profit and Loss. Even in such elementary accounting, it is considered that not every change in proprietorship is shown in Profit and Loss. This conception has perhaps been worked out most minutely in questions of probate, where a life interest in an estate is left to one person while the body of the estate goes to some other legatee. Here it is of vital importance to distinguish between the income going to the tenant for life and the body of the estate going to the remainder-man. In this relation the conception has been introduced of there being a growth or increase in the body of the estate which does not constitute a part of the income. Conversely there may be a loss of part of the principal without effect on the income derived from the remainder. The theory, while well worked out in detail in its application to the settlement of estates, is recognized as being peculiar to probate law, and while interesting to the accountant is not applicable to commercial accounts.[4]

Capital Changes and the Double Account Balance Sheet

In England the discussion has been clearer than in the United States. It has been especially favored by the exceptional form for the balance sheet provided for parliamentary companies. The fact that the Capital account is here kept separate, as in the simple form:

Capital Account

Capital assets	£ 95,000	Shares	£100,000
Balance	5,000		
	£100,000		£100,000

Balance Sheet

Balance of Capital Account	£ 5,000	Notes Receivable	£15,000
Accounts Payable	20,000	Cash	15,000
Profits	5,000		
	£30,000		£30,000

seems to encourage the idea that the Capital account, or at least the plant purchased with receipts from capital have little or nothing to do with the profits exhibited in the balance sheet. The inference is easily drawn that there can be a

[4] *Cf.* Merchants' Loan and Trust Co. *v.* Smietanka, 255 U. S. 509, 521 (1921).

loss in the value of the capital assets which would affect only the Capital account and which would leave the profits of the year undisturbed. Doubtless, because of being accustomed in double accounts to treat capital as a thing by itself, the English courts have been more ready to take advanced ground on the general problem.

Whatever decision may ultimately be rendered by accountants, the problem at least is clear. Recognizing the loss of certain assets, say by fire, or by shipwreck, by default of securities, or by normal exploitation, the only point of debate is as to the channel through which that loss shall be shown. In accounting terms it is simply whether a given, recognized loss is to be debited to Profit and Loss, or to some other account which would indicate a deduction from net wealth but which would say nothing about current revenues. To a certain extent it is a question of terminology; in part, it is a question of law. Does the term net profits mean the net change in wealth, due to whatever cause, or does it mean only those changes due to a certain set of business factors? Does the law allow dividends to be made of the surplus of certain receipts (realized or constructive) over certain expenses (whether paid or merely recognized), or is it the surplus of present assets over the net assets of a year ago which may be divided?

Alternative between Income and Surplus

As shown above, the alternative to entering the change in proprietorship in the current Income account is not always limited to charging it to the Capital account. Although excluded from the current Income account, it may still be recognized as income, rather than an addition to capital, but income to be attributed to some other period, or income of a nature to be differentiated from that which is ordinarily shown in the Income account. With much reason it may at times be urged that a given loss, suffered, or at least made manifest during the current year, may be held to lessen the profits attributed to past years, appearing under Surplus. It may be thought undesirable (under the urge of expediency rather than of logic) to allow a loss, exceptional in amount, to fall in its entirety on the present year, and, on the other hand, a gain may for legal or other reasons be so unavailable for dividends that it may well be placed in some special account bearing a rubric which unmistakably indicates that so much of a real, although perhaps unrealized, profit is not, in the immediate future, to be distributed to the stockholders.

Exclusion from Income of Abnormal Changes

The circumstances which lead to the exclusion of some actual gain or loss from the current Income account are various. At times it is due to the idea that the Income account should show only the changes due to the operations of the business which the corporation conducts. The line of demarcation here is, as in so many accounting matters, extremely vague. There is in most cases some reference, either open or implied, to the regularity of such income, or to its being normal. Some of the distinctions are made more prominent in connection with the negative side of profits. Thus, for instance a concern engaged in manufacture would consider the regular and normal depreciation in the value of its machinery due to wear and tear as an item affecting profits. But if in a given year its plant were destroyed by fire or earthquake, many accountants would present a statement showing the income of the year unaffected by this abnormal occurrence.

The differentiation here rests sometimes upon whether the gain or loss is of an unusual or exceptional character. Sometimes it relates rather to the amount of change which has taken place, particularly where the change is a loss. Thus, where part of the capital assets, for instance, a piece of real estate, is sold at an increase over the cost, this gain might be excluded from the showing of profits purely on the ground that it arose from an exceptional and unusual circumstance and this would be true whether the gain were large or small. An illustration of an item being excluded from the showing of profits merely because of the amount involved, may be found in the case of fire losses. In any extended plant there will from time to time be minor losses from fire. These would undoubtedly be included as one item in the profit and loss statement. But if the fire loss is an overwhelming one, even though it be of the same nature as the losses which previously have been considered in ascertaining profits, it is quite common to set it up as a separate item which at least does not affect present profits. In one case the item excluded from Profit and Loss is exceptional because of its character or source; in other cases it is exceptional in quantity.

Profits and Profits Available for Dividends

Another use of the term profits limits it to so much of the increment in proprietorship as may, in accordance with legal provisions or the maxims of business expediency, be distributed as dividends of a corporation. In legal discussions the term profits of a corporation frequently means profits available for dividends, a restriction in the use of the term which has caused much confusion. The Income account is frequently used to indicate profits in this restricted sense. When this is the case it is obvious that a gain which is considered not thus available, even though clearly pertaining to the events of the current year, must be excluded from the Income account. It must, as stated above (4) appear in some other account indicating, it is true, a gain, but a gain not available for dividends. This account may well have a descriptive title, such, for instance, as Surplus Arising from Sale of Capital Assets.

There is, accordingly, a series of dilemmas which the accountant must face when he is attempting to record the profits of a given period. Granting that the assets at the end of the period are actually in excess of those at the beginning, questions arise: (1) Is the increment to be looked upon as income or as an increase in the capital? (2) Granting that the increment is to be regarded in some sense as income, is it to be recorded in the current Profit and Loss account or is it to be entered into some other account which clearly represents some phase of profits, but one which is to be kept separate from the profits ordinarily exhibited? (3) Are the credits to be made, not so much with a view to showing the economic or the accounting interpretation of the increment in proprietorship, as to bring out clearly in the accounts whether that which is shown as profits may be legally distributed?

When Are Profits Realized?

Another difficulty is as to when the profits arise, or, as it is more commonly expressed, as to when profits are realized. This is a somewhat cognate but different problem from the one just referred to. Agreement might be reached that an increase of proprietorship due to a favorable sale of merchandise is a form of income properly to appear in the Income account, or that a decline in the value of investment securities held by a trustee is to be shown as a reduction of capital. But there still remains the question as to when the profit from sale comes into being, as to what evidence is necessary in order to establish the decline in the capital invested in bonds.

Unrealized Profits

It is a common assumption that profits exist only when the increment in wealth is realized. In this opinion there is rather unusual agreement of many accountants, jurists, and economists.[5]

It is not always clear, however, whether a writer considers that there are unrealized as well as realized profits, the latter only being of interest to the accountant, or whether there is no such thing as unrealized profit. If the latter is true the phrase realized profits is evidently tautological.

Much of the discussion of realized profits is confused by an uncertainty as to whether the writer, perhaps a judge rendering a decision, means that profits are not in existence until realized, or that profits are not available for distribution unless they have been realized. The economist is more likely to

---

[5] Thus Sir Arthur Lowes Dickinson says, "In the widest possible view profits may be stated as the realized increment in value (*op. cit.*, p. 67)"; Charles E. Hughes argued, "It is the essence of income that it be realized. . . . Income necessarily implies separation and realization (Eisner *v.* Macomber, 252 U. S. 195)"; and Irving Fisher emphasizes this point of view throughout his *Capital and Income*. See also, Jennery *v.* Olmstead, 13 N. E. 926 (N. Y. 1885); Sexton *v.* C. L. Percival Co., 177 N. W. 83 (Ia. 1920).

take the former ground, the jurist even when his language refers in more general terms to profits, is probably thinking of profits available for dividends, a subject discussed in the following chapter.

Unrealized Increase in Capital Assets Excluded from Income

The opposition to considering an unrealized increase in capital assets as income has in it much of practical value. An orchard of trees as it increases in growth from year to year undoubtedly becomes more valuable, but it is more valuable primarily because the larger trees yield a larger supply of fruit. The increasing yield is a cause of larger income. It in itself constitutes the larger income and this income can be distributed or divided or consumed by the owner. The increased value of the orchard as such is a reflection of this increased income but practically it is the crop income which is available as dividends and not the increased value of the orchard. Similarly, if a piece of business property increases in value, this is presumably due to the fact that because of the growth or shifting of population, stores or offices located upon this particular piece of land will rent for a higher price. The increased income thus derived is profit available for dividend and it flows in in the form of cash receipts. The capitalization of that income as represented by the increased value of the land is nothing available for dividends. Indeed to consider both the increased receipts and the capitalization of the receipts as available for dividends to a certain extent is giving double recognition to a single factor.[6]

In the case of the growth of standing timber, the objection to considering the increment as income before it is cut and sold is not quite so obvious. While this would be spoken of as an appreciation of capital assets, it is more nearly a case

---

[6] This view has been brought out, although in an entirely different connection, by J. H. Bickley in *Journal of Land and Public Utility Economics,* I, p. 414. There is, however, a distinction between having an additional income of $1,000 for the following year and having that income not only for the next year, but an assurance that it will be continued perpetually. It may not be unreasonable to say that this distinction might properly be exhibited in accounts.

of an increase in the value of salable merchandise. The income yielding capital, that is the land itself, is not increasing in value. The product is becoming yearly more valuable. The increased value, if unquestioned, is akin to the increasing value of a discounted note which by most authorities is counted as income available for dividend even though it has not as yet been converted into cash.

Realization of Profits

But while there is a widespread agreement that the accountant is concerned primarily with realized profits, unfortunately there is failure to agree as to when profits are realized or as to the circumstances or conditions which constitute realization. Three answers are given to this question.

1. Cash Basis

The first answer is, when they have been converted into cash. This is a rigidly conservative view but one which is occasionally presented. It is to a certain extent often accepted by the naïve business man and is distinctly set forth in some legal decisions. Among such cases which have at least a curious interest is People *v.* San Francisco Savings Union, where the court stated:

> It is not easy to comprehend how *profits* or *surplus profits* can consist of earnings never yet received. The term imports an excess of *receipts* over *expenditures* and without *receipts* there cannot properly be said to be profits. Money earned as interest, however well secured or certain to be eventually paid . . . does not constitute *surplus profits* within the meaning of the statute.[7]

Even so late as 1902, Justice Kekewich gave an opinion so remarkable as to deserve quoting at some length:

> If it is a mere question what were the profits made in a particular year, it seems to me that the duty is to ascertain what cash has been received and what cash has been expended, and, if that is fairly done, you know the profits of the year. If there is a large outstanding liability which cannot be settled, the partners will estimate that, and it will not be considered as part of the profits. If there is a large

[7] 13 Pac. 500 (Cal. 1887).

outstanding possible loss, and there is a large sum due to a client, then you would provide for that. But in ascertaining what is really actually divisible for the year fairly, you take the cash account as it stands. . . .

A merchant in London consigned a cargo to some foreign port for sale in 1901. Suppose the payment is made by bill perhaps at six or three months, it may run into 1902. Now, are they to treat that as concluded in 1901 and consider that business as attributable entirely to 1901 when the bills may not be met at maturity? Are they to consider those as so much cash for the purposes of that business? It seems to me that that would be entirely wrong in the absence of a special agreement. For the purposes of the balance sheet, no doubt, they would estimate that there is an outstanding asset which they hope to realize; but for the purpose of ascertaining the profit and loss—that is to say, what is to be divided it seems to me that they must consider only what they have received, because those bills will only come in when met at maturity in 1902.[8]

In a dissenting opinion, Justice Brandeis goes even further and suggests that profits can never be determined with certainty until a business adventure has been completely liquidated except in the case where the returns have at least exceeded the capital originally invested.[9] But in general, the decisions of the courts in this respect have been more satisfactory to accountants. A leading English case held that cash need not be on hand and that obligations of the Confederate government honestly estimated as good were a proper basis for determining profits as dividends.[10] A number of American cases have satisfactorily held that profits are not necessarily limited to money received,[11] and it is to be presumed that the conflicting expressions of other courts will not be repeated in the future.

The idea that income is to be counted only as received in cash has had considerable vogue in some business circles. It has also at times appeared in provisions of income taxation, but there more as a matter of administrative convenience than as an expression of correct theory. Accountants are agreed,

---

[8] Badham *v.* Williams, 86 L. T. R. 191 (1902).

[9] Eisner *v.* Macomber, 252 U. S. 230.

[10] Stringer's case, L. R. 4 Ch. App. 475 (1869).

[11] Jones *v.* Davis, 21 Atl. 1035 (N. J. 1891); Slayden *v.* Coal Co., 25 Mo. App. 439 (1887); Van Dyck *v.* McQuade, 86 N. Y. 38 (1881).

in this one matter at least, that income is concerned with accruals rather than with receipts.

On the negative side, that is that expenses are to be reckoned as incurred rather than when paid, the argument is even stronger than when it relates to earnings and receipts. The principle may be the same in both cases, but in regard to accruing expenses logic is backed up by the love of conservatism so marked among accountants. The crude idea, often held by those unversed in accounts, that the income can be ascertained by a comparison of cash receipts and cash payments has, of course, no validity.

2. When Sale Is Made

Probably the most generally accepted view is that profits are realized when a sale has been made. It does not imply the receipt of cash but at least an actual contract involving the establishment of a valid claim against the purchaser. The general acceptance of this test of profits being realized is probably due in large part to the fact that it offers objective evidence of the correctness of the estimated profit. It does not depend merely upon the opinion of the proprietor as to the value of his own assets, but the opinion has been corroborated by an outsider and has been manifested by the giving or receipt of cash, or by the making of an enforceable contract. It matters not whether the amount realized is represented by cash, by the note of the purchaser, or by accounts receivable, provided there is no valid doubt as to the real value of the actually acquired asset. If the claim against the purchaser is good, profit has been realized; if the claim is not good, there is not only an absence of profit but a further loss representing the original investment. To recognize part of this sum as good and to discriminate against the other larger part is clearly illogical. Illogical is the attitude of the California court that the claim for 1 per cent interest against the government may not be counted good, while the 100 per cent of principal still stands among the assets at its full value.

There is some difference of opinion as to the point at which realization takes place, among those who maintain that realization depends upon the making of a contract. It is sometimes expressed that profit is not actually realized upon the sale of goods until legal title to the goods has passed to the purchaser. This is an extreme view, however, and does not correspond with ordinary accounting practice. If payment has been received for goods, ordinary bookkeeping technic would indicate that profits have been made even though there might be a slight delay before the goods passed into the hands of the purchaser. The other view is that as soon as a contract has been entered into which gives to the vendor an enforceable right against the purchaser, profit may be considered as realized. This is of particular importance in connection with contracts covering a long period of time. Even those who object to the recognition of profits upon ordinary merchandise not yet delivered, admit that it is proper to show profits at the end of the year upon a partly completed ship being built on contract, although title to the ship will not pass for perhaps two years upon completion of the work. The reckoning of profits on uncompleted contracts, while refusing to do so on merchandise sold for future delivery, is probably a sacrifice of consistency for expediency such as is often found in accounting practice. The inconvenience of waiting two or three years before reckoning profits in the case of building a ship would be so great that conservatism and consistency are both rejected.[12]

3. When Assets Appreciate

This view while logical is not generally accepted, for the accountant is peculiarly conservative. Even where he knows that profit has been made, he is sometimes unwilling to admit the fact. This attitude of course leads to admitted inconsistencies.[13]

One may have bought $10,000 Second Liberty Loan bonds and $10,000 Third Liberty Loan bonds when both issues were

[12] Montgomery, *Auditing, Theory and Practice,* 3d ed., I, p. 315.

[13] The accountant transcends the conservatism of the proverb, "Do not count your chickens before they are hatched," saying, "Here are a lot of chickens already safely hatched, but for the love of Mike use discretion and don't count them all, for perhaps some will die."

selling at 90. Somewhat later, when both have risen, he may sell his block of the third issue at par and buy, at the same figure, a block of the second issue. If this has been done, he is conventionally allowed to show that the more recently acquired bonds are worth par and that he has made a 10-point profit in the transaction. But the identical bonds which he bought at an earlier date, in accordance with the foregoing rule, must still be valued at 90 showing no profit from appreciation.

Those who object to the recognition of profits where no sale has taken place seldom apply this rule so as to prohibit the recognition of accruing interest as an element of profit. The refusal so to recognize accruing interest in the case of the San Francisco Savings Union (cited above) does not meet with the approval of accountants and in the court decision probably turned more upon the phraseology of the statute than upon any recognized principle. The denial that profit can exist without a sale and the simultaneous recognition of accruing interest as profit is another of the many inconsistencies in accounting practice. The exception in favor of accruing interest probably rests upon the idea that it is definitely calculable, its amount may be accurately determined. But if this is a satisfactory basis of differentiation, the rule for recognizing profits should be expressed in terms of calculability or certainty rather than made dependent upon the existence of a contract.

In the case of government bonds referred to above, the present value is a matter of absolute certainty. It is constantly being expressed in terms of $\frac{1}{32}$ of 1 per cent. The exactness of value here is probably more demonstrable than in the calculation of accrued interest which in many cases involves a possibility of a default in payment, but this and other inconsistencies in accounting must be recognized even though they should be deplored.

It is stated above that there is oftentimes doubt in the accountant's mind as to whether the increase in the value of the net assets should be considered an item affecting profits or should be credited to some special account which may perhaps be included under the general title of surplus. An illustration of such a problem arises particularly in connection with the appreciation in the value of capital assets which is discussed in the next chapter. Other instances relate to premium received upon capital stock. Even in cases where such premium may be legally distributed as dividends, it would not generally be considered that premium should be included in the current income account. A somewhat similar problem relates not to an actual increase in the amount of net assets, but to an increase in the excess of assets above the outstanding capital. This arises when part of the previously outstanding capital stock is canceled. In such cases the question must be raised as to the proper recording of this item.

For bibliography see note to Chapter XII.

CHAPTER XI

DIVIDENDS AND CAPITAL LOSSES

Availability

The question as to the amount of profits available for dividends is one which frequently arises and has perhaps entered into legal disputes more than any other accounting matter. The question of availability for dividends has however, a twofold aspect.

Financial Aspect

The first relates merely to the expediency of paying a dividend in given circumstances. It is a financial rather than a legal or accounting problem. Thus, a manufacturing establishment, which during a year had made unquestioned profits of $100,000 might have invested this entire sum in an extension of plant. All of its resources are thus tied up in business operations and it has no free funds. The profits amounting to $100,000 which would appear in the balance sheet are clearly not available for dividends unless it is possible and financially expedient for the corporation to borrow funds for making such payment. Availability for dividends in this sense implies therefore, a careful consideration of business conditions, a comparison of liabilities to be met and funds with which to meet them, a forecast of general business conditions, and an intimate knowledge of the specific needs of the particular concern. Light may be thrown upon some of these questions by a study of the accounts, but final determination must rest upon business judgment rather than upon accounting principles or statutory provisions.

Legal Restriction as to Source

The second phase of the question of profits available for dividends is more limited and definite. It raises the question as to whether the funds on hand have come from a source which in accordance with law make a dividend permissible. The general conception of a corporation, even without specific statutory restrictions, is that it is not empowered to declare dividends except out of profits. If not distinctly prohibited by statute, a payment by the directors of dividends without profits would at least be *ultra vires.* This may be illustrated by the case of a corporation organized with $100,000 capital stock which was paid in full. Of the cash received, $80,000 was expended in construction of the plant and in providing the ordinary working capital. It is found that the needs of the business are so limited that $20,000 of the contributed capital can not be profitably employed and is lying in idle cash. It is obvious that although this cash is not needed in the business, it is not legally available for dividends as its source is the capital contribution of the stockholders and not profits. No doubt could arise in so obvious a case, but real difficulty is found in other instances and these will be discussed at some length. Thus, it has been a much disputed matter as to whether the net receipts from operating a mine may legally be distributed as dividends. Many contentions have been raised as to whether the gain realized by sale of property either contributed by stockholders or purchased by funds paid in for capital stock, constitutes profits available for dividends; and similar questions arise in connection with undisputed increase in proprietorship due to the receipt of premium on an issue of capital stock. These are all matters which have given rise to legal contests and which have puzzled the brains of both accountants and jurists. The difficulty has been increased by the fact that the courts, while using the same words, are not always speaking the same language as the accountants, and by the fact that the judges, while passing on matters which really involve accounting principles, are unfortunately not always as well versed in accounting as they are in law.

Legal Restrictions as to Amount Distributable

A second element in the legal availability of profits for dividends relates not to the source of the profits but turns upon the point whether some portion of the profits, no matter whence derived, must be withheld from distribution. A clear illustration is found in the provisions of the National Bank Act that one-tenth of the profits of any year must be withheld from dividends and carried to surplus until the surplus amounts to 20 per cent of the capital stock. Similar provisions relating to all corporations and not merely to banks, are found in the statutory provisions of continental countries. Here the restriction is an arbitrary one, enforced by statute. In other cases, it may arise from a contract entered into by the corporation itself. Thus not infrequently the contract with bondholders provides that each year a certain sum shall be set aside from profits to establish a sinking fund or to pay off the debt directly. The sum thus set aside does not in any sense cease to be profits, but it is of course not available for dividends. The sinking fund contract practically provides that dividends shall be paid only from the excess profits over the sinking fund requirements. While the profits are in no way affected by such transactions, in almost all cases the balance sheet will show a clear differentiation between that part of the profits reserved for sinking fund purposes and the remainder which is available for dividends.

Confusion in Terminology

Much of the confusion is doubtless due to a mere difference in terminology and oftentimes the term profits in legal use means profits available for dividends. The courts may well place certain restrictions on the payment of dividends which would not at all correspond with the accountant's limitations of the concept of profits. Indeed, this is in many cases done by statute; and is true in a number of the Spanish American republics, which prescribe that only liquid profits may be paid as dividends. It may be accepted that it is incorrect to base a dividend on unrealized profits, or indeed that an unrealized gain is not profit, but "the hope of profit."[1] There is good business conservatism in the argument of Dupin, "One

[1] J. H. Pim, in *Accountant*, XXIV, p. 679.

does not divide hopes, however well-founded; one does not divide a phrase, but money. A dividend before going out of the treasury of the company, ought first to have come into it.''[2]

Wasting Assets

One of the most debated problems regarding profits available for dividends has arisen in connection with corporations with wasting assets, which have been defined as ''material assets, such as mines, which diminish in value with removal of their product, or immaterial assets, such as patents, which theoretically diminish in value by reason of a fluction of time.''[3]

Illustration

The problem may be illustrated by assuming a case of relative simplicity where a company is organized to purchase a coal mine and to exploit and sell the coal. Waiving the question of the difficulty of making an intelligent estimate of the value of the coal deposit, it may be assumed that $250,000 is paid for the property and that this is an equitable price for the million tons of coal which the mine contains. On these terms the selling price should return the principal, pay all the operating expenses, and yield a fair profit on the original investment. The proceeds of each year's sales obviously should considerably exceed the annual cost of operating the mine; but it is perfectly clear that the excess of receipts over annual expenditures will not all be profits. Out of the price received for each ton of coal 25 cents is a return of a similar sum paid originally for the coal *in situ;* and allowance for this cost price must inexorably be made before profits can correctly be determined. With the assumptions made, the

---

[2] Quoted in Bastide, *Des dividends fictifs*, p. 36.

[3] Committee on Terminology, A.I.A., in *Journal of Accountancy*, XXXV, p. 466. Accountants consider standing timber a wasting asset analogous to the ore deposit in a mine. Curiously the Supreme Court of the United States has stated that this is only a superficial analogy and that the logging of timber property may be treated differently from the depletion of a mine. Doyle *v.* Mitchell Bros. Co., 247 U. S. 179, 188 (1917).

mining company can no more legitimately treat the net annual receipts as net profits than can the merchant neglect the cost price of his commodity, or the manufacturer disregard the factory cost of his product in his estimate of profits. Thus assuming that the total cost of mining and selling coal, including all the direct outlay for operation, amounts to 55 cents per ton, the company, after exploiting 100,000 tons, should show in its Profit and Loss account:

Profit and Loss

Expenses	$55,000	Sales	$100,000
Depletion of Mine	25,000		
Balance available for dividends	20,000		
	$100,000		$100,000

and having paid out the full profits the balance sheet should show:

Balance Sheet

Cost of Mine	$250,000	Capital	$250,000
Cash, etc.	25,000	Allowance for Depletion	25,000
	$275,000		$275,000

The same process being continued until all the coal is disposed of the balance sheet should be:

Balance Sheet

Mine—cost price	$250,000		Capital	$250,000
Less Depletion	250,000			
Cash, etc.		$250,000		
		$250,000		$250,000

During the course of business the net cash receipts amount to $450,000, but because of charging to Profit and Loss a sum representing the cost price of the coal, the total profits shown and distributed amount only to $200,000, while there steadily accumulates in the treasury a sum which at the end of operations equals the original cost of the mine.[4] This would serve to return the contributed capital.

The Lee Case

Such treatment of the accounts met with the practically unanimous approval of accountants, when in 1889 the accounting world was startled by the now historic decision in the English case, Lee *v.* Neuchatel Asphalte Company, Limited (L. R. 41 Ch. Div. 1). Here action was brought by a shareholder to prevent a company formed to work certain asphalt deposits from paying dividends without making allowance for the exhaustion of the deposits. But the court refused to interfere. Unfortunately for the peace of mind of accountants, jurists, and company directors, the decision itself was somewhat vague in principle, contradictory in detail, and difficult of apprehension. But the case at least decided the principle that there is no requirement compelling companies to limit their dividends to an amount remaining after making allowance for the exhaustion of their capital invested in "wasting" assets.

So counter was this to the teaching of textbooks, and the practice of accountants that it immediately attracted attention and criticism. In the current discussion in the *Accountant,* the organ of the Chartered Accountants, it was almost universally condemned. It was claimed that the decision showed "a feeble grasp of the fundamental principles of accounting" and to be "utterly at variance with the views of all practical accountants and prudent men of business."[5] The *Dictionary of Political Economy* appearing soon after the decision maintained that it "contradicts every sound principle of business and bookkeeping."[6] Palmer, one of the most eminent authorities on company law, has said: "The views on Lee are

---

[4] For the sake of simplicity the question of interest accruing on this fund is disregarded.

[5] A. W. Payne, *Accountant,* XVIII, p. 143.

[6] I, p. 222.

not shared by some other learned judges and they do not commend themselves to the common sense of accountants, economists, or business men in general,''[7] and he declares its system of ascertaining profits to be "obviously unsound."

In face of such united criticism coming from such varied authorities it requires some temerity to argue in favor of the decision; especially so since the decision, while it has frequently been followed in England and the United States,[8] has been said to have really no bearing on the question of the treatment of wasting assets as in reality the value of the remaining deposits was greater than the original price paid for the concession.[9] It should be borne in mind that the decision was not expressed in accounting terms, nor was it a decision as to what constituted profits,[10] but merely that a company, organized to work a wasting property might, in accordance with the terms of its own articles, distribute the net annual receipts without withholding a sum to represent the exhaustion of the mineral deposits, there being no creditors who were thereby harmed.

Policy of Dividends from Wasting Assets

The question as to the business policy of distributing the net proceeds of mining operations as dividends without making allowance for depletion is somewhat independent of the legality of such action. It has already been shown how the decision in Lee *v.* Neuchatel Asphalte Company was almost universally criticized. Even Pixley in his latest edition of *Duties of Auditors,* styles the payment of such dividends "a

---

[7] *Company Precedents,* I, p. 757.

[8] See, *e.g.,* People *ex rel.* United Verde Copper Co. *v.* Roberts, 51 N. E. 293 (N. Y. 1898); Excelsior Water and Mining Co. *v.* Pierce, 27 Pac. 44 (Cal. 1891); Goodnow *v.* American Writing Paper Co., 66 Atl. 607 (N. J. 1907); Mellon *v.* Mississippi Wire Glass Co., 78 Atl. 710 (N. J. 1910).

[9] Bond *v.* Barrow Hæmatite Steel Co., [1902] 1 Ch. 353, and Wilmer *v.* McNamara & Co., [1895] 2 Ch. 245. Strictly speaking the Lee case did not involve the actual depletion of mineral resources, as the company held only a lease entitling it to exploit the deposit and did not itself own the deposit.

[10] See statement of Fletcher-Moulton, *In re* Spanish Prospecting Co., [1911] 1 Ch. 92, 102.

suicidal policy and contrary to the practice of soundly managed public companies."[11]

Despite the high authority of the critics cited there is strong reason for justifying the payment of dividends without making allowance for the exhaustion of the mine. The discussion reduces itself to the question whether mining and similar enterprises are to be regarded as permanent undertakings, the capital of which should be maintained, or as temporary ventures corresponding to the character of the natural resources, from which capital as well as profits may be withdrawn as quickly as may be possible without injuring creditors or impairing credit. Those holding the former view claim that so much of the receipts as represents the return of capital should be reserved by the company, and invested so that at the time of the final exhaustion of the mine it would own other assets equaling the entire amount of the capital stock.

This view seems entirely to overlook the essential character of the enterprise. A mining venture is always a speculative undertaking. Subscribers to the capital know well that in the nature of things it cannot be a permanent undertaking, and presumably they are aware of its speculative character. Their sole object is to exploit a given deposit of mineral, and the logical thing seems to be to have the fruits of such exploitation turned back to the subscribers as quickly as may be. Granting that creditors are not misled nor harmed (and protection can easily be secured by contract) it seems absurd to require that a body of capitalists willing to invest in a peculiar speculative enterprise should be forced to form what is practically a trust company to invest part of the annual receipts against some far distant day of accounting. If one prefers a speculative enterprise with possible large gains, what is more unreasonable than to require that this venture should gradually be transformed into something entirely different, an investment in long-time and low-rate securities. Better by all means, unless it is thought that paternalistic laws should force him willy-nilly to become conservative, to

---

[11] 11th ed., p. 477.

turn back to him the proceeds of the exploitation and allow him to make another similar venture if he sees fit.

Moreover, the very nature of the organization probably is an argument against the accumulation of a reserve. The officers of the mining company presumably were selected because they knew how to mine. But this so far from supporting, furnishes a presumption against, the supposition that they are desirable persons to keep and administer a large trust fund. From all points of view it seems much more sensible to allow the gradual return of capital invested in an enterprise which by its nature is terminable, than to demand the accumulation of a reserve fund.

A dictum of the United States Supreme Court, although given in other circumstances, is pertinent to this discussion:

> A stockholder [said Mr. Justice Davis] enters into a contract with the company that his interest shall be subject to the direction and control of the proper authorities of the corporation to accomplish the object for which the company was organized. He does not agree that the improvement to which he subscribed should be changed in its purposes and character at the will and pleasure of a majority of the stockholders so that new responsibilities and, it may be, new hazards are added to the original undertaking. He may be willing to embark in one enterprise and unwilling to engage in another.[12]

This statement was made regarding an extension of a line of railroad out of profits which otherwise would have been distributed to the stockholders. If it applies to a mere extension of a similar enterprise, much more should it hold as regards enterprises so utterly divergent in character as the speculative exploitation of a mine, and the establishment of a trust fund.

On the other hand there are certain circumstances in which it might be highly desirable for the company to withhold a sum corresponding to the exhaustion of the wasting capital and reinvest in other similar enterprises. Thus a manufacturing company owning its own coal or iron mines might most wisely reinvest in new mines as the old ones were depleted.

---

[12] Clearwater *v.* Meredith, 68 U. S. 40 (1863).

But this is a special case. All that is claimed is that there should be no general rule that there must be a withholding of receipts. Even a reinvestment in a similar enterprise requires special justification; the creation of a fund to be invested in outside securities of an entirely different nature is much less to be favored.

In the above case the question related solely to the treatment of the income of a company specifically organized for the exploitation of wasting assets, or as it is loosely phrased, with wasting capital. The nature of such an enterprise precludes its permanence. The more successful its operation, the shorter its life. Like Nancy Etticoat[13] of the childish riddle, the more brilliant its career, the sooner it ends; the more efficient its management, the more quickly will its resources be exhausted. Such an enterprise differs radically from an ordinary commercial undertaking where the element of permanence and continuity is implied. The decision in the Lee case, therefore, did not necessarily apply to any enterprise other than those with wasting assets.

Dividends and Capital Losses

Verner Case

Five years later a decision almost equally important was given which greatly extended the idea that losses might be suffered without affecting the Profit and Loss account. This was in the case of Verner *v.* The General and Commercial Investment Trust, Limited ([1894] 2 Ch. 239). This concerned a company organized to purchase stock of various other companies, the sole function of the trust being to make speculative investments dividing the net income as dividends to its own stockholders. The investments made were in diverse

---

[13] When this was first written, it was thought that the allusion would be familiar to every one. Experience of the last nineteen years has, however, shown that at least so far as the average college student is concerned, there is a deplorable ignorance of our heritage of English literature. For elucidation the ignorant are respectfully referred to: *Harleian MSS.*, No. 1960; or to the *Publications of the Percy Society,* IV, part 4, p. 93 (1842); or *Mother Goose* (Rackham ed.), N. Y., 1913, p. 112.

enterprises and were made purely for the sake of the income to be derived therefrom. In this particular instance, nearly $5,000,000 had been raised by shares and debentures, all of which had been invested. But some of the investments had been poorly selected, their market value had fallen greatly, and some of them were known to be absolutely worthless. It was admitted that there was an irrecoverable loss of $375,-000. Receipts of interest and dividends, however, largely exceeded the current expenses, and the case turned on the legitimacy of paying these net receipts as dividends, instead of using them to make up the loss due to the decline in the value of the investments. The decision held that such dividends were proper, despite the general legal principle that dividends may not be paid out of capital.

Here there was, of course, no question of wasting assets. Investments were not made for the purpose of exploitation and exhaustion, but for permanent income. In the decision, Lord Justice Lindley held that while in general dividends cannot legally be paid out of capital, yet that does not imply that in all cases the loss of capital must be made up before dividends may be paid. A distinction was made between the loss of what was termed fixed capital and of circulating capital. Dividing the income of a company, without the replacement of the circulating capital consumed in producing the income, is a payment of a dividend out of capital, such as is prohibited by law.

> Fixed capital may be sunk and lost and yet the excess of current receipts over current payments may be divided, but floating or circulating capital must be kept up, as otherwise it will enter into and form part of such excess in which case to divide such excess without deducting the capital which formed part of it will be contrary to law.

Other Decisions Concerning Capital Losses

In this decision the principle that capital need not be kept up before declaring dividends, which in Lee *v.* Neuchatel Asphalte Company was applied only to wasting capital, was extended to so-called "fixed capital" permanently invested in a peculiar enterprise known as an investment trust. In the following year the doctrine was extended in the case of Wilmer *v.* McNamara and Company ([1895] 2 Ch. 245) where a decline in the value of the goodwill of a company was held not to interfere with the payment of dividends on the ground that this loss also was one of fixed and not of circulating capital. Even more far reaching was the decision in the Kingston Cotton Mill Company case ([1896] 1 Ch. 348) that the rulings, which in Lee and Verner were applied to companies of a peculiar nature, would also apply to an ordinary manufacturing concern.

A recent decision has similarly held that dividends might be paid despite the loss of value in the fixed plant of a railroad.[14]

The doctrine laid down in Verner seems to be well established, although its significance has at times been somewhat lessened as by the important case of Bond *v.* Barrow Hæmatite Steel Company ([1902] 1 Ch. 353). In this case the court accepted the earlier decisions regarding the loss of fixed and wasting capital as binding. But it took the remarkable ground that the rules regarding losses of fixed capital did not apply to damages to iron mines and the destruction of blast furnaces and workmen's cottages, as these were all losses of circulating capital.[15]

Policy of Dividends with Capital Losses

The policy of paying dividends despite the loss of capital where the investment was in other than wasting property is not so easily defended. Here there is a real loss, not a return of capital; here the enterprise is normally a permanent not a terminating one; here the whole purpose of the enterprise is not to exhaust and return the capital but to use it in business.

Circumstances may, however, justify even such a payment

[14] Lawrence *v.* W. S. Mineral R. R. Co., [1918] 2 Ch. 250.

[15] The principle involved in the Verner decision has also been somewhat questioned in a Scottish decision (City Property Investment Trust *v.* Thorburn, Court of Sessions cases, 1897, p. 361). But in this case the court held that the investments which had declined in value were really circulating rather than fixed assets.

of dividend. For instance, an individual's entire income is derived from ten houses each worth $10,000 and each yielding 10 per cent net income. If two of these houses burn down, uninsured, the common sense view is that the proprietor's income is thereby cut down from $10,000 to $8,000 per annum, and that coincidentally there is a loss of capital of $20,000. It rarely occurs to the owner that he must consider his income as entirely cut off until the principal can be restored through earnings. Similarly it might be an act of cruelty to dependent stockholders to stop dividends entirely until an exceptional loss is reimbursed. The main difficulty is that in a corporation such an occurrence really calls for a reduction of the nominal capital, a cancelation of part of the capital stock. The red tape and legal expense of doing this, perhaps, too, the bad effect on the company's credit of giving public notice that there has been an encroachment on capital, make directors loath to do so. The criticism properly to be made is not so much that dividends are paid before restoring the capital (*i.e.*, increasing the assets until they again equal the capital), but rather that the capital stock has not been reduced to correspond with the amount of remaining assets, before the dividend is paid. To allow dividends to be paid when assets have fallen below the nominal capital seems to render nugatory all the legal provisions regarding the reduction of capital stock. Why enact such careful legal restrictions and yet suffer the same results to be reached by the methods permitted in the case of the General and Commercial Investment Trust? The hardship of going entirely without dividends for a series of years may perhaps be considered only a fair return for the exceptional privileges granted to stockholders.

A significant recognition of the impropriety of paying dividends despite previous losses is found in the revision of the New York Stock Corporation Law which provides that no stock corporation shall declare or pay any dividend which shall impair its capital or capital stock nor while its capital or capital stock is impaired.[16]

[16] Laws 1923, chap. 787, sec. 58.

Dividends and Operating Losses

Early Decisions

So far there has been considered the question as to whether the profits of the year are to be calculated without reference to the depletion of wasting assets or to the loss of so-called fixed capital. In the case of the National Bank of Wales ([1899] 2 Ch. 629) a decision was given which was more sweeping in its effect. There the loss which had occurred was one which might be considered a loss of circulating capital, for it was due to the shrinkage in the value of loans made by the bank. But the decision sanctioned the payment of dividends in a year when profits had been earned despite the fact that the losses of previous years were still uncovered. Soon afterwards Justice Wright relying probably on this decision, stated in the case of Crichton's Oil Company ([1901] 2 Ch. 196): "I do not think that there is any rule of law that profit on one year's trading cannot be divided merely because in the Profit and Loss account there is a deficit over on the balance of former years."

The adoption as a general rule of the principle enunciated in these decisions would be to treat each year as a separate unit, and if a judicious arrangement of the accounts could be made so as to show alternately net annual profits and losses, to allow a continued distribution of dividends despite the fact that there was a constantly growing deficit due to the loss of circulating as well as fixed capital.[17]

The validity of the decision in the National Bank of Wales case was for many years seriously questioned, for although the decision was upheld in the House of Lords,[18] the judgment in the last court was based entirely on technical grounds, and in no way vouched for the correctness of the doctrines relating to profits. Furthermore, each one of the lords rendering an opinion in the latter case, took unusual pains to call attention to the fact that his approval of the decision of the lower court did not imply approval of the

---

[17] See F. B. Palmer, *Company Precedents,* I, p. 764.
[18] Dovey *v.* Cory, [1901] A. C. 477.

doctrine, therein enunciated, as to the treatment of lost banking capital. But that the decision in the National Bank of Wales case is legally binding was definitely asserted nearly twenty years later in the important and startling decision in the Ammonia Soda Company, Limited *v.* Chamberlain ([1918] 1 Ch. 266).

The Ammonia Soda Company Case

This involved a company which was engaged in extracting brine and manufacturing salt. In the earlier years, the company, allowing for depreciation upon its plant, had run at a loss, but an unexpected deposit of rock salt was discovered which undoubtedly added to the value of the property a sum greater than the net deficit. The company reorganized upon the basis of this higher value and proceeded to pay dividends out of subsequent earnings. Objection was made that it was improper to mark up the value of the property, thus canceling out the deficit, and that it was also improper to distribute earnings of a given year if the operations of preceding years had resulted in a deficit. The court, however, decided that the dividends were legitimate, holding both that the marking up of the value of the fixed assets was proper and, what is more pertinent to the present discussion, that even if the property had not thus been marked up, there was no law requiring that previous deficits should be made up before distributing profits. The latter argument was based upon the decision in the National Bank of Wales case. It was held that this decision had never been reversed. It is true that doubt was thrown upon it by the *obiter dicta* rendered in Dovey *v.* Cory, but the decision in the latter case was made upon the technical question of the responsibility of a director and did not pass upon the question as to the legitimacy of distributing profits despite a previous deficit. In the Ammonia Soda Company case, the court held that as the decision in the National Bank of Wales case had stood for twenty years without having been reversed by a higher court, it was incompetent to disregard it merely because of the *obiter dicta* in Dovey *v.* Cory. The decision is probably an unsatisfactory one to accountants. They generally considered the opinion in the National Bank of Wales case, as to losses of circulating capital, unsound. The fact that the justices had gone so far out of their way to question the earlier decision was generally accepted as discrediting, if not reversing it; but the decision stands and doubtless will continue to have great influence in accounting matters. Accountants, however, generally would agree with the statement of Pixley that so long as a deficit resulting from a loss on trading exists "no dividend should be paid to the shareholders although in law it may be allowable."[19]

Criticism of Legal Decisions

Many of the court decisions emphasize the unsatisfactoriness of the distinction which the courts have attempted to draw between a loss of fixed and one of circulating capital. If by this is meant a loss of fixed and circulating *assets,* there is, of course, the difficulty already alluded to of determining in any concrete case which class of assets has been lost. As the Lord Chancellor said in Dovey *v.* Cory, "The distinction between fixed and floating capital, which may be appropriate enough in an abstract treatise like Adam Smith's 'Wealth of Nations' may with reference to a concrete case be quite inappropriate."

In no system of classification known to economists from Adam Smith down is an iron furnace included, as it has been included by the court, in the list of circulating capital. But the objection to this distinction from the technical viewpoint of accounting is even more serious. Part of the assets may be lost, but no particular asset is an embodiment of any particular credit in the balance sheet. The asset in question may, indeed, have been bought with the cash paid in on subscriptions to capital stock, or from the proceeds of an issue of bonds, or by incurring floating debt, or by investing the profits of the business. But the destruction of this particular

---

[19] *Duties of Auditors,* 11th ed., p. 541. In the earlier editions of this work, which appeared before this decision, the clause "although in law it may be allowable" is omitted.

asset is not thereby made specifically a loss of capital, or of funded debt, or of current liabilities, or of profits. To the accountant the distinction between the credit items in the balance sheet and the assets is vital. They represent entirely different conceptions and are not to be confused.

Capital Losses in the Balance Sheet

The critics generally assume that the courts justify the Neuchatel Asphalte Company and the General and Commercial Trust in presenting accounts misleading and incorrect. Thus Palmer in his masterly work on Company Law says:

> The views expressed in Verner *v.* General and Commercial Investment Trust involve the proposition . . . that the Balance Sheet need not disclose the true condition of the company. It deals as regards the assets not with existing facts but with past history. It shows what the particular assets cost, not what they are worth. Thus if a company buys a property for £10,000 and the value has fallen to £1,000, it will properly be entered on the Balance Sheet as property that cost £10,000; and it will remain at that figure, even though each year, by consumption or otherwise, it depreciates more and more.[20]

But this opinion, which is shared by many another critic, not merely ignores the possibilities of accounting technic, but more strangely disregards the express words of the decision itself in which Lord Justice Lindley states: "It is obvious that capital lost must not appear in the accounts as still existing intact; the accounts must show the truth and not be misleading or fraudulent."[21] Similarly in the later case of Barrow Hæmatite Steel Company ([1900] 2 Ch. 857) Justice Cozens-Hardy very clearly intimates that, although a loss of capital may not prevent the Profit and Loss account from showing a balance available for dividends, the balance sheet would at the same time show or imply the loss which had taken place.

---

[20] 11th ed., pp. 220-1.
[21] [1894] 2 Ch. 267.

While the professional accountant sometimes advises a client as to the legality of certain transactions, the language of accounting is itself not concerned with legal technicalities. Whether or not the law permits a company to hold its own stock, to issue stock or bonds below par, to make stock dividends, or as in the case here to pay dividends while assets are less than the nominal capital is an important, but purely legal matter. If the transaction named has taken place, the question as to its technical legality has not—or at least should not have—anything to say as to the statement of facts by the accountant. It may be logical to claim that *all* losses or gains, however caused, should go to Profit and Loss, and not direct to some other proprietorship account. But such a claim, while logical enough, does not at all conform to accounting practice of any land or time. Once granted that some losses need not appear to the debit of Profit and Loss, the duty of the accountant is plain, and his task is simplicity itself. The loss—say that cited by Palmer—being excluded from Profit and Loss must appear elsewhere. If law requires or permits the reduction of nominal capital stock, and that is done, the loss is deducted immediately from the Capital account. Thus a company which at first shows:

Balance Sheet

Plant	$10,000	Capital Stock	$22,000
Miscellaneous Assets	15,000	Profit and Loss	3,000
	$25,000		$25,000

will after the unfortunate experience, have as its balance sheet:

Balance Sheet

Plant	$1,000	Capital Stock (reduced)	$13,000
Miscellaneous Assets	15,000	Profit and Loss	3,000
	$16,000		$16,000

If the legal steps necessary to reduce the nominal capital have not been taken, the showing should be:

Balance Sheet

Property	$ 1,000	Capital Stock	$22,000
Miscellaneous Assets	15,000	Profit and Loss	3,000
Loss on Capital Account	9,000		
	$25,000		$25,000

Some other descriptive term may be used in place of Loss on Capital Account, the only requirement being that it be not misleading. And greater explicitness can be introduced by indicating the shrinkages, perhaps as follows:

Balance Sheet

Property			Capital Outstanding	$22,000	
Original Cost	$10,000		Less Shrinkage, per contra	9,000	
Less Shrinkage	9,000				
		$ 1,000			
Miscellaneous Assets		15,000			$13,000
			Profit and Loss		3,000
		$16,000			$16,000

Deficits in the Balance Sheet

Even in the extreme case such as that set forth in Dovey *v.* Cory, the proper form of preparing the accounts is clear. It may be assumed that at the end of a year a corporation has the following balance sheet:

Balance Sheet

Miscellaneous Assets	$ 90,000	Capital Stock	$100,000
Deficit	10,000		
	$100,000		$100,000

During the following year the business is profitable and the books would accordingly show:

Balance Sheet

Miscellaneous Assets	$ 90,000	Capital Stock	$100,000
Deficit	10,000	Net Operating Profit	25,000
Cash, etc.	25,000		
	$125,000		$125,000

This implies that which the courts seem to have recognized, the possibility of there being a loss upon previous operations and profits arising from the operations of the current year. While the preceding deficit is not looked upon by the courts as being a loss of capital, it is obviously of that character for where there has been a net deficit, the shrinkage can fall only upon contributed capital. Therefore, in this case as well as in one where the loss was specifically a loss of capital assets, the previous deficit, if it is held not to encroach upon the amount available for dividends, should be shown in the balance sheet as a reduction of capital as follows:

Balance Sheet

Miscellaneous Assets	$ 90,000	Capital Stock	$100,000	
Cash	25,000	Less Previous Losses	10,000	
				$ 90,000
		Profits for the year		25,000
	$115,000			$115,000

The matter is simple—all that is needed is clearness and honesty—and the facts can be presented in various satisfactory forms. The undesirability of paying dividends while capital is diminished has nothing to do with the necessity of truthfully showing what has taken place. That such is seldom or never done is perhaps unfortunately true, but it does not depend altogether on the much criticized decisions of the courts.

Accounting Where Accuracy Is Impossible

The rule that a shrinkage of capital should be shown in the balance sheet is, perhaps, to be modified in cases where the loss is incapable of exact, or even approximate, estimation. Thus the cost of an oil well represents wasting capital which logically should be written off as the oil is exhausted. But the estimate of the oil supply is so much a matter of guesswork that it may be better to retain the known cost, without attempting any estimate of the depletion.

Were the amount of shrinkage accurately known, it should be shown. But where the accuracy of a valuation is specious, where the only ascertainable value is the original cost, it may be less harmful for the balance sheet to show the cost, indicating that it does not represent the present value. The interested persons can then make their own allowances for shrinkage of capital assets. Before the Federal income tax, depletion of wasting assets was rarely shown in American balance sheets. But at present it is the prevalent practice to make such allowance, as is done, for example, in the balance sheet of the Union Oil Company, printed in Form 8.

Profits and Depreciation

The relation between depreciation and the amount available for dividends has already been discussed in Chapter V. The principles of accounting have in the last twenty-five years gained such increased recognition that it is almost universally admitted that one cannot speak of profits in any sense until depreciation has been allowed, and if no profits, there of course can be no profits available for dividends. This has at last come to be recognized even by the courts, and the apparent exceptions, such as the payment of dividends by a corporation with wasting assets discussed above, implies rather an admission that in certain circumstances part of the capital may be returned to stockholders rather than that profits exist irrespective of the depreciation of wasting assets.

For bibliography see note to Chapter XII.

CHAPTER XII

PROFITS AVAILABLE FOR DIVIDENDS

Realized Appreciation of Capital Assets

In the preceding chapter there was discussed the problem as to whether dividends could be paid in spite of shrinkage of capital. A somewhat more interesting question is as to whether in all cases an increase in proprietorship is divisible as profits. In the preceding chapter the concept of a loss of capital as something distinct from the loss of revenue was introduced. The converse that capital or proprietorship may increase without affecting the showing of profit is to be considered here.

This has arisen in the first place in regard to an increase in the value of the so-called capital assets. Discussion has been somewhat confused by not clearly distinguishing between an appreciation which has been realized, and one which is estimated only. But where the gain is actually realized, it certainly may be credited to Profits, although if the gain be exceptional it would conservatively be placed to some Surplus or Reserve account. This doubtless is inconsistent with the doctrine of Lee *v.* Neuchatel Asphalte Company. Indeed one argument given by the court in favor of excluding the shrinkage in value of capital assets was that a contrary rule would imply that dividends might be paid out of the increase in value of capital, which was said to be "contrary to all practice and to principle."[1] But this very doctrine, in so far as it relates to a realized gain, was soon

[1] An interesting illustration is found in the accounts of the Pennsylvania Railroad Company which in 1906 showed profits from the sale of some of its securities which had been held as permanent investments. Of the $15,000,000 profit thus gained, $13,000,000 was canceled by charging against it the cost of constructing the New York tunnel and the balance was carried to Extraordinary Expenditure Fund.

fully admitted in Lubbock *v.* British Bank ([1892] 2 Ch. 198) which has since been followed in various decisions.

Spanish Prospecting Company Case

An interesting decision was rendered in 1911 in a case [2] where an officer of the company was entitled to salary only in case of there being sufficient profits arising from the business to provide for its payment. The operating profits were meager and insufficient to provide for the salary. The company, however, disposed of the bulk of its property for cash and securities of another company. The company was later wound up and the securities were sold at a figure which more than covered past deficits. A suit was brought to compel the payment of salaries out of this excess. The company contended that there had been no profits in operating the business, that up to the time of liquidation there had been no realized profits, and that the excess gained by the sale of the securities was not profits. The court, however, held that profits had arisen from the sale of the securities, and though at the time of the sale the value of the securities was not definitely known, and hence the amount of profits could not be shown, the proceeds when the securities were sold were rightly brought into the Profit and Loss account.

American Decisions

The same question has been decided in an American case,[3] where a company which had invested its capital in a leasehold and goodwill sold these at a considerable advance over cost. It was held that the realized appreciation was profit which could be divided. Somewhat similarly, it was held that, for taxing purposes, profit realized upon the sale of capital assets was to be considered income and not an increase of capital.[4]

Another important decision related to a railroad which

[2] *In re* Spanish Prospecting Co., [1911] 1 Ch. 92. See also Cross *v.* Imperial Gas Assoc., [1923] 2 Ch. 553.

[3] People *ex rel.* Mercantile Safe Deposit Co. *v.* Sohmer, 143 N. Y. S. 313 (1913).

[4] Merchants Loan and Trust Co. *v.* Smietanka, 255 U. S. 509 (1920).

sold at an advance various stocks which it had held. The claim was made that this was an accretion to capital and not profits. Despite the fact that the company was not authorized to deal in securities, and so the transaction could not be looked upon as an ordinary merchandising gain, the court held that the gain was clearly a profit and distributable as such.[5] However successfully the courts attempt to distinguish between capital and revenue, or even between a shrinkage of capital and a loss of revenue, there is now no effort to differentiate between a realized gain due to the appreciation of capital assets and other income.[6]

Unrealized Appreciation of Capital Assets

More delicate is the question of unrealized profits. In the discussion of the inventory in Chapter II, it was shown that mere fluctuations in value are disregarded and that generally a permanent appreciation in the value of fixed assets is similarly left out of account. Opinions and decisions on this latter point are, however, not uniform. An attempt is made to differentiate between the fixed or capital assets and merchandise in discussing the recognition of an appreciation in value. The accepted view has been that where fixed assets are concerned an appreciation in value should be altogether disregarded inasmuch as such appreciation cannot be realized so long as the business continues to be a going concern. Thus Finney states: "There is no principle of accounting more firmly established than the one which prohibits taking a profit by writing up a fixed asset which is not being sold";[7] and Couchman says that the mark-up of a patent "is not profit nor anything akin to profit and has no more real tangibility than the thinnest of thin air."[8] The argument of Couchman that it is futile to show an appre-

---

[5] Equitable Life Assurance Society *v.* Union Pacific R. R. Co., 106 N. E. 92 (N. Y. 1915). For other cases bearing on this subject, see Reiter, *Profits, Dividends and the Law,* pp. 206 *ff.*

[6] Some exceptions to this may be found in case of the final distribution of assets of liquidated concerns.

[7] *Journal of Accountancy,* XXXI, p. 389.

[8] *The Balance Sheet,* pp. 127 and 45.

ciation in the value of fixed assets because such increased value would not be usable in any form is unsound. The recognition of an actual increase in the value of real estate might have considerable use as a basis for securing additional credit. Sir Arthur Lowes Dickinson admits that at times it may be

> unfair to one business to maintain original cost values as compared with another whose assets have been created at widely varying costs . . . in fact there are well-known cases in which by far the larger part of the ultimate profits of a corporation over a long series of years has been due not to the results of its activities but to the large unearned increment on its capital assets. This condition must be recognized and is frequently met by means of careful appraisals of all properties, the resulting increase (or possibly decrease) being taken up as a special credit or debit to Profit and Loss account (or Surplus) and shown as entirely distinct from the operating results.[9]

And Leake holds that an increase in the value of government securities is a capital profit which may be treated as income whether or not the government securities are about to be sold at the end of the year.[10]

There has also been a series of decisions justifying the inclusion of an appreciation of the capital assets in estimating profits;[11] on the other hand, the Supreme Court of the United States says that it is a logical incongruity to mark up property acquired for permanent employment in business.[12]

Until recent years, the marking up of the value of fixed assets was almost unknown among reputable accountants, but in recent years there has been a tendency, because of the provisions regarding taxation, to show such appreciation

---

[9] *Accounting Practice and Procedure,* p. 81.

[10] Great Britain, Royal Commission on the Income Tax (1919-20), *Minutes of Evidence,* par. 3605.

[11] Meyer *v.* Nethersole, 75 N. Y. S. 987, 990 (1902); *in re* Spanish Prospecting Co., [1911] 1 Ch. 99. See also criticism of this decision, *Accountant,* XLIV, p. 367; Ammonia Soda Co. *v.* Chamberlain, [1918] 1 Ch. 266. See also criticism of this case, *Accountant,* LVII, pp. 81, 217, 417, 458.

[12] La Belle Iron Works *v.* U. S., 256 U. S. 393 (1921). See also So. Calif. Home Builders *v.* Young, 188 Pac. 586 (Cal. 1920); and U. S. *v.* Phellis, 257 U. S. 156 (1921).

in the balance sheet. Where this is done, however, the corresponding credit is not made to Profit and Loss but to a special reserve. If this appreciation is gradually realized, as by a sale of mineral deposits, the appropriate amount is debited to this reserve and carried to the general Surplus account. An example of a balance sheet showing such appreciation is that of the Union Oil Company, printed in Form 8.

Unrealized Appreciation of Circulating Assets

In the matter of unrealized appreciation of circulating assets, particularly of merchandise, there is a somewhat similar difference of opinion and there has been a somewhat similar change in practice. As stated in the discussion in Chapter II, it was, in this country, only quite recently considered very objectionable to show any unrealized appreciation in inventories. Even Sir Arthur Lowes Dickinson, who admits the possibility of showing an appreciation in fixed asset, expresses himself strongly against such a procedure in regard to merchandise, saying, "Sound commercial principles require that no credit be taken for profits until they are realized."[13] And Kester states, "no refinement of logic can obscure the obvious fact that goods are bought to be sold and that no profit arises until the sale takes place."[14] But as stated in the discussion in Chapter II there are some daring and rigidly logical accountants who declare that the function of the balance sheet is to show actual values and that this should be done even where the present value of merchandise exceeds its cost. Foremost among such accountants are Paton, Stevenson, and Montgomery. The latter is less thoroughgoing in support of this doctrine and has apparently been influenced by the startling changes in price level which have accompanied the Great War. But even those writers who approve marking up the value of unsold merchandise disapprove of making a corresponding credit in the current Profit and Loss account.

---

[13] *Op. cit.*, p. 94.
[14] *Accounting*, 1st ed., II, p. 227.

Booking of Appreciation

The bookings in case of a shrinkage in capital assets, whether due to the depletion of wasting assets or to some exceptional loss which is regarded as a loss of capital rather than of income, have already been discussed. The procedure to be followed in the case of increases in the value of capital assets where these are regarded as not entering into the ordinary Profit and Loss account, is similar. If, for instance, it is decided to exhibit an unquestioned increase in the value of real estate held, this would best be accomplished by a journal entry substantially as follows:

Increase in the Value of Real Estate	$100,000	
Surplus Arising from Marking up the Value of the Real Estate		$100,000

In the balance sheet the original cost of the real estate and the appreciation in its value should each be shown in an interior column with the sum of the two extended. In this way the exact status is clearly shown and it is difficult to see how any one could in any way be misled. In case the property is subject to depreciation, there would each year be a reduction in the book value of the real estate and at the same time transfer from the account, Surplus Arising from Marking up the Value of the Real Estate, to the general Income account. If appreciation of merchandise is taken into account at all, the counter entry should similarly be in a reserve account, the amount being transferred to Surplus only as the goods are sold.

Profits on Unfinished Contracts

There is some question as to whether dividends may be based upon estimated profits upon a partly finished contract. In general this is thought to be undesirable and indeed improper.[15] But where the contract is one covering a considerable period of time with partial payments made as the work progresses, as for instance in the case of building a ship, ac-

[15] Hutchinson *v.* Curtiss, 92 N. Y. S. 70 (1904); So. Calif. Home Builders *v.* Young, 188 Pac. 586 (Cal. 1920).

countants consider it proper to estimate the amount of profits included in the payments received, conservative allowances being made for contingencies which may arise before completion.

Limitations on Decisions of the Courts

The whole discussion of the form in which profits are received involves the frequently recurring confusion to which reference has been made, between assets and the credit side of the balance sheet. The assets cannot be distinguished as being this capital and that profit. All the assets together equal capital and profits. Hence as Mr. Ernest Cooper has pointed out, the question as to whether the profits are liquid or not cannot legitimately be raised.[16]

Furthermore, it is quite possible for a company to pay dividends even though it has no cash. Thus the Dutch East India Company regularly paid part of its dividends in spices. More modern instances are the dividends declared after the Great War by several companies and paid in Liberty bonds, then held in the treasury.

But it certainly would be unwise for a court to compel the payment of a dividend in the absence of liquid assets, and the decisions cited are based on this practical objection rather than on any recognized principle that profits exist only when in cash. In charity to the courts the decisions cited are to be interpreted not as meaning that only cash earnings are profits, but that the courts will not compel a company to pay a dividend when the absence of cash or its equivalent might compel a perhaps disadvantageous borrowing, or a loss due to a forced sale of some of the assets.

Dividends from Borrowed Funds

The limitation of profits to cash receipts is closely connected with the question of borrowing funds with which to pay dividends. If profits have really been earned, the replenishment of the cash account through borrowing removes

[16] *Accountant,* XIV, p. 746.

any objections which the accountant might have to the declaration of a dividend. But Lord Justice Lindley characterized the payment of dividends with borrowed money as being "as unjustifiable in point of law as it would be reckless and blameworthy in the eyes of business men."[17]

Here again the decisions are discordant. In some cases the payment of dividends with borrowed funds has been condemned,[18] but the lucid decision in Williams *v.* Western Union Telegraph Company (93 N. Y. 162 [1883]) held that where the surplus had been invested in the plant, the company "could borrow money on the faith of it and divide that (p. 192)."

The same doctrine was clearly brought out in Excelsior Water and Mining Company *v.* Pierce (27 Pac. 44 [Cal. 1891]) [19] where improvements were paid for out of profits, and the company later borrowed funds which it used to pay dividends.

The court said:

> The result is precisely the same as if the money had been borrowed sooner and the identical money borrowed paid out on the tunnel. Nothing has been accomplished beyond what the directors had a right to do, and surely the mode in which it has been done can make no difference. In fact, the transaction may be regarded as a temporary borrowing from the dividend fund of the sum necessary to meet an immediate demand, with the advantage to the corporation of keeping its money employed and saving it the payment of interest.

Dividends from Premiums

A question which as yet has received no authoritative answer is whether premium received on capital stock constitutes a fund which may be used for the payment of dividends. In England, by the dictum of Lord Romer in Hoare and Company ([1904] 2 Ch. 213), premium received on the issue of shares may be legally applied to the payment of dividends. This has been generally accepted by accountants as expressing

---

[17] Verner *v.* General and Commercial Trust, [1894] 2 Ch. 266.

[18] Davis *v.* Flagstaff Silver Mining Co., 2 Utah 74; Belfast etc. Co. *v.* Belfast, 1 Atl. 362 (Me. 1885).

[19] See also Mills *v.* Northern Ry., etc., (L. R. 5 Ch. App. 621 [1870].

the present legal status, although English accountants generally do not consider such a treatment advisable.

The exact legal status in the United States is somewhat indefinite. There is in general legal objection to paying dividends out of capital stock. Unfortunately the term capital stock, as many other accounting terms, is used with diverse meanings. Its meaning when used in statutes and court decisions frequently refers to the assets contributed by the stockholders. In this it approximates the original use of the term in economic writings. Stock or capital stock or capital, as used by early economists, referred to the actual assets used by the owner in carrying on his business. Its meaning is similar to that still in use when one speaks of stock of merchandise.

Premium on Stock: Statutory Provisions

Statutory regulations prohibiting the disbursement of capital stock therefore frequently refer to the items which appear upon the left-hand side of the balance sheet, rather than to capital stock as used by the accountant. Thus in California, capital stock has been legally defined as including "the entire proceeds of sales by a corporation of its own stock, even when sold for more than par value."[20] Where such a definition of capital is accepted, obviously premium is not a part of profits available for dividends. Furthermore in a number of states dividends are limited by statute to "profits arising from the business." Premium hardly seems to come under this category, yet even here the decisions are not altogether in accord. The courts of New York and of California show an apparent difference in interpreting a similar restriction. In the California case, just cited, the payment of dividends out of premium on stock is held to be altogether illegal, but in New York in a case not altogether so conclusive[21] premium received on an issue of additional

---

[20] Merchants and Insurers Reporting Co. *v.* Youtz, 178 Pac. 540 (Cal. 1918).

[21] Equitable Life Assurance Society *v.* Union Pacific R. R. Co., 106 N. E. 92 (N. Y. 1915).

stock was held to be "part of such accumulation of profits and surplus and distributable as such." Other decisions bearing upon the subject consist largely of *obiter dicta* or are otherwise inconclusive.

For the purposes of the Federal income tax, premium on stock issued is not income nor can a corporation realize gain or loss from the purchase or sale of its own stock.[22] But this is of course a ruling relating to the limited sphere of income-tax procedure and need not be considered at all authoritative in ordinary commercial accounting. Premium received upon stock of railroads is, according to the rules of the Interstate Commerce Commission, not to be credited to income, although provision is made in the rules for the booking "in case the accounting company is permitted and elects to distribute all or any part of the net premium on its capital stock to its stockholders." In one case, however, premium upon additional issues of stock may be credited to income. This is where stock is issued by a company paying regular dividends at some time other than the date of dividend payments, as for instance where a corporation paying dividends January 1 and July 1 issued stock on April 1. In so far as the premium paid for the new stock issued April 1 is considered to represent the amount of regular dividends accrued between January 1 and April 1, it is credited to income and used as a basis for the regular dividend paid July 1. This seems equitable as the stockholder whose interest began April 1 properly participates only in the earnings after that date. If on July 1 he is paid the regular dividends, he will be receiving more than he is entitled to unless so much of the dividend as was earned before he became a stockholder is offset by the premium paid when he acquired the stock. The principle here involved should properly apply also to any premium paid by new stockholders which offsets previously accumulated surplus.

[22] Regulations 65, art. 543. Montgomery considers that any gain arising from the purchase and sale of stock of the company in the open market should appear in the Income account but that gain from the sale of donated stock is not income but an addition to capital. *Auditing, Theory and Practice*, 3d ed., I, p. 292.

The surplus of a corporation is in ordinary cases clearly available for dividends. If the new stockholder pays a premium on each share of stock equal to the surplus attributable to the share of old stock, it would seem entirely proper that such premium should be considered available for distribution. While this view has not been clearly recognized in statutes or regulations, it is implied, although somewhat inaccurately expressed, in a Wisconsin case.[23] In this case a bank had stock with a book value of $153.50 per share. So much of the premium paid on the new stock as was necessary to equalize the surplus already accumulated was held to be of the same nature as that surplus and hence, although the court did not distinctly say so, would be available for dividends. The effect of this decision is however confused by the fact that it held that the excess premium, that is the difference between the book value of the old stock and the price paid for the new, was profit available for distribution.[24]

Dividends from Premium Opposed by Accountants

The whole matter of the relation between premium on stock and dividends is in an unsettled and unsatisfactory state. Almost all accountants are opposed to regarding premium as so available, but many of them admit that in ordinary cases a dividend may legally be declared out of premium. Unquestionably the accountant should object to including premium in any account which would seem to indicate that it was a part of the annual profits. It should in any case be looked upon as something which is not a part of profits, but this does not imply that even from the accountant's viewpoint a return to the stockholders of premium is improper in the absence of statutory or contractual prohibition. Criticism may therefore properly be made of the statement of Montgomery when he says, "There is just as much

---

[23] Miller *v.* Payne, 136 N. W. 812 (Wis. 1912).

[24] Other cases discussing the availability of premium on stock for dividends are Smith *v.* Cotting, 120 N. E. 177 (Mass. 1918); Boston and Maine R. R. Co. *v.* U. S., 265 Fed. 578 (1920); Hyams *v.* Old Dominion Copper Co., 89 Atl. 37 (N. J. 1913). These discussions are of interest although the dicta may not be authoritative.

moral turpitude in paying a dividend out of so-called capital surplus as out of capital, because in every way, except the bare legal distinction, they are the same and should be equally safeguarded."[25] But the legal distinction is the essential matter. Creditors make loans to a corporation presumably upon the basis that they are protected by a definite amount of contributed capital. It is of course unjust if this guaranteed fund upon which the creditors rely is reduced without their consent, but it is a matter of fact and not of morals as to whether the amount upon which they may rely is the entire sum originally contributed by the stockholders or a sum expressed by the par value of the capital stock. There is nothing inherently wrong or inconsistent in an arrangement whereby stockholders subscribing for $100,000 capital stock at $200 do so with the understanding that $100,000 must be left permanently with the company as a guarantee to creditors, but that the additional $100,000 may, if circumstances make it desirable, be withdrawn by the stockholders. Creditors would have no just complaint and the procedure might be a thoroughly desirable one.

Summary by Prosper Reiter

The situation has been admirably summarized by Prosper Reiter, as follows: (1) Premium paid in on the original issue of a company of capital stock constitutes paid-in surplus. Distribution of this premium would be permissible in the absence of special restrictions. (2) If a company with but one class of stock issues additional stock at a premium corresponding to the book value of the old stock, premium thus paid should be credited to paid-in surplus, and such surplus may properly be distributed as dividends. (3) If the additional stock is issued at a premium higher than the book value of the old stock "the additional premium would seem to have the earmarks of paid-in surplus, but it has been specifically held by a court of law that it is distributable as profits." (4) Since premium on capital

[25] *Auditing, Theory and Practice,* I, p. 276.

stock cannot be classed as a profit "arising from the business" it could not be paid as a dividend in states with this limitation. (5) The question of dividends from premium may be affected, where there are two classes of stock, so as to maintain the relative rights of preferred and common stockholders.[26]

Dividends from Donated Surplus

It seems to be legally permissible to distribute among the stockholders a donated surplus. In sanctioning such a distribution the courts have at times attempted a difficult differentiation, holding that the dividing of such a surplus among the stockholders is not a dividend in the technical sense.[27]

Dividends from Premium on Bonds

Premium received on bonds differs in its nature from premium on stock. Logically, it is part of the money borrowed and so partakes of the nature of a liability rather than of surplus.[28] The proper treatment of premium on bonds is discussed above in Chapter IX.

Premium is properly speaking not profit of any period, although in ordinary bookkeeping technic it often is amortized in such a way as to act as an offset to excessive charges made against income through interest. It is, however, not uncommon to find the premium credited to the general surplus account, and if the amount received is small it would be hypercritical to demand that it be minutely divided through a long series of years. According to Pixley, the payment of dividends out of premiums on debentures is not

---

[26] *Profits, Dividends and the Law,* p. 232. The above summary is a condensation of that given by Reiter. Those interested in a further study of this difficult subject should read all of Chapter XIX of this work.

[27] People *ex rel.* North American Trust Co. *v.* Knight, 89 N. Y. S. 72 (1904). A similar interpretation that a distribution paid out of premium on stock is not a "dividend" is found in People *ex rel.* Queens Co. Water Co. *v.* Travis, 157 N. Y. S. 943, 945 (1916).

[28] Paton, *Accounting Theory,* p. 234; and *contra,* Bentley, *Journal of Accountancy,* XIV, p. 171; and Pixley, *Accountancy,* p. 225.

prohibited by English law, but such a procedure is more than questionable from the viewpoint of accounting. If such a policy is adopted, it would be consistent to pay as dividends the entire amount of money borrowed provided the debtor repaid the debt in annual installments charging each installment as an expense of the year when paid. This would be showing a surplus in the first year when nothing was gained, offsetting it by charging to each subsequent year an expense never really suffered.

Dividends from Surplus from Forfeited Stock

As shown in the discussion in Chapter VII the forfeiture of capital stock creates a surplus in so far as the net assets exceed the reduced amount of outstanding capital stock. But such action in no way creates a surplus above the amount contributed by the stockholders, and contributed distinctly as capital rather than as premium. An early American case [29] held that such a surplus was not profit. But in Strong *v.* Brooklyn Cross Town Railroad Company (93 N. Y. 426 [1883]) it was held that if, after the reduction of capital stock, the assets exceeded the reduced capital and liabilities, such excess was distributable.[30] If the forfeited stock is resold, any excess above the par value received through the payments by the original subscriber and his successor is of the nature of premium and would be subject to the rules relating to the payment of dividends from premium.

Dividends and Unpaid Debts

A curious doctrine has sometimes been announced by the courts to the effect that "all the debts (other than funded debt . . .) are debts to be paid before the profits can be ascertained." [31] This theory has been expressed even in the Supreme Court of the United States which quoted with ap-

[29] Gratz *v.* Redd, 43 Ken. 178 (1843).

[30] Montgomery suggests that while a surplus thus created might legally be distributed, it could not be considered a dividend, but a return of capital. *Auditing, Theory and Practice,* 3d ed., I, p. 295.

[31] Corry *v.* Londonderry & Enniskillen Ry. Co., 29 Beaven 263 (1860).

parent approval the above decision and also an American decision which defined profits as "what remain after defraying every expense, including loans falling due as well as the interest on such loans."[32] Taken literally, the notion that debts must be paid before profits are ascertained is of course absurd. The decisions probably need to be interpreted as meaning that a dividend would be unwise in circumstances in which a payment of a dividend would so encroach upon the available cash of a company as to make it impossible to meet an impending debt. In such circumstances, the court might properly refuse to sanction the payment of the dividend and to such a decision no objection can be made. It is only to be regretted that in taking a commendably conservative position, it should be done at the cost of confused terminology and questionable theorems. Recent decisions clearly state that debts do not need to be paid before declaring a dividend.[33]

The accountant cannot disregard the decisions of the courts, or he may find that he has led his clients into an action for which they may be held liable. But it is evident that many of the decisions to which reference has been made are, at least on the face, opposed to what the accountant considers fundamental principles of his profession. Some of these contradictions can be smoothed over by recognizing that the courts and the accountants are attaching quite different meaning to the technical terms of commerce. Difficulty may be avoided by the accountant's continuing to lean, as in the past he has generally done, toward conservatism, for while the courts, as in the question of loss of capital, sometimes permit, they never compel an excessive estimate of profits. But for a more perfect rationalization of the legal dicta concerning profits, it will probably be necessary to await the day when the growing dignity of the profession of accounting shall cause its principles to permeate the ranks of bench and bar.

---

[32] Mobile etc. R. R. *v.* Tenn, 153 U. S. 486 (1894).
[33] See O'Shields *v.* Union Iron Foundry, 76 S. E. 1098 (S. C. 1912).

Bibliographical Note

Bastide, J.—*Des dividends fictifs* (Toulouse, 1903).

Buckley, H. B. (Lord Wrenbury)—*The Law and Practice under the Companies Acts* (10th ed., London, 1924).

Charpentier, J.—*Étude juridique sur le bilan dans les sociétés par actions* (Paris, 1906).

Cole, W. M.—*The Fundamentals of Accounting* (Boston, 1921), chap. xvii.

Dickinson, A. L.—*The Profits of a Corporation* (New York, 1904). A brief but comprehensive and most valuable treatise.

Dicksee, L. R.—*Auditing* (13th ed., London, 1924), chap. viii.

Kester, R. B.—*Accounting, Theory and Practice* (2d ed., New York, 1925), II, chaps. xxiv, xxv.

Palmer, F. B.—*Company Law* (11th ed., London, 1921). Contains an extended review and a criticism of the English decisions in the Lee series.

Paton, W. A.—*Accounting* (New York, 1924), chaps. xxv-xxvii.

Pixley, F. W.—*Auditors, Their Duties and Responsibilities* (11th ed., London, 1918), chap. xiv.

Reiter, J., Jr.—*Profits, Dividends and the Law* (New York, 1926). The most important work on the subject giving both the legal and the accounting aspects.

Saunders, A. F.—"The Ascertainment of Profits," *Accountant,* L, p. 413.

CHAPTER XIII

SURPLUS AND RESERVES

Capital Adjustments in Corporation Accounts

In the accounts of individual traders the Profit and Loss account is, at stated intervals, closed out, and the balance is carried to the credit of the proprietor's Capital account. Profit and Loss is thus in practice, as well as in theory, a mere temporary subdivision of the main proprietorship account, and at the close of the year is indistinguishably merged with the latter. In corporation accounting it is necessary to keep the accretions of wealth separate from the original capital contributions. Nevertheless there is customarily a closing of the books, and an apportionment of the annual profits of corporations similar to that which takes place in the books of the individual or of the partnership. At such a time a part of the profits is normally voted as dividends and immediately passes out of the control of the corporation. But it is unusual to distribute all of the profits earned, and there is ordinarily further action by the directors or stockholders deciding to retain part of the profits. The accounts of corporations therefore differ from those of the individual trader or partnership in two respects:

1. The initial proprietorship is not always shown in the capital account but may comprise, as explained above in Chapter VII, a nominal figure expressed in that account and an addition shown in an account called Premium or Surplus or a subtraction shown as Discount on Capital Stock.
2. Accretions to proprietorship in corporations are not added to the nominal capital but are kept distinct.

Surplus: General Definition

The excess of net assets over the capital stock of a company is in a general and somewhat nontechnical way called surplus, but even in this most general use one exception is to be noted. If the capital stock was originally issued at a discount, surplus is the excess of net assets over the amount originally contributed by the stockholders rather than over the par value of the capital stock.[1] Consistency would demand that in case the stock is originally issued at a premium a surplus exists only when the net assets exceed the sum of the par value and the premium paid thereon. But accountants generally have not attempted to preserve this consistency. The premium paid by the stockholders is not considered part of the base from which the surplus is measured but as in itself constituting part of the surplus.

Surplus is, however, used in several more restricted, technical senses among which are the following:

Surplus: Restricted Meaning

1. Surplus is sometimes used in the balance sheet not as the name of a specific account but as a subtitle including some, but not all, of the items indicating an excess of net assets above the capital stock. This is well illustrated in the balance sheet prescribed by the Interstate Commerce Commission printed as Form 13. This grouping excludes premium on capital stock which is more generally considered a part of the surplus.

2. Surplus is often used as the title of a specific account as, for instance, in the balance sheets of national banks. In this case it is used in contradistinction to sinking fund reserves and other specific reserves. It does, however, include the profit and loss balance, and may or may not include appropriated surplus.

3. Surplus is often used with a modifying word or phrase as, for instance, in accounts entitled, Donated Surplus, Capital Surplus, Surplus from Forfeited Stock, and Appropriated Surplus. These descriptive titles generally carry with them the implication that such portions of the surplus are not to be distributed as regular dividends.

---

[1] Goodnow *v.* American Writing Paper Co., 73 N. J. Eq. 692 (1908).

4. Surplus, when not modified, is by some writers defined as the amount available for dividends,[2] although those who attach to the term this definition do not at all times rigidly adhere to it. As thus used it often implies profits earned by the company and, somewhat even more strictly, profits earned through the ordinary course of the business. When used in this last sense it would exclude sums received as premium and at times such unusual gains as may have arisen through the sale of capital assets. Perhaps this is due to the idea that such unusual gains, even though legally distributable, should not be paid out as dividends, and so are to be excluded from the Surplus account.

Reserves

The word reserve is frequently used to designate parts of the corporate surplus in its most general significance. Thus, we find such accounts as Sinking Fund Reserve and Reserve for Extension. These represent parts of a real surplus which have been appropriated for a specific purpose; they indicate that while a surplus exists it is not to be used for dividends but is reserved for the purpose specified. Such reserves properly fall within the grouping of the Interstate Commerce Commission known as Appropriated Surplus.

Asset Reserves

In the above nomenclature, reserve seems to be appropriately used. Its name signifies that something has been held back and, properly speaking, this should relate to profits or other sources of income which, though available for distribution as dividends, have been retained by the company. Most unfortunately reserve is, however, frequently used in an entirely different sense. Some writers have classified reserves as asset reserves, liability reserves, and proprietorship reserves.[3] In the sense used above the reserve is a proprietorship reserve and it would be well if the term could

---

[2] Montgomery, *Auditing, Theory and Practice,* 3d ed., I, p. 309; Gilman, *Principles of Accounting,* p. 301.

[3] *E.g.,* Couchman, *The Balance Sheet,* pp. 209 *ff.*

be limited to that class. Those who use the classification of asset reserves, use it in the sense of a valuation or offset account such as a Reserve for Depreciation. It does not, despite the phraseology so frequently found in accounting texts, indicate that part of the assets have been set aside, but, as has been fully explained in the chapter on depreciation, merely that the nominal value of the asset as shown, for instance, by the debit balance in the Machinery account, is not actually in existence. Instead of representing something held in reserve it represents something which is nonexistent. Less obviously the Reserve or Allowance for Doubtful Accounts represents that in the best judgment of the accountant part of the value expressed by the face of the receivables is not real. The difference between an account which represents the withholding of profits from dividends and one which represents a subtraction to be made from assets is so clear that it seems eminently desirable not to use the same term for both categories.

Liability Reserves

The phrase liability reserve is also misleading. This is very frequently found in such titles as Reserve for Wages or Reserve for Taxes. If these titles stand for anything, they indicate a liability for the sums named. There is no more reason for calling the estimated liability for accrued wages a reserve than there is for using the phrase Reserve for Wages to indicate the amount of accrued wages. The calculated obligation for accrued wages and other similar items should appear among current liabilities under the simple title Wages Accrued. The phrase, Reserve for Taxes, has been justified by some who would object to using the phrase, Reserve for Wages. The argument is that while the amount of wages accrued is definitely ascertainable, the amount to be paid as taxes can be only roughly estimated, but as stated in Chapter IX it is after all an estimate of a debt due to the government. One should make the best possible effort to secure as accurate an estimate as possible, but unavoidable inaccuracy in making the estimate does not change the character of a liability. One may wrongly estimate the value of a piece of real estate, but an error in that estimate does not change the real estate into merchandise on hand or into accounts payable.

Various Uses of Term Reserve Illustrated

The varying uses of terms applying to surplus and the difficulties which arise in the interpretation of so-called reserves may be illustrated by taking the case of a company whose books at the end of a year make the following showing:

Trial Balance

Plant at cost	$50,000	Capital	$50,000
Accounts Receivable	50,000	Bonds	50,000
Expenses	50,000	Trading Profits	85,000
Miscellaneous Assets	35,000		
	$185,000		$185,000

This shows an apparent gain of $35,000, but no allowance has as yet been made for depreciation, nor have taxes accruing during the year been entered on the books. Assuming the depreciation to be $5,000, and the accrued taxes to be $300, the revised balance sheet may show:

Balance Sheet

Plant at cost	$50,000	Bonds	$50,000
Accounts Receivable	50,000	Capital	50,000
Miscellaneous Assets	35,000	Reserve for Depreciation	5,000
		Reserve for Taxes	300
		Profits	29,700
	$135,000		$135,000

NOTE: The Reserve for Depreciation account is purposely left on the credit side instead of being subtracted from the valuation of the plant in order to emphasize the distinction made below.

The directors or stockholders decide that the business is so profitable that it will be desirable to extend the plant within a few years, and in preparation therefor vote to withhold $5,000 of the profits as the beginning of a fund with which to make the expected extensions; and in order to be on the safe side they vote to reserve $1,000 to cover any possible future loss which may occur when attempt is made to realize on the accounts receivable. They also, in accordance with the terms of the bonds, establish a sinking fund of $5,000 out of the profit and place that sum in the hands of sinking fund trustees and vote a dividend of $8,000. The balance sheet then reads as follows:

Balance Sheet

Plant at cost	$50,000	(1) Capital	$50,000
Accounts Receivable	50,000	(2) Bonds	50,000
Miscellaneous Assets	30,000	(3) Reserve for Depreciation	5,000
Cash in Hands of Sinking Fund Trustees	5,000	(4) Reserve for Taxes	300
		(5) Reserve for Extensions	5,000
		(6) Reserve for Doubtful Accounts	1,000
		(7) Sinking Fund Reserve	5,000
		(8) Dividends Declared	8,000
		(9) Surplus	10,700
	$135,000		$135,000

Reserve for Depreciation and Reserve for Extensions

In examining a balance sheet, such as is shown above, it is most important clearly to distinguish between items of which Reserve for Depreciation (3) is the type and those of which Reserve for Extensions (5) is the type. The real distinction between them is radical and the use of the term reserve to apply to both, while not uncommon in American accounting practice and even approved by recognized authorities is still to be deplored.[4] The Reserve for Extensions (5) is, on the contrary, a part of the profits. It represents an addition to the original net worth shown in the Capital account. It shows that assets have increased.[5] In order to make

[4] See "Report of Committee on Terminology, A. I. A.," *Journal of Accountancy*, XXXIV, p. 312. In some systems of accounts the allowance for depreciation is combined in a single account with an appropriation of profits sufficient to provide for replacement at a higher price. For discussion see above, p. 145.

[5] "Surplus net profits is not changed by calling it 'Reserve.' . . . Whatever they do about it, so long as it is not actually paid out,

this distinction clearer, the use of the phrase Allowance for Depreciation, instead of Reserve for Depreciation, found in the balance sheet of the United States Steel Corporation is to be commended.

Reserve for Doubtful Accounts

The Reserve for Taxes (4) as explained above, represents a liability and there is no propriety in applying the term reserve to any liability. Item (6), Reserve for Doubtful Accounts, is perhaps even more difficult to classify. There has been no wear and tear. No one of the accounts is known to be bad; no single one of them is even suspected. Each is carried on the books at its full value, and perhaps no one of them would be sold at a discount of 2 per cent. Yet ordinary common sense and business experience show that a loss is likely to occur, and a Reserve is provided so that if a loss should take place it need not be charged against the current profits. From the outside it is impossible to say whether this is nearer akin to depreciation or to a reservation of profits. If under the law of probabilities the loss is practically certain to take place, it is logically a deduction for an unrealized but existing loss. If the creation of the reserve was based on a minimum of certainty and a maximum of prudence it represents a reservation of profits. In many recent balance sheets, for instance that of the International Harvester Company, the title Allowance for Doubtful Accounts is used in place of Reserve for Doubtful Accounts. This is to be commended as it makes clearer the fact that this item is not like Reserve for Extensions, a part of the surplus. Item 8 has ceased to be a part of the surplus and has become a current liability due to the stockholders.

Sinking Fund Reserve and Surplus

Sinking Fund Reserve (7) is part of the surplus where that term is used in the broader sense. It differs only from

---

it must remain in fact 'Surplus Net Profits.' Mere bookkeeping entries cannot affect it.'' Bassett *v.* U. S. Cast Iron Pipe & Foundry Co., 70 Atl. 929, 932 (N.J. 1908).

item 5 in that instead of devoting the accumulated profits to further extension of the plant they are to be used in the payment of debt. As the payment of debt is not in any sense a reduction of proprietorship, an appropriation to provide for such payment in the future cannot lessen the real surplus of the company. Surplus (9) is here used in the restricted sense and indicates accumulated profits which not only are legally available for dividends but have not been specifically appropriated by the directors to other purposes.

Surplus Classified as to Source

Confusion is also caused by the different systems of classifying portions of the surplus. According to one they are given descriptive titles which relate to the purpose of their establishment, according to the other they are labeled in accordance with the source whence they were derived. Thus the Sinking Fund Reserve and Reserve for Extensions relate to the purpose while Donated Surplus and Capital Surplus refer to the source. The fact that surplus was derived from donated stock does not at all indicate whether it is to be used for extension of plant, for payment of debt, or for other specific purposes. There is perhaps an implication when a source, other than ordinary profits, is specified in the title of reserve that it is not intended, and perhaps not even considered proper, that that portion of the surplus should be distributed as ordinary dividends. On the other hand, one cannot by examination of the balance sheet determine which of the various reserves really represent ordinary profits if some of them are designated in accordance to the purpose to which they are devoted. In the form provided by the Interstate Commerce Commission, there is found included in the group, corporate surplus, an account entitled Additions to Property through Income and Surplus. The caption is not a happy one, as an addition to property is an asset item. While a surplus account may properly represent that surplus has been devoted to making additions, it does not conform with the ordinary rules of accounting thus to confuse asset and proprietorship items. But aside from objections to the title, attention is called to the fact that this account by definition includes "income and surplus definitely appropriated . . . and expended . . . in the acquisition of property" and also "the amount of donations in aid of construction . . . and not subject to distribution as dividends."[6] Part of the account, therefore, represents actual earnings and these despite their appropriation and investment might legally be made a basis of dividends. The mere fact that they are represented by fixed assets rather than by cash is immaterial. It would presumably be possible for the railroad to borrow a sum representing the amount of such appropriation and from the cash thus derived to pay a dividend. This would be legal as representing a distribution of earned profits.[7] On the other hand, there is a strong presumption that so much of this surplus as is represented by donations is not subject to distribution as dividends.

1. Surplus from Profits

Surplus, using the term in its most general sense, as representing the excess of proprietorship over the capital stock (or in some cases over the amount originally contributed by the stockholders), may arise in three different ways: by accumulation, by contribution, and by cancelation of capital stock. The normal source of surplus is, of course, by the accumulation of ordinary profits derived from the business of the enterprise. In so far as profits are earned and as a matter of fact are not all distributed to the stockholders, there is by that very act an accumulation of a surplus. It is not necessary here to discuss the extent to which it is desirable for a corporation to limit its dividends to a part of the profits earned and thus to build up an increasing surplus. It suffices to say that in all conservatively managed corporations, this is the normal procedure. Because of the fact that surplus is thus normally derived from business profits, there has often been an implication that where the term surplus appeared in the balance sheet it indicates that

---

[6] Account No. 779.
[7] See p. 286 above.

profits had been earned and retained in business. It is because of this implication that some of the authors have sought to exclude from the Surplus account accretions of wealth otherwise acquired. While the accumulation is ordinarily derived from the profits of business, it may also arise through unusual gains. But the line between business profits and unusual gains is difficult to draw. The gain from the sale of capital assets and perhaps that from speculation not directly connected with the main business of the enterprise would be considered unusual gains. The accumulation of surplus may also come through a recognition of the appreciation of capital assets even where there has been no sale. If this is shown at all, accountants generally agree that it should not appear among the current profits but must be put in some surplus account, perhaps with a distinctive title indicating its peculiar source.

2. Contributed Surplus

Surplus may be accumulated by contribution. This occurs most frequently through the payment of a premium on capital stock. This is particularly common in the case of national banks, many of which start with an initial surplus in part due to the fact that the statutes require that only part of the annual profits may be distributed as dividends until the bank has accumulated a surplus of 20 per cent of its capital stock. While uncommon in other corporations, the issue of stock at a premium and the consequent establishment of an initial surplus is occasionally found in this country and has been a rather common practice in some of the continental countries. A less common method of contributing surplus is by donations which generally are in the form of donated stock discussed above in Chapter VIII. Finally, a surplus may be contributed through assessments levied upon the stockholders.

3. Surplus from Cancelation of Stock

The establishment of a surplus by a cancelation of capital stock sometimes occurs particularly where a corporation has had some unsuccessful experiences and possibly a deficit appears upon its balance sheet. If permission can be obtained to reduce the capital stock by an amount exceeding the deficit the latter will be wiped out and at the same time a surplus created.

Purpose of the Surplus

Surplus, using the term in its broadest sense, may be established for any of the following purposes:

1. To provide a permanent increase of capital:
   (*a*) As an additional guaranty to creditors.
   (*b*) To provide for extension of its fixed or other capital assets.

2. To provide a means for covering unusual losses or to provide for other emergencies without encroaching on the nominal capital.

3. To provide for equalizing dividends by retaining part of one year's profit to be used to make up for scanty profits of other years.

1. Surplus to Increase Capital

The best example of surplus established to provide additional security to creditors is found in the compulsory surplus required by the National Bank Act referred to above.[8] Somewhat similarly but more comprehensively the laws of Germany and France[9] require all corporations, not alone banks, to establish a compulsory surplus by reserving a percentage of the annual profits and in addition certain specified receipts, as for example premium on stock. In both of these cases the purpose of the law presumably is to furnish additional security to the creditors of the corporations concerned. Another example is the establishment of a so-called sinking fund reserve to provide for the payment of bonds as discussed in the following chapter. This, according to current practice in the United States, is ordinarily an accumulation of profits

---

[8] Pullen *v.* Corporation Commissioner, 68 S.E. 155 (N.C. 1910).
[9] *D. H. G. B.*, sec. 262; *Code de Commerce*, Law 24th July, 1867, art. 36.

to act as additional protection to creditors. The accumulation of surplus for the purpose of extending the business is of more frequent occurrence; indeed, it may be said that the normal provision for expansion of business is by retaining part of the profits earned in the business. The practice is of early origin. The Bank of Saint Ambrose established in Milan in 1593 made a practice of distributing only one half of its profits and thus accumulated a large surplus. A striking instance was that of the Chemical National Bank of New York which at one time with $300,000 capital stock showed a surplus of $6,000,000. An instance which caused considerable discussion was the Wells Fargo Express Company which had $8,000,000 capital and over $16,000,000 surplus. The latter became a bone of contention, some of the stockholders thinking that it was unnecessary and should be distributed. In foreign countries the accumulation of surplus is an even more generally accepted practice than in the United States.

In some cases the profits are retained for the purpose of providing some definite, specific expansion. In such cases it is ordinarily indicated by some title such as that used by the United States Steel Corporation which at one time carried upon its books an item of $25,000,000 which represented profits retained for the specific purpose of constructing a plant at Gary, Indiana. While this bore the specific title "Construction Fund for Account Gary, Indiana, Plant," it was of course one of the items going to make up the surplus of the company.

2. Surplus to Cover Losses

The second purpose for which a surplus is established is not to provide for an extension of the enterprise but to prevent its curtailment should it meet with unusual or perhaps partially anticipated losses. At times portions of the surplus are specifically labeled to indicate the sort of calamity against which it provides. In such cases it is likely to be called a reserve, as for instance, the reserve created by a steamship company to replace vessels, should any be lost at sea. Another corporation in 1903 suffered loss to its property by the hurricane in Jamaica, a loss surely not distinctly anticipated, yet one which was most conveniently covered by a previous surplus.

Such provision against unforeseen emergencies may perhaps be construed as one form of a protection for creditors, and the legal reserves mentioned above are, as a matter of fact, sometimes used to cover exceptional losses. But this provision inures as well to the benefit of stockholders, and in many cases the establishment of a Reserve for Contingencies is inspired by regard for the stockholder rather than for the creditor—if indeed the two interests can be separated. Among such emergency reserves may be mentioned a Reserve for Personal Injuries of a coal mining company; a Reserve for Accidents not unreasonably provided by a manufacturer of powder; and an Accident Fund of a street railway company.

In some of these cases it may be difficult to say whether the item labeled reserve and established to provide against some unfavorable contingency, logically represents a part of surplus or whether it represents a loss implicit in the business but which has not yet been made manifest. If experience shows, for instance, that a certain number of vessels are lost each year at sea or that a hurricane recurs at fairly regular intervals it is entirely proper to say that the apparent profits up to a given date are not actual, for there should be charged against the earnings of these earlier years, a share of the loss which is bound to occur in the future. If the enterprise were to cease business on the date of the balance sheet, such a deduction would not need to be made, and the reserve against hurricanes would really represent a part of the accumulated surplus; but accounts are not kept to show what would be the status were the enterprise to cease business, but rather on the basis of the going concern. There is always a difficulty in deciding whether such a reserve should be considered as representing profits actually gained which merely as an evidence of extreme conservatism are reserved from distribution to the stockholders or whether at best they represent the share of a future anticipated loss which should properly be charged against present earnings.

3. Surplus to Equalize Dividends

The third purpose for which a surplus is accumulated is to equalize dividends. The individual shareholder is probably benefited by receiving a fairly constant dividend from year to year. Thus, if a corporation over a series of years has profits alternating regularly 9 per cent in one year and 3 per cent in the next, it would be better for the private investor to have 6 per cent paid regularly rather than to have a regular alternation of dividends corresponding to the fluctuation in profits. If the stockholder receives in the first year a dividend of 9 per cent he not only is likely to expect to receive 9 per cent in the second year but to adjust his scale of living to a 9 per cent basis. The drop to 3 per cent in the following year is a real hardship. He would be much better off to have the dividends maintained at the regular rate of 6 per cent. Most corporations attempt to maintain a somewhat regular dividend rate although, of course, this cannot always be realized. Thus, the United States Steel Corporation maintained its dividends at 5 per cent upon common stock in 1921 and 1922, although the earnings of those years, available for such dividends, were less than 3 per cent. Many other corporations in those trying years paid dividends altogether or in part out of the surplus of preceding years.

For bibliography see note to Chapter XIV.

CHAPTER XIV

SURPLUS: ITS APPROPRIATION, INVESTMENT, AND DISTRIBUTION

Creation of Reserves

Assuming that the corporation has undistributed profits amounting to a million dollars, it is within the discretion of the directors either to distribute them as dividends or to devote them to some other purpose. No action is necessary to withhold them from dividends. Dividends cannot be paid without action of the directors and a mere failure to vote a dividend is *ipso facto* a withholding of the profits from distribution and the establishment of a reserve. It is, however, entirely proper for the directors to take more definite action and, as it were, to indicate to the stockholders the reason why a certain portion of the earned profits is retained by the corporation and also that stockholders are not to expect that this particular portion of the profits will at any time in the near future be distributed. This is accomplished by a vote "placing in reserve" a portion of the profits which would be indicated through a journal entry as follows:

Profit and Loss (Income, or Surplus)	$50,000	
Reserve for Extensions		$50,000

Results Not Assured by Creation of Reserve

But there is no assurance that even after such action the reserve will be devoted to the purpose for which it was created. The establishment of a reserve for extensions is at best merely a declaration of the present intentions of the existing board of directors and both intentions and boards are subject to change. In some cases assurance that the purpose will be carried out may be secured by distinct segregation of funds corresponding to the amount of reserve and a quasi-alienation of these funds so as to prevent diversion for other purposes. This is definitely accomplished in the case of a sinking fund reserve by depositing funds in the hands of a trustee so that they are no longer at the disposition of the company or its directors. Such an arrangement is ordinarily the result of a specific contract between the company and the bondholders. The mere laying aside of certain assets corresponding in amount to the reserve does not assure the carrying out of the original plan. This aspect of reserve is discussed more fully on a later page. Even where it is not intended that dividends should be paid from a given reserve the restriction is a limited one for a loss which otherwise might have prevented dividends may be charged against this reserve. Thus a company may have accounts showing the following:

Trial Balance

Assets	$615,000	Capital	$400,000
Expenses	80,000	Reserve for Contingencies	70,000
		Bonds	125,000
		Earnings	100,000
	$695,000		$695,000

If both the ordinary expenses and an unexpected loss of $25,000 are charged against earnings, there would result a showing of an operating deficit of $5,000. With such a showing it would not be considered proper to pay a dividend. But by charging the unusual loss against the reserve for contingency the following balance sheet would result:

Balance Sheet

Assets	$590,000	Capital	$400,000
		Reserve for Contingencies	45,000
		Bonds	125,000
		Undivided Profits	20,000
	$590,000		$590,000

a showing which makes the legitimacy of a dividend unquestionable.

Specially Covered Reserves

A surplus being a reservation of profits must be represented by equivalent assets. It is the increase of assets that creates all profit, and necessarily that portion of the profits reserved from distribution. To speak of a surplus without equivalent assets is, therefore, self-contradictory. But with the ambiguous use of the term reserve, question often arises as to whether, being a surplus, it represents assets or being a valuation or offset account, it merely signifies the depreciation in value of some of the assets. Objection has already been made to the use of reserve in the latter sense and Allowance for Depreciation or some similar title has been recommended in its place. Some writers have gone further and demanded that the term reserve should never be used unless it represents, not merely the existence of equivalent assets, but that certain specific assets of a particular character have been set aside to cover the reserve. Such action is occasionally taken. Where part of the surplus is reserved to provide a sinking fund it is almost universally the case that there is a simultaneous setting apart of cash ordinarily paid into the hands of sinking fund trustees in order that current funds will actually be available when the time comes for retiring the bonds. Such a setting aside of cash is a part of the contract with the bondholders, but even where there is no such contractual obligation, assets may of course be set aside corresponding to the reserve created out of profits. Thus at the time when the directors of a corporation vote to establish a reserve for extension of $5,000, a similar amount of cash could be laid outside either by putting it in a separate bank account, by investing it in outside securities, or even by placing it in the hands of trustees. Such an action rests upon the assumption that if it is desirable to reserve profits in order to provide for a future expenditure, it is likewise desirable to take action that will provide not merely that the profits are not disbursed, but that the assets representing the reserve will be in the form of cash or other current funds when the time comes for making the extension.

According to the accounting nomenclature now generally accepted, specific assets thus set aside to cover a reserve may properly bear in their title the word fund, as for instance, Sinking Fund or Extension Fund in the circumstances described above. Occasionally they may bear a more descriptive title as for instance, Cash in Hands of Sinking Fund Trustees or Investment of Reserve for Extension. The earlier practice of using fund in the title of a credit balance is no longer recognized as good accounting practice. It should always refer to the concrete assets and not to the portion of surplus which the assets represent.

Objections to Assumption That a Reserve Implies a Reserve Fund

The question whether a reserve should always be covered or, in other words, whether the appearance of a reserve on the credit side of the balance sheet should always imply a corresponding reserve fund appearing among the assets, demands further attention.

1. Confuses Assets and Proprietorship

Primary objection to such an assumption is that it implies a confusion of the two sides of the balance sheet, of asset accounts and proprietorship accounts. The debit side of the balance sheet lists certain specific assets, the value of which, less liabilities, equals the sum of the various proprietorship accounts; but there is ordinarily no specific asset corresponding to specific credits. Bonds may have been issued to purchase plant, preferred stock to purchase present goodwill, common stock to represent the estimated additional earning power of the consolidation, but the balance sheet does not make a separate equation of these three pairs. It suffices to show that Plant + Goodwill = Preferred Stock + Common Stock + Bonds.

It is true that the equating of the various items is in part secured by the double account form of balance sheet required of certain English companies, where the receipts from capital stock and bonds are balanced against the more permanent investments. There is also a comparison made, though not a definite equation between various subheads frequently introduced into modern balance sheets, as for instance between capital assets and capital liabilities and between current assets and current liabilities. But even in such cases there is no real equivalence stated between a given credit and some other debit item. The equivalence of the balance sheet is that between the sum of the items representing proprietorship and liabilities and the sum of those representing assets. The groups into which these assets are subdivided and the various subdivisions into which proprietorship is for convenience divided, are divergent systems of classification and should not be confused. In the varied shifting of form which continually takes place in the assets, an original correspondence between certain credits and debits becomes lost and the connection can no longer be traced. Undoubtedly every depositor and stockholder in a bank contributed some particular money or other asset equivalent to his deposit or his subscription; but the identity is lost at once upon the title passing to the bank and there is no specific asset representing the particular claim of A although, for convenience, there may be a comparison, though not a balancing of the items of Deposits and Cash Reserve, or of Deposits and Discounts.

2. *Specially Covered Reserves Not More Secure*

Secondly, the setting aside of a specific asset does not make the reserve any more secure, any more available. For instance, a balance sheet shows:

Balance Sheet

Miscellaneous Assets	$120,000	Capital	$100,000
Investment of Reserve	5,000	Debts	20,000
		Reserve for Extensions	5,000
	$125,000		$125,000

A debt becomes due, which because of financial stringency cannot be renewed or placed elsewhere. Unless the investments of the reserve have been specifically placed in trust, they will in such an emergency probably be sold to provide cash to pay the debt. The balance sheet becomes:

Balance Sheet

Miscellaneous Assets	$120,000	Capital	$100,000
		Debts	15,000
		Reserve for Extensions	5,000
	$120,000		$120,000

The specific investment has not made the Reserve for Extensions any more available than it otherwise would have been, and it remains despite the disappearance of the specific investment.

On the other hand, the reserve is made no more secure because of the specific investment, for supposing that the business of the year following the showing results in a net loss of $5,000, the balance sheet then becomes:

Balance Sheet

Miscellaneous Assets	$115,000	Capital	$100,000
Investment of Reserve	5,000	Debts	20,000
		Reserve for Extensions	0
	$120,000		$120,000

so that while the specific investment is still intact the reserve has disappeared as effectively as possible. It would be illegitimate to show:

Balance Sheet

Miscellaneous Assets	$115,000	Capital	$100,000
Investment of Reserve	5,000	Debts	20,000
Loss	5,000	Reserve for Extensions	5,000
	$125,000		$125,000

for the reserve indicates that there has been a reservation of part of the profits amounting to $5,000 while the Loss items show there are no profits to be reserved. This is shown even by Pixley who, himself, argues strongly in favor of a specific investment.

3. Assumption Leads to False Theories

And finally, although this pertains to corporation finance rather than to accounting, the identification of reserve with specific assets lends itself easily to two false theories: (*a*) That an outside investment is a better holding for the corporation than an investment in extending its own plant, and (*b*) that where a fund of cash, or other liquid assets is desirable as a provision for emergencies, such provision need not be made out of capital, but only as profits accumulate. The first of these views is undoubtedly true in certain circumstances, as where provision is being made for an emergency demanding ready funds, but as a general principle it is without validity. The second view is altogether unsound and vicious in principle and in practice.

Opinions of Foreign Authorities

In such matters, where personal opinion and taste have much weight, it may be well to quote two leading authorities, one German and the other English. Says Rehm:

> A reserve is not an asset but merely a technical indication of property in such. It signifies that a given value of assets may not be distributed or disbursed; but as it is not assets it cannot be an item on the asset side of the balance sheet, and accordingly it also cannot be transferred into assets and invested in given securities.[1]

Dicksee similarly says:

> It cannot be too strongly advanced that the question as to whether or not any given reserve is represented by assets consisting of marketable securities outside the business or by less readily marketable assets employed in the business as fixed (or working) capital, is comparatively speaking of little importance. The most casual perusal of any balance sheet will show at a glance, even to the least informed, by which class of assets the reserve is represented.[2]

---

[1] *Die Bilanzen*, 571. See also H. V. Simon, *Die Bilanzen der Aktiengesellschaften*, § 60.

[2] *Auditing*, 13th ed., p. 278. See also N. H. Humphrys in *The Gas World*, LX, p. 170, and subsequent correspondence and editorial comment.

In the case of Hoare and Company [3] before the Court of Appeals, Vaughan Williams, L. J., implies there is no reserve unless the assets are specifically set aside, but Romer and Cozens-Hardy, L. JJ., speak of a reserve where there is no separate investment. Somewhat more specific is the provision in the revised form of Table A of the English Companies Act. In this it is provided that reserves for any purpose may at the discretion of the directors "either be employed in the business of the company or be invested in such investments (other than shares of the company) as the directors may from time to think think fit." [4]

Covered Reserves in American Practice

In accounting practice much diversity is found. The great majority of reserves in the balance sheets do not show a corresponding special investment. Where there is such an investment it is generally given some distinguishing title such as Contingent and Insurance Fund Assets (Bethlehem Steel Company) or Sinking and Reserve Fund Assets (United States Steel Corporation). In some cases the assets thus specially set aside exactly equal in amount the reserve on the other side of the balance sheet, but in other cases there is no such equivalence, only a portion of the reserve being specifically invested (as in the case of the United States Steel Corporation).

Distinction between Reserve and Reserve Fund

There has been much confusion in the use of the terms Reserve and Reserve Fund. In America accounting terminology in this respect at least has happily become somewhat crystallized. The definition of fund as "a sum of money or its equivalent employed in, set aside for, or available for a specific or general purpose," made by the Committee on Terminology of the American Institute of Accountants,[5] may now be said to represent the better American practice. It

---

[3] [1904] 2 Ch. 208, 213.
[4] The Companies (Consolidation) Act, 1908, 1st schedule, 99.
[5] *Journal of Accountancy*, XXXV, p. 388.

follows, therefore, that reserve fund is to be used only as describing an asset while reserve may be used as a credit item. This usage has not been so generally adopted in England where reserve fund frequently appears as representing what in this country would be called a reserve. Some English accountants, however, attempt to differentiate, using both terms to describe items upon the capital and liability side of the balance sheet, but limiting reserve fund to indicate such reserves as have been specially covered.[6]

Appreciation of Assets in Reserve Fund

A difficulty arises when the assets in which a specially covered reserve is invested increase in value. If this increase is realized by the sale of the assets there is doubt as to whether the increment should be added to the reserve or be carried to the general Profit and Loss or Surplus of the corporation. If the situation is looked upon as analogous to a trust fund, there is a colorable argument that the increment adds to the corpus of the fund and would accordingly result in an increased credit to the reserve. This is the opinion of Sir Arthur Lowes Dickinson,[7] but there is an equally strong argument to the effect that the corporation's purpose was to reserve only a certain amount and that the incidental gain due to appreciation of investments does not necessarily require a corresponding increase in the amount reserved. From this viewpoint the increment would properly be credited to Profit and Loss or Surplus, and it seems altogether more satisfactory to hold that the increase of the reserve is optional and not compulsory.

Reserves in Banking and Insurance

Much confusion is also caused by the fact that the term reserve is used in connection with banking and insurance in an entirely different sense from that in general bookkeeping practice. Thus the National Bank Act, general banking literature, and at times even the balance sheets of the

[6] Pixley, *Duties of Auditors,* 11th ed., p. 516.
[7] *Accounting Practice and Procedure,* p. 87.

banks use reserve as indicating the entire cash on hand or deposits in certain banks deemed by law or custom equivalent to cash. A condensed balance sheet, such as is published for advertising purposes, may read:

Condensed Balance Sheet

Loans and Discounts	$11,100,000	Capital	$ 2,000,000
Bonds	1,500,000	Surplus and Undivided Profits	1,100,000
Reserve	7,000,000	Deposits	16,500,000
	$19,600,000		$19,600,000

Reserve in this sense evidently has nothing to do with profits, and its maintenance is in no wise dependent upon the existence of accumulated profits; but in law and in banking practice it is proportionate to the deposits, not to profits. Similarly reserve in insurance has a specific meaning referring to certain classes of assets which must be kept on hand to cover the actuarial value of outstanding risks. Again this is proportionate to a given item of liabilities, not to profits. The reserve of the bank is really cash and deposits with approved reserve agents and is thus correctly stated in the detailed balance sheet. The reserve of the insurance company is really cash, bonds, and similar items, while reserve, as it appears among the liabilities, is merely an indication that part of the accumulated profits is not to be distributed as dividends. It is not the assets themselves but represents at most a state of mind regarding certain assets. The exceptional use of reserve in banking and insurance literature may sometimes be confusing, but the matter is so simple that it should cause no serious misunderstanding.

Secret Reserves

A surplus exists when an increment of assets is withheld from distribution to the stockholders or proprietors; that is, whenever the excess of the total value of the net assets over the original capital is retained by the company. It is an economic fact and is independent of whether the accounts show the existence of such a surplus or not. In corporations desiring to be considered conservative, or wishing to escape taxation, or to conceal large profits, it is not uncommon purposely to conceal the existence of such a surplus. This is actually done whenever there is an undervaluation of assets, or less frequently when there is an overstatement of liabilities. In such cases there is said to be a secret reserve. Thus in a company whose balance sheet shows:

Balance Sheet

Plant, etc.	$90,000		Capital	$90,000
Less Depreciation	5,000		Profits	5,000
		$85,000		
Cash		10,000		
		$95,000		$95,000

if an additional depreciation of $5,000 is reckoned, one not represented by an actual loss or decline in value, the balance sheet will read:

Balance Sheet

Plant, etc.	$90,000		Capital	$90,000
Less Depreciation	10,000			
		$80,000		
Cash		10,000		
		$90,000		$90,000

Despite the statement here made the net value of the assets is really $95,000, which exceeds the capital by $5,000. As no profits appear in the balance sheet, no dividends can be declared, and the $5,000 cash, which might otherwise have been distributed, is perforce reserved as an addition to the working capital of the concern. Such a condition may also be produced by treating as expenses, or by charging direct to Profit and Loss account, payments which really represent the purchase of new assets. If the $5,000 is spent in making some unquestioned improvement or addition to the plant, the normal entry is to charge the amount to Plant or to some synonymous account. A change in the form of assets held from cash to plant does not affect profits, or surplus. But if the payment is treated as though it were an expense, the total assets are apparently diminished when the cash is paid, and no showing is made of the new asset gained by purchase. Whether the charge is made originally to Expense and thus indirectly diminishes profit, or whether the charge is made direct against Profit and Loss, or against some special or general reserve, the effect is the same. In one way or another the assets held are understated and to an equivalent amount the showing of accumulated profits is less than the correct amount.

Secret Reserves in American Practice

Banks are especially given to this practice, doubtless with the purpose of being able to cover losses without disclosing them to the public. Thus the First National Bank of New York City is said to have covered a defalcation of $690,000 because it had so large a secret reserve. This could be done by bringing into the balance sheet enough of the assets representing the secret reserve to cover the unusual loss.

Railroads, too, in earlier years, have at times acted similarly either by violently marking down the value of the road, as was done by the Chicago and Northwestern Railway in 1893; or by charging to operation and maintenance sums representing very material additions to the physical property, as was done by the same road to the extent of nearly $5,000,000 a year for the seven successive years from 1900 to 1906. An even more striking charge, one of $13,000,000, part of the expense of constructing its tunnel, was made by the Pennsylvania against a special surplus in 1906.

Objections to Secret Reserves

Again appears a case of justifying a practice abhorrent to accounting principles, yet not without certain practical merits. In the anxiety to escape the prevalent temptation to exaggerate the value of the assets, which in many cases has led to such disgraceful results, conservative financiers applaud an equally erroneous, but perhaps less dangerous tendency to understatement. But the creation of a secret reserve is not without its dangers. It may be used as a means of refusing to pay dividends really earned, which so far as it applies to holders of income bonds or noncumulative preferred stock, may work an irreparable loss. Even where there are no such divisions of interests it may lead ignorant stockholders, thinking the balance sheet correct, to dispose of their stock at less than its real value.

The position which the Interstate Commerce Commission has taken against the practice of charging to operating expenses payments really of the nature of betterments is decidedly healthful. This has been attacked by the technical press, and has been spoken of as "casting to the winds the whole system of conservative finance which has been the boast of many American railroad companies."[8] This is curious as coming from the organ of the Chartered Accountants, whose council had previously taken ground that the existence of secret reserves makes the balance sheet criminally false. To identify conservative finance with incorrect statements is a dangerous precedent, for the use of untruth in a good cause is likely to induce an attitude of mind in which untruthfulness becomes chronic and ineradicable. It is hard to believe that so good a cause as financial conservatism needs such unholy allies as misrepresentation and deception.

Secret Reserve Held Legal

An extreme type of a secret reserve, one which the directors were authorized to expend without accounting to the stockholders therefor, was brought to notice in connection with the Birmingham Small Arms Company. The articles of the company authorized the directors to set aside, out of the profits, an internal reserve fund which need not be disclosed by the balance sheet, the directors to use the reserve

[8] *Accountant,* XXXVII, p. 80.

fund in any way which they think will promote the interests of the company without giving any information to the shareholders regarding the amount or application of this reserve. In discussing this provision, Justice Buckley said:

The special resolutions in the present case provide that the balance sheet shall not disclose the internal reserve fund; it must, therefore, omit on the assets side of the balance sheet the assets which make up the amount standing to the credit of that fund and the contra item—namely, the credit balance of the fund—on the liability side. The result will be to show the financial position of the company to be not as good as in fact it is. If the balance sheet be so worded as to show that there is an undisclosed asset, the existence of which makes the financial position better than shown such a balance sheet will not, in my judgment, be necessarily inconsistent with the Act of Parliament. Assets are often by reason of prudence estimated, and stated to be estimated, at less than their real value. The purpose of the balance sheet is primarily to show that the financial position of the company is at least as good as there stated, not to show that it is not, or may not be better. ([1906] 2 Ch. 378.)

Cancelation of Surplus

A surplus being ordinarily accumulated profits, its disbursement is secured in any way in which profits are disbursed save where some particular statute or by-law prevents. More strictly speaking there occurs a cancelation rather than a disbursement of surplus, for a Surplus in the sense of an account on the credit side of the balance sheet cannot itself be disbursed. Certain tangible assets may be paid out and this may work a cancelation of the credit. The bookkeeping entries in connection with such cancelation remain for consideration.

Losses Charged against Reserves

A reserve created to provide against some unusual loss logically remains intact until such loss occurs. This may be a loss by fire or other accident, a loss due to default by trade debtors or on securities held, a loss due to unfavorable results in business operations. Such a loss would otherwise be charged to Profit and Loss, or to Capital, but where a reserve exists the unusual loss may appropriately be charged against such reserve, leaving the current profits from ordinary business still available for dividends. Similarly, where the reserve is used to pay a dividend, otherwise unearned, there results a cancelation of some part of the reserve, just as a dividend paid in ordinary circumstances works a cancelation of the credit balance to Profit and Loss. Whether the charge for dividend is made direct to the reserve account, or whether part of the reserve is transferred back to the Profit and Loss account from which it originated is immaterial so far as the final showing is concerned. The reserve being a reservation of profits, may either be used to cancel any loss, as current profits would be used; or at any time may be canceled by retransference to Profit and Loss, which simply signifies that profits for a while *reserved* are no longer so, but are to be treated in the usual way.

Extensions Not Properly Chargeable to Reserve for Extensions

But it has been shown that sometimes—and frequently—a reserve is created not to cover a loss or make possible a dividend but to provide additional plant, to cover an exchange, not a profit and loss transaction.

Thus in the following case:

Balance Sheet

Plant	$ 90,000	Capital	$100,000
Cash	20,000	Reserve for Extensions	10,000
	$110,000		$110,000

the reserve may have been created for the specific purpose of purchasing an additional machine. The time has come when this is needed, and the reserve is just sufficient to cover the cost. Cash is lessened by $10,000 when the machine is purchased, but this expenditure is no loss, as a machine of equal value is received in exchange. Consequently the balance sheet should show:

Balance Sheet

Plant	$90,000		Capital	$100,000
Additions	10,000		Reserve for Extensions	10,000
		$100,000		
Cash		10,000		
		$110,000		$110,000

In many cases, however, Cash is credited and Reserve for Extensions is debited showing merely:

Balance Sheet

Plant	$ 90,000	Capital	$100,000
Cash	10,000		
	$100,000		$100,000

But this is a case of creating a secret reserve, which has already been criticized. There is no justification in charging to reserve anything which could not legitimately be charged against profits. The purchase of a machine, an exchange transaction, should not thus be charged.

Transfer of Reserve to Surplus

It may, however, be desirable to make some change in the reserve item. It seems somewhat absurd to have a reserve to provide for something already secured. Consequently the credit to Reserve for Extensions may be canceled and a corresponding credit made either to the general Surplus account or to some specifically labeled reserve or surplus account. If the latter is desired there can appear the cumbrous but minutely accurate title, Reserve Created by Purchasing Machinery out of Profits. In the terminology of the Interstate Commerce Commission it should be credited to account No. 779, Addition to Property through Income and Surplus. It is undesirable to credit the current Profit and Loss with this item, for it has nothing to do with the operation of the current year. Crediting it to the general Surplus is entirely legitimate but seems to indicate a change in policy. The policy originally adopted was to provide the machinery at the expense of dividends. If a sum is now credited back to Surplus, it would seem to be available for dividends. If the surplus is then distributed, the machinery would not have been purchased from reserved profits, but from other sources.

The payment of debt, like the purchase of assets, is not a loss transaction, and similarly is not a logical charge against a reserve. The treatment of a reserve provided for the payment of debts, should, therefore, be identical with that of a reserve for extensions described above.

Booking in Case of Specially Covered Reserve

It is to be noted that the booking is identical whether the reserve is specifically covered or not. Where specific investments are held, presumably they will be sold to provide cash with which to cover the payment. Thus with a balance sheet showing:

Balance Sheet

Plant, etc.	$ 90,000	Capital	$100,000
Investments	10,000	Reserve for Extensions	10,000
Cash	10,000		
	$110,000		$110,000

the company may make the addition to its plant contemplated when the Reserve for Extensions was established. Whether the payment is made from the cash on hand or from $10,000 realized from the sale of the investments, is immaterial so far as it affects the rest of the balance sheet. In either case the item Plant is increased by $10,000, and the treatment of the reserve is the same. The amount of the latter remains unaltered, although the term used in the balance sheet may be changed as suggested in the preceding paragraph. Even when specific investments are held to cover the reserve it may be that a flurry in the investment market makes it undesirable to sell them, and the purchase is made with cash already in hand or even by credit. In the last-named case the balance sheet becomes:

Balance Sheet

Plant, etc.	$100,000	Capital	$100,000
Investments	10,000	Notes Payable	10,000
Cash	10,000	Reserve for Extensions	10,000
	$120,000		$120,000

This again emphasizes the fact that the booking of reserve is practically independent of the existence of specific assets.

Reserve for Insurance

The item Reserve for Insurance is frequently found in balance sheets. It generally occurs where a company, whose plant is so widely scattered that there is little likelihood of large loss by a single fire, decides not to carry any insurance but to stand its own loss should one occur. In such circumstances it is assumed that the insurance premiums saved will more than cover losses as they occur. To carry out this policy an annual charge, perhaps equivalent to regular insurance premiums, is made against earnings, and an equivalent amount is credited to Reserve for Insurance. There may or may not be a specific investment made to cover the reserve. It is somewhat difficult to determine whether such a reserve is really a part of profits. Were the company to go into liquidation, or to change its policy and provide for future losses by carrying regular insurance, the balance then standing to the credit of the Reserve for Insurance would unquestionably represent an addition to profits which could be distributed as dividends. But so long as the company maintains its business and refrains from insuring, the reserve is closely allied to a provision for depreciation or for bad debts. If the plant is sufficiently large and scattered, the law of probabilities makes certain that a loss will some time occur. If an accurate estimate shows that there will be an average loss of $20,000 each ten years, it is clear that the accountant should charge $2,000 (ignoring the compounding of interest) as the share of such loss properly to be allocated to each year's business. And the accumulation of such charges is not so much a part of net profits as a representation of a loss logically anticipated but as yet unrealized.

BIBLIOGRAPHICAL NOTE

DAWSON, S. S.—"Reserves and Reserve Funds," Article in *Encyclopædia of Accounting,* V, pp. 482-8.

DICKSEE, L. R.—*Depreciation, Reserves, and Reserve Funds* (3d ed., London, 1912).

FINNEY, H. A.—*Principles of Accounting* (New York, 1924), chaps. xlv, xlvi.

KESTER, R. B.—*Accounting, Theory and Practice* (2d ed., New York, 1925), chap. xxvi.

MEADE, E. S.—"The Management of the Surplus Reserve," *Publications of the American Economic Association,* 3d series, V, p. 245.

NEUKAMP, E.—"Das Dogma von der 'Bilanzwahrheit,'" *Goldschmidts Zeitschrift f. d. gesamte Handelsrecht,* XLVIII, p. 450. A strong argument in favor of secret reserves.

WILDMAN, J. R.—*Principles of Accounting* (New York, 1922), chaps. xxi, xxii.

CHAPTER XV

SINKING FUNDS

Definition

A sinking fund is defined as "a sum of money periodically set aside to accumulate through deposit or investment so that at a given date the total accumulation will approximately equal the amount of the obligation for the redemption or retirement of which the fund was created."[1] In accounting, however, the use of the term has not been thus strictly limited for in many cases the term sinking fund is found upon the credit side of the balance sheet and does not indicate an asset as is called for by the definition, but represents part of the corporate surplus. In this matter, however, accounting practice is becoming somewhat more uniform and it may now be accepted that the term sinking fund is to be applied solely to the assets themselves and that some other name is to be applied to the credit item if such appears in the balance sheet. An indication of the change in practice is found in the reports of the United States Steel Corporation which formerly used the title Sinking Fund for the credit balance, but in 1921 changed to Sinking Fund Reserve. The railroads which in earlier years similarly used Sinking Fund as a credit item now follow the terminology prescribed by the Interstate Commerce Commission and use the phrase Sinking Fund Reserve. This is in accordance with the acceptance of the rule that in accounting the word fund, whether sinking fund or fund for some other purpose, shall be used only as

---

[1] Committee on Terminology, A. I. A., in *Journal of Accountancy*, XXXV, 389. The term sinking fund is also occasionally used as applying to a fund provided for renewal of assets. This is particularly common in the case of mining property. See *e.g.*, Dawson and de Zouche, *Accounting*, p. 259.

applying to assets; while the corresponding credit item includes either the word reserve or allowance in its title. Where sinking fund is used to apply to the credit, the corresponding assets are generally headed Sinking Fund Assets and that title is still used in the balance sheet of the United States Steel Corporation.

Sinking Funds in the Balance Sheet

Items relating to a sinking fund including not merely the assets themselves but as well a corresponding reserve appear in various combinations in published balance sheets. (1) In some cases the sinking fund is found among the assets with no specifically related credit. (2) In other cases, sinking fund reserve appears among the proprietorship items without any specifically related asset. (3) In other balance sheets, items relating to the sinking fund appear simultaneously on both sides of the balance sheet, not infrequently in exactly similar sums, and finally (4) a corporation may actually maintain a sinking fund and have no reference thereto appear in the balance sheet. The significance of each of these methods of handling a sinking fund is as follows:

1. Sinking Fund as an Asset

A given sum of money is annually paid to sinking fund trustees or otherwise set aside to accumulate at compound interest until the time when the bonds mature. The payment is not regarded as a loss or an expense, which indeed it is not, for the payment of debt not being an expense certainly the preliminary setting aside of a fund with which to pay the debt is no more so. Assuming a corporation whose balance sheet shows:

Balance Sheet

Plant, etc.	$ 99,000,000	Capital Stock	$ 50,000,000
Cash	2,000,000	Funded Debt	50,000,000
		Surplus	1,000,000
	$101,000,000		$101,000,000

the payment to the sinking fund trustees of an installment of $500,000 produces the following condition:

Balance Sheet

Plant	$ 99,000,000	Capital Stock	$ 50,000,000
Cash in Hands of Sinking Fund Trustees	500,000	Funded Debt	50,000,000
Cash	1,500,000	Surplus	1,000,000
	$101,000,000		$101,000,000

In this case cash has been taken out of the general funds and put aside to provide means for the future payment of the bonds. There is no indication as to its relation to profits. The legal requirement by contract with the bondholders is that funds be thus set aside and separately held. So long as this is done it is immaterial to the bondholders whether the cash is obtained from the stockholders, from loans obtained elsewhere, from the conversion of capital assets, or from accumulated profits. The sinking fund here is a fund of assets, analogous to a bank reserve and not a reserve in the sense of reserved profits. This form is used, for instance, by the American Agricultural Chemical Company.

2. Sinking Fund and Sinking Fund Reserve

Railroads are accustomed to charge the amount of the sinking fund installment to the Income or Profit and Loss account. In this case a distinct reserve is created by withholding part of the accumulated profits. Where this is done the balance sheet becomes:

Balance Sheet

Cost of Road, etc.	$ 99,000,000	Capital Stock	$ 50,000,000
Cash in Hands of Sinking Fund Trustees	500,000	Funded Debt	50,000,000
		Sinking Fund Reserve	500,000
Cash	1,500,000	Surplus	500,000
	$101,000,000		$101,000,000

which is the form prescribed by the Interstate Commerce Commission. The name given to the account varies somewhat in the different reports, but the essential thing is to note that a reserve, specially covered by cash in the hands of the trustees, has been established, and that both sides of the balance sheet show the amount of the sinking fund.

3. Other Variations in Accounting for Sinking Fund

The other forms are variations of the two just given, and depend on the method of employing the funds paid to the trustees, and of booking the transactions. The purpose of the sinking fund being to provide means which shall serve to wipe out a given issue of bonds at a certain time, this end can be gained either by leaving the cash on deposit in a trust company, by investing it in outside securities, or by buying up some of the company's own bonds. The first plan is objectionable because of the small rate of interest received, the second involves the possibility of risk, the danger of misappropriation of the large sums of securities held by trustees, and a relatively low rate of interest, for the trustees will prefer bonds whose greater security means lower returns. Investment in the company's own securities is therefore the most desirable as well as the customary method, and so far as practicable the bonds purchased are part of the very issue to be covered by the sinking fund. Here the question of security cannot arise, for the purchase of the bonds in itself secures the desired end; misappropriation can be prevented by canceling or by rendering the bonds otherwise non-negotiable; and the interest will be higher than could be gained by any investment of approximately equal security.

Where outside investments are made the securities held must appear in the balance sheet as part of the assets of the company, under the heading Cash and Securities Held by Sinking Fund Trustees, or an equivalent phrase; but where bonds of the company are purchased different methods of booking the transaction are employed. Sometimes they too are included among the assets embraced in the heading just given, but in other companies bonds so held are not counted as assets, and are therefore necessarily canceled from the bonds listed among the liabilities. This is treating the bonds purchased for the sinking fund as a payment of a debt, and a debt paid as a rule no longer appears in the accounts. Assuming that the sinking fund has been invested in the company's bonds, and that these bonds are canceled, the balance sheets given above become respectively:

Balance Sheet

Plant, etc.	$ 99,000,000	Capital Stock	$ 50,000,000
Cash	1,500,000	Funded Debt	49,500,000
		Surplus	1,000,000
	$100,500,000		$100,500,000

Balance Sheet

Cost of Road, etc.	$ 99,000,000	Capital Stock	$ 50,000,000
Cash	1,500,000	Funded Debt	49,500,000
		Sinking Fund Reserve	500,000
		Surplus	500,000
	$100,500,000		$100,500,000

Sinking Fund without Specific Investment

While the original idea of the sinking fund implied an annual investment of cash, which would be allowed to accumulate at compound interest, in its more recent use the term is occasionally used where there is no specific investment in a strict sense, but the funds representing the sinking fund reserve are used in extension of the plant, or for the general purposes of the business. This is true of the sinking fund of the Glasgow Railway and of the Fairmont Coal Company. While such a procedure does not directly provide liquid funds for payment of the debt at maturity, it is argued that the creditor is benefited by the increased assets protecting his loan and indeed that such a method is preferable in that sums invested in the business itself yield a better return than could be obtained from profits on outside securities.[2]

[2] See article by Marwick, *Accountant,* XXXIII, p. 285; T. A. Welton, *ibid.,* XLV, p. 679.

Comparison of Methods of Showing Sinking Fund

A comparison of the four methods shows that an item representing the sinking fund appears in the first form only among the debits, in the second in both debits and credits, in the third in neither debit nor credit, and in the fourth in the credit side alone. The creditors are given the security in the first case, of certain segregated assets, but no assurance that the total assets of the company will be increased. In the second case the reserved assets at the same time constitute an increase in the total assets of the company, gained by a reservation of profits, or at least there is the guaranty that the stockholders take no dividends unless profits are first withheld sufficient to provide for repayment of the debt. In the third method no specific assets are withheld and the gross assets may even decline, but the outstanding claims are reduced so that the margin of security is increased. In the fourth there is a similar reduction in liabilities, but in this instance accompanied by a guaranty, not found in the third method, that the gross assets will at least be constant while the net assets are being increased by paying debts with profits.

Sinking Fund Reserve Not a Charge against Earnings

Payment of debt is in no sense an expense or loss and is not to be reckoned in ascertaining net income. Still more the mere provision for the future payment of a debt cannot be considered an expense, yet in many cases sinking fund installments have been treated in the accounts as being analogous to interest charges and hence a deduction before arriving at the net income. This was probably due to the fact that both sinking fund installments and interest are fixed charges which must inevitably be paid by the corporation, but the model set by the Interstate Commerce Commission has not merely changed the practice of railroads but has had a beneficial effect on the practice of other corporations. According to the Commission's rules, payments to sinking fund under the title, Income Applied to Sinking and Other Reserve Funds, are a disposition of net income along with dividends, and appropriations of net income for investment in the road. Furthermore the sinking fund reserve, being in all senses a part of the surplus, is now included as one of the items in the total corporate surplus in the balance sheets of American railways.

The older view of sinking fund transactions was clearly expressed by M. M. Kirkman, vice-president of the Chicago and Northwestern Railway.

> Sinking fund is unrepresented capital. It is not chargeable against income account any more than any other capital expenditure. The reason why we so often find it included in the income account is because of the conservatism of proprietors. It is another way they have of strengthening their properties. It is similar in effect to making improvements with net earnings. The fact that it is done by sagacious and practical business men is, in itself, sufficient evidence that it is proper.[3]

But the analogy here given is not quite correct. In charging improvements to net earnings the item disappears entirely from the balance sheet and constitutes a secret reserve. This is apparently never done in regard to the sinking fund. The payment does not disappear but is either held among the assets or what is equivalent is deducted from outstanding debt. The alternative, so far as the showing in the balance sheet is concerned, is between retaining an unappropriated balance to Income and a special reserve, not between creating a secret and an open reserve. Charging to income reduces the unappropriated balance and doubtless lessens the clamor for extra dividends which might appear as that balance is augmented, but which would be less insistent where it appears as Sinking Fund Reserve. To charge to gross rather than to net income affects only the showing in current income accounts, not at all the cumulative sum in the balance sheet, but even the showing of the annual profits at a sum larger than can advisedly be distributed is at times embarrassing. While the net profits of the Chicago and Northwestern Railway were unquestionably larger than the amount shown, the amount

[3] *Science of Railways*, III, p. 104.

of Net Profits Available for Dividends was not larger. The compulsory nature of the sinking fund has some bearing, it is true, but neither national banks nor foreign corporations consider the compulsory establishment of a surplus a reason for understating the annual net profits, and they do not charge the required percentage of their profits as if it were an expense, but show it properly as an appropriation of profits. So the compulsory nature of the sinking fund, while lessening the amount which may be available for dividends, should not diminish the net profits shown. Even the decisions of the courts, that profits are ascertained after the payment of sinking funds,[4] like the similar decisions regarding the payment of the principal of the debt, are, as is shown in Chapter XII, to be explained as a ruling against forcing dividends rather than as a scientific definition of the nature of profits.

Interest on Sinking Fund

The theory of the sinking fund involves the compounding of interest on the invested installments. Where outside investments are made this is simply done by leaving in the hands of the trustees the interest received. Where the company's own bonds are purchased it involves the payment of interest on the entire issue of bonds, including those held by the sinking fund, and regardless of whether these bonds are canceled and subtracted from the liabilities or not.

Formerly it was the custom when interest was collected by the sinking fund trustees merely to debit Cash in Hands of Sinking Fund Trustees (or Sinking Fund) and credit Sinking Fund Reserve. In this way, the gain from interest did not appear at all in the general income statement of the corporation. This customary but incorrect procedure has been abolished, so far as railroads are concerned, by the rules of the Interstate Commerce Commission, in which income from sinking and other reserve funds is included in non-operating income, requiring a separate charge against net income if it is appropriated for sinking fund purposes.

---

[4] Belfast & Moosehead Lake R'y. *v.* Belfast, 1 Atl. 362 (Me. 1885); Excelsior Water and Mining Co. *v.* Pierce, 27 Pac. 44 (Cal. 1891).

Payment of Bonds from Sinking Fund

In the normal course when the time comes for the retirement of bonds covered by the sinking fund the funds so held are applied to the payment of the debt. It is not always the case that the company is under obligation to appropriate to the sinking fund an annual sum which will gradually accumulate to the entire amount of the outstanding debt. The bondholders may feel sufficiently protected if the funds accumulated in the hands of the trustees amount, at the time of the maturity of the debt, to some considerable percentage of the amount then due. If, in the first instance, investors were willing to lend a given sum upon the general credit of the company they might feel fully protected if 80 per cent of the bonds were paid at maturity out of the sinking fund as presumably the general assets of the company would then be more than adequate to protect the remainder of the debt.

If, however, the provisions were such that a sum equal to the entire amount of the outstanding bonds is in the hands of the trustees when the bonds mature, the balance sheet would be as follows:

Balance Sheet

Cost of road, etc.	$ 99,000,000	Capital Stock	$ 50,000,000
Cash in Hands of Sinking Fund Trustees	50,000,000	Funded Debt	50,000,000
Cash	1,500,000	Sinking Fund Reserve	50,000,000
		Surplus	500,000
	$150,500,000		$150,500,000

At this point the bonds are presented to the trustees of the sinking fund and paid by them. The balance sheet then becomes:

Balance Sheet

Cost of road, etc.	$ 99,000,000	Capital Stock	$ 50,000,000
Cash	1,500,000	Sinking Fund Reserve	50,000,000
		Surplus	500,000
	$100,500,000		$100,500,000

Sinking Fund Reserve after Payment of Bonds

It perhaps seems unreasonable to continue the Sinking Fund Reserve under that title, now that the debt has been redeemed and canceled. The entire sum could with propriety be credited back to Surplus, whence it all originally came. To most accountants, however, it appears better to continue it as a special reserve, perhaps under some such descriptive title as that proposed by Dicksee, "Accumulations of Revenue which have provided the wherewithal to Redeem Loans," or so far as accounting is concerned, it can legitimately be capitalized, and a stock dividend issued for it to the stockholders. Economically it means that by a period of prolonged abstinence the stockholders, formerly having only a half interest in the economic capital, have bought out the bondholders' interest of $50,000,000, making payment out of their accumulated profits or savings.

Where the sinking fund is invested in the bonds of the company and such bonds are canceled and disappear from the balance sheet, the final condition will be the same as that shown above.

Where no special Sinking Fund Reserve is shown in the balance sheet the final payment of the debt does not require any further alteration of the balance sheet, for the payment of bonds, either gradually or in mass, has not been charged against income, and there is no need for reëstablishing that depleted account.

Journal Entries for Sinking Fund

The journal entries involved in sinking fund transactions may be illustrated as follows: In accordance with the contract with bondholders, a corporation at the end of each year turns over $10,000 to sinking fund trustees. This is immediately invested by the trustees in 5 per cent bonds of the company, purchased at par. On the 1st of July, the coupons on these bonds are collected by the trustees and as the funds are insufficient to purchase another bond, they are put on deposit at 2 per cent interest. At the end of the year a similar donation is made to the sinking fund. Interest on bonds and on bank deposits is collected and a new purchase of bonds is made by the trustees. The entries are as follows:

Dec. 31		
Net Income	$10,000.00	
Sinking Fund Reserve		$10,000.00
Jan. 1		
Cash in Hands of Sinking Fund Trustees	10,000.00	
Cash		10,000.00
Bonds in Hands of Sinking Fund Trustees	10,000.00	
Cash in Hands of Sinking Fund Trustees		10,000.00
July 1		
Cash in Hands of Sinking Fund Trustees	250.00	
Income from Sinking and Other Reserve Funds		250.00
Dec. 31		
Cash in Hands of Sinking Fund Trustees	252.50	
Income from Sinking and Other Reserve Funds		252.50
Income from Sinking and Other Reserve Funds	502.50	
Non-operating Income		502.50
Net Income	10,502.50	
Sinking Fund Reserve		10,502.50
Cash in Hands of Sinking Fund Trustees	10,000.00	
Cash		10,000.00
Jan. 1		
Bonds in Hands of Sinking Fund Trustees	10,500.00	
Cash in Hands of Sinking Fund Trustees		10,500.00

In the above entries, for the sake of clearness, separate accounts have been established distinguishing between cash in the hands of the sinking fund trustees and the bonds in the hands of the sinking fund trustees. These might, in the balance sheet and even in the general ledger of the corporation, be included in the general term Assets in Hands of Sinking Fund Trustees, as in the case of the United States Steel Corporation, or simply under the title Sinking Fund.

Formula for Sinking Fund

The calculation of the amount required for a sinking fund is as follows: The problem being the amount payable at the end of each year, which invested at a given rate of interest (i) will be sufficient to pay off the principal (P) in n years. In this calculation the interest annually paid on the bonds is neglected, that being a regular charge against the earnings of the company, the sinking fund installment being separately handled.

A payment of $1.00 invested at the end of the first year will accumulate at compound interest until the end of the sinking fund period of n years. Its accumulated value will therefore be $(1+i)^{n-1}$, the second installment will accumulate for one less year and so on, for a series, the next to the last installment drawing interest for only one year, the last installment made at the time when the bonds mature accumulating no interest. The series then becomes:

$$(1+i)^{n-1} + (1+i)^{n-2} \ldots (1+i) + 1$$

which may be simplified to

$$\frac{(1+i)^{n}-1}{i}$$

Dividing the total amount of bonds to be retired (P) by this sum, the amount of the annual sinking fund installment is obtained, and:

$$\text{Sinking Fund Installment} = \frac{iP}{(1+i)^{n}-1}$$

In these calculations the accountant and the investor must have in mind that there is bound to be some delay in reinvestment and that the rate to be obtained is almost certain to decline through any protracted period.

It is, however, by no means necessary that the sinking fund should equal the entire principal to be retired. A provision which amounted to 80, 60, or any other considerable percentage of the funded debt would in the case of a perpetual enterprise, such as a railroad, offer security sufficient to satisfy the creditor; for if to-day the road can borrow $100,000,000, the presumption is that twenty years hence it will have no difficulty in borrowing half that sum, if it should prove necessary to refund the debt not covered by the sinking fund. Where the enterprise is not perpetual, as where it is dependent on a limited franchise, the adequacy of the sinking fund provision is more important and the failure to realize the calculated interest may be a decided injury to the bondholder.

Sinking Fund and Depreciation

The relation of the sinking fund to depreciation has led to protracted discussion, especially in connection with the legal restrictions on municipal borrowing. The English requirement is that the municipality, desiring to borrow for public service utilities must provide out of the revenue both for a sinking fund with which to retire the bonds at maturity, and also for a depreciation fund with which the plant can be replaced when worn out. But assuming that the life of the plant and the duration of the bonds are the same this leads to an exact doubling of the proper charges against revenue. Whatever good effect this may have in preventing reckless undertaking of municipal enterprises, it clearly does not lead to a correct showing of the profitableness of the undertaking. The relation between sinking fund and depreciation is better understood by accountants. Thus for instance the certificate of the public accountants attached to the balance sheet of the American Hide and Leather Company contains the following: "The appropriation out of profits for the purposes of the sinking fund is in our opinion, sufficient to take the place of provision for depreciation."

This by no means implies that depreciation does not take place when a sinking fund provides for bonds. It does not even imply that the balance sheet is in all respects correct for that represents the plant as still worth its cost value, while in reality it has greatly depreciated. If true at all, it is so only in the sense that if the showing of profits of the concern has been understated because there has been debited to Profit and Loss an item which properly does not belong in that account, the error is not increased but rather offset by the omission from the Profit and Loss account of an equal charge for depreciation. It is a case of two errors securing a correct result. But in so far as the credit to Sinking Fund Reserve appears in the balance sheet as part of the surplus while the allowance for depreciation is by the better practice clearly differentiated from proprietorship, the result is altogether misleading.

Advisability of Sinking Funds

Much discussion has taken place in the fields of both public and private finance as to the economic effects of adopting a sinking fund policy. The use of a sinking fund originated in connection with the public debt of England and when introduced, some of the enthusiasts seemed to think that they had found the magic wand by which a debt could be paid without burden to the taxpayers. On the other hand, opponents of the sinking fund method of paying debt say that a sinking fund is necessarily and, from a purely actuarial basis, extravagant as compared with a direct serial payment.[5]

While both of these extreme views are incorrect, it is of course true that the employment of a sinking fund is an indirect and somewhat cumbersome method of retiring debt. It involves in some cases the possibility of unwise investment, of misuse of funds by trustees, and the failure to obtain the expected results because of a lowering of the current rate of interest.

Investment of Sinking Fund

The sinking fund may be invested in three different ways:

1. In outside securities.
2. In bonds of the issue which is to be protected by the sinking fund.
3. In other bonds issued by the same company.

The first method is relatively unknown although the Pennsylvania Railway has at times invested part of its sinking fund in municipal securities. Investment in bonds of the issue to be retired through the sinking fund has the advantage of securing absolute safety so far as sinking fund purposes are concerned, while the rate of interest received (in

---

[5] A. D. Chandler, "Amortization," *American Economic Review,* III, p. 875.

reality a saving in interest paid) is presumably higher than could be secured in outside bonds having the maximum degree of safety. Investment in other bonds of the same company is not infrequently resorted to, perhaps as a protection against having to pay an excessive price if holders of the bonds know that the company is compelled to buy in a certain amount of a limited issue each year.

It has frequently been assumed that the protection to the outside bondholders is the same whether the sinking fund is invested in outside securities or bonds of the particular issue. This is true only in case that the other property of the corporation has not declined in value, but this is the very contingency against which the sinking fund system seeks to provide. This may be illustrated by assuming the case of two corporations each with $10,000,000 bonds and a sinking fund of half that amount. In one corporation, the sinking fund is invested in outside securities; in the other, in its own bonds. If the company then goes into bankruptcy and, for the sake of simplicity it is assumed that all other assets are worthless, the difference in the situation of the bondholders is this: Holders of $10,000,000 bonds in the first case would each receive fifty cents on the dollar while in the second case, $5,000,000 of the bonds originally issued would already have been redeemed but the persons holding 50 per cent of the issue outstanding at the time of bankruptcy would receive nothing.

Bibliographical Note

Chase, H. S.—"Governmental Sinking Funds, Serial Bonds and Depreciation Reserves," *Journal of Accountancy,* XXVI, pp. 253-68.

Dewing, A. S.—*Financial Policy of Corporations* (New York, 1920), III, pp. 125-45.

Dicksee, L. R.—*Depreciation, Reserves and Reserve Funds* (3d ed., London, 1912), pp. 57-65.

Kester, R. B.—*Accounting, Theory and Practice* (2d ed., New York, 1925), II, chap. xxvii.

Lawton, W. H.—"Treatment of Sinking Funds," *Journal of Accountancy,* XVIII, pp. 80-2.

LUDLAM, C. S.—"Treatment of Sinking Funds," *Journal of Accountancy,* XVII, pp. 165-76.

SPRAGUE, C. E.—*The Accountancy of Investment* (New York, 1914).

TURNER, S. H.—"Depreciation and Sinking Funds in Municipal Undertakings," *Economic Journal,* XIV, pp. 47-56.

VINAL, E. R.—*Mathematics for the Accountant* (3d ed., New York, 1924), pp. 75-80.

CHAPTER XVI

TRADING, MANUFACTURING, AND INCOME ACCOUNTS

Advantages of Subdividing Income Account

The profits of a year can be accurately shown without an elaborate set of books, all that is necessary being a carefully prepared annual inventory. The herdsman telling the tale of his sheep, the miser counting over his hoard, compares the figures of a preceding period and learns what has been his annual increase. The contribution which double entry bookkeeping has made to accounting science is largely that it has introduced a separate Profit and Loss account which, though it may not show the net results any more accurately, does present them in greater detail. Even the simpler forms of the Profit and Loss account exhibit such details as the gain from merchandise, the amount of expenses, the interest earned or incurred, wages, rent, and other sources of profit and lines of expense. With greater complexity of business organization there comes a demand for a more logical, or at least a more practical classification of profit and loss items.

An elementary subdivision of the Profit and Loss account is one which merely separates the items relating to the immediate trafficking in merchandise from the other items affecting proprietorship. The first grouping is ordinarily called the Trading account, while the other items would be grouped under the title Profit and Loss account. In some cases, however, the two sections both bear the title Profit and Loss account, the first part being differentiated as the trading section. By some accountants the Profit and Loss account is subjected to a more complicated subdivision. Two illustrations are given below, the first being that presented by Lisle.[1]

[1] *Accounting in Theory and Practice*, p. 57.

Lisle's Form

FORM 16

PROFIT AND LOSS ACCOUNT

1st Section—Trading Account

To Cost of goods used (including freight inward and after deducting purely trade discounts)	$100,000	By Sales (after deducting purely trade discounts)	$125,000
To Expenditure directly connected with sales or which reduces the price realized for the goods such as:			
Commission and salaries of travelers and travelers expenses	2,500		
Wages of salesmen	2,000		
Wages of porters	1,200		
Outgoing freight	600		
Cash discounts allowed on sales	1,500		
To Balance carried down being Gross Profits	17,200		
	$125,000		$125,000

2d Section—Ordinary Business Profit and Loss Account

To Fixed Charges not directly connected with sales and not varying much with the turnover such as:		By Balance brought down being Gross Profits	$ 17,200
Rents, taxes, etc.	$ 1,100	By Income not directly connected with sales such as:	
Repairs and other office expenses	1,200	Rent of stores or premises let to tenants	600
Salaries of office staff and management	3,000	Revenue from royalties	400
Depreciation	500		
To Business losses such as:			
Bad debts	200		
Defalcations	50		
To Balance carried down being Profit on Ordinary Business	12,150		
	$ 18,200		$ 18,200

3d Section—The Net Profit Account

To Expenses connected with Capital, such as:		By Balance brought down being Profit on Ordinary Business	$ 12,150
Interest on loans	$ 720	By Income connected with capital such as:	
To Balance carried down, being Net Profit	13,480	Revenue from investments	1,100
		Interest earned	150
		Cash discounts obtained which depend on the amount of capital in the business	800
	$ 14,200		$ 14,200

4th Section—The Profit and Loss Appropriation Account

To Allocation of Profit:		By Balance brought down being Net Profit	$ 13,480
Interest on capital	$ 3,000		
Profit allocated to capital	10,000		
To Profit unappropriated carried forward	480		
	$ 13,480		$ 13,480

The subdivisions in the above form are all significant although the first is, perhaps, less so than the others. In the first the comparison between the sales and the costs directly connected with the sales brings out the so-called trading profit. In the second section expenses and income connected with business operations, but not immediately pertaining to the sales, are brought into the account and the balance indicates the profits which the business as such has made. This is one of the most important facts to be brought out. It emphasizes what the concern as an economic unit has gained from carrying on the enterprise in which it was interested. It is not concerned with the method by which the enterprise was financed, which is left to the following section. It is important to know that the capital actually invested in the business enterprise has, as a result of all of its activities, made a gain of a certain amount, in the illustration $12,150. This condition is irrespective of whether the capital was furnished by the stockholders or whether part of it was borrowed. The proportion of the actual investment borrowed and the rate of interest paid for borrowed funds, of course, affects the profits to the owners of the business but does not affect the gain which has come from the use of the actual capital in the business. These two concepts, the gain which comes to the economic unit and the gain which comes to the proprietors of the enterprise are both of significance in any enterprise. The former is of particular importance in enterprises where the rates are subject to legal control such as public utilities.[2]

The third section modifies the economic gains made by items of the nature of interest. It serves to indicate whether the business suffers from being undercapitalized. The balance properly indicates the profits earned by the stockholders or proprietors during the fiscal period. The last section sometimes called the Allocation account shows what disposition has been made of the profits of the year.

Form Proposed by American Institute of Accountants

A somewhat similar arrangement, differing principally in that it provides a separate section for indicating the Federal income tax, has been suggested by the Committee on Terminology of the American Institute of Accountants. The Federal income tax section is credited with the "net profit before charging Federal income tax," and is debited with the amount of the tax. The balance representing net profit is carried to the Appropriation section. This is illustrated in the following pages.

---

[2] In the above discussion, "economic unit" relates to the aggregation of actual capital engaged in carrying on the enterprise. Thus in case of a street railway, it refers to the rails, the power plant, the cars, the necessary cash for current use and any other assets involved in operating the road. Ancillary operations are not considered. The corporation as a financial unit may have purchased bonds as an investment or speculation. Unless it is necessary to have the bonds as an incident to operating the road, the income derived from that source is not considered a gain of the economic unit. The point to be emphasized in the accounts is how much does such a plant, including of course any subsidiary assets in the form of working assets, earn as a result of its operations. Difficulty arises where a corporation is actually engaged in more than one line of activity.

FORM 17

Profit and Loss Account

Trading Section

Cost of Goods Sold	$182,000	Net Sales	$230,000
Salesmen's Salaries	7,000		
Salesmen's Commissions	230		
Salesmen's Expenses	5,000		
Freight Outward	500		
Advertising	7,000		
Packing	400		
Miscellaneous Selling Expenses	600		
Gross Profit	27,270		
	$230,000		$230,000

General Section

General and Administrative Expenses	$ 12,000	Gross Profit	$ 27,270
Bad Debts	250	Rents	600
Fire Loss	500	Sundry Profits	430
Net Operating Profit	15,550		
	$ 28,300		$ 28,300

Financial Section

Interest on Bonds	$ 3,000	Net Operating Profit	$ 15,550
Amortization of Discount on Bonds	120	Interest Earned	350
Loss on Investment	500	Income from Investment	600
Net Profit before charging Federal Income Tax	12,880		
	$ 16,500		$ 16,500

Federal Income Tax

Income Tax	$ 500	Net Profit before charging Federal Income Tax	$ 12,880
Net Profit	12,380		
	$ 12,880		$ 12,880

Appropriation

Dividends	$ 5,000	Net Profit	$ 12,380
Reserve for Contingencies	5,000		
Unappropriated Surplus	2,380		
	$ 12,380		$ 12,380

NOTE: This follows the form suggested by the Committee on Terminology in the *Journal of Accountancy,* XXXVI, p. 226, except that two earlier sections are here omitted. These are entitled the manufacturing section and the finished product section. They are reproduced on p. 362.

Report Form of Income Account

Both of the above statements are in what is called the account form, which signifies that the debits and credits are arranged in the conventional double columns. This corresponds to the account as it appears in the ledger and is occasionally used in preparing the formal published reports of corporations. Objection to presenting a statement to stockholders and the public in this form is sometimes made on the grounds that it is too technical and not easily understood by the lay reader.[3] It is, therefore, becoming increasingly common, especially in the United States, to present the exhibit of profit and loss or income in what is called the report form, in which the main facts follow one after another in a single vertical column—additions or subtractions being made at any point in order to emphasize important features. An additional merit of the report form is its much greater flexibility and the convenience with which explanatory details can easily be introduced in one or more indented columns.[4] The profit and loss statement which appears in an account form in Form 16 if presented in the report form would be as follows:

[3] *E.g.*, Paton, *Accounting*, p. 456.

[4] What is here called the report form of profit and loss statement is frequently spoken of in textbooks as a profit and loss statement in contradistinction to a profit and loss account. The phraseology is perhaps not the best as both of these forms as well as many others used in accounting are statements. Statements may, however, with propriety, be differentiated as being in an account form and in a report form respectively.

FORM 18

PROFIT AND LOSS STATEMENT

Sales		$125,000
Cost of goods used (including freight inward and after deducting purely trade discounts)	$100,000	
Expenditures directly connected with sales or which reduce the price realized for the goods such as:		
Commission and salaries of travelers and travelers' expenses	2,500	
Wages of salesmen	2,000	
Wages of porters	1,200	
Outgoing freight	600	
Cash discounts allowed on sales	1,500	107,800
Gross profits		$ 17,200
Income not directly connected with sales:		
Rent of stores or premises let to tenants	$ 600	
Revenue from royalties	400	1,000
		$ 18,200
Fixed charges not directly connected with sales and not varying much with the turnover such as:		
Rents, taxes, etc.	$ 1,100	
Repairs and other office expenses	1,200	
Salaries of office staff and management	3,000	
Depreciation	500	
Business losses such as:		
Bad debts	200	
Defalcations	50	6,050
Profit on ordinary business		$12,150
Income connected with capital such as:		
Revenue from investments	$ 1,100	
Interest earned	150	
Cash discounts obtained which depend on the amount of capital in the business	800	
	$ 2,050	
Less: Expenses connected with capital such as:		
Interest on loans	720	1,330
Net profit		$ 13,480
Allocation of profit:		
Interest on capital	$ 3,000	
Profit allocated to capital	10,000	13,000
Profit unappropriated		$ 480

Deductions from Sales

The profit and loss statement in the report form sets forth as the first item the amount received from sales. This may be modified by making such deductions as are necessary to reduce the gross sales to net sales. There is considerable disagreement as to the item to be subtracted from the net sales; three different procedures are recognized:

1. To subtract the purchase price of the goods sold or, if the goods are manufactured by the establishment, a sum representing the manufacturing cost of the goods sold. The remainder after such a subtraction is generally entitled gross trading profit.

2. To subtract from the net sales a sum which represents the cost of the goods and in addition, to use Lisle's phrase, such other expenses as are "roughly proportionate to the amount of the turnover." This would certainly include such items as salesmen's salaries and salesmen's commissions, etc. If this sum is subtracted from the net sales the remainder is ordinarily entitled net trading profit.

3. To subtract a sum representing the cost of the goods and all other expenses which have to do with the operation of the business. These latter are frequently grouped under the subheads: selling expenses and general expenses; although they may at times be divided into a larger number of subdivisions. The remainder left after such a subtraction is generally entitled net operating profit or net operating income.

Variations in Practice Illustrated

The variations in procedure may be illustrated by giving a statement reduced to the simplest terms of a concern which sells for $100, merchandise which cost $40, with selling expenses of $10, and general and administrative expenses of $15. These facts could be presented in any one of the following forms:

I[5]

Net sales	$100
Deduct—Cost of goods sold	40
Gross trading profit	$ 60
Deduct—Selling Expenses	10
Net trading profit	$50
Deduct—General and administrative expenses	15
Net operating profit	$35

[5] Finney, *Principles of Accounting*, II, chap. liii, p. 5.

II[6]

Net sales		$100
Deduct—Cost of goods sold	$40	
Selling expenses	10	50
Net trading profit		$50
Deduct—General and administrative expenses		15
Net operating profit		$35

III[7]

Net sales		$100
Deduct—Cost of goods sold		40
Gross trading profit		$60
Deduct—Selling expenses	$10	
General and administrative expenses	15	25
Net operating profit		$35

IV[8]

Net sales..	$100
Deduct—Cost of goods sold, selling expenses, and general and administrative expenses..........................	65
Net operating profit....................................	$35

It is impossible to attempt any categorical statement as to which of these methods is to be preferred. Each has its merits and each is subject to certain criticism. Gross trading profit as used in the first and third forms is a convenient figure in that it immediately compares two facts which are ordinarily easily ascertainable, namely, the price paid for merchandise and the price for which it is sold. But the difference between these two is in no sense profit as only part of the expenses are deducted from the sales. Net trading profit, as used in both the first and second forms is also a somewhat unconvincing term and there is difficulty in determining just what items are to be included in selling expenses. Commissions paid to salesmen are presumably proportionate to the amount of their sales. The salaries of salesmen are less accurately proportionate; both of these are ordi-

[6] Lisle, *Accounting in Theory and Practice*, pp. 57-8.
[7] Federal Reserve Board form; also Dickinson, *Accounting Practice and Procedure*, p. 64.
[8] U. S. Steel Corporation.

narily included in the trading section, when it is constructed in accordance with Lisle's model. But wages of bookkeepers are also to some extent, at least, "roughly proportionate" to the amount of turnover. To be sure it does not require any more service on the part of the bookkeeper to record a sale of ninety dollars than to record one of ten dollars but it does require considerably more service to record one thousand sales than to record one hundred. But the wages of bookkeepers are perhaps universally excluded from the selling expenses. The second form differs from the first only in that it fails to emphasize the gross trading profit. The third form differs from the second in that selling expenses instead of being added to the cost of goods sold is added to general and administrative expenses and in that it shows, as does the first form, a figure representing gross trading profit. The fourth form does not give figures which are in any sense misleading, but on the other hand, it fails to bring out and emphasize either the gross trading profit or the net trading profit as is done in the other forms.

Inventory Value in the Trading Account

In whatever way the Trading account is formed, it implies a combination of the cost of merchandise, the closing inventories, and sales. The introduction of the closing inventories is frequently said to be for the purpose of ascertaining the cost of the goods sold which when compared with the sales would indicate the gross trading profits. But this is only true when the inventory is taken at cost price.

Where the closing inventory is taken on any other basis than the cost price, the Trading account does not indicate trading profits. This may be illustrated in rudimentary form as follows:

Trading Account

Cost of merchandise	\$200,000	Sales	\$125,000
Gross trading profits	15,000	Inventory	90,000
	\$215,000		\$215,000

In this case, let it be assumed that the sales covered half of the merchandise purchased, but the inventory, while representing half of the purchases, is valued at market rather than cost. The Trading account apparently shows gross trading profits of $15,000. But a more correct statement of the situation would be that there was a trading profit of $25,000 due to the sale for $125,000 of goods which cost $100,000, and that coincident with this trading profit there had been a loss because goods purchased at $100,000 are now estimated to be worth only $90,000. Less clearly may objection be made to the trading profit in the above instance as $15,000, where the inventory varies from the cost price of unsold goods, not because of a change in price but because of shrinkage in the amount of goods actually on hand. If through pilfering, damage through the action of the weather, or other similar causes, the amount of goods on hand is less than the amount of purchased goods still unsold, it might still be considered that $25,000 had been made upon the sale of goods with the coincidental loss due to wastage of $10,000. But it would be less objectionable to consider that this loss in bulk was a function of the selling process and therefore might, either altogether or in part, be taken into account in calculating the trading profits.

Journal Entries for Changes in Value of Merchandise

In the above case a correct and satisfactory showing of shrinkage in value could be produced by the following journal entry:

Merchandise inventory, Dec. 31	$90,000	
Profit and loss (shrinkage on inventory)	10,000	
Trading account (unsold goods at cost)		$100,000

In case the merchandise on hand had increased in value, it would probably be considered better not to carry the profit representing such appreciation in value to the Profit and Loss account but to credit an account entitled, perhaps Reserve for Appreciation of Inventory.

The journal entry in the case described would therefore be:

Merchandise inventory, Dec. 31	$110,000	
Trading account (unsold goods at cost)		$100,000
Reserve for appreciation of inventory		10,000

If desired, the fact that appreciation is taken into consideration could be still further emphasized by dividing the item in the balance sheet showing the value of the merchandise inventory so as to show:

Merchandise inventory at cost	$ 90,000	
Appreciation	10,000	$100,000

This treatment is sometimes described as using a different basis for the inventory in the balance sheet, from that used in the Trading account. More strictly it should be described as taking the inventory, which will appear in the balance sheet at present value, making adjustment through some supplementary account, and ascertaining the trading profit by subtracting from sales the actual cost of the goods sold, rather than the difference between cost of purchases and closing inventory value.[9]

Non-Operating Income

The difference between the four methods described above consists merely in the number of steps to be taken before reaching the final result. Certain subtractions are to be made from the net sales. These are: the price paid for the goods, the costs directly connected with selling, and the other expenses of the business. Whether these items are subtracted in a series or grouped in various arrangements of subtotals, they are all sooner or later subtracted and all lead to the same figure. This represents the profits which the business as an economic unit has made irrespective of expenses to which the organization may have been put in order to obtain the neces-

[9] Kester, *Accounting, Theory and Practice*, 2d ed., II, pp. 153-6.

sary funds and of income which may have been derived from the investment of surplus funds not utilized in the business as such. Some slight variation is also found in the arrangement after the obtaining of the net operating income. Two variations may be noted:

1. To the net operating income is added other income received (generally representing the yield from capital invested outside of the business proper) giving a figure often called gross income. From the gross income is subtracted payment of interest and similar items, the remainder being entitled net income or profits.

2. Instead of adding other income and subtracting interest payments, these two items are compared and the net result is, as the case may be, either added to or subtracted from the net operating income. This, of course, gives the same result for net income or profit and differs from the preceding method only in that there is no figure indicating what is called gross income in the previous arrangement.

The first method is that called for by the Interstate Commerce Commission. The second form is frequently found in published reports, as for instance, in that of the Studebaker Corporation.[10]

Interstate Commerce Commission's Form

The profit and loss statements of public utilities are similar in essential characteristics to those of manufacturing and trading concerns but differ somewhat in form because of differences in the nature of the business. In this country the forms prescribed by the Interstate Commerce Commission are in general use and have been adopted with slight modifications by many of the state commissions. An illustration of the form prescribed by the Commission is shown on the following pages:

---

[10] A similar treatment is followed by Finney, *Principles of Accounting,* I, chap. iii, p. 4; Bentley, *Journal of Accountancy,* XIV, p. 175.

FORM 19

Income Account (*Abridged*)

Operating Income:		
Railway operating revenues	$102,358,892.95	
Railway operating expenses	61,713,161.02	
Net revenue from railway operations		$40,645,731.93
Railway tax accruals	$4,449,290.83	
Uncollectible railway revenues	9,547.58	4,458,838.41
Total operating income		$36,186,893.52
Nonoperating Income:		
Rent	$1,300,396.92	
Dividend income	10,554.05	
Income from funded securities	39,520.88	
Income from unfunded securities	1,029,259.92	
Income from sinking fund	2,900.10	
Miscellaneous income	11,519.97	
Total nonoperating income		2,394,151.84
Gross income		$38,581,045.36
Deductions from Gross Income:		
Rents	$1,585,311.43	
Miscellaneous tax accruals	13,165.26	
Separately operated properties—Loss	41,887.85	
Interest on funded debt	7,038,490.72	
Amortization of discount on funded debt	55,163.52	
Miscellaneous income charges	756.60	
Total deductions from gross income		8,734,775.38
Net income		$29,846,269.98
Disposition of Net Income:		
Income applied to sinking funds	$1,817,679.41	
Dividend appropriations of income	8,867,128.00	
Income appropriated for investment in physical property	4,431,359.81	
Fund for accrued taxes—not yet due	2,400,000.00	
Miscellaneous appropriations of income	6,000,000.00	
Total appropriations		23,516,167.22
Income balance transferred to credit of Profit and Loss		$ 6,330,102.76

PROFIT AND LOSS ACCOUNT

CREDITS:		
Credit balance at beginning of fiscal period		$ 97,879,653.81
Credit balance transferred from income		6,330,102.76
Profit on road and equipment sold		840,298.89
Delayed income debits		
Unrefundable overcharges		
Donations		16,690.00
Miscellaneous credits		753,423.00
Total credits		$105,820,168.46
DEBITS:		
Debit balances at beginning of fiscal period		
Debit balances transferred from income...		
Surplus applied to sinking and other reserve funds		
Dividend appropriations of surplus		
Surplus appropriated for investment in physical property		
Stock discount extinguished through surplus		
Debt discount extinguished through surplus		
Miscellaneous appropriations of surplus ..		
Loss on retired road and equipment	$719,198.00	
Delayed income debits..................		
Miscellaneous debits	12,694.00	
Total debits		731,892.00
Balance carried to balance sheet......		$105,088,276.46

This statement is prepared in report form and the first part of it is called the Income account, Profit and Loss account being restricted to that part of the statement exhibiting the distribution and appropriation of net profits and various adjustments of profits not strictly pertaining to the operations of the current year, or of so unusual a character as not properly to represent normal conditions.

Form Recommended by Sir Arthur Lowes Dickinson

A simple form, suitable for general application, is that suggested by Sir Arthur Lowes Dickinson at the Congress of Accountants held at St. Louis in 1904. The form is exhibited on the following page.

FORM 20

Gross Earnings (whether sales of products, transportation earnings, professional earnings, etc.)		$........
Deduct—Cost of Manufacture or Operation:		
(*a*) Manufacture (for a manufacturing concern):		
Labor	$........	
Material	....	
General Manufacturing Expenses....	....	
(*b*) Cost of Operation (for concerns not manufacturing)		
(Under suitable headings according to the nature of the business)	$........	$........
Gross Profits		$........
Other Earnings		....
Deduct—		
Expenses of sale (manufacturing business only)	$........	
Expenses of management (if distinct from operation)	....	
		$........
Net Profits from Operation		$........
Deduct—		
Interest on Bonds	$........	
Other Fixed Charges	....	
		$........
Surplus for year		$........
Extraordinary Profits (detailed)		....
Surplus brought forward from preceding year...		....
		$........
Deduct—		
Extraordinary charges not applicable to the operations of the year	$........	
Interest and Dividends on Stocks	....	
		$........
Surplus carried forward		$........

The Manufacturing Account

The statements whether in account or report form given above on pages 346-53 relate to a trading concern. In these one of the most significant items is the cost of the goods sold. If, however, the concern manufactures the goods which it sells it is customary to introduce into the account form of the profit and loss statement one or more preliminary sections exhibiting the cost of manufacturing and furnishing a net figure of manufacturing cost analogous to the purchases of a trading concern. Assuming for simplicity of illustration that the manufactured goods are sold as soon as completed, this figure would correspond to the cost of goods sold appearing in the Trading account. Thus, in the form used by Lisle, there would come before the Trading account a Manufacturing account in substantially the following form:

FORM 21

Manufacturing Account

Raw material		Manufacturing cost carried to Trading account	$100.000
Inventory, Jan. 1	$ 9,000		
Purchases	70,000		
	$ 79,000		
Less inventory, Dec. 31	12,000		
	$ 67,000		
Wages	28,000		
Rent and taxes, factory	3,600		
Depreciation, machinery	800		
Miscellaneous	600		
	$100,000		$100,000

NOTE: Lisle, *Accounting in Theory and Practice*, pp. 62-3.

Somewhat similarly the Committee on Terminology [11] recommends that in the case of a manufacturing concern the Trading account presented on page 349 be preceded by two sections:

[11] *Journal of Accountancy*, XXXVI, p. 226.

FORM 22

Manufacturing Section

Inventory of raw material and work in process, Jan. 1	$ 39,200	Raw material and work in process:	
Raw material purchases	118,000	Inventory, Dec. 31	$ 30,000
Inward transportation	800	Sales of by-products	800
Productive labor	48,400	Cost of production	183,200
Manufacturing overhead (including depreciation)	7,600		
	$214,000		$214,000

Finished Product Section

Cost of production	$183,200	Inventory of finished products, Dec. 31	$ 25,000
Inventory of finished products, Jan. 1	20,000	Balance—Cost of goods sold	182,000
Storeroom expenses	3,800		
	$207,000		$207,000

Federal Trade Commission's Form

Where the income statement is presented in report form, the items entering into the cost of manufacture are sometimes set forth in detail in the income statement itself. Where there are many items entering into the cost, this makes a somewhat confused statement. Another treatment is to place in the income statement only the net figure for the cost of manufactured goods showing the details in a subsequent exhibit. This is illustrated in the forms given below which have the approval of the Federal Trade Commission.[12]

Whichever form of statement is used, two points should be made clear. These are the cost of goods manufactured during the year and the cost of the goods sold. It is important to express each of these clearly as each is a fact of importance in the administration of the business and one which lends itself to statistical treatment.

[12] *Fundamentals of a Cost System for Manufacturers.*

FORM 23

Profit and Loss Statement for Month Ended January 31, 1916

Gross Sales		$13,485.60
Sales Returns	$ 865.20	
Sales Allowances	50.00	
Outbound Freight	120.00	1,035.20
Net Sales		$12,450.40
Cost of Sales	$ 8,204.41	
Reserve for Overhead	189.11	8,393.52
Gross Profit		$ 4,056.88
Shipping Expense	$ 237.19	
Selling Expense	1,120,53	
General Expense	1,180.67	
Discount on Sales	95.00	
Bad Debts	70.00	2,703.39
Net Earnings		$ 1,353.49
Discount on Purchases		165.40
Net Profit		$ 1,518.89

Statement of Factory Operations for Month Ended January 31, 1916

Material:		
Inventory at First of Month	$ 3,000.00	
Purchases	7,800.00	
Freight and Express In	284.32	
Total	$11,084.32	
Less Inventory at End of Month	4,600.00	
Direct Material Used		$ 6,484.32
Direct Labor		4,444.67
Factory Overhead, per detail below:		
Department A	$ 1,207.34	
Department B	1,311.96	
Department C	662.70	
Total Factory Overhead		3,182.00
Total Material, Labor, and Overhead		$14,110.99
Add Inventory at First of Month:		
Work in Process	$ 2,000.00	
Finished Goods	3,754.00	5,754.00
		$19,864.99
Less Inventory **at End of Month:**		
Work in Process	$ 4,024.86	
Finished Goods	7,635.72	11,660.58
Cost of Sales, per Profit and Loss Statement		$ 8,204.41

Manufacturing Profit

In connection with the Manufacturing account there is one point of some considerable technical significance upon which accountants do not, altogether, agree. This turns on the question as to the value at which manufactured goods are to be carried down to the trading section. Where these sections are kept separately two distinct views are presented; the first is that goods should be valued at the net manufacturing cost; the other is that instead of being valued at the actual cost these would be carried down to the trading account at a figure which represents a fair market price. That is the figure which would have been paid had the goods been bought from some other manufacturer instead of being produced within the establishment. If the latter procedure is adopted the accounts in condensed form would appear as follows:

Manufacturing Account

Costs	$100,000	Trading account	$110,000
Manufacturing profits	10,000		
	$110,000		$110,090

Trading Account

Merchandise at trade price	$110,000	Sales	$125,000
Expenses	7,800		
Trading profits	7,200		
	$125,000		$125,000

This exhibits manufacturing profit of $10,000 and trading profit of $7,200 while if the merchandise had been brought down at the cost of manufacturing there would be shown only a single item of profit of $17,200. The advantage of distinguishing between the two elements of profit is indisputable. Where the concern purchases part and manufactures part of the merchandise which it sells, this information is of especial importance, as it aids in determining the policy to be followed in an expanding business. The management will in this way be directed as to whether it is desirable to erect a new factory building to supply the growing market or whether the additional supply would better be purchased from other manufacturers. It brings clearly to light the relative efficiency of the different branches of the business. It may be that the selling organization is so well ordered that the profits are largely attributable to that department. In this case additional supply might well be secured from other manufacturers but the reverse might be true, the real success of the enterprise being due to the skill of the factory manager and foremen.

Accounting for Unrealized Manufacturing Profit

A difficulty arises when the manufactured goods are not all sold during the year in which they are produced. Wherever the amount of manufacturing profits included in the closing inventory exceeds the amount included in the opening inventory the result is a showing of unrealized profit. This may be illustrated by taking the illustration already used, but assuming that only four-fifths of the manufactured goods were sold during the year. Where manufactured goods are brought down at trade price the accounts would show:

Manufacturing Account

Costs	$100,000	Carried down to Trading account	$110,000
Manufacturing profit	10,000		
	$110,000		$110,000

Trading Account

Merchandise at trade price	$110,000	Sales	$100,000
Expenses	7,800	Inventory at trade price	22,000
Trading profit	4,200		
	$122,000		$122,000

Where the manufactured goods are brought down at cost the acccunts would show:

Manufacturing Account

Costs	$100,000	Carried down to Trading account	$100,000
	$100,000		$100,000

Trading Account

Merchandise at cost	$100,000	Sales	$100,000
Expenses	7,800	Inventory at cost	20,000
Trading profit	12,200		
	$120,000		$120,000

By the first procedure the Profit and Loss account would be credited with $10,000 manufacturing profits and with $4,200 trading profits, a total of $14,200 instead of $12,200 shown by the second method. The difference is of course due to having marked up the unsold goods from $20,000 to $22,000.

The problem here is the same one that arises when inventorying any merchandise, namely: Shall stock on hand be taken at cost or at market price? As has been shown in Chapter III, the taking of a higher market price is generally condemned as opening the doors to imaginary profits. The criticism applies to the taking of an assumed manufacturing profit as well as to the profit taken on still unsold merchandise purchased. But there is a real advantage in showing the manufacturing as distinct from the trading profits, in that it gives information which serves as a guide for future management. And the objection to showing the unrealized profit may not be conclusive, for it is possible to put the profits thus shown into a special reserve, thus removing them from the sum available for dividends and lessening the danger of overvaluation. As has been shown, valuation at the present market price is in reality the logical course in accounting, but in ordinary cases logical consistency is sacrificed as a practical expedient to prevent overvaluation. In treating the Manufacturing account, the real advantage of distinguishing the part of the profits derived from manufacturing is so great as to lead many accountants to return to the logical scheme of valuation, elsewhere abandoned from motives of conservative prudence. This is recommended by both Dicksee [13] and the *Encyclopædia of Accounting.*[14] It is a case where advantages are to be weighed against dangers, with the additional complication of logical principles pulling against consistency of treatment.

---

[13] *Auditing,* 13th ed., p. 261.
[14] V, p. 4.

CHAPTER XVII

PROBLEMS OF THE INCOME ACCOUNT

Discounts on Sales: Conventional Treatment

In addition to the divergent practices in regard to the general arrangement of the profit and loss statement there are several matters of some theoretical importance in regard to the proper handling of individual items. The most important of these are: discounts on sales, discounts on purchases, interest, insurance, taxes, and depreciation. The conventional way of handling discounts on sales has been to record the sale at its full invoice value, making no record at the time of discounts offered for early payment, the customer's account being charged for the full amount of the invoice. If the customer takes advantage of the offered discount the journal entry at the time of payment would be as follows:

Cash	$98.00	
Discount on Sales	2.00	
Accounts Receivable		$100.00

If the customer does not avail himself of the discount, no record of the fact appears in the accounts. According to this procedure only those discounts which have been taken are recorded in the books; those which were offered but of which the customer did not avail himself are altogether left out of account. A more recent treatment which is discussed later places emphasis not upon the discounts taken but upon those offered and not taken.

Location of Discounts in the Income Statement

At the end of the year the account Discounts on Sales will show a number of entries recording all of the discounts availed of by the customers. In closing the books at the end of the fiscal period, the balance standing to the debit of Discount on Sales has been treated in three different ways:

1. As a subtraction from gross sales before obtaining net sales;

2. As an operating expense; and

3. As a charge against income, ordinarily in the same section with interest, appearing as a reduction of operating profits.

The reason for each of these three methods is as follows:

1. The subtraction of discounts allowed from gross sales is a simple recognition that the seller received only the reduced sum. If two sales are made, one over the counter for cash and another on account to a customer who avails himself of the discount, it seems misleading to book the transactions in a manner which will show a different price for the two transactions.

2. Discount when recorded as an operating expense is regarded by some as analogous to advertising and other selling expenses which are considered necessary inducements to secure sales. By others it is looked upon as an expense incurred in order to avoid the increasing likelihood of bad debts arising when the term of credit is extended. If all goods were sold say on sixty days, there would be a certain percentage of the sales (a percentage which could perhaps be rather definitely calculated as a result of statistical records), which would not be paid. It is proper therefore to make a regular charge to Profit and Loss crediting Allowance for Doubtful Accounts. If in any case a customer were induced to pay cash for the goods when he receives them, by offering him a discount from the regular price, it is clear that the risk of loss is entirely obviated and to that extent, the discount allowed is an offset to the charge necessary to provide for bad debts. The provision for bad debts is generally made by charging the amount to operating expenses.

A still greater refinement is at times attempted by those who argue that the discount allowed includes both interest and offset to bad debts. The rate is obviously much higher than the rate ordinarily paid on loans. Some attempt, therefore, to divide discounts on sales into these two elements with an appropriate charge for each part. The division of discount on purchases is somewhat more difficult. While the discount represents an insurance against risk to the creditor, that can hardly hold on the books of the debtor and if he pays more than the net price, it is presumably a premium which he pays for the use of capital and analogous to interest.

3. Discount when recorded as a charge against income, that is, as a deduction from operating profits, is looked upon as being very similar to interest payments. The merchant, needing funds, has presumably the alternative of either borrowing from his bank (in which case he would of course pay interest) or of inducing his customers to make early payments in which case a discount would be granted. In the minds of many accountants these seem closely analogous. It is convenient to have interest expenses appear as offsets for interest gains, and, in so far as discount on sales resembles interest, there is reason for treating it as a deduction from income.

Discounts on Purchases

Discounts upon purchases are ordinarily considered the converse of discounts on sales. Thus, if discount on sales is an operating expense, one would expect to find discount on purchases appearing as part of the income from operations. Where discount on sales is treated as a charge against income, discount on purchases would seem to be an item of income to be added to operating income. And where discount on sales is subtracted from gross sales, it would seem logical to subtract discount on purchases from purchases. While this comparable treatment of the two items is followed by many accountants, this is not always the case. Some, as for instance Lisle in the statement printed above, treat discount on sales as one of the selling expenses but show discount on purchases as an element of non-operating income, analogous to interest. Those who treat the two forms of discount in dissimilar fashion explain their apparently inconsistent action on the ground that the taking of the discount upon the sale is an action beyond the control of the seller while the availing himself of discount on purchases is a matter within his own control. This argument though frequently advanced is not altogether convincing. The divergent practice in handling discounts may also be explained by the conservative tendency of showing unrealized losses while omitting profits which have not yet been realized. If the discount on purchases is not shown as a deduction from purchase price, there is apt to result an overvaluation of the inventory and a showing of unrealized profit; but it makes little difference whether the discounts on sales are shown as a reduction of earnings or as an expense of the business.

Discounts Not Taken

In the more recent method of handling discounts referred to above, emphasis is placed on the cases where the customer has not taken the discount instead of those where he has done so. This treatment is more scientific and significant but has not as yet been generally adopted in accounting practice. In the conventional treatment the sale is looked upon as normally being at the invoice price, the discount representing an exceptional reduction or an expense of the business. The other treatment looks upon the net cash price as representing the normal sale price and all sales and purchases appear at net figures. Where the customer fails to take advantage of the discount and pays more than the net cash price, the difference is treated as an element of income in addition to profit on sales. Of course in the customer's account the gross figure must appear, as that is the amount stated in bills rendered. But this can be adjusted by having the offset account, Discounts Offered, showing the total reductions which would be made if all customers took advantage of discounts offered. When the customer pays promptly for his purchases and therefore secures a discount, no entry is made which in any way affects sales or profits; but when he fails to take advantage of the discount and pays a price higher than that which was reckoned in booking sales, the additional sum thus paid is put in the same section of the Profit and Loss statement as interest. The reverse is true when the merchant pays an amount greater than that charged to purchases because he has failed to avail himself of the discount offered.

Journal Entries for Discounts Offered

Where this treatment is used, the journal entries where goods are sold with 2 per cent discount if paid within ten days, might be as follows at the time of sale:

Accounts Receivable	$1,000	
Sales		$980
Discounts Offered		20

If the customer takes advantage of the discount offered, the journal entries at the time of payment would be:

Cash	$980	
Discounts Offered	20	
Accounts Receivable		$1,000

If the customer fails to take advantage of the discount, the entries at the time of payment would be:

Cash	$1,000	
Accounts Receivable		$1,000
Discounts Offered	20	
Discounts on Sales Not Taken		20

Corresponding journal entries would be made when the discount relates to purchases rather than to sales.[1]

Interest in the Income Statement

A rather fundamental difficulty arises in regard to the treatment of interest in accounts. It turns upon the question as to whether interest is one of the expenses of the business or virtually a share in the profits (or at least a share of the income) allocated to creditors. This is of particular significance in the case of a manufacturer, for if interest is an operating expense it enters into the cost of goods manufactured and in so far as manufactured goods are not sold it results in an increase in the value of inventories rather than

[1] For a thorough discussion of this subject see Jackson, "Neglected Commercial Discounts," *Journal of Accountancy,* XXX, p. 321.

a charge in the Profit and Loss statement. Discussion on this point has been almost interminable and has been participated in by economists and accountants alike. There is hardly opportunity here to enter fully into this discussion. The view that interest is not a part of operating expenses has been strongly argued by Sir Arthur Lowes Dickinson,[2] the opposite view is presented by C. H. Scovell,[3] and by J. O. McKinsey,[4] who includes all financial expenses in operating expenses.

Insurance and Taxes

The treatment of insurance is also a matter of disagreement. It is sometimes treated as an operating expense, sometimes as a deduction from income. The same divergence is found in regard to the treatment of taxes, but the treating of taxes as an operating expense is becoming increasingly common and it has the support of the Supreme Court.[5] The Interstate Commerce Commission provides for a still different booking treating taxes as a deduction from revenue, as is shown in the income statement printed above. In this form there is an intermediate category introduced—net revenue from operations. From this, taxes and uncollectible revenues are subtracted to obtain what is called Railway Operating Income. The distinction here made between revenue and income is not a common one, although each of these terms is used with rather widely divergent connotation. Some accountants make a discrimination on this basis, charging general taxes as an operating expense and considering income taxes as a deduction from net income.[6] According to this view the government is in a sense looked upon as one of the proprietors of the enterprise entitled to a share of the profits but this distinction is not made by the Interstate Commerce

---

[2] "The Fallacy of Including Interest and Rent as Part of Manufacturing Cost," *Journal of Accountancy,* XII, p. 588.

[3] *Interest as a Cost,* N. Y., 1924.

[4] *Managerial Accounting,* p. 199.

[5] Willcox *v.* Consolidated Gas Co., 212 U.S. 51 (1909).

[6] Thus, Kester, *Accounting, Theory and Practice,* 2d ed., II, p. 107, and Paton, *Accounting,* p. 465.

Commission and some accountants treat all taxes as a deduction from income.[7]

It is impossible to say that any one of these views is absolute and exclusive. Perhaps even the system of taxation may influence the decision as to the proper treatment of taxes in accounts. A strong argument can be made in favor of the view that taxes are really a part of profits and not a deduction from earnings to be made before determining profits. In so far as the stockholder is concerned it turns on two facts: whether the taxation of the road exempts the stockholders from other taxation; and whether the capitalist would escape taxation on other investments. If the stockholder has his dividends lessened by the taxes paid, but in all probability would pay no taxes were his funds invested, say, in bonds or mortgages, the taxes are, from his point of view, in no sense a distribution of profits. But where there is an income tax uniformly enforced, and the payment of taxes by the road works merely as a stoppage of that part of the income, it is not illogical to consider the tax as a distribution of part of the net profits derived from operating the road.

Depreciation in the Income Statement

Of much greater importance is the treatment of depreciation. In a preceding chapter it was shown that depreciation, despite conflicting usage and authority, is a charge which should invariably be made. Here the question is as to the section of the Profit and Loss account—using the title in its broadest sense—in which depreciation should appear. Almost all possible arrangements are found. There is probably a growing tendency to subtract depreciation from gross earnings making it prior to determination of net earnings. This may either be by actually including it in operating expenses as required by the Interstate Commerce Commission or by showing it as a separate item coördinate to operating expenses, as it appears in the statements of the United States Steel Corporation. In other cases it is grouped with interest

[7] *E.g.*, Esquerré, *Applied Theory of Accounts*, p. 436.

and deducted from net earnings in order to obtain net income as in the statement of the American Smelting and Refining Company. In still other cases the deduction is made from what would ordinarily be called profits as by the Republic Iron and Steel Company. Depreciation charges are thus variously regarded, as partaking of the nature of expenses, of a deduction from operating income, and of profits reserved or placed in surplus.

Those who have followed the argument of this treatise will agree that it is a radical error to treat depreciation as anything else than a deduction to be made before profits are ascertained, and that, allowing for variations in the use of terms, it must inexorably appear in the Income account before the balance called net income is reached.

The strong position taken by the Interstate Commerce Commission is theoretically correct, for depreciation is really an expense. In the formal statements of manufacturing concerns depreciation of the plant should appear in the Manufacturing account, the depreciation of office and store equipment in the Trading account rather than among the fixed charges as a deduction from net earnings.

Even to treat depreciation as analogous to interest charges, though that is a great improvement over regarding it as an optional disposition of profits, is illogical. Depreciation represents an expense not only preceding profit to the stockholders as such, but prior also to the earnings on the invested capital as a whole, whether that capital is represented by bonds or stock. Whether a road costing $100,000,000 is financed by issuing $100,000,000 stock, or by issuing only half that sum in stock and an equal amount in bonds, the invested capital (using capital in the economic, but not in the accounting, sense) is the same, and the earnings of that investment should appear the same in the Income account. No change of form of capitalization affects these earnings. Interest charges may increase, but the earnings *ceteris paribus* remain unchanged. But not so with depreciation. A smaller charge shows indeed larger apparent earnings, but such a showing is false and deceptive. Depreciation, therefore,

FORM 24

BETHLEHEM STEEL CORPORATION

Comparative Income Account

YEARS ENDED DECEMBER 31, 1923 AND 1922

	1923 *	1922 †	Increase or Decrease	
Gross Sales and Earnings	$275,213,422.65	$131,866,111.39	$143,347,311.26	*Inc.*
Less — Manufacturing cost, administrative, selling and general expense, and taxes..	239,115,639.82	114,957,170.61	124,158,469.21	*Inc.*
NET OPERATING INCOME	$ 36,097,782.83	$ 16,908,940.78	$ 19,188,842.05	*Inc.*
Interest, dividends and other miscellaneous income	1,275,445.17	2,884,771.92	1,609,326.75	*Dec.*
TOTAL INCOME	$ 37,373,228.00	$ 19,793,712.70	$ 17,579,515.30	*Inc.*
Less—Interest charges, including proportion of discount on, and expense of, bond and note issues	12,322,997.53	8,689,193.32	3,633,804.21	*Inc.*
BALANCE	$ 25,050,230.47	$ 11,104,519.38	$ 13,945,711.09	*Inc.*
Provision for depreciation, obsolescence and depletion	10,676,078.25	6,499,188.84	4,176,889.41	*Inc.*
NET INCOME FOR THE YEAR	$ 14,374,152.22	$ 4,605,330.54	$ 9,768,821.68	*Inc.*

* Includes the results of the operations of the properties acquired from Cambria Steel Company and Midvale Steel and Ordnance Company after March 30, 1923.

† Includes the results of the operations of the properties acquired from Lackawanna Steel Company after October 10, 1922.

is not logically to be treated as coördinate with interest charges.

It is even more erroneous to treat the interest charges as superior to depreciation. Unquestionably there is an insistence about interest charges which appeals to the directors in a way in which a charge erroneously called a "mere bookkeeping entry" is not regarded. But the compulsion to make a payment has nothing to say regarding the position of the charge in the Income account. Needed repairs may, perhaps, be deferred for years, while the payment of a collateral note is imperative and unavoidable. But the inclusion of repairs among expenses is never even questioned, while the payment of a note has no place whatever in the Income account, does not in the least affect the determination of profits. A sound

FORM 25

FORM RECOMMENDED BY THE FEDERAL RESERVE BOARD

Comparative statement of profit and loss for three years ending . . 19 .

	Year ending—		
	19—	19—	19—
Gross sales	$......	$......	$......
Less outward freight, allowances, and returns	......	......	......
Net sales	......	......	......
Inventory beginning of year	......	......	......
Purchases, net	......	......	......
	......	......	......
Less inventory end of year	......	......	......
Cost of sales	......	......	......
Gross profit on sales	......	......	......
Selling expenses (itemized to correspond with ledger accounts kept)	......	......	......
Total selling expense	......	......	......
General expenses (itemized to correspond with ledger accounts kept)	......	......	......
Total general expense	......	......	......
Administrative expenses (itemized to correspond with ledger accounts kept)	......	......	......
Total administrative expense	......	......	......
Total expenses	......	......	......
Net profit on sales	......	......	......
Other income:			
Income from investments	......	......	......
Interest on notes receivable, etc.	......	......	......
Gross income	......	......	......
Deductions from income:			
Interest on bonded debt	......	......	......
Interest on notes payable	......	......	......
Total deductions	......	......	......
Net income—profit and loss	......	......	......
Add special credits to profit and loss	......	......	......
Deduct special charges to profit and loss	......	......	......
Profit and loss for period	......	......	......
Surplus beginning of period	......	......	......
	......	......	......
Dividends paid	......	......	......
	......	......	......
Surplus ending of period	......	......	......
	......	......	......

FORM 26

GENERAL MOTORS CORPORATION AND SUBSIDIARY COMPANIES

Income Account

	Year Ended Dec. 31, 1922	Year Ended Dec. 31, 1921
Net earnings for year before deducting interest, but after all expenses of manufacturing (including maintenance), selling and administration, as well as ordinary taxes, insurance, depreciation ($13,584,788.95 in 1922; $6,750,674.54 in 1921) of plant and equipment	$ 66,781,613.52	$ 13,246,523.30
Less: Provision for employes' bonus.....	$ 1,341,997.52	———
Provision for employes' savings and investment fund	1,477,216.28	$ 2,174,080.00
Interest on notes and accounts payable	1,351,155.40	5,281,084.67
	$ 4,170,369.20	$ 7,455,164.67
	$ 62,611,244.32	$ 5,791,358.63
Less: Write-down of inventories to cost or market, whichever is lower (in 1922 carried direct to operations in accordance with usual practice)	———	$ 16,603,073.25
Employes' housing development....	———	5,600.00
Provision for refunds due dealers and distributors on account of price reduction effective January 1, 1922	———	2,441,376.07
Adjustments and losses in excess of reserve created at the close of previous years	$ 4,553,796.10	11,421,102.78
	$ 4,553,796.10	$ 30,471,152.10
	$ 58,057,448.22	*$24,679,793.47**
Less: Provision for Federal taxes and extraordinary expenses	6,250,000.00	———
	$ 51,807,448.22	*$24,679,793.47**
Less: Special reserve established December 31, 1921, to cover anticipated losses and unforeseen contingencies	———	14,000,000.00
	$ 51,807,448.22	*$38,679,793.47**
General Motors Corporation proportion thereof	$ 51,496,135.65	*$38,680,770.05**
Debenture dividends at rate of 7%	$ 1,860,936.41	$ 1,807,490.09
Debenture dividends at rate of 6%	3,597,570.05	3,531,515.50
Preferred dividends at rate of 6%	970,721.50	971,004.00
	$ 6,429,227.96	$ 6,310,009.59
Amount earned on Common stock	$ 45,066,907.69	*$44,990,779.64**

* Deficit.

system of accounting will therefore not make depreciation subsequent to fixed charges merely because of the imperative nature of the latter payments.

FORM 27

PACKARD MOTOR CAR COMPANY

AND SUBSIDIARY COMPANIES

Comparative Income Account

	Year Ending August 31, 1924		Year Ending August 31, 1923	
Factory Sales:				
Carriages, Service Parts, Marine and Aviation Engines..		$46,003,679.26		$55,670,464.51
Deduct—Cost of Sales		39,463,110.43		44,446,930.78
Gross Profit		$ 6,540,568.83		$11,223,533.73
Add—Other Income:				
Discount on Purchases	$180,789.03		$ 81,464.73	
Rentals	60,954.55		59,887.78	
Interest Earned ...	546,859.73		534,621.47	
Discount on Preferred Stock Purchased for Retirement	134,800.61		—	
Miscellaneous	91,709.68	1,015,113.60	181,385.59	857,359.57
		$ 7,555,682.43		$12,080,893.30
Total Gross Profit and Income:				
Deduct—Selling, General and Administration Expenses...		2,636,937.10		2,433,374.62
Profit before deducting interest and financial charges		$ 4,918,745.33		$ 9,647,518.68
Deduct:				
Interest	$ 11,177.68		$ 424,847.59	
Proportion of bond discount and expense	—		889,022.43	
Provision for Federal income tax	590,699.79		648,715.08	
Provision for Contingencies	912,803.21	1,514,680.68	2,000,000.00	3,962,585.10
Profit from Factory Operations		$ 3,404,064.65		$ 5,684,933.58
Profit from Operation of Branches and Subsidiary Companies ...		1,401,109.89		1,396,945.02
Net Profit for the Year		$ 4,805,174.54		$ 7,081,878.60

Finally placing depreciation charges after net profits is not only incorrect in theory, but tends to the vicious policy of making the amount of depreciation depend on the amount of profits and of omitting it altogether when there are no net profits against which it may be charged.

In the advertisements of corporation bonds, statements are frequently made leading to a sum which is denominated, "Amount Available for Interest, Depreciation and Divi-

FORM 28

SEARS, ROEBUCK AND CO.

Consolidated Income Account

YEAR ENDING DECEMBER 31, 1924

Gross Sales	$222,174,743.75		
Less Returns, Allowances, Discounts, etc.	22,628,881.47		
Net Sales		$199,545,862.28	
Sales by Factories and Other Income		6,884,665.14	$206,430,527.42
Less:			
Purchases, Including Difference in Inventories, Wages, General and Selling Expense, Advertising and all Administrative Charges.......		$183,517,333.69	
Repairs on Plant and Equipment	$ 848,912.60		
Depreciation on Plant.	1,379,157.39	2,228,069.99	185,745,403.68
Net Profit from Operations			$ 20,685,123.74
Deduct:			
Reserve for Taxes ...		$ 3,158,530.22	
Payment of Company's Contribution to Trustees of Employees' Savings and Profit Sharing Pension Fund for Year Ending December 31, 1924....		3,172,196.45	6,330,726.67
Net Income for Year....			$ 14,354,397.07

dends." This statement while not untruthful is highly objectionable as it groups together two dissimilar items and exhibits neither the earnings nor the profits of the enterprise.

Variations in Purpose of the Income Statement

There is a fundamental lack of agreement as to what it is that the profit and loss statement is designed to show. Does its balance represent the change in the amount of proprietorship which has taken place during the fiscal period? This would mean that just to the extent that the net assets at the end of the year exceed the net assets at the beginning of the year, the difference is adjusted through the balance of profit and loss. This to some extent corresponds with the definitions of profits occasionally given by economists as by Alfred Marshall.[8]

[8] See above, p. 242.

From another point of view, the legalistic, profits are apt to be limited to the sum which a corporation may legally or perhaps even advisably distribute as dividend. The distinction is not always clearly made and much confusion arises as to the relationship of profits and profits available for dividends. It is not always clear which of these is meant or which it is that should be exhibited in the profit and loss statement. A still further refinement is attempted corresponding to the definitions of the economist. The net increase of wealth accruing to the proprietor is analyzed so as to indicate how much of it represents interest upon his capital investment and how much of it profit in the more restricted economic sense. Thus the net increment in wealth is to be reduced by excluding extraneous additions such as increment in the value of land which is not connected with the operations of the business as such, and also by subtracting interest which is looked upon as a return upon the capital rather than the result of business operation.

In discussing the variations in practice one ruling principle is to be kept constantly in mind. The form of the profit and loss statement should be adapted to the needs of the individual establishment and cannot be prescribed by any hard and fast rules. Its purpose being to give a better insight into the operations of the establishment to the end of enabling the managers to limit waste and prevent unprofitable ventures, the subdivisions to be made and the decision as to the particular section into which any one item should appear, turn largely on the particular information which the management desires to secure, and on the business and physical organization of the plant itself. Thus, for instance, of two manufacturing establishments one may be considering the relative desirability of increasing its plant or of purchasing, from other manufacturers, part of the goods it sells. The other, having no opportunity to purchase the finished commodities, might, however, consider whether it is better to continue its sales department or to turn its entire product over to some jobbing or commission house. In the first case it is desirable to show the exact cost of manufacture, to compare it with the price at which goods can be purchased elsewhere; in the other the point of emphasis is the cost connected with selling. It is quite conceivable that the system of accounting which best brought out one set of figures would not most economically give the information desired in the second establishment.

Again, the nature of the organization itself is a factor in determining the form of accounting. The separation or juxtaposition of the factory and the office, the location of the warehouses at one or the other place, the degree to which the labor of employees is specialized, and the number of branch establishments are all examples of facts which enter into the question of the proper grouping of items. What is desired is to be able to put the finger on some point and say, "Here there is relative inefficiency." If manufacturing is distinct from trading, the separation of the two in the accounts seems to facilitate the localization of responsibility; if the two are combined, but there are separate plants each manufacturing and selling, the line of cleavage is evidently different. As in all accounting matters, while certain general principles hold good, the main difficulty is their application to a particular problem which must be individual and perhaps unique.

Bibliographical Note

Cropper, L. C.—*Accounting* (London, 1924), chap. ii.

Dickinson, A. L.—"The Fallacy of Including Interest and Rent as Part of Manufacturing Cost," *Journal of Accountancy,* XII, p. 588.

Finney, H. A.—*Principles of Accounting* (New York, 1923), chaps. ii, iii.

Kester, R. B.—*Accounting, Theory and Practice* (2d ed., New York, 1925), II, chap. v.

Lisle, G.—*Accounting in Theory and Practice* (Edinburgh, 1906), pp. 53-63.

McKinsey, J. O.—*Managerial Accounting* (Chicago, 1924), chap. x.

"Revenue Accounts and Balance Sheets," article in *Encyclopædia of Accounting,* VIII, pp. 249-326. Contains an interesting collection of Revenue accounts of British companies.

Scovell, C. H.—*Interest as a Cost* (New York, 1924).

CHAPTER XVIII

COST ACCOUNTS

Definition

Perhaps the most important contribution which the present generation has made to the science of accounting is the development of cost accounting. The subject combines much theoretical matter with a mass of technical detail. Many comprehensive works have been written on the subject, to some of which reference is made in the bibliographical note at the end of this chapter. While the subject is too complicated and too technical for a general treatise on accounting such as the present volume, it is nevertheless appropriate briefly to consider the purpose of cost accounting and some of the features of theoretical importance.

Attention has been called to the fact that the manufacturing and trading accounts have been developed because of a desire to distinguish between the elements of profit which are due to industrial and commercial activities respectively. But the stress of modern business and the very keenness of competition make necessary a more minute analysis and a closer estimate of the factors affecting profits. Not only must it be known what is the cost of manufacturing the annual product; but this must be so analyzed as to indicate the cost of each commodity, of each process performed in production, even of each part, minute though it be, of which the commodity is composed. Systems designed to secure such information are known as cost accounts.

The attention given to such investigations is of recent origin. The first reference to its desirability is said to be that of Charles Babbage in his *Economy of Manufacture*, published in 1832,[1] but half a century elapsed before factory

[1] Church, *The Proper Distribution of Expense Burden*, p. 9.

managers began on any extended scale to introduce systems of cost accounts. Since then increased attention has been given to the subject, particularly under the influence of engineers, to whom, rather than to professional accountants, the credit of inaugurating and developing cost accounting is perhaps due.

Purposes of Cost Accounting

More specifically the purposes of cost accounting are as follows:

1. To indicate the probable actual cost of production so as to enable the manufacturer to determine the price at which he can profitably sell. This is particularly important in engineering work where so much is done on contract rather than by producing stock goods for the open market. Thus, for instance, a system of cost accounts, accurately kept, should enable a shipbuilder to give an estimate of the cost of constructing a vessel which would be something more than guesswork.

2. Identical in principle is the value of cost accounts in indicating whether the manufacturer shall produce goods for the open market where the price is already fixed by competition. Without such information manufacturers have undoubtedly continued to produce and sell certain lines of goods which, at least to them, were unremunerative and a source of loss. Perhaps the market price is fixed by some competitor whose peculiar advantage in production gives profits at prices unremunerative to less favored rivals; or perhaps the price is due to ignorance on the part of the competitors who are themselves selling at a loss while fancying that they are making profits. A clear understanding as to whether the manufacturer can produce so as to realize a fair profit at current prices is of advantage not merely to the individual, but also to society, as it serves to prevent the misdirection of capital and the great loss which occurs when readjustment becomes necessary.

3. Cost accounts have a further advantage in determining the advisability of introducing a new process, or of substitut-

ing machine for hand labor. They have shown, for instance, that it is profitable to run a drill so rapidly as to wear it out in a single day, although at a slower speed it would have drilled twice as many holes before destruction.[2] They show at what prices of machinery and of skilled labor it is profitable to substitute an automatic machine in a process which can interchangeably be performed by a skilled laborer on a less costly machine. Thus throughout the industrial process cost accounts substitute facts and intelligence for the rule of thumb and blind guessing.

4. Finally, cost accounts furnish a convenient method for checking the efficiency of factory management. If it appears that the cost of producing a given form of pinion has increased, it helps the manager in his effort to locate the cause. It may be that the change is unavoidable, due to higher cost of raw material or to higher wages. But, on the other hand, investigation may show carelessness on the part of the foreman, and ill-advised redisposition of labor, or wastefulness in the handling of material—evils which are already far on the way toward correction when once their existence is shown. Slight losses of this kind may well escape attention if only general results are studied; or the losses in one department may easily be offset—but by no means canceled—by a new economy elsewhere. The subdivision of accounts makes it more easy to detect changes, and gives a constant incentive to foremen and superintendents to reduce costs.

Prime Cost, Factory Cost, Total Cost

The discussion of cost accounting is rendered more difficult by the rather vague and varying terminology employed. There are many different costs depending on the point of view. The terms used to designate these differing costs—prime cost, factory cost, total cost, etc.—are not uniformly defined either by economists or accountants. This may be illustrated by the case of a factory which desires to learn the

---

[2] Lauer, "The Importance of Cost Keeping to the Manufacturer," *Annals of the American Academy of Political and Social Science*, XXII, p. 467.

cost of producing, say, a pair of shoes. To produce this the following factors are involved: (1) The raw material used. (2) The wages of the laborers directly employed in making the shoes. (3) The expenses of operating the factory as a whole which are not particularly assigned to this pair of shoes, as for instance the wages of watchmen, the repairs on the building, the cost of the power used for various purposes, etc. (4) The expenses of the establishment outside of the factory. (5) More questionably the normal rate of profit, whether separated or not from the normal rate of interest on invested capital. In a broad sense profit is a necessary cost of the permanent continuance of the industry; for, if normal profits are not secured, new factories will not be started, and an adjustment of prices will be ultimately secured whereby profits as well as wages will be covered by the selling price.

By some writers the first and second items mentioned above are collectively called prime cost, while the first three items together make up factory cost. Other writers use prime cost to indicate the same as factory cost just defined, and these employ no specific term to indicate the sum of the cost of material and labor directly employed. The sum of the first four items is sometimes called total cost, sometimes "cost to make and sell." Accountants universally exclude profits from cost, but use as a comprehensive term, including all five items enumerated above, the phrase selling price. In addition to these differences in terminology there is divergence in regard to the treatment of certain particular items, such as interest, rent, taxes, etc., involving the principles discussed in Chapters II and XVII.

Without attempting to decide between the various usages, each of which has the support of high authority, and therefore no one of which can be declared wrong, the real problem may be faced, namely: What share of the total expenses, covering as they do the production of various commodities, is to be assigned to the cost of some one commodity, or to some single process? As to the first two items, wages and material, there is no doubt as to the principle and little difficulty in practice. The material actually used and the wages of laborers directly employed in producing the given commodity are obviously an integral part of the cost of producing that article. The connection is so clear that the use of the phrase prime cost seems in a measure to be justified in describing these two fundamental and easily ascertainable elements of cost.

Distribution of Factory Overhead Expense

The first point of difficulty comes in attempting to distribute the indirect factory costs, generally spoken of as "factory overhead," among the various commodities produced. Various principles are used, among which may be mentioned the following:

1. The indirect factory expenses, which include such items as wages of workmen employed in general labor such as watchmen, cleaners, firemen, etc., the wages of foremen and superintendents, light, heat, rent, and repairs of factory and its equipment, depreciation, etc., are apportioned among the various jobs or processes in the proportion which in some particular exists between the given job and the total operations of the factory. But the basis on which the comparison is made is variously chosen, and it may rest either on

(*a*) The direct wages paid.

(*b*) The hours of labor spent.

(*c*) The material used.

(*d*) The direct wages paid plus the cost of material (prime cost).

(*e*) The units of product.

Other bases may also be taken, and one of them, the machine rate, is reserved for further discussion, but the five mentioned above are those most generally used.

Taking, as purely arbitrary figures, those given below, it is seen that each of the methods may produce quite different results, the figure in the last column indicating the amount of the total indirect factory expenses of $12,000 to be apportioned to the particular job on each of the five bases of distribution mentioned.

COMPARISON OF METHODS OF DISTRIBUTING OVERHEAD

BASIS USED	IN ENTIRE FACTORY	ON THIS JOB	APPORTION-MENT
(*a*) Wages paid	$24,000	$100	$ 50.00
(*b*) Hours of labor	60,000 hours	400 hours	80.00
(*c*) Material used	$16,000	$50	37.50
(*d*) Wages plus material...	$40,000	$150	45.00
(*e*) Units produced	400,000 units	4,000 units	120.00

Doubtless in actual practice the divergence in results reached by the different methods would not be so great, as in the figures given above. But it is clear that unless all work is of a practically uniform character, the costs obtained must vary according to the basis of distribution selected. Unfortunately for scientific accuracy it is impossible to pick out any one of the methods named as being logically correct or uniformly accurate. The first one, which distributes factory expenses in proportion to direct wages paid, is probably more frequently used than any of the others. It is, however, obviously incorrect where there is great divergence in rates of wages paid, or where there is a difference in the degree in which automatic machinery is used in the various processes. But it is simple of application, and this fact in itself probably explains its more general use.

Distribution in proportion to hours rather than to cost of labor is favored on the ground that much of the indirect cost, such as foremen's wages, light, heat, etc., is dependent on the hours of work, and that other general charges, such as rent, depreciation, etc., have a direct relation to time. But its critics point out the fact that it makes the same charge upon the labor of a boy running a fifty-dollar machine that it does on that of a man with a thousand-dollar machine, "the grotesqueness of which procedure will not be enlarged upon." Apportionment of indirect factory expenses on the basis either of material or of the sum of wages plus material has the obvious objection that there does not seem to be any logical connection between an increase in the cost of material used and an added charge for indirect factory costs.

Apportionment in proportion to the units of product may be most convenient of application in certain kinds of production, and is frequently used in foundry practice, the ease with which this system is used being held to more than offset any theoretical objection on the ground of the absence of strict logical accuracy.

Machine Cost as a Direct Expense

The foregoing methods have all considered wages and material as the only charges directly apportionable to the particular product or operation, and have made all the indirect charges a function of labor or material. A different conception is one which recognizes to a greater or less degree that in modern factory production there is a third element of cost, namely, that of the machinery employed. This theory has had various applications. In some it has merely determined the direct cost of the machinery, including depreciation, repairs, and interest, and from this obtained an hour rate by dividing the total of such costs by the assumed number of hours which the machine runs. This method, of course, merely gives an apportionment of part of the indirect expenses of the factory and leaves probably the larger part still to be allocated. Furthermore, it does not give correct results where the machinery is idle for part of the time, for the rate charged is on the basis of the machine running the assumed number of hours. Sometimes the method has involved dividing all the indirect expenses by the total number of hours which the machines run, or are supposed to run, thus obtaining a uniform hour rate without differentiation between different classes of machines. This is similar to dividing the indirect expenses according to the hours of labor spent on the particular operation, the difference being that in one case the hours of labor, in the other the hours of machine operation, are taken as the basis of distribution.

The obvious objection here is that many of the indirect expenses have no more to do with the cost of running the machines than they have to do with wages or the cost of material. For instance, in a factory in which all the work was done by hand there would still be indirect charges covering the cost of the factory itself, the watchmen, light, and fuel necessary for keeping the building warm in winter. These certainly cannot be machine costs, where no machinery is used, and part of similar expenses in a modern factory equally relate to labor rather than to machinery. Or again some of the indirect expenses relate to the material used, as, for instance, the additional watchmen required where the material is costly and portable and hence easily stolen. Probably the indirect expenses of an establishment for polishing diamonds have no close relationship to the use of machinery.

In the more improved methods of obtaining machine rates the attempt is to determine not merely part, but all of the charges which attach to the running of a given machine, and to make an hour rate which correctly distributes all such expenses. In other words, it is an extension of the costing system to the operation of the individual machines themselves, so as to determine scientifically what is the real cost of running each one of them for an hour.

Church's Theory of Production Centers

This system has been strongly advocated by A. Hamilton Church, who outlines it as follows:

First we consider each machine as an independent production center, allocating to such centers all the expenses and charges which can on reasonable analysis be considered as chargeable as a composite rent or machine rate for all the factors of production therein concerned. Second, we charge to a monthly shop-charges account all charges whatever incurred by that shop, including all the items specifically represented in fractional detail by the machine rates, and also including, of course, such general items as cannot be represented in the machine rates, of which the most obvious item is the supervision of a head or foreman.

Then as each machine is occupied on jobs, the latter are debited with so much per hour as machine rate, and at the end of the month the total amount so earned by the machines *is deducted from the total shop expenses,* leaving a balance which is distributed over the same jobs as a *supplementary rate.* The ratio of the supplementary rate to the amount distributed by the machine rates forms a varying barometer whose fluctuation is an index of the efficiency of the shop.

It will of course be obvious that when the machines are all running full time the supplementary rate will consist of the general charges alone, such as the foreman's wages, which have not any individual connection with the particular machines. This will be the condition of maximum efficiency in the shop. In proportion as all machines are not kept full of work all the time, this ratio of the supplementary rate to the amount distributed by the machine rates will begin to rise. The same effect will occur if any general kind of expenditure is increased.[3]

Items Entering into Machine-Hour Rate

In determining the special hour rate to be applied to a given machine the following method is advocated by Church. First, the costs of the factory building as such are determined. These include interest, insurance, depreciation and repairs on the building, ground rent, if any, and taxes on the real estate. All these expenses are apportioned between the various machines on the basis of the floor space occupied. This rate may be further varied by distinguishing between space occupied in one or another part of the building. Second, the cost of lighting is determined, which is also distributed according to floor space where there is general overhead lighting, with special charges for individual lights for a particular machine. Third, the cost of power, which includes fuel, boiler and engine costs, wages of firemen and engineers, etc., all of which is reduced to a rate per horsepower hour, which is then charged to each machine on the basis of the estimated power used by each machine. Fourth, the cost of the machine itself, which as before stated includes interest, depreciation, etc., and all of which is apportioned according to the estimated annual working hours.[4] The several factors just enumerated give a machine-hour rate, different for each type of machine, which is supposed with some degree of accuracy to cover all the costs of operating that machine, assuming that the machine is fully occupied. But it still leaves two elements of indirect cost not yet appor-

---

[3] *Op. cit.*, pp. 56-7.
[4] *Ibid.*, chap. iv.

tioned. One of these covers the general expenses of the factory which cannot with any show of reason be considered part of the cost of operating the machine, and the other that element of expense which remains unapportioned because the machines are not run to their full estimated capacity.

Church's Treatment of Other Factory Costs

It is apparent, therefore, that even the elaborate scheme of machine costs proposed by Church does not entirely remove the problem as to the distribution of indirect factory costs. It has, however, made that problem of much less practical importance, for instead of considering all the expenses over and above the wages and cost of material as indirect expenses, the apportionment of which must be largely by a crude and unscientific ratio, the bulk of the general factory expenses are found to be directly attributable to particular jobs through the machine rate, and there remains as unallocated expenses only the two items mentioned in the last paragraph—those by nature not assignable to a machine rate, and those due to idle plant.

Idle Time

The treatment of the unassignable expenses is relatively unimportant, for it cannot constitute a very large proportion of the total expenses. Church suggests that the apportionment be on the basis of the hours spent on the various jobs. But where there is a considerable margin due to idle plant the apportionment of this sum is of some theoretic interest.

The illustration given by Church assumes a factory with four machines on which the machine rate was based on the assumption that they would each work 200 hours, the rate charged to each machine being 40, 30, 20, and 10 cents respectively. Had each of the machines been used for the full assumed time the charges would have covered the total indirect expenses of $200, but because of idleness there remains a balance of unassigned charges amounting to $58, the charges to each machine being as shown in the following table:

Machine	Time Used	Rate per Hour	Amount Charged
A	120	$0.40	$48.00
B	134	0.30	40.20
C	169	0.20	33.80
D	200	0.10	20.00
	623		$142.00

In this case, the author argues, the $58 may either be apportioned on the basis of the hours employed, making a supplementary rate of 9⅓ cents per hour, or on the basis of the amount of the machine charges, making a supplementary rate of 40.8 per cent.[5] Whichever method is used, the result is that the cost of production is increased because of the idle machines.

Other Opinions Regarding Idle Time

To this some critics vigorously object. If the costs are taken as the basis for making estimates, or bids, it leads to the illogical result that at the very time when, because of an idle factory, it is most desirable to get new work, the accounts will show that the work cannot profitably be done except at a price higher than normal. Whitmore, therefore, urges that these costs representing idle time should not be charged up against the goods produced. In his opinion they should be put in a separate account which would be treated as a general expense of the establishment, not as part of the immediate cost of manufacturing.[6] But the practical results are the same whether supplementary charges are treated as Whitmore suggests or are all distributed over the goods produced. So long as the elements representing idle machines are shown in a supplementary rate, attention is clearly drawn to the loss that comes from idle plant. There is the same incentive to try for new business whether that loss appears among the manufacturing costs or is separately shown as one of the general expenses of the establishment.

[5] *Ibid.*, p. 58.

[6] "Factory Accounting as Applied to Machine Shops," *Journal of Accountancy*, III, p. 28.

Past Costs or Present Costs

A vital difference in method of estimating cost turns on the point whether the indirect factory expenses which are apportioned to different jobs are the actual expenses incurred during the period in which the operations are performed, or whether they are to be based on the experiences of past operations. For instance, in a given factory it may be desirable to treat the indirect costs as a percentage to be added to the prime cost. This may be done by taking account, say, at the end of each month of all such expenses and accurately apportioning them to the work then in progress. But others, as for instance Oberlin Smith and Nisbet, recommend that the added charge be based on the experience of a preceding year, or series of years, so that the charge can at any time be made without waiting for the results of the current period.

To some it seems that by taking the current figures a greater degree of accuracy is obtained. But it should be remembered that for certain purposes what is desired is not so much the actual amount which it cost to produce a certain commodity, as an estimate of what it will cost to produce more of the same kind of goods. This is particularly true where special contracts are undertaken. Just what experience will give the best indication of future costs may be debatable. It does not necessarily follow that the experience of the present month is any better criterion than that of last year.

General Establishment Charges

The distribution of general establishment charges offers somewhat similar difficulties. These expenses include the office expenses, the expenses of selling, and the general expenses of financing and managing the whole enterprise. Alternative methods of dividing these expenses among the products are to apportion them in proportion to:

1. The wages cost;

2. The factory cost, *i.e.*, the cost of wages, material, and the indirect factory expenses; or

3. The hours consumed in manufacturing the product;
4. The selling price.

The second method seems the most logical, for it apparently covers all the elements for which the establishment exists. Church, however, advocates employing the hours as the basis, making, however, certain modifications in the rates charged to different classes of commodities.

In the preceding pages have been discussed the problems concerning the distribution of indirect charges in general. Further difficulties arise in reference to the apportionment of certain special costs. One of these, relating to the cost of patterns, requires particular mention. Not only is there the general question as to how far the costs of designing and making patterns should be charged to expense, and how far the patterns should be considered an asset, but there is a further difficulty. After having decided that a given amount is really an expense, is it to be allocated to the particular products made from the pattern or treated as a general expense of the factory? This is particularly clear where unsuccessful patterns or designs are made. Are these all to be charged against the cost of the article made from a later satisfactory model, or do the preliminary attempts represent merely general expenses of the factory as such? Somewhat similarly: is the cost of making a special pattern for an article made on contract to be considered as cost of completing the contract or is there a residual value representing the serviceability of that same pattern for future possible contracts?

Expense Involved in Cost Accounts

Three points of uncertainty arise even in regard to the best system of cost accounting. The first is whether the information acquired is after all worth the expense of acquiring it. This is more than doubtful in some of the more elaborate and expensive systems of cost keeping that are occasionally introduced. To take a flagrant and notorious case, the cost system introduced into the Government Printing Office seems to have cost decidedly more than it was worth. In this instance the committee investigating the system reported that it is principally to be criticised upon the score that in an attempt to secure all classes of detail, the amount of labor entailed upon each employee for the purpose of recording necessary facts, and the amount of labor required for subsequent tabulation, were so great as to make the system almost prohibitive.[7]

Inaccuracy of Cost Accounts

The second point of doubt is as to the degree of accuracy which may be obtained and the danger which arises from treating as actual what is merely hypothetical. It has been shown that even the division between the Manufacturing account and the other portions of the Profit and Loss account is with difficulty drawn and can never be regarded as of absolute value. Much more it is true that the detailed apportionment of expenses among the different processes or the various commodities is to some extent a matter of estimate. To be sure accounts can be prepared, though with great difficulty and much expense, in which every cent expended will be allocated to some unit of product. But it must be remembered that this rests on estimates which can never be exact. To illustrate: It is difficult to determine the exact cost of power in a factory. Coal and wages may be known, but depreciation of plant is an estimate merely. But granting a substantial accuracy as to the cost of the total power, this can be divided to the last cent by some system of machine rates. But much of this ostensible accuracy is specious. It is a rough estimate at best which attempts to divide the horse power among the different machines, and the degree of accuracy obtained in the final results can never surmount this fundamental defect. And the whole system of fixing the machine rate depends on an incorrect estimate of the hours during which the machine will be at work. As Burton said, "Cost accounts based on separate charges for each machine employed must be generally hypothetical, and in many if not the majority of cases they must be delusively hypothetical."[8]

---

[7] LX Cong. 1. Sess. H. Doc. 974, p. 11.
[8] *Engineers' and Shipbuilders' Accounts,* p. 91.

Application of Results of Cost Accounts

A third point bears on the application which is to be made of the result. Are they to be used in determining whether capital shall go into a given industry? If so, it is evident that what is wanted is a correct estimate of the net income after deducting all interest on capital and other items frequently, indeed generally, excluded from the cost accounts themselves. The information necessary to show whether an enterprise is ultimately successful is very different from that which shows whether an enterprise once established should be continued. Cost accounts as they are frequently prepared confuse these two points of view. Thus Whitmore criticizes the inclusion of idle-machine cost as not showing whether to a new concern it is desirable to undertake certain work. The idle-machine cost, says he, is incidental to the establishment of a new concern and should not be included in an estimate which shows whether goods can be produced profitably at a certain price.[9] But the same author includes interest on the cost of machines and buildings in his estimate of machine costs, while these have nothing to do with the cost of producing further goods by a factory already established.[10] As is well known in railroad practice, when a road is once permanently constructed it is better to carry freight at a price not covering interest than to refuse traffic. The same principle, of course, applies to a factory. If, as seems to be the opinion in discussing idle-plant costs, the purpose of the cost account is to show the figure at which the established factory can afford to produce, it is clearly illogical to include in this figure interest, which indeed bears on the ultimate profitableness of the enterprise, but not on the desirability of undertaking a given contract.

Different Establishments Need Different Systems of Cost Accounts

As to the technic of cost accounting little can here be said. It is impossible to frame a system of cost accounting appli-

[9] *Op. cit.*, II, 256-7.
[10] *Ibid.*, III, p. 21.

cable to establishments of different character. Iron works producing a single form of staple commodity, a factory making a few standard grades of cloth, each involving a succession of separate processes, works manufacturing special machines where it is desirable to learn the cost of the entire machine and of each of its parts, and a shipyard undertaking special contracts, each needs an entirely different system of keeping its cost accounts. No general scheme of forms can be outlined which will apply to all of them. Nor can a scheme be outlined which will apply in detail to the different individual establishments of a single class of undertakings. As Dicksee has said:

> It need hardly be pointed out that the requirements of undertakings carrying on a similar business are by no means uniform. Special and local considerations have to be taken into account, and the most desirable system for any particular undertaking can only be ascertained after a full and detailed inquiry has been made into its peculiar circumstances and conditions.[11]

Even to describe a system serviceable to a particular establishment, while it might have illustrative and suggestive value, would require so extended a treatment as to exclude it from a treatise on the general principles of modern accounting.

Bibliographical Note

Armstrong, G. S.—*Essentials of Industrial Costing* (New York, 1921).

Arnold, H. L.—*The Complete Cost-Keeper* (New York, 1912).

Atkins, P. M.—*Textbook of Industrial Cost Accounting* (New York, 1924).

Castenholz, W. B.—*Cost Accounting Procedure* (Chicago, 1922).

Church, A. H.—*Manufacturing Costs and Accounts* (New York, 1917).

——— *Production Factors in Cost Accounting and Works Management* (New York, 1910).

——— *The Proper Distribution of Expense Burden* (New York, 1913). An elaborate presentation of the "improved machine cost" system and a criticism of other systems of cost accounting.

---

[11] *Advanced Accounting*, 6th ed., p. 280.

Dohr, J. L.—*Cost Acoounting, Theory and Practice* (New York, 1924).

Eggleston, De W. C.—*Business Costs* (New York, 1921).

Jordan, J. P.—*Cost Accounting, Principles and Practice* (2d ed., New York, 1925).

Lawrence, W. B.—*Cost Accounting* (New York, 1925).

National Association of Cost Acountants—*A Bibliography of Cost Books* (New York, 1921).

Nicholson, J. L.—*Cost Accounting* (New York, 1919).

Webner, F. E.—*Factory Accounting* (Chicago, 1917).

CHAPTER XIX

PARTNERSHIP ACCOUNTS: ORGANIZATION

Nature of Partnership Accounts

Partnership accounts constitute no separate system of accounting. Whether the proprietorship is vested in one or more persons the general principle of double entry bookkeeping, that there is an equation between the sum of the proprietorship accounts and the excess of assets over liabilities, holds true. The mere subdivision of the proprietorship into various individual accounts introduces no new accounting principle.

The discussion in the present chapter does not profess to treat any problems save those which seem peculiar to the status of partnership. While in the keeping of partnership accounts questions will arise as to the most convenient method of booking certain transactions, these are ordinarily mere questions of general bookkeeping technic and not peculiar to partnership. Or problems may arise as to the amount of profits to be divided, but these are all matters of accounting principles elsewhere discussed, say under valuation, depreciation, or profits; questions all of which refer to corporation and individual accounts as well as to those of partnership. The partnership problems, as such, are generally involved in the correct interpretation of the partnership agreements, perhaps ambiguously drawn up or even resting on a vague oral agreement, and have to do primarily with the essential relationship of the individual partners, the terms on which they unite, the division of profits, the adjustment of unpaid capital contributions through allowances for interest, and the final distribution of assets, all of which transactions must conform to the rules of the partnership agreement.

Establishment of Partnership

The first class of difficulties arises in connection with the establishment of the firm. When an individual first opens a set of books there either is no difficulty in knowing how much capital he contributes, or if there be a doubt it is of no particular moment so far as it concerns ultimate distribution of wealth. If A begins business with $5,000 cash and certain real estate he should, of course, attempt to place correct valuation on the latter in estimating his net wealth. But if he fails to do so it evidently does himself no injury. But if two persons join in a partnership, one furnishing cash and the other real estate, it is necessary to know what value is placed on the latter. To be sure the original entry is the same whether it be in the books of a single trader or those of a partnership, as in either case Real Estate is debited and the Capital account of the one contributing it is credited. This may be illustrated by assuming the following opening:

Balance Sheet

Cash	$ 5,000	A, Capital	$ 5,000
Real Estate	5,000	B, Capital	5,000
	$10,000		$10,000

in which the cash is contributed by A and the real estate by B. Any other valuation of the real estate would not, in itself, affect the credit of A's Capital account; nor would it, in the absence of special agreement, affect the division of profits, B being entitled to half of the profits whatever the value of his contribution. But the value at which the contributed property is admitted is, nevertheless, of vital importance in a partnership for having once been accepted by the firm any subsequent shrinkage in the value of the real estate is a loss to be divided between the two partners, and not one to be borne by the contributing partner alone. Conversely a sale of the real estate for $10,000 gives to A as well as to B one half of the appreciation, \$2,500. It is evident then that it is essential in accounting to understand the nature of the contribution which each partner makes, to interpret accurately the terms of the partnership agreement, for "in the absence of special agreement the rise or fall in the value of fixed plant or real estate belonging to a partnership is as much profit or loss of the partnership as anything else." [1]

Necessity of Determining Amount Contributed

It is essential that there should be a clear understanding of just what values are contributed by the several persons organizing a partnership and this is true whether the partners contribute tangible assets such as cash and real estate, or goodwill. If in forming a partnership it is distinctly agreed that A shall contribute real estate valued at \$5,000 and goodwill valued at \$1,000 and that B is to contribute \$6,000 cash, the entry to be made is simple and obvious. Unfortunately, however, in many cases the articles of partnership do not distinctly specify the value of goodwill even though the value of the tangible assets is mentioned. Thus, it may be specified that A shall contribute certain tangible assets, having at least a book value of \$5,000, and that B is to contribute \$6,000 in cash with the condition that he thereby acquires a one-half interest in the new partnership.

Distinction between Share in Business and Share of Profits

Here it is necessary to distinguish between a provision that a partner is entitled to one half of the profits (carrying with it a liability to stand half of the losses) and the provision that the partner has a half interest in the business. The interpretations by the courts are somewhat confusing in this matter. However, it is difficult to see how in a partnership where one member of the firm contributes \$25,000 and the other makes no contribution, the latter can be said to have

[1] Robinson *v.* Ashton, L. R. 20 Eq. 28 (1875).

a half interest in the business even though he is, as is normally the case, entitled to half the profits. The phrase half interest or equal interest should imply a contribution of one half of the total capital as well as the right to receive half the profits.

Contributed Goodwill

If a partnership is formed, A contributing real estate worth $5,000 and B $6,000 cash, profits to be shared equally, the opening entries are simple and unquestioned. The contributed assets would be debited and each partner's capital account credited for the amount of his contribution. The resulting balance sheet would be as follows:

Balance Sheet

Real Estate	$ 5,000	A, Capital	$ 5,000
Cash	6,000	B, Capital	6,000
	$11,000		$11,000

Exactly the same entries and the same resulting balance sheet would be given in case profits were to be divided in any other ratio. Indeed the balance sheet gives no indication whatever of the ratio in which profits are to be divided but merely shows the share which each partner has in the estimated value of the assets of the partnership.

But if in the illustration previously given, B is to acquire a half interest in the partnership by the contribution of $6,000, it is only reasonable to assume that A must in some form or other also have contributed $6,000. This of course may be justified by assuming that despite the former book value of the real estate, it is now worth $6,000. But if the value of $5,000 is accepted, the ordinary interpretation is that A has matched B's contribution by contributing both real estate worth $5,000 and goodwill worth $1,000. If this interpretation is accepted the balance sheet of A and B would be as follows:

Balance Sheet of A and B

Real Estate	$ 5,000	A, Capital	$ 6,000
Goodwill	1,000	B, Capital	6,000
Cash	6,000		
	$12,000		$12,000

If desired the same relationship can be represented with goodwill eliminated as follows:

Balance Sheet of A and B

Real Estate	$ 5,000	A, Capital	$ 5,500
Cash	6,000	B, Capital	5,500
	$11,000		$11,000

Similarly if the arrangement specifies that B's contribution of $6,000 gives him a three-fifths interest in the business, not merely three-fifths of the profits, and the merchandise still being accepted as worth $5,000, B must be construed as bringing into the firm business connections, or other elements of goodwill, to such a value that his total contribution represents one and a half times the value of A's merchandise, or:

Balance Sheet of A and B

Real Estate	$ 5,000	A, Capital	$ 5,000
Goodwill	1,500	B, Capital	7,500
Cash	6,000		
	$12,500		$12,500

or again eliminating the goodwill:

Balance Sheet of A and B

Real Estate	$ 5,000	A, Capital	$ 4,400
Cash	6,000	B, Capital	6,600
	$11,000		$11,000

Booking without Including Goodwill

The same result can be reached by a slightly different method of calculation. If it is agreed that A is to contribute real estate worth $5,000 and B $6,000 cash, the total contribution (if goodwill is excluded) is $11,000. If, according to the agreement, each partner is to have a one-half interest he can immediately be credited with one half of this sum by means of the following journal entry:

Real Estate	$5,000	
Cash	6,000	
A, Capital		$5,500
B, Capital		5,500

Or in the case that B is to have a three-fifths interest, A could be directly credited with two-fifths of $11,000 or $4,400 and B with three-fifths or $6,600. The first point in partnership accounting to be ascertained is what is the exact nature of the partnership agreement? What does each partner actually contribute? What is the division of interest between the partners?

Buying an Interest in Partnership

The admission of a new partner into a firm already established does not differ materially from the creation of a new partnership. There are, however, likely to arise some additional difficulties in interpreting the agreement. One of the points of difficulty is in distinguishing between one who buys say a third interest in a firm from one or more members of the firm and one who enters a partnership making such a contribution as will entitle him to a third interest. Thus, if A and B are in business together with the following showing:

Balance Sheet of A and B

Miscellaneous Assets	$60,000	A, Capital	$20,000
		B, Capital	40,000
	$60,000		$60,000

C might, if it were mutually agreed on, buy a third interest in the firm from B, paying therefor $20,000, which would give as the balance sheet of the new firm:

Balance Sheet of A, B, and C

Miscellaneous Assets	$60,000	A, Capital	$20,000
		B, Capital	20,000
		C, Capital	20,000
	$60,000		$60,000

But if he were admitted to the firm with a one-third interest the showing, provided he contributed the book value of his share in the business, would have to be as follows:

Balance Sheet of A, B, and C

Miscellaneous Assets	$60,000	A, Capital	$20,000
Cash	30,000	B, Capital	40,000
		C, Capital	30,000
	$90,000		$90,000

Goodwill of Old Partnership

Where the incoming partner contributes an amount in excess of the book value of the interest which he acquires, he is presumably making the additional payment to offset goodwill existing in the old firm, but not shown upon the books. In such a case there is no objection to writing into the book of the old firm the estimated value of the goodwill. The general rule that goodwill is not to be entered into the books except where there is a purchase, is not violated, for with the admission of the new partner the old firm has ceased to exist and all of its assets including, of course, goodwill, have virtually been sold to the new partnership.

Adjusting Shares of Partners

Where profits are shared in proportion to the contributed capital the adjustment is easily made. If the arrangement with C had been that he was to contribute $45,000 to the firm, acquiring thereby a third interest, the implication is that the total value of all of the assets tangible and intangible, held by A and B must be equal to twice the amount contributed by C, that is, they would have a total value of $90,000. If only $60,000 of this is represented by the tangible assets, A and B are presumably contributing goodwill valued at $30,000. This increase in the value of the assets of A and B, like any ordinary gain, would be distributed one-third to A and two-thirds to B, and the balance sheet after the admission of C would accordingly be as follows:

Balance Sheet

Miscellaneous Assets	$60,000	A, Capital	$30,000
Goodwill	30,000	B, Capital	60,000
Cash	45,000	C, Capital	45,000
	$135,000		$135,000

Similarly, if C had bought a third interest in the firm from B, paying therefor $45,000, it would be fair to assume that the total value of all of the assets held by A and B, including their goodwill, were worth $135,000. As the tangible assets amount only to $60,000 this would imply goodwill of $75,000, increasing A's capital account by $25,000 and B's by $50,000. After the transfer had taken place, the balance sheet of A, B, and C would be as follows:

Balance Sheet

Miscellaneous Assets	$60,000	A, Capital	$45,000
Goodwill	75,000	B, Capital	45,000
		C, Capital	45,000
	$135,000		$135,000

Where the division of profits is not in proportion to the amount of contributed capital the value of the goodwill can similarly be estimated where the incoming partner contributes to the new firm. Assuming similar transactions but profits shared equally between A and B, the balance sheet after the admission of C would be:

Balance Sheet

Miscellaneous Assets	$60,000	A, Capital	$35,000
Goodwill	30,000	B, Capital	55,000
Cash	45,000	C, Capital	45,000
	$135,000		$135,000

If, however, C purchases from B a one-third interest in the existing firm, it is not possible from that statement alone to determine the amount of goodwill. In such cases it is customary in the absence of further information merely to transfer a part of B's capital to C, producing a balance sheet similar to that given above on page 404, and without attempting to show the goodwill.[2]

Problem in Adjusting Shares of Partners

An interesting problem arises where an agreement is made that an incoming partner shall buy from the firm say a one-third interest, but in such a way that each of the former partners shall also have an equal one-third interest. This may be illustrated by a problem which has been discussed in accounting publications for at least eighty years, but which seems even yet a matter upon which accountants do not all agree.[3]

The problem as it has been given practically without change during all that period is as follows: A and B have bought a

[2] The reason for this is that the price paid for half of B's interest represents the payment for his share of the assets and also for an estimated value of whatever additional profits he receives. To make this estimate it is necessary to make a specific calculation of the value of B's goodwill which, as his profit-sharing ratio is different from his share of the contributed capital, is not a proportionate share of the total goodwill of the firm. For a full discussion of this difficult problem which is theoretically interesting but not of great practical importance, see the forthcoming work on partnership accounts by Professor C. C. Staehling.

[3] It was raised at least as early as November, 1844, in a communication to Hunt's *Merchants' Magazine* of that date. It was raised so late as August, 1924, by a correspondent from Brazil writing to the *Journal of Accountancy*.

boat for $8,000, A contributing $5,000 and B $3,000; profits in the enterprise to be shared in proportion to capital contributions. It is now proposed that C shall buy from A and B a one-third interest in the boat, the money paid being so distributed between A and B that each of the three partners will have a one-third interest. The proper solution of the problem is as follows:

If one-third interest in the boat is now worth $4,000, the most elementary student in arithmetic could attribute to the entire boat a value of $12,000 and the books may be written up to record this valuation. There being an increased value of $4,000, this would be divided between A and B in the ratio of five to three. The accounts would then show a balance sheet as follows:

Balance Sheet

Boat	$12,000	A, Capital	$7,500
		B, Capital	4,500
	$12,000		$12,000

If C is to acquire a third interest, leaving to both A and B each a third interest, he would evidently acquire from A a share amounting to $3,500 and from B one worth only $500 and the payment of $4,000 should be made accordingly. The problem could of course have been solved without marking up the value of the boat by figuring that a third interest in the boat has a book value of $2,666⅔, and that amount should be retained by both A and B. C's purchase would therefore be as follows:

From A	$5,000	— $2,666⅔	=	$2,333⅓
From B	$3,000	— $2,666⅔	=	$ 333⅓
Total				$2,666⅔

For this, he pays $4,000 or 150 per cent of its nominal value. He would therefore pay to A 1½ times $2,333⅓ or $3,500, and to B $500. If the terms of the original partnership had been that profits were to be shared equally, the distribution of the $4,000 would of course be different. The appreciation in the value of the boat being divided equally between A and B would show credits to their respective capital accounts of $7,000 and $5,000. C would accordingly buy from A a share valued at $3,000 and from B a share valued at $1,000, the cash payment being distributed accordingly.

Interest on Partners' Capital

To some extent in this country and almost uniformly in England, calculations are made allowing to the several partners interest upon their capital contributions. Where capital is contributed in different amounts by the several partners, but profits are shared equally, allowance for interest seems reasonable. Each partner may be considered as equally concerned in the success of the business and contributing by his personal efforts equally in obtaining profits. But the partner who contributes a larger amount of capital is to that extent rendering additional service which may well be compensated by allowing interest. Perhaps the argument for interest upon partners' capital is even stronger where the amount contributed varies from the amount which the partner was supposed to furnish in accordance with the articles of partnership. For illustration, it may be assumed that a partnership needs $200,000 to carry on its business and the articles call for the contribution by each partner of half that sum. If one of the partners, however, provides only $80,000, it may be necessary for the firm to borrow $20,000. As it must pay interest on this loan, it seems equitable that the partner who is responsible for this burden should be charged interest on the amount of his deficiency. The same argument, *mutatis mutandis,* would apply to a partner who has contributed more than the specified amount.

Two Bases for Allowing Interest

Interest allowance is made in two different forms: (1) Interest is allowed to each partner upon the entire amount of capital contributed by him; (2) Interest is allowed for any capital contributed by a partner in excess of the amount which in accordance with the articles of partnership he has agreed to furnish and conversely, each partner is charged for any deficiencies in capital contributions below the amount specified in the articles.

Interest on Entire Capital: First Method

Where profits are shared in proportion to such contributions, an allowance of interest upon the entire capital has no effect on the relative shares of the different partners. The burden of whatever interest is allowed to the partners must be borne by them in the same ratio and the net result is to leave the partners' accounts at the same figure as they would have been had interest not been calculated. Such an allowance may of course be made for the purpose of bringing to light the extent to which the profits of the business in a narrow sense exceed the amount which might have been expected from an investment of the capital at an ordinary rate of interest. But where the ratio in which profits are shared differs from the ratio of contributed capital, an allowance of interest affects the equities of the several partners. Thus, assuming partners who contribute as follows, A $100,000; B $60,000; C $50,000, interest at 5 per cent to be allowed on the entire capital contributions and the profits to be shared equally, the accounts concerned will be as set out as follows:

A, Capital Account

⅓ of interest allowed	$ 3,500	Cash	$100,000
Balance	101,500	Interest on $100,000 at 5%	5,000
	$105,000		$105,000
		Balance	$101,500

B, Capital Account

⅓ of interest allowed	$ 3,500	Cash	$ 60,000
Balance	59,500	Interest on $60,000 at 5%	3,000
	$ 63,000		$ 63,000
		Balance	$ 59,500

C, Capital Account

⅓ of interest allowed	$ 3,500	Cash	$ 50,000
Balance	49,000	Interest on $50,000 at 5%	2,500
	$ 52,500		$ 52,500
		Balance	$ 49,000

Interest Account

Allowed on partners' capital:			By A	$ 3,500
A	$5,000		By B	3,500
B	3,000		By C	3,500
C	2,500	$ 10,500		
		$ 10,500		$ 10,500

NOTE: As these accounts are to show only the effect of the interest transactions the Interest account has been closed directly into the Capital accounts instead of being carried to the Profit and Loss account and appearing indirectly in the balance of Profit and Loss carried to the partners.

The result of this allowance is to add to A's equity $1,500 and to diminish that of B by $500 and that of C by $1,000.

Interest on Entire Capital: Second Method

The same result may be secured with somewhat less bookkeeping and without encumbering the Profit and Loss account by the following method: The amount contributed by each partner is compared with the share of the total contributed capital corresponding to the share which the partner has in the profits. In this case the total amount of capital contributed by the three partners is $210,000. Each partner is entitled to one-third of the profits and accordingly each partner's capital contribution is compared, for the purpose of calculating interest, with one third of the total contributed capital. Accordingly A shows an excess of $30,000 and B and C show deficits of $10,000 and $20,000 respectively. Interest being calculated on these sums at 5 per cent, the adjustment would be made by the following journal entry:

B	$ 500	
C	1,000	
A		$1,500

It is to be noted that had the basis of profit sharing not been one third to each but in some other proportion, say, 2:1:1, the basis of comparison, by which excess contributions are measured, would be correspondingly modified. Thus A's contribution being compared with two fourths of $210,000 or $105,000 he is charged with interest on $5,000 or $250; B showing an excess of $7,500 over $52,500 (*i.e.,* one fourth of $210,000) receives $375; and C pays $125. These entries produce the same results as though the entire capital had been credited with interest and the total interest, $10,500, had been divided in the proportion last named.

Interest on Excess or Deficient Contributions: First Method

Where the partnership agreement calls for interest only upon capital contributions in excess of the amount specified in the articles of partnership, the calculations can of course be made by the longer and more complicated method. Thus if the partners had agreed to contribute as follows: A, $100,000; B, $60,000; C, $50,000, but in fact paid $70,000, $73,000, $25,000 respectively, if profits were to be shared in proportion to the agreed on contributions of capital (that is, in the ratio of 10:6:5) the accounts would show:

A, Capital Account

Interest on $30,000 deficit	$ 1,500	Cash	$70,000
Balance	69,500	10/21 of interest received	1,000
	$71,000		$71,000
		Balance	$69,500

B, Capital Account

Balance	$74,250	Cash	$73,000
		Interest on $13,000 excess	650
		6/21 of interest received	600
	$74,250		$74,250
		Balance	$74,250

C, Capital Account

Interest on $25,000 deficit	$ 1,250	Cash	$25,000
Balance	24,250	5/21 of interest received	500
	$25,500		$25,500
		Balance	$24,250

Interest Account

To B on $1,300		$ 650	On A's deficit	$ 1,500
Balance to partners:			On C's deficit	1,250
A, 10/21	$1,000			
B, 6/21	600			
C, 5/21	500	2,100		
		$ 2,750		$ 2,750

Booking of Interest on Excess Contribution: Second Method

In the above case the shorter and simpler method of adjusting the equities of the partners could have been employed. The method of calculation is as follows: The total amount of capital actually contributed is $168,000. A was supposed to contribute 10/21 of the entire capital. That proportion of $168,000 is $80,000. He actually contributed $70,000. A charge of 5 per cent interest upon the deficit of $10,000 would burden his account with $500. Similarly B's contribution of $73,000 being compared with 6/21 of $168,000 shows an excess of $25,000, entitling him to a credit of $1,250 and C similarly would be charged with 5 per cent on a deficit of $15,000 or $750. The entire adjustment could, therefore, be made by the following journal entry:

A	$500	
C	750	
B		$1,250

Where the interest is calculated only on excesses and deficiencies, but the division of profits is not in the same ratio as the agreed-on contribution of capital, the shorter and simpler method of making adjustments between the capital accounts cannot readily be used, and the charges and credits should go through the books in detail in accordance with the methods shown on page 411.

To sum up: When interest is allowed on the *total* capital, entries may be through the Interest account, or the adjustment may be made directly between the Capital accounts by allowing interest on excesses and deficits relative to the proportion of total contributed capital corresponding to the individual partner's share of profits. But where interest is allowed only on *excesses* and deficits, the shorter method can be used only where profits and assumed capital contributions are proportionate. Otherwise the adjustment of excesses must be made by the longer form of putting entries through the interest or other similar account.[4]

Withdrawal of Partner

Withdrawal by a partner of any of the assets of the partnership is to that extent a reduction of his proprietary interest. It is customary, however, not to charge such withdrawals immediately to the partner's capital account but to place it in a drawing or personal account. Sometimes this is done with an agreement between the partners as to the amount which may be withdrawn during the year and perhaps provisions as to the conditions in which interest is to be charged. The drawing account may also at times be credited perhaps for an allowance in the nature of salary or for interest upon contributed capital. The balance of the partner's drawing account in most cases should be carried to his capital account when the books are closed. There can be no absolute rule in this matter as in some partnerships the intention is to make a marked differentiation between the partner's capital and other credits and debits of a more personal character. By some accountants, the partner's share of profits at the end of the year is carried to his personal or drawing account. A preferable procedure, and one which seems to be rather gen-

---

[4] Accountants are inclined to consider interest on partners' capital as a division of profits rather than as an expense. While this would affect the location of the interest item in the income statement, it does not materially alter the treatment of the problems discussed above.

erally accepted in England, is to carry the partner's share of profits to his capital account and also to carry to the same account the debit balance of his drawing account if such there be. A credit balance of a partner's drawing account, especially where it represents a part of a regular salary allowance not withdrawn, may with better reason be carried into the opening balance sheet as a separate account.

For bibliography see note to Chapter XX.

CHAPTER XX

PARTNERSHIP ACCOUNTS: LIQUIDATION

Final Distribution of Assets

Problems frequently arise regarding the final distribution of assets when a partnership liquidates. Here great confusion exists, even in the decisions of courts. To illustrate, there may be taken a partnership between A and B in which A furnishes $2,000 and B $500, profits to be shared equally. But losses having been suffered, the total assets amount to only $1,000, the balance sheet showing:

Balance Sheet

Cash	$1,000	A, Capital	$2,000
Deficit	1,500	B, Capital	500
	$2,500		$2,500

It is a common assumption that in such a case the partners would divide the cash or the remaining assets in the ratio in which profits were shared. Others assume that the cash would be divided in the ratio of the capital contributions so that A would receive $800 and B $200. Neither of these views is, however, correct. The proper calculation of the share of the cash to go to each of the partners is as follows: The net loss amounts to $1,500. By the terms of the agreement this is to be shared equally. Each partner's capital account should therefore be debited with $750, after which the accounts would appear as in the balance sheet on the next page.

This shows that A is not only entitled to all the cash, but has a valid claim against B for $250. A moment's consideration will show that this is the only solution that satisfies the requirement that losses are to be shared equally. A

Balance Sheet

Cash	$1,000	A, Capital	$1,250
B, deficit	250		
	$1,250		$1,250

contributed $2,000. If he receives all of the cash on hand and $250 additional from B, his net loss will be $750. B originally contributed $500. None of this is returned to him, but he must pay to B the additional sum of $250, making his loss equal to that suffered by A.[1]

Distribution Where One Partner Is Insolvent

Somewhat more complicated, but similar in principle, is the case where three partners are concerned and the one whose account shows a deficit proves to be personally insolvent. Assuming a condition as follows:

Balance Sheet of A, B, and C

Cash	$2,200	A, Capital	$2,000
Deficit	4,800	B, Capital	500
		C, Capital	4,500
	$7,000		$7,000

dividing the deficit gives:

Balance Sheet

Cash	$2,200	A, Capital	$ 400
B, deficit	1,100	C, Capital	2,900
	$3,300		$3,300

If now, B is found to be insolvent and the claim against him worthless, a great variety of opinions are given as to the proper division of the remaining assets between A and C.

[1] Legal support of this solution is found in Nowell *v.* Nowell, L. R. 7 Eq. 538 (1869); and Livingston *v.* Blanchard, 130 Mass 341 (1881).

Some argue that A is entitled to 1/2 of the cash, or $1,100. Others say to 20/65 or $676.92, and others to 4/33, $266.66.

The correct solution is, however, easily reached if the procedure illustrated above is continued. There being only $2,200 cash with which to pay the $3,300 due to A and C, the two together must inevitably suffer a further loss of $1,100, which, according to the terms of the partnership, is to be borne equally. Charging this additional loss equally to A and C gives:

Balance Sheet

Cash	$2,200	C, Capital	$2,350
A, deficit	150		
	$2,350		$2,350

whereby A, instead of receiving any of the cash on hand, is compelled to pay C an additional sum of $150.

Some objection has been made to this treatment on the ground that the default by B is not a loss arising from the business and therefore should not be apportioned among the remaining partners in accordance with the rule for distributing business losses. This view unfortunately has been adopted by the leading English case [2] relying largely on the phraseology of the statute. There is some difference of opinion as to what other basis should be chosen in making the final adjustment and accountants generally consider that the decision in this case was at least unfortunate.[3] The correctness of the solution given above is, however, generally recognized by American accountants and has been sanctioned by a series of decisions in the American courts.[4] It also corresponds with the provisions of the Uniform Partnership Act generally adopted by the American states. This provides in section 18a that each partner "must contribute toward the

[2] Garner *v.* Murray, [1904] 1 Ch. 57.

[3] The decision is discussed in a series of communications in the *Accountant,* XXXII, XLVIII, LIII, LXIII; Dicksee, *Advanced Accounting,* 6th ed. p. 78; Cropper, *Accounting,* p. 512.

[4] Raymond *v.* Putnam, 44 N.H. 160 (1862); Whitcomb *v.* Converse, 119 Mass. 38 (1875); Woelfel *v.* Thompson, 53 N.E. 819 (Mass. 1899).

losses, whether of capital, or otherwise, sustained by the partnership according to his share in the profits.''

The foregoing discussion shows the futility of the question frequently raised as to the basis on which assets are to be divided, the ratio in which losses are shared being already given. Such a question involves a misconception or else is purely gratuitous. If all losses are shared according to the agreed proportion, the capital accounts of the several partners show the amounts which they are severally to receive or pay. Evidently a firm starting with an equality of assets and capital will, by the most elementary principle of bookkeeping, have assets still equaling the balances of the proprietorship accounts if all shrinkages are deducted from the original credits. One need not estimate proportions, the absolute amounts will appear in the accounts themselves. To determine the final distribution of assets it is necessary only to determine profits and losses, to divide these in the agreed proportion, and to discharge the remaining capital balances, collecting from the debtor, and paying to the creditor partners.

Installment Distribution in Liquidation

In one set of circumstances, there arises a somewhat more complicated problem relating to the division of assets between partners. This arises in liquidating a partnership which has suffered losses and whose partners have contributed capital in some other ratio than that in which profits are shared. When liquidation is begun, it may be impossible to know just how much the loss will finally prove to be. The process of realizing on the assets of the firm may take considerable time and until the last asset has been turned into cash the exact amount of loss is not known. It is, however, undesirable that the partners should be compelled to wait until the realization has been completed before any of the cash is paid to them. Cash amounting to $2,500 may have been received and the question arises as to how this is to be distributed. It is highly desirable that the distribution should take place in such a way that it will never be necessary to collect back from one of the partners any of the cash paid to him as liquidating dividend in order that it may be turned over to one of the other partners.

Illustrative Problem in Installment Distribution

The problem involved and the method of its solution may be illustrated by the following case. A, B, and C, being in partnership in which profits are shared equally, have the following:

Balance Sheet

Miscellaneous Assets	$10,000	A, Capital	$ 5,000
Deficit	12,000	B, Capital	7,000
		C, Capital	10,000
	$22,000		$22,000

The partnership decides to liquidate and the miscellaneous assets are realized gradually, cash being received in the following installments:

(*a*)	$2,500
(*b*)	1,500
(*c*)	4,500
(*d*)	300

It is impossible to estimate the rate at which the assets will be converted into cash, or to determine in advance just how much will ultimately be realized. It is, however, thought desirable to distribute the cash as promptly as possible, and the problem is how can the cash be distributed, as received, without incurring a risk of relatively overpaying one of the partners. The solution is given on the next page.

It might well be that at the time of the first distribution when the balances due to A, B, and C are respectively $1,000, $3,000, and $6,000, A and B would object to having all the $2,500 paid to C. It would not be unnatural that they should claim either that a third of the sum should be paid to each partner or that it should be divided, $250 to A, $750 to B, and $1,500 to C. There is probably no legal way of enforcing the scheme of distribution as outlined below. But

TABLE SHOWING INSTALLMENT DISTRIBUTION

	A	B	C
Balances on books after allocation of deficit	$ 1,000	$ 3,000	$ 6,000
$2,500 cash realized. Allocation of loss possible if remaining assets prove worthless ($10,000 — $2,500)	2,500	2,500	2,500
Balances	$—1,500	$+ 500	$+3,500
Allocation of A's deficit	+1,500	— 750	— 750
Balances		$— 250	$+2,750
B's deficit charged off		+ 250	— 250
Balance indicating distribution of $2,500 cash			$ 2,500
Balances on books after distribution of $2,500 cash	$ 1,000	$ 3,000	$ 3,500
$1,500 cash realized. Allocation of loss possible if remaining assets prove worthless ($7,500 — $1,500)	2,000	2,000	2,000
Balances	$—1,000	$+1,000	$+1,500
Allocation of A's deficit	+1,000	— 500	— 500
Balances indicating distribution of $1,500..		$ 500	$ 1,000
Balances on books after distribution of $1,500 cash	$ 1,000	$ 2,500	$ 2,500
$4,500 cash realized. Allocation of loss possible if remaining assets prove worthless ($6,000 — $4,500)	500	500	500
Balances showing distribution of $4,500 cash	$ 500	$ 2,000	$ 2,000
Balances on books after distribution of $4,500 cash	$ 500	$ 500	$ 500
$300 cash realized. Allocation of loss possible if remaining assets prove worthless ($1,500 — $300)	400	400	400
Balances showing distribution of $300 cash	$ 100	$ 100	$ 100
Balances on books after distribution of $300 cash	$ 300	$ 300	$ 300

if, as assumed, there is real uncertainty as to how much would be realized from the remaining $7,500 of miscellaneous assets, it might be unwise to adopt any other basis of distribution than that described. The only recourse, should A or B object, would be to refrain from any distribution until enough had been collected to make certain that subsequent shrinkage would not create a debit balance in the account of any one of the partners.[5]

Schedule for Payments

The method illustrated above clearly determines, at the time that a distribution is to be made, just how it is to be apportioned. It may, however, be advisable to prepare in advance of any collection of cash the procedure which is to be followed. It might for instance be of considerable advantage to A to learn in advance that not until $7,000 has been paid to B and C can he receive any of the proceeds of liquidation, and that thereafter he may receive one third of whatever comes in. This knowledge might be of value to him in planning for financing future operations. It is well, therefore, in such a case to prepare a schedule in advance. In the illustration given above, the three partners are to share losses equally; but if nothing were to come in, the books show that the losses would be as follows: A, $1,000; B, $3,000; C, $6,000. It is apparent therefore that before anything is properly to be paid to A the amount which B and C together have at hazard should be reduced to $2,000. This implies that $7,000 is to be paid to B and C before anything is to be paid to A. But there is no reason why equity should not be established between B and C as rapidly as possible, even though there may be a danger that both of them will lose proportionately more than A. Therefore, the $3,000 should be paid to C before anything is paid to B. The schedule can be, therefore, arranged as follows:

	A	B	C
The first $3,000 is distributed			100 %
The next $4,000 is distributed		50 %	50
Thereafter any receipts	33⅓ %	33⅓	33⅓

Applying this schedule to the receipts in the case given above, the first installment of $2,500 goes entirely to C.

[5] Kester, *Accounting, Theory and Practice*, 2d ed., II, p. 629.

When the next installment of $1,500 is realized, $500 of this goes to C as making up the first item of the schedule, the remaining $1,000 is distributed equally between B and C in accordance with the second item of the schedule. The third installment of $4,500 furnishes the $3,000 necessary to complete the second item of the schedule, leaving $1,500 to be distributed equally between A, B, and C.

Loans by Partners

The courts have generally insisted that in the case of a partnership dissolution, loans to the partnership by one of the members should be first paid out of the assets before any payments are made to the partners on capital account. This is also provided for in the Uniform Partnership Act which specifies that the assets shall be used to liquidate the amounts owed to the partners in the following order: (1) partnership loan or advance, (2) partnership capital, (3) partnership profits.

This statement, however, needs some qualifications. In case the assets are ample so that there is no possibility of there being a debit balance in the capital account of any one of the partners, it is entirely proper that in point of time the repayment of money borrowed from one of the partners should precede payments on account of capital contributions. It is not correct, however, to state that the loan by a partner has priority over the claims of his partners for contributed capital in the sense that the first mortgage takes precedence over a second mortgage or an unsecured loan. This may be illustrated by assuming a partnership in which A has contributed $5,000, and B $3,000, and in addition B has loaned to the partnership $2,000. The agreement provides for the equal division of profits between the two partners. At the time of the liquidation the ascertained value of all the assets is $4,000, but it will require some time before these assets can all be converted into cash. If $2,000 cash is realized, it is entirely proper to apply this as a payment of the note due to B and in that sense it is proper to speak of the partners' loan as having precedence over capital contributions. In other circumstances, however, it would be undesirable to give any precedence to the loan due to B. This may be illustrated by another partnership in which profits are also to be divided equally. At the time of liquidation, the status is as follows:

Balance Sheet

Cash	$ 4,000	A, Capital	$ 7,000
Deficit	6,000	B, Capital	1,000
		B, Loan	2,000
	$10,000		$10,000

Even though cash more than sufficient to pay B's note is already at hand, it would not be proper to pay it. If this were done and the deficit appearing upon the books were divided in the agreed ratio, there would result the following balance sheet:

Balance Sheet

Cash	$ 2,000	A, Capital	$ 4,000
Due from B	2,000		
	$ 4,000		$ 4,000

If equity is to be secured to A, it will be necessary not only to pay to him the remaining $2,000 cash but to collect back from B just the sum that was paid to him on account of his note. The recovery of this may be difficult or impossible. In any case, it seems undesirable that cash, which ultimately should go to A should be temporarily handed to B, placing upon A the necessity of taking action for recovery.

The proper way of handling such cases is to disregard entirely any distinction between the capital account and the loan account. When liquidation begins, the loan to or from any partner should be respectively debited or credited to his capital account. The ascertained loss should also be charged to the capital account in the regular way. If this were done in the case assumed, the resulting balance sheet would appear as follows:

Balance Sheet

Cash	$ 4,000	A, Capital	$ 4,000
		B, Capital	0
	$ 4,000		$ 4,000

From this it would be clear that all the $4,000 should be paid to A and the inconveniences caused by treating the note separately would be avoided. Where the assets are of a somewhat uncertain value and will be realized by a gradual process of sale, the treatment of the loan by one of the partners involves the same points which have been discussed above in the question of serial liquidation. Before payment is made, either upon the note or upon capital contributions, precaution should be taken so that there will be no danger of paying to one of the partners, on either account, any money which in the case of further shrinkage would have to be recovered from him for the benefit of another partner.

Partners' Drawing Accounts

In case of liquidation, the treatment of the drawing accounts of the partners, whether showing a debit or credit balance, should be handled in a manner similar to that recommended in respect to a partner's loan. Unless there is complete assurance that no one of the partners' capital accounts will ever show a debit balance, payments should not be made to a partner because of a credit to his drawing account. Drawing accounts and loan accounts should, if there is any uncertainty, be both carried to the partner's capital. The loss when definitely ascertained, should then be charged to the several partners and the balances then outstanding will indicate clearly the amount to be paid to or by each partner. If the final loss is not definitely ascertainable in advance, but, at best, is merely an uncertain estimate, installment distributions of assets in liquidation should be made only after taking the precautions proper to any serial distribution.

Transfer of Partnership to Corporation

It is an ordinary business occurrence for a corporation to take over the business of a partnership. The recording of such a transaction in the accounts does not differ in principle from recording any other ordinary purchase made by a commercial concern. The subject has, however, been referred to in discussing the issue of capital stock for property. Similarly the taking over of the business of one partnership by another calls for no peculiar accounting procedure. Mention may, however, be made here of the entries in the books of the partnership at the time of such a sale. This may be illustrated by assuming a partnership between A and B, profits being shared equally. The status of the partnership is as follows:

Balance Sheet of A and B

Cash	$ 3,000	Accounts Payable	$ 6,000
Accounts Receivable	5,000	A, Capital	14,000
Merchandise	10,000	B, Capital	10,000
Furniture and Fixtures	4,000		
Real Estate	8,000		
	$30,000		$30,000

A contract is made to sell the business, the purchaser taking over all of the assets, assuming the accounts payable, and in addition paying $4,000 for goodwill. There is no reason for presuming that the purchaser will take all the assets at the book value appearing in the accounts of A and B. As a result of bargaining, the following values are agreed upon: merchandise $9,000, real estate $12,000, furniture and fixtures, $3,600, accounts receivable at book value, less allowance of 5 per cent for doubtful debts. On the other hand, the accounts payable are estimated at 2 per cent less than the face amount, that being the price at which they may be discounted. The simplest adjustment in the books of A and B would be secured by the journal entries shown on the next page.

Purchaser	$30,470	
Accounts Payable	6,000	
Assets (listed in detail)		$30,000
Profits on Sale of Business		6,470
Profits on Sale of Business	6,470	
A, Capital		3,235
B, Capital		3,235

If the purchaser pays the purchase price in cash and this is distributed to the two partners, the books would be closed by the following entries:

Cash	$30,470	
Purchaser		$30,470
A, Capital	17,235	
B, Capital	13,235	
Cash		30,470

If payment had been made in stock of the purchasing corporation or by giving to A and B an equivalent partnership interest in a new partnership the items given above under the title of cash would be correspondingly changed.

Adjustment of Values before Transfer

Many accountants, however, think that it is desirable before making the transfer to adjust the values on the books of A and B so that they will correspond to the values which are entered upon the books of the new firm or the purchasing corporation. While this may perhaps be desirable it is not in accordance with ordinary routine accounting procedure. The merchant selling for $1,200 merchandise valued upon his books at $1,000 does not mark up the goods before sale so that the sale transaction itself appears merely as an exchange of goods worth $1,200 for the same amount of cash. If, as in the illustration above, net assets having a book value of $24,000 are sold for $30,470, it would seem satisfactory simply to record the fact that the sale had produced a profit. But the record might be considered more complete if changes were made in the books of A and B, particularly so in respect to recording the item of goodwill which is sold for $4,000 but which at the time has a book value of *nil*. Those preferring the more elaborate record could secure it by the following journal entry:

Loss and Gain on Sale of Business	$1,650	
Merchandise		$1,000
Furniture and Fixtures		400
Accounts Receivable		250
Real Estate	4,000	
Accounts Payable	120	
Goodwill	4,000	
Loss and Gain on Sale of Business		8,120
Loss and Gain on Sale of Business	6,470	
A, Capital		3,235
B, Capital		3,235

The entry for the sale could then be put through the books in terms of the prices agreed upon with the purchaser. An abbreviated form of journal entry would be:

Purchaser	$30,470	
Accounts Payable	5,880	
Assets (listed in detail)		$36,350

When the purchase price is paid and distribution made to the partners the entry would be identical with those given above.

Bibliographical Note

DAWSON, S. S., and DE ZOUCHE, R. C.—*Partnership Accounts* (London, 1913).

DICKSEE, L. R.—*Advanced Accounting* (6th ed., London, 1921), chap. viii.

FINNEY, H. A.—*Principles of Accounting* (New York, 1923), chaps. vi, xvi-xix.

KESTER, R. B.—*Accounting, Theory and Practice* (2d ed., New York, 1923), I, chaps. xxxiii-xxxvii.

LINDLEY, N.—*A Treatise on the Law of Partnership* (8th ed., London, 1912).

PIXLEY, F. W. (Editor)—"Partnership Accounts," in his *Accountants' Dictionary* (London, 1922), pp. 737-71.

POWELSON, J. A.—*Introductory Accounting* (New York, 1926), chaps. xv-xvii.

STAEHLING, C. C.—*Partnership Accounts* (in preparation).

WOODBRIDGE, F. W.—*Elements of Accounting* (New York, 1925), chaps. xviii-xxi.

CHAPTER XXI

THE STATEMENT OF AFFAIRS AND DEFICIENCY ACCOUNT [1]

Purpose of the Statements

These statements, while somewhat outside of the regular scheme of accounts, are sufficiently important to deserve some notice. The statement of affairs is a statement drawn up when a concern becomes insolvent, and designed to indicate to creditors the probable amount which will be realized in liquidation. The deficiency account is a supplement to the statement of affairs and serves to explain how the deficiency shown by the statement of affairs has been caused.

The use of these forms is of English origin and depends on the provisions of the Companies Acts which prescribe the form in which they shall be made out. In the United States the laws are less exact regarding bookkeeping forms, and the statements submitted to the courts are generally not in strict accounting form. But despite the absence of legal authorization, the advantage which results from a clear and formal presentation of the status of the involved concern is great, and the use of these approved forms is to be commended.

Illustrative Problem

The matter may be made clear by presenting an example applying to a typical problem but one which contains only a few items and is free from complications.[2]

---

[1] While recognizing the strength of the argument made by J. T. Madden (*Publications of the A. A. U. I. A.*, IX, p. 158) that a discussion of the statement of affairs should have no place in a work on accounting, the author nevertheless includes this chapter, influenced by the power of convention which has always had so marked an influence in accounting matters.

[2] This problem was given in the examination of the American Institute of Accountants, June, 1917. A solution to the problem, differing slightly

A B finding himself financially embarrassed, is forced to go into liquidation. A statement drawn from his books shows the following balance sheet:

Balance Sheet of AB

Real Estate		$140,000.00	Capital		$229,652.00
Equipment	$75,150		Mortgages on Real Estate		75,000.00
Less Depreciation	821	74,329.00	Accounts Payable		124,615.24
			Notes Payable		80,000.00
Patents		54,700.00			
Investments		33,500.00			
Cash		4,348.64			
Notes Receivable		2,479.75			
Accounts Receivable		31,108.15			
Inventories		81,423.70			
Goodwill		40,000.00			
Trading Losses		47,378.00			
		$509,267.24			$509,267.24

A further examination discloses the following facts:

The real estate is valued at $90,000, the equipment at $30,-000. The patents are considered worthless, with the exception of one thought to have a market value of $5,000. Bonds, with a par value of $27,500, were pledged to secure a collateral loan of $25,000. These have, however, shrunk in value so as to be worth at present prices only $22,000. Included in investments are $5,000 other bonds which are clearly worthless; the other investments have a doubtful value of 50 per cent. The notes receivable are thought to be good. Of the accounts receivable $10,000 are known to be good, $5,000 are known to be bad, and the remainder are expected to pay 80 per cent. The inventories are estimated as worth not more than half of their book value. Goodwill is purely fictitious. Interest accrued on the mortgage is $800, on notes payable, $523. Wages accrued are $1,200. It is further estimated that the expenses of liquidation will amount to $3,000. With these facts and estimates, the statement of affairs and deficiency account would be as follows:

from that here presented, is given by Seymour Walton, in *Journal of Accountancy,* XXIV, p. 468.

STATEMENT

ASSETS

Adjusted Book Values		Expected to Realize
$ 4,348.64	Cash	$ 4,348.64
31,108.15	Accounts Receivable	
	Good $10,000.00	10,000.00
	Doubtful (valued at 80%) 16,108.15	12,886.52
	Bad 5,000.00	
2,479.75	Notes Receivable	2,479.75
33,500.00	Investments	
	Pledged to secure loan .... 27,500.00 (estimated worth $22,000 see contra)	
	Unpledged (estimated 50%) 1,000.00	500.00
	Bad 5,000.00	
81,423.70	Inventories (estimated 50%)	40,711.85
74,329.00	Equipment (less depreciation)	30,000.00
140,000.00	Real Estate, estimated 90,000.00	
	Less Mortgage $75,000	
	Interest 800 75,800.00	14,200.00
54,700.00	Patents	5,000.00
40,000.00	Goodwill	0.
		$120,126.76
	Deduct estimated cost of liquidation	3,000.00
	Available assets	$117,126.76
	Deduct preferential claims for wages	1,200.00
	Assets available for general creditors	$115,926.76
	Deficiency	67,211.48
$461,889.24*		$183,138.24

* The item Trading Losses, $47,378.00, appearing in the balance sheet is subtracted from the capital as shown contra.

OF AFFAIRS

LIABILITIES

Adjusted Book Values			Expected to Rank
$124,615.24	Accounts Payable		$124,615.24
80,000.00	Notes Payable		
	Partly secured	$25,000.00	
	Less securities, see contra	22,000.00	3,000.00
	Unsecured		55,000.00
523.00	Interest on Notes Payable		523.00
800.00	Interest on Mortgages deducted, see contra		
75,000.00	Mortgages on Real Estate deducted, see contra		
1,200.00	Wages accrued deducted, see contra		
179,751.00	Capital (net) †		
$461,889.24			$183,138.24

† This is obtained by subtracting from the capital as shown on the balance sheet, the following items: Trading Losses, $47,378; Interest Accrued, $1,323.00; Wages Accrued, $1,200.

Deficiency Account

Trading losses as per balance sheet.	$47,378.00		Deficiency brought down	$ 67,211.48
Interest accrued	1,323.00		Capital as per balance sheet	229,652.00
Wages accrued	1,200.00			
		$49,901.00		
Estimated shrinkage in value of assets:				
Real Estate	$50,000.00			
Equipment	44,329.00			
Patents	49,700.00			
Investments	11,000.00			
Accounts Receivable	8,221.63			
Inventories	40,711.85			
Goodwill	40,000.00			
		243,962.48		
Estimated expenses of liquidation		3,000.00		
		$296,863.48		$296,863.48
Net free assets	$115,926.76			
General creditors	183,138.24			
Estimated percentage payable to general creditors	63.3%			

Variations in Arrangement

Considerable variation is, however, found in the arrangement of such statements. In the form given above it is noticed that the liabilities are given on the left hand, just as they appear on that side in English balance sheets. By some accountants this order is reversed. Similarly there is a disagreement as a result of that same arrangement of the sides of the deficiency account, some placing the deficiency and capital items on the debit side, and the items showing how the losses occurred on the credit side of the account, as is done above, while others reverse this order. The variations may be classified as follows:

VARIATIONS IN ARRANGEMENT OF STATEMENT OF AFFAIRS AND DEFICIENCY ACCOUNT

	Statement of Affairs		Deficiency Account	
	Left Column	Right Column	Left Column	Right Column
I.	Liabilities	Assets	Capital and Deficiency	Shrinkages, etc.
II.	Liabilities	Assets	Shrinkages, etc.	Capital and Deficiency
III.	Assets	Liabilities	Shrinkages, etc.	Capital and Deficiency

Of these various forms, I corresponds to the schedules of the English Companies Acts and is most generally used in England. The second arrangement is approved by Lisle, Bennett, and Cole. The third form is probably the most commonly used in this country and is recommended by Esquerré, Finney, and Kester.[3] Some of the authors mentioned above have argued at some length in favor of one or another arrangement. Much ingenuity has been exhibited in showing that the arrangement liabilities-assets has some particularly logical justification when used in the statement of affairs. But historically it doubtless arose as that arrangement of the balance sheet customary in England but not elsewhere followed. It may furthermore be noted that in Forms I and III the deficiency in the statement of affairs is carried to the opposite side of the deficiency account, just as a balance of any ledger account is thus transferred to the opposite side. But in Form II, the deficiency item appears on the same side of the two accounts.

Treatment of Valuation Accounts

No set rules can be laid down for the formulation of the statement of affairs and deficiency account. These are both somewhat artistic productions, the whole point of which is

[3] For specific references to the variations in forms mentioned above, see Bibliographical Note at the close of this chapter.

to present certain facts in such a way as best to bring out the desired information. In the infinite variety of circumstances, there is room for an infinite amount of discretion as to the most artistic way of presenting the results. There are some few things, however, which are in general desirable. Valuation accounts, although appearing as credit balances in the ledger, should be subtracted from the assets to which they relate. The actual book value of the machine is the amount appearing as a debit balance in the machinery account less the amount appearing as a credit balance in the allowance for depreciation. The shrinkage, if any takes place in the process of realization, would be a shrinkage from the depreciated value and not from the original cost. It is always desirable, where this can be arranged, to link up the statement of affairs with the balance sheet of the company. This is done in the model form printed above by use of the columns headed adjusted book values. This serves as a convenient check to be sure that everything has been taken into consideration.

Showing Previous Operations in Deficiency Account

In some cases, the deficiency account may reach back to an earlier period so as to show the history of the company not merely in the process of liquidation but during the preceding years. The company, when it started out, had its capital intact. The deficiency account may be so formed as to show how that original capital has been dissipated and not merely the changes that have taken place since the preparation of the last balance sheet. A deficiency account constructed in this manner might be as shown on the opposite page.

Offsetting Debts and Collateral

Liabilities fully secured by specific assets should be subtracted from such assets. Thus a note for $10,000 should be subtracted from the $11,000 Liberty bonds placed as collateral for that note. If in the books there are separate accounts showing land $50,000, and building $100,000, against which there is an outstanding loan secured by mortgage for $80,000,

Deficiency Account

Operating deficit, 1924	$ 5,000		Capital, Jan. 1, 1921		$100,000
Operating deficit, 1925	15,000	$ 20,000	Profits, 1921	$ 8,000	
			Profits, 1922	10,000	
			Profits, 1923	1,000	19,000
Dividends paid, 1921	$ 7,000		Deficiency brought down		31,000
Dividends paid, 1922	8,000	15,000			
Shrinkage in assets (in detail)		115,000			
		$150,000			$150,000

the two accounts representing the value of the real estate should be added and from their total the amount of the mortgage should be subtracted. Preferential claims such as wages are in a way secured by all of the assets of the concern and should be subtracted as in the illustration printed above from the total of the assets rather than from cash on hand as is the practice of some accountants.[4] On the other hand, where a loan is partially secured by the pledge of specific assets, the assets so pledged should be subtracted from the face of the liability, extending only the unsecured portion of the loan.

Alternative Grouping of Liabilities

Accountants sometimes prefer to group the liabilities not in the way in which they are ordinarily presented in the balance sheet, but in the three groups: fully secured liabilities, partially secured liabilities, and unsecured liabilities. This has some advantages and in most cases can be accomplished by the exercise of a little ingenuity. It should not be attempted, however, where the result is an added complexity which de-

[4] This rule can not be rigidly applied. Thus taxes upon real estate are immediately secured by a lien upon the property. But it is in most cases better to treat taxes as a preferred liability to be subtracted from the total of the assets rather than to show it as a subtraction from the value of the real estate.

tracts from rather than increases the intelligibility of the statement.

Bibliographical Note

Bennett, G. E.—*Advanced Accounting* (New York, 1922), pp. 511-7.

Cole, W. M.—*The Fundamentals of Accounting* (Boston, 1921), pp. 355-9.

Couchman, C. B.—*The Balance Sheet,* chap. xv.

Cropper, L. C.—*Accounting* (London, 1924), pp. 415-28.

Dicksee, L. R.—*Advanced Accounting* (6th ed., London, 1921), chap. xiii.

Esquerré, P.-J.—*Applied Theory of Accounts* (New York, 1914), chap. xxxix.

Finney, H. A.—*Principles of Accounting* (New York, 1923), I, chaps. xxi, xxii.

Kester, R. B.—*Accounting, Theory and Practice* (2d ed., New York, 1925), II, pp. 644-59.

Lisle, G.—*Accounting, Theory and Practice,* pp. 82-95.

CHAPTER XXII

CONSOLIDATED BALANCE SHEET

Consolidation in Business

Business, in recent years, has been characterized by the tendency to form larger industrial and financial units. Corporate organization had already in the middle of the last century begun to supplant the individual trader and the partnership, because it was better adapted than either of these for securing relatively large amounts of capital. Toward the end of the century there appeared a tendency to consolidate previously existing corporations, securing thereby still larger units, with the expectation that greater efficiency would thereby be secured.

It is not necessary to recount the arguments in favor of larger business units, nor to discuss how far the expected advantages have been gained, nor how far the advantage to the organization represents a loss or gain to the consumer and the public. To the accountant it suffices to see how the movement toward consolidation has been reflected in accounting practice.

Two Methods of Consolidating Corporations

There are two principal forms in which the combining of previously separate, and perhaps competing, concerns has been brought about. In one, those interested in effecting the combination buy from one or more concerns their plants and other assets just as any purchaser may at any time buy a single article of merchandise. The transactions are identical in principle and even the differences in detail are relatively simple. The purchase may be for cash or it may be paid for by issuing to the vendor securities of one kind or another. The purchaser may pay the full purchase price, or, as is so often the case in the purchase of real estate, he may pay part of the price and assume some already existing liability of the vendor.

In the other method the assets of the existing concern are not bought. Indeed, at least formally, there is no transaction between that concern and the organization attempting to bring about a combination. The transaction is one between the combining corporation, ordinarily called the holding company, and the individual stockholders of previously existing corporations. Here again the transaction while at times novel in purpose and startling in magnitude, is, so far as accounting goes, exactly the same as any other purchase of stock, in large or small amount. The former stockholder sells his shares and the purchaser makes payment therefor in such medium as is mutually satisfactory.

Balance Sheets after Consolidation

These two methods of securing control may be illustrated in extremely simple form by assuming that Corporation H is organized with $1,500,000 capital stock which is used to make a combination of Corporations A and B whose balance sheets are respectively:

Balance Sheet of A

Plant and other assets	$600,000	Capital Stock	$300,000
		Surplus	300,000
	$600,000		$600,000

Balance Sheet of B

Plant and other assets	$300,000	Capital Stock	$300,000

The agreement made is that three shares of stock of Corporation H shall be given in exchange for each share of stock in A, that $400,000 stock shall be given for the plant, goodwill, and other assets of B, and that the remaining stock of H is to be issued to subscribers for cash at par.

Assuming that the bargain is an equitable one all around,

the balance sheets of the three corporations, after the transactions, will be:

Balance Sheet of H

Stock of Corporation A 3,000 shares at $300	$900,000	Capital Stock	$1,500,000
Plant, etc.	300,000		
Goodwill at cost	100,000		
Cash	200,000		
	$1,500,000		$1,500,000

Balance Sheet of A

Plant and other assets	$600,000	Capital Stock	$300,000
		Surplus	300,000
	$600,000		$600,000

Balance Sheet of B

Stock of Company H 4,000 shares of $100	$400,000	Capital Stock	$300,000
		Surplus	100,000
	$400,000		$400,000

The balance sheet of A is unchanged as the transaction was between H and the individual shareholders. The balance sheet of B shows stock of H held as the only asset. Remembering the assumption made above, that the consolidation is in all respects equitable, which implies that full par value is given and received, B must show a surplus (profit) of $100,000 for it sold its assets at an advance of that amount over their book value. H shows the stock of A, which it bought of the shareholders, but not the assets of A which still belong to the latter corporation, the only change being a shifting in the personnel of the stockholders. But it shows not only the assets which formerly appeared in the balance sheet of B but also the goodwill which it bought, which was not listed as an asset by B but which is legitimately included in those of H.

It is furthermore clear that the stock of H might have been issued at a premium, or a discount, and that any possible variation in terms and prices could occur without affecting the principles elucidated in this most simple illustration. As to the legality of the combination under statute law the present discussion is not concerned, but providing a consolidation is effected in the manner specified, the accounting should be as given above.

The balance sheet of H is technically correct and corresponds with the accounts appearing on its ledger. But the picture thereby presented is, from many points of view, unsatisfactory. It shows the material assets, the actual plant, and the cash, and together with these a large holding of an investment security. Legally and technically this corresponds with the facts, but from the viewpoint of the industry what actually exists is a combination of the plants of both A and B into a larger economic unit, working for a common end and under uniform management. It is true that A still maintains its juristic existence, the assets still belong to that corporation, it is still taxed, the real estate still is recorded as belonging to A. But since H holds all the stock of A it evidently is in a position to choose all its directors, and being sole owner has undivided interest in all its earnings.

Consolidated Balance Sheet

There has accordingly been devised a form of statement, known as the consolidated balance sheet, which attempts to present a picture of the economic unit as a whole, rather than an exact representation of the accounts of the legally independent corporations. If this were done in the assumed case the consolidated balance sheet would be:

Consolidated Balance Sheet of H and Subsidiary Companies

Plant, etc.	$900,000	Capital Stock	$1,500,000
Cash	200,000		
Goodwill	400,000		
	$1,500,000		$1,500,000

Rules for Preparing Consolidated Balance Sheet

The procedure involved in preparing such a consolidated balance sheet is simple in principle although its application in complicated cases may be extremely difficult. The rules may be stated as follows:

1. Assets and liabilities of the subsidiary companies are substituted for their stock appearing as an asset in the balance sheet of the holding company.

2. Where the value attached to the stock of the subsidiary in the balance sheet of the holding company does not correspond to the value of the net assets on the books of the subsidiary, adjustment is made in the consolidated balance sheet. When, as is generally the case in American corporations, the value attributed to the stock as an asset exceeds the book value of the net assets which it represents, the difference is entered in the consolidated balance sheet as goodwill. The statement of this rule of procedure does not imply that it is proper, but merely that it is customary.[1]

3. If a credit in the balance sheet of one company represents a debit in the balance sheet of another company (within the consolidation) the two items are canceled one against the other in preparing the consolidated balance sheet. Debts due from one company to another are thus eliminated.

Illustrative Problem

In the illustration given above all of the stock of the subsidiary company was purchased at more than its book value. This accordingly represented only one possible combination for the holding company might acquire not all but only a major part of the stock of the subsidiary company and this might be purchased either at its book value or below or above that figure. The application of the rules just given to all six conditions of purchase are discussed below. It is assumed

---

[1] Saliers makes the admirable suggestion that instead of charging the amount to Goodwill, it should be charged to a distinctive account such as "Cost of Stock of Subsidiary in Excess of its Book Value." *Accountants' Hand Book,* p. 1118.

that Corporation H is organized with $300,000 capital stock, its object is to secure a consolidation of two existing corporations whose balance sheets at the time are as follows:

Balance Sheet of A

Mine	$90,000	Capital Stock	$100,000
Accounts Receivable	10,000	Accounts Payable	20,000
Cash	20,000		
	$120,000		$120,000

Balance Sheet of B

Factory	$ 70,000	Capital Stock	$ 50,000
Merchandise	25,000	Surplus	50,000
Accounts Receivable	30,000	Accounts Payable	35,000
Cash	10,000		
	$135,000		$135,000

The $10,000 accounts receivable held by A are due from B. H issues its stock in exchange for stock of the subsidiary companies to the amount required and issues its remaining stock at par for cash. The different terms of consolidation illustrated below are as follows:

1. H buys all of the stock of A at par and all the stock of B at 200.
2. H buys all of the stock of A at 120 and all of the stock of B at 250.
3. H buys $90,000 (par value) of the stock of A at 100 and $40,000 of the stock of B at 200.
4. H buys $90,000 (par value) of the stock of A at 120 and $40,000 of the stock of B at 250.
5. H buys all of the stock of A at 80 and all of the stock of B at 150.
6. H buys $90,000 of the stock of A at 80 and $40,000 of the stock of B at 150.

Solution to Problem

The consolidated balance sheets resulting from the first four transactions are exhibited in the table given below. Two variations in the treatment of transaction four are given.

CONSOLIDATED BALANCE SHEETS RESULTING FROM TRANSACTIONS 1 TO 4 ABOVE

	1	2	3	4a	4b
Cash	$130,000	$ 85,000	$160,000	$122,000	$122,000
Accounts Receivable	30,000	30,000	30,000	30,000	30,000
Merchandise	25,000	25,000	25,000	25,000	25,000
Factory	70,000	70,000	70,000	70,000	70,000
Mine	90,000	90,000	90,000	90,000	90,000
Goodwill		45,000		45,000	38,000
	$345,000	$345,000	$375,000	$382,000	$375,000
Capital Stock	$300,000	$300,000	$300,000	$300,000	$300,000
Accounts Payable	45,000	45,000	45,000	45,000	45,000
Outstanding Stockholders:					
A			10,000	12,000	10,000
B			20,000	25,000	20,000
	$345,000	$345,000	$375,000	$382,000	$375,000

Discussion of Solution

The problems stated above are so simple as to require little explanation. In column 1, the book value of the assets held by A and B is substituted for the stock of these two companies held by H and no further adjustment is needed inasmuch as the stock was acquired at its book value. The only modification made was the cancelation of the $10,000 due from B to A.

In column 2 the entire business of A was purchased for $120,000. The book value of the net assets, however, was only $100,000. Assuming that the values attached to the several tangible assets are correct, it is assumed that the additional $20,000 paid by H must represent the purchase of goodwill. In the case of B, $125,000 was paid for a business whose book value is only $100,000 and this is taken to represent a payment of $25,000 for goodwill. Accordingly in column 2 the item goodwill appears among the assets of the consolidated balance sheet valued at the sum of these two figures or $45,000. In column 3 there appears an item showing the interest in the consolidation belonging to the stockholders of A and B whose stock has not been sold to H. Company H in purchasing $90,000 of the stock of A, really acquired an equity of 9/10 of the mine and a similar proportion of the accounts receivable and the cash belonging to A, but for the purposes of the consolidated balance sheet it is undesirable to show among the assets only that portion in which H has an equitable interest. The assets are accordingly listed at their full value and the entire ownership is shown as made up of two items: that represented by the capital stock of H and that represented by the stock of A held by individuals who have not sold their holdings to H. The interest of outstanding stockholders in A is $10,000, in B $20,000, the latter represented by capital stock with a par value of $10,000, to which there attaches an equal interest in the surplus of the company as shown upon its books.

Outstanding Shareholders' Interest in Goodwill: First Method

In columns 4a and 4b are shown two different treatments where the holding company acquires only part of the stock of the two subsidiaries but pays for such stock more than its book value. In 4a the calculation of the value of goodwill is the same as that exhibited in column 2. The actual value of A stock, as evidenced by the price paid by H, is 120. As all shares of stock are equal it is calculated, just as in column 2, that the total value of the business must be $120,000, giving rise to the insertion of goodwill of A of $20,000. By similar calculation, the goodwill of B must be worth $25,000. The outstanding stockholders of A have a 1/10 equity in all of the business, including the goodwill, or $12,000. Similarly the outstanding stock of B being 1/5 of all of the stock presumably is worth 1/5 of $125,000, or $25,000. This calculation implies a hypothetical writing into the balance sheet of A and B of the goodwill and a corresponding increase in the amount of surplus shown on their books. If this change were actually made, instead of being implied, the balance sheet of B would be as follows:

Balance Sheet of B

Factory	$ 70,000	Capital Stock	$ 50,000
Merchandise	25,000	Surplus representing goodwill	25,000
Accounts Receivable	30,000	Surplus	50,000
Cash	10,000	Accounts Payable	35,000
Goodwill	25,000		
	$160,000		$160,000

With a balance sheet such as this it is obvious that the ownership of $10,000 capital stock would represent a total value of $25,000. In preparing the consolidated balance sheet it might even be desirable to indicate the interest of the outstanding stock more in detail, as for instance:

Outstanding Stockholders of A

Par value	$10,000	
Surplus	10,000	
Share of goodwill	5,000	
		$25,000

Outstanding Shareholders' Interest in Goodwill: Second Method

The calculation upon which 4b is based is as follows: Company H bought 9/10 of B. The book value of this 9/10 interest was $90,000. For this H paid $108,000, the difference, $18,000, being held to represent purchased goodwill. Similarly H bought 4/5 of B with a book value of $80,000 for which it paid $100,000. The difference in this case is held to represent goodwill worth $20,000, making a total sum paid for goodwill of $38,000. In this column, the interest of the outstanding stockholders is taken merely at the book value of such interest without any estimate of recognized goodwill.

Probably the majority of accountants prefer to follow the form set forth in 4b, calculating as the value of goodwill only the excess of the price paid by the holding company above the book value of the share purchased by it. It is argued that there is a generally accepted rule that goodwill is to appear in the balance sheet only where it has been purchased and only at the purchased price. As the outstanding stockholders of A and B have purchased no goodwill, it is argued that only that which has been purchased by Corporation H can legitimately appear in the consolidated balance sheet.

This argument seems to rest upon a mere verbal interpretation of formal accounting rules. Accountants in preparing the balance sheet of a corporation have been so often brought to task for exhibiting goodwill, which has not been subject to a distinct purchase and sale, that they think the same objection applies even in the case of a consolidated balance sheet. But a consolidated balance sheet is not an actual balance sheet and it violates other even more fundamental accounting rules. Certainly no one would justify a corporation presenting a balance sheet in which are included assets belonging to some other corporation. But in the consolidated balance sheet of a purely holding corporation, all of the assets, technically and legally, belong not to the holding but to the subsidiary companies. In the ordinary balance sheet, it would be highly improper to cancel accounts receivable against accounts payable, but this is properly done in a consolidated balance sheet. Inasmuch as in the consolidated balance sheet the full value of each of the assets is shown, although the holding company has only a fractional interest therein, it seems needlessly inconsistent in regard to the single asset goodwill to show only part of its value and to neglect entirely that portion representing the equity of the outstanding stockholders. And finally, it is certainly inconsistent and contradictory to assume that when the value of 900 shares has been established at 120 by an actual purchase and sale, the remaining 100 shares of exactly similar stock may not have the same value attributed to them.

Form of Balance Sheet Where Stock Is Purchased below Book Value

There remains to be considered the form of the balance sheet representing transactions where the stock of the subsidiary corporations is bought at less than its book value. In American consolidations, it has almost universally been the case that the stock of the holding company exceeds both the sale value and the book value of the stock for which it is issued. The assumption in such cases is that the excess value represents purchased goodwill. How is the difference between the purchase price and the book value to be treated where the latter exceeds the former?

Three methods[2] of handling the problem are: (1) to consider an element of negative goodwill; that is, that the goodwill acquired in the purchase of other companies is to be diminished; (2) to show upon the consolidated balance sheet a capital surplus due to the fact that a greater value of assets has been acquired than the amount of par value of the stock issued therefor; (3) to introduce into the balance sheet a valuation account entitled possibly Reserve Representing Overvaluation of Assets of Subsidiaries.

1. *Negative Goodwill*

The first rests upon the consistently logical argument that if the excess of the new stock represents goodwill the underissue represents something which may be designated as negative goodwill. But the conception of negative goodwill is a rather difficult one and accountants are inclined to apply it with but a halting and imperfect consistency. The item of negative goodwill is not shown upon the balance sheet but is subtracted from goodwill already owned or acquired in the purchase of some other subsidiary. Thus, if a holding company had purchased the stock of one corporation on such terms as to indicate goodwill valued at $50,000, but had bought all of the stock of another company with a book value of $100,000 for $80,000, the consolidated balance sheet, it is argued, should show goodwill valued at $30,000. This means that a positive goodwill of $50,000 acquired from one company is offset by a negative goodwill of $20,000, the difference between these two sums only appearing in the balance sheet.

---

[2] Montgomery, *Auditing, Theory and Practice,* 3d ed., I, 346.

It does not, however, seem proper to adjust the divergence between the book value of the acquired stock and the price paid therefor by changing the value of other assets acquired in another transaction. This is equivalent to the following: A corporation acquires a plant valued upon the vendor's books at $100,000 but actually worth in tangible value without any estimate of goodwill $200,000. For this the purchaser pays $200,000. It acquires from a second company a mine whose book value is $200,000 but whose actual value (without the introduction of any such unnecessary conception as negative goodwill) is only $100,000 and pays that sum for the mine. It is obvious that in the balance sheet of the purchasing corporation the mine should be listed as worth $100,000 and the manufacturing plant at $200,000. There would be no argument in favor of subtracting from the actual value of the plant the amount which should be subtracted from the book value of the mine. From the viewpoint of accounting theory the same argument applies to the question of the valuation to be attached to goodwill acquired from one company when there is a question as to the proper valuation to be attached to the assets of another subsidiary. There is no connection between the two subsidiaries save through the element of stockholdership.

2. Premium on Stock of Holding Company

The second method implies that the stock of the holding company has been issued at a premium. While this is, of course, a possible arrangement it would in almost every case be far removed from the actual facts.

3. Recognition of Overvaluation

The third method is probably more nearly correct. If the acquired stock of the company is not worth its book value presumably the net assets are not worth the sum of the individual values attached to them in the books of the vendor. It may not be known which one of these assets is overvalued, but the fact of a general overvaluation can be adequately represented by crediting the difference to Allowance Representing Overvaluation of Assets of Subsidiaries which in the balance sheet should properly be treated similarly to an allowance for depreciation and subtracted from the sum of the shown assets. This treatment is not inconsistent with the concept of negative goodwill, for the item overvalued may well be goodwill. But overvaluation of assets, while more frequent in the case of goodwill, may also occur in real estate and other assets.

In these matters there is, however, irreducible inconsistency. The accountant is asked to assume, where the stock of the subsidiary is purchased at more than its book value, that the stock of the holding company is worth par value and also that the tangible assets of the subsidiary companies are worth just the values attributed to them in the books of the subsidiary. Both of these statements can, however, not be true where stock is issued to an amount less than the book value of the acquired stock. If it is legitimate in one case to show a premium or surplus arising from the issue of the stock of the holding company, it would be proper to show a discount where the stock is issued in excess. If the assets are to be marked up in one case, they should be marked down in the other. The difficulty is, of course, that in most cases the stock issued has in reality been put out at a discount, but those concerned are unwilling to show this fact as it might imply a responsibility upon the part of the recipients of the stock for the amount of the discount.

The problem would be somewhat clearer and simpler if the stock of the holding company were issued to subscribers for cash and the stock of the subsidiaries were paid for in cash and not in stock. If this were the case it would be clear that where control of a subsidiary is secured by purchasing its stock at less than its book value, there is either an element of negative goodwill or the book value of the assets is overstated and a reappraisal is necessary. In preparing the consolidated balance sheet it may not be possible to make such reappraisal, but the fact of overvaluation can be adequately represented by crediting an allowance for overvaluation as indicated above.

Surplus of Subsidiary at Time of Consolidation

Another matter on which accountants disagree relates to the treatment of a surplus shown upon the books of a subsidiary company at the time that the holding company acquires the stock. Reducing to even more simple terms the treatment shown above, the situation of two corporations may be as follows:

Balance Sheet of Corporation B

Miscellaneous Assets	$100,000	Capital Stock	$ 50,000
		Surplus	50,000
	$100,000		$100,000

Balance Sheet of Corporation H

Stock of B at 200	$100,000	Capital Stock	$100,000
	$100,000		$100,000

The question at issue is whether the consolidated balance sheet should appear as follows:

Consolidated Balance Sheet

Miscellaneous Assets	$100,000	Capital Stock	$100,000
Goodwill	50,000	Surplus	50,000
	$150,000		$150,000

or:

Consolidated Balance Sheet

Miscellaneous Assets	$100,000	Capital Stock	$100,000
	$100,000		$100,000

The first form is advocated, although perhaps not in the bald form in which it is here presented, by accountants of high repute. The argument, although not always clearly expressed, in favor of this procedure is probably that it is desirable in the consolidated balance sheet to indicate that there is somewhere a surplus of $50,000 which is available for distribution and, if this surplus appears in the consolidated balance sheet, the gap on the asset side is filled by the insertion of purely fictitious goodwill. But this rests upon a misconception. It is true that Corporation B is in a position to make a dividend of $50,000, but the consolidation as a whole may not do so. If Corporation B should make a cash dividend of its entire surplus, that item would disappear from its balance sheet but it would not create a credit to Profit and Loss nor to Surplus upon the books of Corporation H. After such a dividend was paid, the balance sheets of the two corporations should be as follows:

Balance Sheet of Corporation B

Miscellaneous Assets	$ 50,000	Capital Stock	$ 50,000
	$ 50,000		$ 50,000

Balance Sheet of Corporation H

Stock of B at cost	$100,000		Capital Stock	$100,000
Less Dividend	50,000			
	$ 50,000			
Cash	50,000			
	$100,000			$100,000

The $50,000 received by H as dividend is in no sense profit. It represents part of the capital investment. The stock of B at the time of purchase was worth 200, presumably because it carried an equity in assets of that amount, but this equity has been reduced by one half at the time that the cash dividend is paid.[3] The consolidation as a whole, therefore, has no surplus, it cannot pay any dividends and the mere transfer of cash from the treasury of one corporation to another is not anything which can be reflected in a consolidated balance sheet.

[3] *Cf.* May in *Journal of Accountancy,* XL, p. 251.

CONSOLIDATED BALANCE SHEET—WORKING SHEET

ASSETS	A	B	H	Total	Eliminations	
Mine	$ 90,000			$ 90,000		$ 90,000
Factory		$ 70,000		70,000		70,000
Accounts Receivable	10,000	30,000		40,000	(a) $ 10,000	30,000
Cash	20,000	10,000	$ 55,000	85,000		85,000
Merchandise		25,000		25,000		25,000
A, Stock			120,000	120,000	(b) 120,000	
B, Stock			125,000	125,000	(c) 125,000	
Goodwill					(b) *20,000** (c) *25,000**	45,000
	$120,000	$135,000	$300,000	$555,000	$210,000	$345,000
LIABILITIES AND CAPITAL						
Accounts Payable	$ 20,000	$ 35,000		$ 55,000	(a) $ 10,000	$ 45,000
Capital Stock	100,000	50,000	$300,000	450,000	(b) 100,000 (c) 50,000	300,000
Surplus		50,000		50,000	(c) 50,000	
	$120,000	$135,000	$300,000	$555,000	$210,000	$345,000

*** Italicised items are to be added.**

Probably those accountants who have adopted the first of the two treatments described above would not advocate it in so flagrant a case as is given here, but the principle is not affected by the amounts or ratios involved. The holding company may, of course, acquire a surplus, in the form of premium on capital stock if, in buying the stock of the subsidiary company, it acquires assets exceeding in value the par of the holding-company stock issued in exchange. But this is irrespective of surplus on the books of the subsidiary. Thus a company might have assets actually worth $110,000. If a holding company acquired all the stock of the subsidiary by issuing $100,000 of its own stock, there would arise a premium on stock which would appear on the books of the holding company and also on the consolidated balance sheet. This surplus would appear whether the books of the subsidiary company showed $100,000 nominal capital and $10,000 surplus, $110,000 capital and no surplus, or $120,000 capital and a deficit of $10,000. Clearly the surplus acquired by the holding company and shown in the consolidated balance sheet is not that shown on the books of the subsidiary company.

Working Sheet

In the technic of preparing a consolidated balance sheet it is customary, when the accounts are at all complicated, to make use of a working sheet somewhat as shown in the form on page 454.

Bibliographical Note

Couchman, C. B.—*The Balance Sheet* (New York, 1924), chap. xxi.

Esquerré, P.-J.—*Applied Theory of Accounts* (New York, 1914), chap. xxxviii.

Finney, H. A.—*Consolidated Statements* (New York, 1922). The most complete treatment of the subject.

Garnsey, G. F.—*Holding Companies and Their Published Accounts* (London, 1923). The most complete treatment from the English viewpoint.

Kester, R. B.—*Accounting, Theory and Practice* (2d ed., New York, 1925), II, chaps. xxi-xxxiii.

Montgomery, R. H.—*Auditing, Theory and Practice* (3d ed., New York, 1922), I, chap. xviii.

CHAPTER XXIII

INTERPRETATION OF THE BALANCE SHEET

The Meaning of Accounts

Accounting is not merely the working out of an intricate puzzle consisting in carefully matching debits and credits so that they will form a nicely balanced equation. It is an attempt by the means of debits and credits to present a picture of business conditions which will be of significance to all concerned. This is not to be looked upon as a mere set of figures, but as the embodiment of essential financial facts. The work of accounting is not accomplished until the accounts as presented are interpreted. Some attention, therefore, may well be given to the procedure to be followed in extracting from the balance sheet the significant meaning which it contains.

Comparison of Assets and Liabilities

The balance sheet both historically and practically is primarily a statement showing the relation between assets and liabilities. The most obvious fact displayed is the relation between these two categories. The recent improvement in the form of balance sheet makes such a comparison easier in that all the liabilities are subsumed in a single total which can be compared with another total showing the net assets. The separation between proprietorship and liability items on one side and the subtraction of valuation accounts from the assets on the other bring out more clearly the figures to be compared, and for this reason that arrangement is to be commended.

The Current Ratio

In many cases the most significant fact is, however, not the relation between all of the assets and all of the liabilities, but rather the relationship between the current assets and the current liabilities. In obtaining a loan from a bank or credit from a wholesaler, this ratio is of prime importance, for neither the bank nor the wholesaler is particularly worried about the bonded debt due many years hence, but they both wish very precise information regarding the debts which will shortly demand payment and the funds from which payment is to be made. The making of the comparison between these two items is facilitated by exhibiting in the balance sheet a subtotal for each of these categories. The ratio between them is ordinarily called the current ratio and in a very loose and inaccurate way banks and credit men have assumed that a ratio of two to one is fairly normal. In computing the current ratio, it has been customary to include among current assets, merchandise and other working assets as well as cash and receivables. Some critics also include prepaid expenses. This is justified, if at all, on the ground that although prepaid expenses are not a source for paying debt, their existence in the balance sheet indicates that just so much cash, which otherwise would have to be used for paying running expenses, will be available for meeting debts.

The "Acid Test"

A more rigid comparison is sometimes made between the sum of cash and receivables (possibly including also marketable securities held instead of cash) and current liabilities. Again, there has been a crude rule of thumb that the normal ratio between these two sums should be one. This ratio is commonly spoken of as the "acid test."

The Seven Ratios

In very recent years, the attempt to analyze and interpret balance sheets has been more seriously undertaken and attention is called to other ratios in addition to the current ratio. Among those which have been especially emphasized are the following: receivables to merchandise, net worth to fixed assets, sales to receivables, sales to merchandise, sales to net worth, total liabilities to net worth.[1] The significance of the first of these ratios lies in the fact that while receivables are perhaps more available as a means of payment than unsold merchandise, yet they involve an element of profit which is thought by some to distort the picture, for the substitution of receivables for merchandise does in itself automatically raise the current ratio. The ratio between net worth and fixed assets is significant as bearing upon the accepted notion that the owners of the business should normally furnish most of the fixed investment, calling upon the banks only for aid in securing the current and working assets. Where there are long-term bonds issued for securing a plant, this ratio is not of so much importance as in the case of a partnership engaged in purely commercial operations.

The ratio between sales and receivables emphasizes the rapidity with which payment is made for purchases and gives an indication as to how soon payments of the outstanding receivables may be expected. The ratio of sales to net worth is significant as indicating how far the concern is efficiently managed in turning over its capital, and the last ratio mentioned, that of total liabilities to net worth, shows the extent to which the owners of the concern have contributed capital as a guaranty fund for the protection of creditors.

It is obvious that no adequate general statement can be made as to the proper ratio in any or all of these matters. The ratio of two to one for the current ratio, despite its wide currency, has no scientific basis. Perhaps the first attempt to seek for a criterion for judging in these matters was that made by Alexander Wall in the article mentioned above. In this he has gathered statistics relating to businesses of many types and located in different sections of the country. These

---

[1] Wall, "Study of Credit Barometrics," *Federal Reserve Bulletin*, V, p. 229. While these ratios apply to balance sheet figures, three of them imply also information regarding the amount of sales, not shown in the balance sheet. Gilman in his *Analyzing Financial Statements*, p. 68, gives nearly the same list but omits the ratio of receivables to merchandise and adds the ratio of sales to fixed assets and the "acid test."

present not any *a priori* idea as to what would be a proper ratio, but a statement as to what the actual ratio is in the various groups and localities examined. Further investigation along this line offers rich return and should attract many accountants.

Charges to Goodwill and to Plant

There are a few other matters to which attention should be given in attempting to interpret any single balance sheet. One of these is the presence of a large sum under the title goodwill. As was stated in the discussion in Chapter I, the presence of goodwill in the balance sheet is, as a matter of fact, always more or less suspicious. In many, if not in most cases, it conceals a deficit and does not represent an asset. Somewhat similarly the presence of large amounts charged to fixed plant raises the question as to whether the distinction between capital expenditures and charges against revenue has been properly maintained. In many cases items which should have been charged as an expense may have been included in cost of plant and there again represent a deficit rather than an asset.

The Comparative Balance Sheet

The attempt to estimate the condition of a concern by a single balance sheet is, however, always difficult. Much better results are obtained by comparing at least two successive balance sheets. The changes which have taken place are oftentimes more significant than the present condition. In any event, an indication of the changes between two balance sheets calls attention to many matters which otherwise would escape notice. The use of the comparative balance sheet form, such as that of the General Motors Company, printed in Form 3, facilitates making a list of the changes occurring in balance sheet items.

The comparison is made even more easy by adding to the comparative balance sheet a third column in which the changes in valuation which have taken place during the year are distinctly set forth so that the reader is saved the onerous and obnoxious task of making a series of subtractions. Such an arrangement is shown below:

COMPARATIVE BALANCE SHEET

The Goodrich Rubber Company

ASSETS	1913	1912		
Plants, patents, goodwill	$71,060,813	$70,685,722	Increase	$ 375,091
Investments	1,768,045	1,635,958	"	132,087
Treasury stock	2,058,700	2,227,117	Decrease	168,417
Inventory	12,614,926	16,226,639	"	3,611,713
Accounts receivable	5,477,195	6,370,890	"	893,695
Bills receivable	586,274	606,944	"	20,670
Cash	723,053	803,225	"	80,172
Prepaid insurance, taxes, etc..	222,950	229,619	"	6,669
	$94,511,956	$98,786,114		
LIABILITIES				
Common stock	$60,000,000	$60,000,000		
Preferred stock	30,000,000	30,000,000		
Bills payable	2,799,736	6,479,411	Decrease	$3,679,675
Accounts payable	489,031	653,185	"	164,154
Accrued liabilities	217,206	547,283	"	330,077
Contingent reserve	300,000	300,000		
Surplus	705,983	806,235	"	100,252
	$94,511,956	$98,786,114		

Statement of Sources and Disposition of Funds

The interpretations of the changes which have occurred is aided by a classification and grouping of the several items. This is set forth in what is generally called a statement of sources and disposition of funds.[2] In this are grouped upon one side decreases of assets, increases of liabilities, and increases of proprietorship. On the other side appear increases of assets, decreases of liabilities, and decreases of proprietor-

[2] This has sometimes been given the less distinctive title, financial statement, as in the earlier reports of the United States Steel Corporation. Professor Cole in the first edition of his *Accounts* uses the title "Where-Got-Gone" statement, but this has apparently been abandoned even by its author. It is a source of regret that a colorful term introduced into the drab literature of accounting should have fallen into disuse. But it hardly seems the function of this treatise to serve as an asylum for a foundling abandoned by its progenitor.

ship. A further subdivision is preferably made so that the assets are divided into current and fixed assets, the liabilities into current and fixed liabilities, and proprietorship into capital and surplus. The totals of these two groups will be equal. The items included in the first group represent the sources from which funds available for the concern have been obtained. The items in the other group show what has been done with these funds. Of course, in each instance only net results are obtained. An increase of $5,000 in the amount of notes payable would appear as an addition to the funds to just that amount. The fact that during the year the concern received $25,000 by additional borrowing and disposed of $20,000 to pay other debts is not brought out in such a statement.

Again, the whole picture is not presented in the following circumstances. Some unusual loss, say the theft of a large amount of cash, has occurred and the loss has been charged against Surplus. In order to replete the treasury, a sum equal to that stolen is borrowed. In the statement of sources and disposition of funds there would be no indication of any transaction involving cash, and there would appear only an increase of liabilities accompanied by a decrease of surplus. Despite such defects the statement is convenient and valuable.

Decrease in Assets

In preparing the statement of sources and disposition of funds any decrease in assets is treated as one of the sources from which funds were derived. In most cases this is obviously correct. If cash has decreased during the year, the net amount which has thus been taken out of the cash drawer has obviously been one of the sources for the expenditures made. Similarly, if the accounts receivable have been reduced, the ordinary inference is that this was the result of payment of the accounts and thus again an actual source is disclosed. In some instances, however, the reduction of an asset is not so evidently a source from which funds are derived. Thus if some of the property has declined in value through fire, theft, or other destructive agency, it in no sense represents a receipt of cash or its equivalent. The justification of treating it as if it were a source is as follows: The increase in the surplus would represent the receipt of cash or other available funds. But if a surplus arose despite the destruction or loss of property, it must mean that in addition to the receipts which swelled the surplus, there must have been other receipts canceling the destruction of property. Thus, for illustration, if a street railroad company received cash fares exceeding the amount of disbursements for operating expenses by $100,000, the accounts would show, in the absence of other transactions, an operating surplus of $100,000 and this would all properly represent a source of funds. If during the same period a destruction of part of the plant amounting to $60,000 had been charged against income or surplus, the operating surplus would then appear as $40,000. The funds available are, however, none the less $100,000 and the correct figures are obtained by adding to the $40,000 increase of surplus, the $60,000 decrease in fixed assets.

Increase in Allowance for Depreciation

Similarly, an increase in allowance for depreciation, although possibly appearing upon the credit side of the balance sheet, should be treated as a decrease of assets. The argument here is the same. Whatever surplus was gained during the year was in spite of a decline in value of the fixed plant through depreciation. To the amount appearing as an increase of surplus must, therefore, be added the amount by which the fixed assets has declined, that is, the amount by which the allowance for depreciation has increased.

The statement of sources and disposition of funds prepared from the comparative balance sheet of the Goodrich Rubber Company is as follows:

Illustrative Statement

Statement of Source and Disposition of Funds

SOURCE OF FUNDS

Current assets decreased:		
Inventory	$3,611,713	
Accounts Receivable	893,695	
Bills Receivable	20,670	
Cash	80,172	
Prepaid Insurance and Taxes	6,669	
		$4,612,919
Capital stock increased		168,417
		$4,781,336

DISPOSITION OF FUNDS

Fixed assets increased:		
Plant	$ 375,091	
Investments	132,087	
		$ 507,178
Current liabilities decreased:		
Bills Payable	$3,679,675	
Accounts Payable	164,154	
Accrued Liabilities	330,077	
		4,173,906
Surplus decreased	$ 100,252	100,252
		$4,781,336

In the above statement there is an apparent irregularity in that the decrease in treasury stock is not listed as a decrease of assets but as an increase of capital stock. Without further knowledge this would seem, however, to be proper. Treasury stock is properly a deduction from outstanding stock rather than a true asset, and a reduction in the amount of treasury stock seems to indicate that part of the stock previously held has been reissued and that funds have in reality been derived from an increase of outstanding capital.

Changes Indicated by Statement of Source and Disposition

A statement will show a number of changes, some of no great importance. It is not possible to pair off the two changes entering into each phase of the year's financial operations, but frequently there will be two changes, relatively large in amount, which evidently are related. Thus, an increase of $1,100,000 in the fixed assets, and an increase of $1,000,000 in bonded debt, would lead to the inevitable inference that bonds had been issued to provide funds for extension of the plant. Had the increase been in short-time notes, instead of bonds, one would infer an unconservative and perhaps dangerous financial policy.

The statement given above presents only a few changes. But using the six essential categories, circulating and fixed assets, circulating and fixed liabilities, capital and surplus, any one of which may be changed either by increase or decrease, a little calculation will show that (bearing in mind the fact that the balance sheet is in essence an equation) there are thirty different combinations of changes which may possibly be brought out in such a statement. These may be arranged for further discussion in ten groups, as follows:

Schedule of Changes in Liabilities, Assets, and Proprietorship

I. Current liabilities increased
- (*a*) Current assets increased
- (*b*) Fixed assets increased
- (*c*) Fixed liabilities decreased
- (*d*) Capital decreased
- (*e*) Surplus decreased

II. Current liabilities decreased
- (*a*) Current assets decreased
- (*b*) Fixed assets decreased
- (*c*) Fixed liabilities increased
- (*d*) Capital increased
- (*e*) Surplus increased

III. Current assets increased
- (*a*) Fixed assets decreased
- (*b*) Fixed liabilities increased
- (*c*) Capital increased
- (*d*) Surplus increased

IV. Current assets decreased
- (*a*) Fixed assets increased
- (*b*) Fixed liabilities decreased
- (*c*) Capital decreased
- (*d*) Surplus decreased

V. Fixed liabilities increased
   (*a*) Fixed assets increased
   (*b*) Capital decreased
   (*c*) Surplus decreased

VI. Fixed liabilities decreased
   (*a*) Fixed assets decreased
   (*b*) Capital increased
   (*c*) Surplus increased

VII. Fixed assets increased
   (*a*) Capital increased
   (*b*) Surplus increased

VIII. Fixed assets decreased
   (*a*) Capital decreased
   (*b*) Surplus decreased

IX. Capital increased
   (*a*) Surplus decreased

X. Capital decreased
   (*a*) Surplus increased

Interpretation of Changes

The various combinations of changes which may appear in the statement of sources and disposition of funds may be interpreted as follows:

I. Current Liabilities Increased

In general the increase of current liabilities means a weakening of the financial condition. Even where the counter change is an increase of current assets, the condition is weakened, for if the normal current ratio is two to one, that ratio will be lowered by the addition of an equal sum to both assets and liabilities. Where the increase of current liabilities has resulted in an increase of fixed assets (I*b*) the position is even worse, for fixed assets, unlike current assets, do not furnish any immediate source for paying debts. The substitution of current liabilities for fixed liabilities is similarly an unfavorable change and in most cases would indicate that fixed liabilities came due at a time when interest rates were abnormally high so that it seemed desirable to pay off the debt by a short-time loan rather than to issue long-time securities at the then current rate. Such a transaction was rather rare in the case of established companies until the financial stringency of 1907 at which time even the standard railroads in many cases issued short-time notes to repay maturing bonds. The other two combinations (I*d*, *e*) imply an extremely unfavorable condition, namely, that debts have been incurred for current expenses to such an extent as to encroach upon the surplus or even upon the capital.

II. Current Liabilities Decreased

The situation here is the reverse of those discussed above and in every instance shows a favorable change. The last two items, however, represent situations which are not likely to occur in business except that an increase in capital accompanying a decrease of current liabilities (II*d*) would appear where the earlier balance sheet showed the item dividends declared which during the following year were paid by means of a stock dividend.

III. Current Assets Increased

In general, increase of current assets no matter what the change may be, shows an improved financial condition. It is not likely to be accompanied by a decrease in fixed assets (III*a*) as a going concern ordinarily does not dispose of part of its plant. The two following combinations indicate that funds have been obtained by a long-time loan (III*b*) or by the issue of additional capital stock (III*c*). The last possibility represents the normal situation where a prosperous concern has made profits during the year which would ordinarily be in the form of current assets.

IV. Current Assets Decreased

This necessarily weakens the financial situation. Where the accompanying change is an increase of fixed assets, there would seem to be poor financing. An exception would be where funds were on hand at the end of a year which had been secured either by accumulation of profits or possibly by the issue of long-time bonds with the express purpose of providing for an extension of plant. If the extension were made in the following year, the change would indicate an increase of fixed assets and a decrease of cash. While the position after the extension has been made is unquestionably less favorable, it is only so because there had previously been an excessive amount of cash on hand. The situation presented in (IV*c*) represents the unusual circumstance of a reduction of capital stock, while the last situation (IV*d*) would in most cases be the normal transaction of the payment of a cash dividend.

V. *Fixed Liabilities Increased*

These changes do not immediately weaken the financial situation, save as it implies an additional burden for the payment of interest upon the debt. Where fixed assets have been secured through the loan (V*a*) it is to be presumed that the earnings of the new plant will more than provide for interest. The substitution of a fixed liability for capital (V*b*) is undesirable in so far as it substitutes a definite obligation to pay interest while previously dividends had been purely optional. An important instance of such a transaction may be found in the history of the United States Steel Corporation which substituted 5 per cent bonds in place of its preferred stock. The weakening of the financial situation was supposed to be justified by the material saving because the rate of interest was so much below the rate of preferred dividends. The last combination (V*c*) would be unusual. It might conceivably represent a payment of dividend by issuing bonds or the replacement of some loss as, for instance, the destruction of a plant, by funds obtained through the issue of bonds.

The complete transaction in this case would have been a decrease of fixed assets and a decrease of surplus followed by an increase of fixed assets and an increase of fixed liabilities. The destruction and replacement of the plant, canceling each other, would show only the increase of liabilities and the decrease of surplus.

VI. Fixed Liabilities Decreased

These combinations are the reverse of those just discussed. The first combination (VI*a*) would be unusual as ordinarily plant is not disposed of to pay debt. It would, however, properly appear in the case of a mining company or company working timber lands if the debt were being gradually paid through the exploitation of the capital investment. The substitution of capital for fixed liabilities (VI*b*) materially strengthens the financial situation. Such transactions have been frequent, since the installation of the income tax, through the issue of preferred stock to take the place of bonds. The motive for such financing in most of the cases was, however, because of the effect which it would have upon excess profits tax. The last combination (VI*c*) is not likely to occur.

VII. Fixed Assets Increased

The two transactions here are both generally favorable as any further investment of capital is an added source of strength to the corporation. Of the two, the first mentioned is somewhat preferable, as there is not the possibility of there being a demand to pay dividends out of a surplus, even though the surplus had been invested in fixed assets.

VIII. Fixed Assets Decreased

The first situation (VIII*a*) would be normal where capital invested in wasting assets is being gradually returned. If part of the wasting assets had been bought through surplus, the second situation (VIII*b*) might arise. Otherwise the combination would represent an unusual transaction, for ordinarily a going concern tends to increase rather than to decrease its fixed assets.

IX. Capital Increased and Surplus Decreased

This would result where a stock dividend is paid.

X. Capital Decreased and Surplus Increased

This would be an unusual combination.

Changes in Individual Items within a Group

The above discussion has related only to the more general groups of balance sheet items. Other changes taking place within a group are sometimes of equal significance. Thus, within current assets, an increase of accounts receivable accompanied by a decrease in cash would be unfavorable as indicating that collections were slow and perhaps throwing some doubt upon the solvency of the debtors. Somewhat similarly, an increase of notes receivable accompanied by a decrease of accounts receivable or of cash would probably indicate that accounts coming due were not paid and the best that could be done was to obtain a note in place of the open account. A different interpretation would similarly be placed upon an increase in current liabilities depending upon whether the item increased was notes payable or dividends declared.

It is evident that no inference can be made from the study of balance sheet changes which is absolutely conclusive. Such a study at least calls the attention to matters on which further information is desirable.

Discussion of Illustrative Statement

The statement relating to the Goodrich Rubber Company, printed above,[3] illustrates at once the advantages and the pitfalls in such an analysis. An examination of the statement shows a large decrease in current assets and a nearly equivalent decrease in current liabilities. This would seem upon the face of it to indicate a healthful though perhaps enforced improvement of the financial situation by a drastic reduction of the debts. The decrease in inventory would seem to imply that in order to pay off the pressing bills payable, inroads had been made upon the merchandise on hand to almost an exactly equivalent amount. The increase in capital stock with a somewhat equivalent decrease in surplus would raise the question as to whether a stock dividend had been declared

---

[3] P. 460.

and paid. From other information, however, it is found that these deductions are in part incorrect. The decline in the inventory is explained in the annual report of the company for 1913 as "due to decreased cost of crude rubber and decreased price of finished product and goods in process of manufacture. It does not reflect any marked change in material or goods on hand." And the decrease in the amount of treasury stock is not due to a sale or issue of such stock but to writing down the value of the preferred stock held in the treasury, the counter entry being a debit to profit and loss. With these explanations, the interpretation must be altered. Despite the business and financial difficulties which the company experienced in 1913, it was enabled very materially to reduce its current liabilities despite the fact that it at the same time suffered a shrinkage in the value of its assets. While the surplus was decreased $100,252, the earnings of the year were apparently large enough almost to cover the shrinkage in assets and also to allow for the payment of dividends. In any case, analysis of this situation must depend upon the acceptance of the statements presented as being correct. Misstatements in published accounts can of course be detected only by outside information not revealed by the balance sheet itself.

Comparison of Ratios

An additional device for bringing out the meaning of the balance sheet is well presented by Stephen Gilman.[4] Instead of showing the changes during a series of years in the amounts of quick assets (cash and receivables), current assets, and current liabilities, he presents these facts in the form of a series of changing ratios, as for instance, the current ratio and the acid-test ratio. Thus, if the condition in respect to these items had been as follows:

---

[4] *Analyzing Financial Statements,* chap. ix.

TABLE OF CHANGES IN ASSETS AND LIABILITIES

YEAR	Quick Assets	Current Assets	Current Liabilities
1922	$14,400	$30,000	$15,000
1923	18,180	31,680	18,000
1924	19,530	31,500	21,000
1925	21,120	31,200	24,000

the situation would be better expressed as follows:

TABLE OF CHANGES OF RATIOS

YEAR	Current Ratio	Acid-Test Ratio
1922	200	96
1923	176	101
1924	150	93
1925	130	88

But the changes are even more clearly brought out if the situation at some given time is taken as the basis and subsequent years expressed in percentages of that basis. Thus, if the situation in 1922 is taken as a basis the table would be as follows:

TABLE OF CHANGES OF RATIOS
(1922 as base)

YEAR	Current Ratio	Acid-Test Ratio
1922	100	100
1923	88	105
1924	75	97
1925	65	92

BIBLIOGRAPHICAL NOTE

BLISS, J. H.—*Financial and Operating Ratios in Management* (New York, 1923).

COLE, W. M.—*Accounts, Their Construction and Interpretation* (Revised ed., Boston, 1915), chaps. xiv-xx. Discusses the interpretation of the accounts of various businesses.

FINNEY, H. A.—*Principles of Accounting* (New York, 1923), I, chaps. iv, v.

GILMAN, S.—*Analyzing Financial Statements* (New York, 1925).

GREENDLINGER, L.—*Financial and Business Statements* (Revised ed., New York, 1921).

GUTHMANN, H. G.—*The Analysis of Financial Statements* (New York, 1925).

KESTER, R. B.—*Accounting, Theory and Practice* (2d ed., New York, 1925), II, chap. xxxiv.

McKINSEY, J. O.—*Managerial Accounting* (Chicago, 1924).

POWELSON, J. A.—*Introductory Accounting* (New York, 1926), chap. xxx.

WOODBRIDGE, F. W.—*Elements of Acoounting* (New York, 1925), chaps. xxv, xxvi.

APPENDIX

QUESTIONS AND PROBLEMS

No attempt has been made to give a series of questions outlining in detail the text of this treatise, as it is thought that such questions tend to stimulate a merely memoriter study of the subject. Answers to the questions imply an application of the principles set forth in the text, rather than a repetition of the words of the text. Grateful acknowledgment is made of the courtesy of Dr. David Friday in permitting the use of many questions published in his *Problems in Accounting* now out of print.

CHAPTER I

1. A balance sheet shows on the debit side the following item: "Earthquake, fire, and strike, $859,983." Discuss the meaning, legitimacy, and future treatment of this item.

2. (*a*) What other account is related to item 5 in Form 12?
(*b*) What is the definition of quick assets as used in this form?
(*c*) How does the primary grouping of items on the liability side of the balance sheet compare with that in Form 2?

3. Classify the arrangement of items in Forms 1 to 15 in respect to the following:

(*a*) Sequence of items—fixed to current—or reversed.
(*b*) Whether total proprietorship is shown in single subtotal.
(*c*) Whether all of the actual liabilities are shown in a single subtotal.
(*d*) Whether valuation accounts are subtracted in all cases from the corresponding asset.
(*e*) Whether goodwill is treated as a fixed asset or as a separate item.

4. Answer the following questions relating to the balance sheet in Form 11:

(*a*) How do you interpret "Reserve for Shrinkages in Inventory Value" (item 7)? What account was debited?
(*b*) In what way is a transaction similar to that indicated by item 8 treated by the U. S. Steel Corporation?
(*c*) To what other item is item 23 related? Is there any inconsistency in the treatment of item 23?
(*d*) How are items similar to 29-33 to be treated in the balance sheet required by the Interstate Commerce Commission?
(*e*) What is the significance of the last three items amounting to $127,618? Do similar items appear elsewhere in the balance sheet? If so, what is the connection between the two?

5. On the debit side of the balance sheet as prescribed by the Interstate Commerce Commission securities appear under "property investment," "working assets," and "deferred debit items." Indicate the basis of differentiation according to which securities are placed in one or another of these groups.

6. Discuss the form of balance sheet recommended by the Federal Reserve Board in respect to the subtraction of goodwill from the proprietorship accounts, instead of showing it as an asset.

7. In what other manner might the last debit item in Form 1 be presented in the balance sheet? Which is the preferable method?

8. *Consolidated Balance Sheet*

(1)	Cash	$ 6,236,251.01	(11)	Accounts Payable	$ 4,821,744.20
(2)	Common Stock, in treasury	3,397,246.95	(12)	Capital Stock of subsidiary companies	987,251.72
(3)	Goodwill	7,934,198.14	(13)	Common Stock	19,874,030.00
(4)	Inventories	18,170,907.21	(14)	First Lien Bonds	10,935,000.00
(5)	Miscellaneous Investments	367,062.80	(15)	Interest, etc., accrued	1,048,970.32
(6)	Notes and Accounts Receivable	3,449,335.45	(16)	Notes Payable	300,000.00
(7)	Patents, etc.	1,508,671.69	(17)	Preferred Stock	18,038,400.00
(8)	Preferred Stock, in treasury	3,053,200.00	(18)	Reserve for Contingencies	2,162,276.49
(9)	Prepaid expenses	412,756.20	(19)	Reserve for Depreciation	3,613,028.52
(10)	Real Estate, Plants, etc.	20,458,977.52	(20)	Reserve for Dividend	262,526.25
			(21)	Surplus	2,945,379.47
		$64,988,606.97			$64,988,606.97

Rearrange the above items in an improved form of balance sheet.

9. What is the significance of the total $460,278,150.28 appearing in Form 2?

10. Discuss the nature of the items appearing under property account in Form 6. Are all of the items there listed a part of the balance sheet? Discuss similarly the items appearing under surplus.

11. Rearrange the following items on a balance sheet:

Accounts Payable	$ 5,090
Bills Payable	5,825
Cash	5,426
Common Stock	60,000
Dividend on Preferred	1,050
Expenditure for Stripping	875
Insurance Fund Assets	1,071
Inventories, Dec. 31, 1909	33,137
Mine Royalties	153
Net Capital Additions, 1909	2,717
Preferred Stock	60,000
Purchases	20,263
Purchase Money Obligations	2,250
Real Estate, Mines, etc.	62,941
Receivables	48,857
Reserves:	
Plant Depreciation and Extinguishment	6,510
Special Maintenance	1,038
Collection Expenses on Receivables	800
Insurance Fund	1,095
Pension Fund	502
Contingent	1,250
Bad and Doubtful Receivables	2,645
Surplus	27,385

12. The following figures are taken from the balance sheet of an English company (Peek, Frean & Co.).

(1)	Allowance for Bad Book Debts	£ 19,743
(2)	Allowance for depreciation of plant	5,370
(3)	Bills Receivable	1,353
(4)	Book Debts	129,276
(5)	Cash	60,104
(6)	Common Stock	200,000
(7)	Creditors	33,228
(8)	Depositors	13,955
(9)	Directors' fees paid	1,575
(10)	Dividend due Jan. 31, 1910	7,062
(11)	Dividends during year	15,000
(12)	First Mortgage Bonds	300,000
(13)	Goodwill	£ 81,416
(14)	Improvements	1,900
(15)	Insurance, unexpired	1,151
(16)	Interest Payable, accrued	5,650
(17)	Interest on Bonds paid during year	12,000
(18)	Investments	27,871
(19)	Land	479,800
(20)	Materials and Stores	120,753
(21)	Plant and Machinery	102,801
(22)	Preferred Stock	300,000
(23)	P. & L. Balance Jan. 1, 1909	36,992
(24)	Profits for year 1909	83,000
(25)	Reserve account	30,000

Rearrange these items in a balance sheet. Note that the balance sheet itself indicates the earnings of the year and their distribution among bondholders, shareholders, and directors. This is similar, although somewhat different in detail, to Form 6. Each item found above should appear somewhere in the balance sheet. Three-column journal paper will be most conveniently used.

13. The following items represent the combined statement of all the national banks. Rearrange them in the form of a balance sheet. You need not follow the form used by the Comptroller of the Currency, but make a balance sheet in the form that seems the most desirable.

Banking house, furniture and fixtures	$ 160,800
Bills of other national banks	31,200
Bills payable	44,700
Bonds borrowed	60,000
Bonds, securities, etc.	700,300
Capital stock paid in	896,400
Cashier's checks outstanding	1,000
Certified checks	1,000
Checks and other cash items	26,900
Circulating notes	551,900
Demand certificates of deposit	1,000
Deposits of U. S. disbursing officers	17,800
Dividends unpaid	1,600
Due from approved reserve agents	614,500
Due from other national banks	334,600
Due from state banks	123,000
Due from the Treasurer of the U. S.	4,700
Due to approved reserve agents	38,100
Due to other national banks	823,000
Due to state banks	395,800
Due to trust companies	337,900
Exchanges for the clearing house	190,600
Fractional currency	2,300
Individual deposits subject to check	4,315,000
Lawful money reserve in banks	701,600
Loans and discounts	4,678,600
Notes and bills rediscounted	14,400
Bonds (other than U. S.) to secure U. S. deposits	68,200
Other liabilities	6,900
Real estate owned other than banking house	20,200
Overdrafts	30,500
Premium on bonds for circulation	14,600
Redemption fund with the U. S. Treasurer	27,300
Reserve for taxes	4,400
State bank circulation outstanding	100
Surplus fund	548,300
Time certificates of deposit	1,000
Undivided profits	186,600
U. S. bonds on hand	7,400
U. S. bonds to secure circulation	557,300
U. S. bonds to secure U. S. deposits	95,600
U. S. deposits	143,300

(American Institute of Accountants, 1917.)

14. What are the four subtotals which enter into the grand total on the credit side of Form 3? What is the nature of each of these subtotals? What is the nature of the items grouped to form each of these subtotals? Is there any criticism to be made of the arrangement?

CHAPTER II

1. Show the radical difference between the payment made for purchasing a machine and an ordinary expense, indicating the significance of the difference in accounting and the difficulties connected therewith. Show in what respects the two are identical rather than different.

2. What is the accepted method of treating payment of expenses, *e.g.*, money paid for repainting of building? In what respect is this treatment technically and theoretically incorrect? How can the accepted method nevertheless be justified?

3. A railway company leases the property of another railway company for a period of fifty years and, as part consideration for the lease, agrees to expend immediately $250,000 on the leased property, in order that it shall have a greater operating efficiency. At the termination of the lease the property is to be returned to the lessor in the same condition as at the time of making the lease, subject to ordinary wear and tear. What entries, if any, would you make on the books of the lessor in respect to the expenditure of the $250,000, and why? What entries required on lessee company books? **(Friday, 111.)**

4. If a company, duly organized, acquires several plants that are found to be in a run-down condition, and to require extensive outlay for repairs and renewals to bring them to the required state of efficiency, should such outlay be charged against Capital or against Revenue?

5. (*a*) A railroad paid $4,869.44 as cost of making a preliminary survey of a branch line designed to prevent construction of a competing line. Neither the branch nor the competing line was built. The cost was charged against operating expenses. Was this correct?

(*b*) The railroad was sued for damages resulting from enlargement of a yard. Should this be charged against revenue or be considered a capital expenditure?

(*c*) The railroad bought W. & T. stock for $104,500. Dividends received from this stock were used to mark down the value on the books, which reached the figure of $13,952.14. Bought Lafayette Stock for $71,750, but did not charge this as a purchase of new stock, but marked up the item W. & T. stock by $71,750, and also by the value of real estate which came with the purchase of Lafayette stock. Later dividends of W. & T. credited to this account. Lafayette stock valueless except to prevent competition. In 1907 received another dividend on W. & T. of $10,405. How should the income account be affected?

(Central of Georgia Ry. Co. *v.* Central Trust Co., 69 S. E. 708.)

6. Which of the following should be charged to Capital and which against Revenue?

The purchase of goodwill.
Loss by fire of uninsured property.
Promotion expenses.
The purchase of a lease.
Replacement of machinery.
Repairs to machinery.
Additional machinery. (Friday, 113.)

7. A suburban traction company, after equipping its line at a very considerable expense for overhead trolley, and operating same for several years, decides to adopt a third-rail system. Extensive changes are necessary in changing power houses, rearranging tracks, and altering cars, involving an expenditure of $25,000. In addition considerable machinery and rolling stock, the original cost of which had been treated as capital outlay and was carried on the books at a valuation of $25,000, are rendered obsolete and are disposed of for $3,500, showing a loss of $21,500. The profits from operation for the year are $18,000.

State how you would recommend that the matter be dealt with in the company's accounts and whether the company can pay a dividend. Give journal entries. (Friday, 119.)

8. A corporation manufacturing explosives is compelled to pay exorbitant rates for a very limited amount of insurance, and in consequence was obliged to install an automatic sprinkler system at a cost of $75,000. This additional fire protection enabled them to secure a full line of insurance, though in mutual companies, and at a much lower rate than was obtained prior to such installation. At the end of the fiscal year the company received dividends from these mutual insurance companies aggregating $2,000. To what account should the cost of the sprinkler system be charged and to what account should this dividend be credited? State your reasons fully. (Friday, 118.)

9. Expenditures are made by a corporation for items of each of the following classes: (*a*) taking down a machine in one part of a factory, moving it, and putting it up in another part; (*b*) expenses of incorporating the company, including state charges and lawyer's services; (*c*) brokerage on purchase of a piece of property; (*d*) commission on an issue of debenture bonds; (*e*) costs attending a mortgage; (*f*) furniture and fitting of a city office and salesroom; (*g*) cost of patents, including solicitor's charges and government fees. Which items should be charged to capital and which to revenue? State reasons for your answer in each case.

(New York, 1900.)

10. A corporation was organized with $20,000 capital fully paid. It bought a mine for $10,000 and paid $10,000 additional for expenses. Later it sold the mine receiving $25,000 in cash, and $25,000 par value of stock in another corporation. Give various forms of balance sheet after the sale has been made.

11. How would merchandise be valued if the rule of taking the "value to the going concern" were strictly followed?

12. The following is the abbreviated balance sheet of a corporation Jan. 1, 1915:

Balance Sheet

Real Estate	$200,000	Capital Stock	$300,000
Plant	100,000	Accounts Payable	25,000
Merchandise	50,000	Surplus	75,000
Replacement Funds	3,500		
Cash	16,500		
Accounts Receivable	30,000		
	$400,000		$400,000

The company immediately carries out the following operations:

(*a*) It builds a new wharf, in a new location, because engineering difficulties are in the way of extending an old wharf to accommodate larger vessels. The present book value (depreciated in ten years from $2,000) of the old wharf abandoned is $500, but no recoverable value remains at abandonment, and the cost of the new wharf is $5,000.

(*b*) It buys, out of the replacement fund, a new machine at a cost of $3,000, to take the place of one originally costing $4,000 (but now selling new for $3,000) and already written down by depreciation to $500 and yielding $30 as scrap in part payment for the new machine.

Show the balance sheet after the changes above—no other transactions taking place and charges, not otherwise provided for, being covered by the issue of notes. Show the entry for each operation, giving alternative treatment where permissible.

13. "We deny that a given object can have a value to its owner in excess of cost." (Gundelfinger.) If this doctrine were rigidly enforced just what effect would it have on a set of accounts? Would it be possible to make a profit on merchandising? What is the cost of a note received in exchange for goods sold?

CHAPTER III

1. How should payments for the following items be treated in estimating the cost of real estate bought for a building site?

(*a*) Examining title.
(*b*) Surveying.
(*c*) Removing old building.
(*d*) Grading.
(*e*) Interest on purchased mortgage.
(*f*) Estimated interest on invested capital.
(*g*) General taxes.
(*h*) Special assessments for street improvement.

2. A real estate company buys a tract of land for $100,000, paying one half cash and giving a 6 per cent note for the remainder. Streets occupying one-tenth of the total area are opened, and dedicated to the city. $20,000 is paid for improving streets, grading same, etc. The property is divided into ten lots valued as follows:

Lot 1	$14,000
Lots 2-4	17,000 each
Lots 5-7	21,000 each
Lots 8-10	24,000 each

Lots 3, 6, 7, 9, and 10 are sold at these prices for cash, less 5 per cent commission to agents. The note is paid with six months' interest. At what figure should the unsold property be inventoried?

3. In auditing the accounts of a corporation you find that the company has utilized its own materials and labor in the construction of extensive additions to its plant, and that it has charged up such work at regular trade prices sufficient to yield to it a substantial profit, which has been credited to the Profit and Loss account. Do you see any objection to this course? Explain fully the theory upon which your answer is based.

4. Should a bank or insurance company holding $100,000 government bonds bought in 19— at 107.15, that being a $3\frac{1}{2}$ per cent basis, make a charge against profits ten years later, when the bonds fall in the market to 102? At this latter date the premium has already been marked down to $4,190, that representing the premium on a $3\frac{1}{2}$ basis.

5. (*a*) "The cost of bonds bought at discount differs from that of bonds bought at a premium in that there is not the same cer-

tainty of the discount being eventually earned as of the premium being lost."

(*b*) In commenting on the above statement, Dr. Sprague says, "'Earned' and 'lost' are not happy expressions here. *The premium is not lost at maturity, but has gradually been refunded to us; and the discount is not earned, but gradually withheld from us.*"

Illustrate and explain fully the *italicized* sentence.

(Friday, 305.)

6. A 6 per cent bond is bought at 111 at which price it yields $4\frac{1}{2}$ per cent. Give the journal entry six months later when interest is collected. At what price would a bond, similar except that it pays 4 per cent, yield $4\frac{1}{2}$ per cent? At what price would a 7 per cent bond yield $4\frac{1}{2}$? Show how these questions can be answered without using the formula or bond-value tables.

7. A 6 per cent bond running four years is bought for $1,073.30, at which price it nets 4 per cent (s/a). Give a table showing the proper valuation to be attached to the bond at each successive six months' interval.

8. An investor buys $100,000, two-year, 3 per cent (semiannual) bonds for $96,238.03 at which price they net 5 per cent (semiannual.) Give the journal entries for purchase and six months later when the first coupon is collected. How would the bonds be listed in the balance sheet at the latter date?

9. The students' bookstore at a university acting upon the recommendation of an instructor, bought 40 Italian books to be used as texts. These cost 40 cents each less 25 per cent commission. Five of the books were sold to students at 40 cents each. Upon what basis should the remaining books be valued when taking the inventory at the end of the year?

10. The following transactions affecting merchandise have taken place.

Jan. 1 inventory		100 units at $1.10
Purchases	Feb. 1	95 units at 1.00
	Apr. 1	90 units at 1.20
	June 1	150 units at .90
Sales	Mar. 1	110 units at 1.20
	May 1	70 units at 1.30
	June 30	100 units at 1.20

What should be the value of the inventory, June 30, according to each of the methods described in this chapter. Give all of the calculations by which your result was obtained.

11. How should a partially completed ship, being built on contract, be valued by the contractor?

CHAPTER IV

1. Discuss the method in which goodwill is treated in the balance sheet recommended by the Federal Reserve Board.

2. Describe the calculations to be made in order to estimate the value of goodwill.

3. Should goodwill be written off? If so in what circumstances should this be done? What is the effect of so doing?

4. If the goodwill of a business with $5,000 excess profits is properly valued at $35,000, how much is the goodwill of another business, similar in all respects save that its excess earnings are $10,000?

5. A mining corporation has assets comprising, among others, leases, goodwill, rent and royalties paid in advance, and patents. How would you deal with them in the balance sheet and income statement? (Friday, 121.)

6. A, B, and C are partners with capital of $90,000, $100,000, and $110,000 respectively. Profits are shared equally. Assuming a normal rate of income of 6 per cent and that excess profits may be capitalized at 10 per cent, what is the value of the goodwill of the firm, when profits are $25,200? How much should one be willing to pay for A's interest in the business? For B's? For C's?

7. A manufacturer obtains two patents at the same time, as follows: (*a*) He purchases outright a patent which has only ten more years to run for the sum of $5,000, which he terms his patent No. 1. (*b*) He invents a contrivance and obtains a patent on same, the cost of which he estimates at $12,000 and which he styles his patent No. 2. At the end of three years he expends the sum of $5,000 in defending his patent No. 2, the decision being given in his favor. One year later he spends $2,000 in a suit he brings against a competitor for infringement of his patent No. 1, which suit he also wins. Without giving the actual figures, state how you would treat all the above transactions and arrive at a valuation of those two patents six years after he had obtained same, giving reasons therefor. (Illinois, 1904.)

8. A company issues $1,000,000 of common stock in payment of patents expiring in ten years. It hopes, by securing additional patents for improvements, to extend the period of protection indefinitely. At the end of one year the company, after all other charges except depreciation of patents, has realized a profit of $100,000. Is there any balance for dividends? If so, how much? If not, how should the company dispose of the $100,000 cash in the treasury?

(New York, 1916.)

9. Compare the method of showing goodwill in Forms 1, 3, 4, 6, 7, 10, 11, 12, commenting on significant features.

CHAPTER V

1. How is depreciation of machinery best shown in the balance sheet? In the profit and loss statement should it be subtracted from gross earnings, from net earnings, from net profits, or from surplus?

2. Discuss the following:

> The theory of plaintiff in this regard seems to be that the life of a plant of this character may be approximated at thirty years, and that a sinking fund of one-thirtieth of the value should be collected from the ratepayers annually and laid aside to be handed to the stockholders upon the sad occasion of its demise, as an alleviating salve to their sorrow. But such a thing is all wrong, for it results in the consumers of water buying the plant and paying for it in annual installments. Consumers of water cannot be charged with cost of construction. They are only to pay a fair interest upon such cost; and as we look at this matter, if this three and one-half per cent [plaintiff's estimate of annual depreciation] is not stowed away in the vaults as a sinking fund to make glad the hearts of the stockholders upon the expiration of the thirty years, which theory cannot be tolerated for a moment, then it must go into the plant as cost of construction, and, therefore, not chargeable against the consumer. (San Diego Water Co. *v.* San Diego.)

3. Recently it has been urged that if the replacement cost of fixed assets is greatly in excess of their cost, depreciation should be computed on the replacement values, so that the reserve for depreciation will be equal to the replacement value when the time arrives for abandoning the old property and acquiring new. It is contended that if this procedure is followed, the company will have sufficient cash to make replacements without impairing the capital. Discuss the various phases of this situation.

4. Discuss the following:

"A conservative corporation should always set aside a portion of the profits to allow for depreciation."

Depreciation is a provision for the replacing of machinery when worn out.

5. Give journal entries where a machine is displaced which originally cost $10,000 and a new machine to supplant it was purchased for $15,000. During the course of ten years, including the year just closing, an allowance for depreciation had been made which amounted to $8,000. The displaced machine was sold for $1,000 cash.

6. A corporation shows:

Balance Sheet

Plant	$ 50,000	Capital	$100,000
Miscellaneous Assets	45,125	Profit and Loss	6,371
Bonds, 6% (cost)	11,246		
	$106,371		$106,371

It is found, however, that no allowance has been made for (*a*) depreciation of plant and (*b*) amortization of bonds. Estimate is made that depreciation is at the rate of 10 per cent (figured on diminishing value). The bonds were bought one year previously and were then estimated to yield 5 per cent (interest payable annually). What changes should be made in the balance sheet to adjust these matters. Supposing no other changes, what further alterations should be made one year later. In both cases give results in form of balance sheets.

7. What is the effect of an excessive allowance for depreciation?

8. What factors other than wear and tear are to be considered in making allowance for depreciation?

9. The State of New York requires telephone companies to maintain a depreciation reserve to take care of the actual depreciation of tangible assets. The treasurer of a certain telephone company reported cash in bank $15,000 among his assets. Among his liabilities he reported a loan from the same bank of $12,000. He was receiving 3 per cent interest on the cash in bank and paying 6 per cent interest on the loan from the bank. When asked why he did not use the cash in bank instead of borrowing, he replied: "Your requirement with respect to Depreciation Reserves prevents me from doing so." Discuss. (Friday, 180.)

10. Through excessive writing down in previous years the book value of the bank building of the Hibernia Savings Bank was reduced to the nominal sum of one dollar. Does the building still depreciate? If depreciation is ignored what erroneous effect is produced in the accounts of each succeeding year? Assuming that it is desirable to continue to carry the building at one dollar, what entries might be made so as to give a correct showing of annual profits in succeeding years?

11. "The method that should be adopted to ascertain the net earnings of a street railway company, is to deduct from the gross earnings,

(*a*) Operating expenses, and maintenance;

(*b*) Interest upon the bonded indebtedness;

(*c*) Depreciation; and

(*d*) Where the city franchise or ordinance operated under is of limited duration, then a sinking fund necessary to retire bonds, when the franchise expires, for then the business ceases."

The above extract is from an "Argument for the Establishment of Rules and Principles That Should Guide the Board of Public Works in Assessing Street Railway Property."

You, as city auditor, are asked to write an opinion on the correctness of the principles above set forth, especially (*d*).

(Friday, 198.)

CHAPTER VI

1. A machine costing $81 declines to $16 in four years. Interest to be reckoned at 5 per cent. Prepare a table showing depreciation by each of the four methods.

2. A machine costing $125 is estimated to last three years at which time it will have a residual value of $27. Prepare a table showing the annual charge for depreciation each year according to the four methods given in the text. Interest to be computed at 6 per cent. $\overline{1.06}^3$ may be taken as equaling 1.191. This may be worked without the use of logarithms.

3. What is the especial significance of each of the four methods of calculating depreciation?

4. What would be included in a system in which the allowance for depreciation is treated in reference to other associated items?

5. Discuss the propriety of apportioning depreciation according to profits.

6. Prepare a table showing the annual charges for depreciation by each of the four methods, in case of a machine costing $10,000, estimated to last ten years with a residual value of $1,000; interest to be computed at 4 per cent per annum.

7. What variations are there in the treatment of depreciation in Forms 1, 3, 7, 9, 10, and 13? Consult also Form 28.

8. An engine installed in a factory Jan. 1, 1914, at a cost of $1,000 is replaced by one of larger capacity Dec. 31, 1917, costing (second hand) $2,800. The discarded machine was sold for $900. The cost of making the change was $200. It has been the practice of the company to charge off 10 per cent depreciation annually (on the diminishing basis) carrying the credit to a Depreciation Reserve account. Make the necessary journal entries.

(Illinois, 1918.)

9. In your examination of the Automobile Delivery Truck account of a company you find the following entries:

Debits	
Jan. 1, 1914, Trucks 1, 2, 3, 4, at $1,200......	$4,800
July 1, 1914, Truck 5	1,500
Aug. 1, 1914, Truck 6	1,500
Credits	
Aug. 1, 1914, Truck 2	$ 900
Sept. 1, 1914, Truck 4	750

Balance, Sept. 1, 1914, $6,150.

The Reserve for Depreciation for Automobile Delivery Truck account stood credited on Jan. 1, 1914, with $1,800.

Upon analyzing the transactions represented by these items, you find the following facts:

(*a*) Truck 5, purchased July 1, replaced Truck 1. The portion of the reserve for depreciation accumulated on Jan. 1 for Truck 1 amounted to $900. Truck 5 was purchased on open account.

(*b*) Truck 2 was traded in for $950 on the purchase of Truck 6 costing $1,500. The difference was paid in cash. The reserve which had been accumulated for depreciation on Truck 2 on Jan. 1 amounted to $300.

(*c*) Truck 4 was totally destroyed by an accident Sept. 1. The reserve for depreciation on this truck amounted on Jan. 1 to $300 and it was insured for $500.

Assume the rate of depreciation to be 25 per cent per year.

Give journal entries which would properly record the above facts and show the balances of all accounts affected, as of Sept. 1, 1914.

(Wisconsin, 1915.)

10. A signs a three year lease by which he is required to pay $100 a year, in advance, payable on January 1 each year. The lease is signed December 15. On December 28 the landlord proposes to his prospective tenant that he make a single payment for all three years. This the tenant is willing to do provided reasonable interest is allowed. Assuming a rate of 10 per cent the amount which A pays January 1 is $273.55. What should the journal entry be at time of payment? What amount should be written off on December 31 of that year? On the theory that "only the amount actually paid" should be written off, what would the amount be?

CHAPTER VII

1. A corporation is organized with capital stock, $500,000. Subscriptions are received for $300,000 at 110 and $150,000 is issued for property valued at $165,000. Subscribers pay all the premium and 50 per cent of the principal of subscribed stock. $175,000 cash is expended on plant. $50,000 stock is donated to the company, of which $40,000 is sold at 105. Prepare journal entries and balance sheet.

2. A company is incorporated with $200,000 common and $150,000 preferred stock. Subscriptions are received for 1,500 shares ($100 each) of the common stock at par, which are paid for in cash. Subscriptions are also received for 500 shares ($100 each) of the preferred stock at par. One quarter of the amount subscribed for preferred stock is paid at the time of subscription, the remainder being due in three equal installments. All subscriptions were paid when due. Organization expenses were incurred and paid by giving 50 shares preferred and 100 shares common. At the end of the year the net profits from operation are $15,000. Dividends of 7 per cent on the preferred stock and 4 per cent on the common stock are declared and paid in cash. Give journal entries covering these transactions.

3. A corporation is organized with $100,000 authorized capital stock. It receives subscriptions for half this amount at 110. A call is issued for payment by subscribers of $60,000 of this covering 50 per cent of the par value of the stock and all the premium; the payment of the above call is made by all subscribers except one who had subscribed for ten shares (of $100 each) who fails to pay; the company pays $1,000 organization expenses. Give journal entries and balance sheet.

4. A corporation is organized with $1,000,000 capital stock. Subscriptions are received for $600,000 at 120. $300,000 capital stock is issued for plant worth $250,000 and goodwill $50,000. Subscribers pay in 70 per cent in cash (70 per cent of par value of stock not of subscription). Remainder of stock is issued at par, subscribers paying one half in cash. Company issues $300,000 bonds at par, paid in full in cash. Pays $750,000 cash for construction of additional plant. Give journal entries and balance sheet.

5. Distinguish between the following:
   (*a*) Capital stock authorized
   (*b*) Treasury stock
   (*c*) Donated stock
   (*d*) Stock outstanding

On which side of the balance sheet will each appear?

6. How are uncalled subscriptions shown in the balance sheet of an English company, and how may they be shown in an American balance sheet?

7. A corporation had outstanding 10,000 shares of no par value preferred for which $80,000 had been paid in. The redemption value is $100,000. It also had outstanding 20,000 shares of no par value common on which $150,000 had been paid in. Surplus was $70,000. How would you present the above data in a balance sheet in order fully to present the important details.

8. A corporation having issued its capital stock at par, buys 1,000 shares at 95. It later sells 500 of these shares at 98, 300 at 85, and 200 at 101. Give the journal entries covering these transactions. How should the items appear on the balance sheet immediately after purchasing the stock and immediately after each of the sales? (American Institute of Accounting, 1917.)

9. How is unissued and treasury stock shown in the several balance sheets following Chapter I?

10. A corporation in a state where no-par stock may not be issued for less than $5.00 per share, issued 300,000 shares at $7.00 a share and later 100,000 shares at $8.00 per share. It subsequently buys 10,000 shares at $6.50; 10,000 at $7.50; and 10,000 at $8.50. Give journal entries for these transactions.

11. Give journal entries if the above corporation:
   (*a*) Sells all of the repurchased stock at $6.00 per share.
   (*b*) Sells them at $9.00 a share.

CHAPTER VIII

1. Discuss Dickinson's statement regarding valuation of property secured in exchange for securities and compare it with decisions in the courts.

2. Why have the courts been so liberal in construing the value put on property received in exchange for securities?

3. From the accountant's viewpoint, how should one treat the transaction in which securities, in excess of the actual value of the property, are issued in exchange for property?

4. Illustrate the argument that an issue of stock below par is not the only way in which an embarrassed company might secure additional funds.

5. What is meant by "stock watering"? What is the principal objection to stock watering?

6. Give an illustration showing the booking proper when a stock dividend has been paid.

7. Discuss the accounting where stock is donated and subsequently sold.

8. (*a*) How should the balance sheet exhibit unissued capital stock, repurchased capital stock held in treasury, capital stock purchased for cancelation, donated capital stock, amount of subscription to capital stock not called for, calls in arrears?
(*b*) What difference is there to be made in the treatment of the premium on bonds sold by a corporation and the premium on the capital stock issued?

9. In a company showing:

Balance Sheet

Plant	$ 95,000	Capital Stock	$100,000
Cash	8,000	Notes Payable	10,000
Deficits	8,000		
	$110,000		$110,000

the stockholders agree to surrender $15,000 of their holdings. Of this $5,000 is sold at 80 and the remainder is canceled. Prepare journal entries and balance sheet.

10. A company with a balance sheet as follows:

Balance Sheet

Plant	$ 95,000	Capital Stock	$100,000
Cash	35,000	Bills Payable	10,000
		Profit and Loss	20,000
	$130,000		$130,000

pays off its note and expends $20,000 in extending plant. A dividend of 10 per cent is declared, one half to be paid in cash, and one half in stock. To enable this to be done $10,000 new stock is issued, $5,000 being issued in payment of dividend. Prepare journal entries and balance sheet.

11. A corporation purchases a mine for $500,000 to be paid for in stock at par. The vendor donates $200,000 stock to the corporation to provide working capital. Soon thereafter $60,000 of this stock is sold at 50 per cent, $100,000 at 60 per cent, and $40,000 at 70 per cent in each case payment being made in cash. Give journal entries for these transactions and balance sheet.

12. A corporation has outstanding $1,000,000 of fully paid stock. Its accumulated surplus is $140,000. The profits for the current year are $100,000. The directors declare a cash dividend of 6 per cent and a stock dividend of 25 per cent:

(*a*) Make journal entries to record these last two transactions.

(*b*) Prepare balance sheet after the dividends are declared.

(Friday, 66.)

13. "A stock dividend is really not a dividend at all." Defend this statement.

(Friday, 69.)

14. "Treasury stock or bonds are merely so many legalized pieces of paper, and cannot in any sense be considered as assets of the corporation creating and issuing them" (Dickinson).

"When stock has been issued fully paid and has been returned to the treasury of the company which issued it through purchase or gift, it is known as "treasury stock," and should appear on the books as an asset. It represents property of more or less value and is not a deduction from the outstanding capital stock unless it is retired by due process" (Montgomery, 1915).

Discuss these two statements.

15. A corporation purchases a sack of United States gold coin, giving therefor 100 shares of its stock, par value $100 per share. How should the transaction be entered in the books? Be sure that your answer would apply in all cases. How does your answer bear on the statement of Sir A. L. Dickinson quoted in note 18, page 207?

CHAPTER IX

1. A railroad company issues $1,000,000 bonds to provide funds for construction. The bonds run twenty years and bear interest at 4 per cent, payable semiannually. They are sold for 87.45 per cent, at which price they net the investor 5 per cent (payable semiannually). How should the discount be treated in the accounts of the railroad?

2. On Jan. 1, 1906, a corporation issued and sold 5 per cent twenty-year bonds, interest payable July 1 and Jan. 1, to the par value of $1,000,000, for $900,000 cash. These bonds contained a sinking fund provision under which the corporation was obliged to call and cancel 2 per cent of the original issue on Jan. 1, 1911, and each year thereafter until maturity. The bonds were callable at 105 and accrued interest.

In conformity with these provisions the corporation called $20,000 of the bonds at 105 on Jan. 1, 1911, and each year since, and expects to continue the practice.

(*a*) What was the original discount on these bonds at the time of issue?

(*b*) What is the unextinguished bond discount on Jan. 1, 1916?

(*c*) What entries would you have made when you paid the bonds which were called on Jan. 1, 1911?

(*d*) What is the effective rate of interest on the capital which the corporation secured from the sale of these bonds?

(Friday, 153.)

3. (*a*) In an unfavorable market a road sells notes instead of long-time bonds, depositing the bonds as collateral security for the notes. Should the discount on the notes be spread over the life of the bonds treating the sale and retirement of both notes and bonds as one transaction?

(*b*) Equipment notes of $5,000, maturing $1,000 each year, are sold at a discount of $350. How should the discount be written off? Are other facts necessary in order to make the entries? What approximate method could be used without further facts?

(See Interstate Commerce Commission, *Accounting Bulletin 15*, Case 172.)

4. What is the logical significance of discount on a non-interest-bearing note payable? What is the relation between discount on a long-time bond, and discount on a non-interest-bearing, short-time note?

5. A corporation issues $100,000 bonds, bearing 6 per cent interest (payable semiannually) at 110. The bonds run twenty years and at the price net 5.19 per cent. It also issues $100,000 bonds, bearing 4½ per cent interest (payable semiannually) at 90. The latter run ten years and at the price net 5.83 per cent. Is it actuarially correct to cancel the premium of $10,000 against the discount of the same amount? Give the journal entries which would make an exactly correct record when interest on both issues is paid six months later.

6. How should the following be treated: Declared dividends, dividends earned but not declared on cumulative preferred stock, dividends on such stock in arrears and not earned?

7. Compare the treatment of discount upon bonds as indicated by Forms 5, 9, 13, 24, and 27.

8. A corporation issues $100,000 bonds at 90. The bonds pay 6 per cent interest, and are repayable in twenty years at 110. Give journal entries at time of sale, and show how the facts should be shown in the balance sheet.

CHAPTER X

1. Give illustrations of what might be considered an increase of capital rather than income.

2. A merchant buys merchandise on Jan. 1 for $10,000; on Feb. 1 the merchandise has risen 10 per cent in value. On March 1, he sells it on account for $13,000 with 2 per cent discount if paid within thirty days. On April 1, the purchaser gives in settlement of account his sixty-day note with 6 per cent interest. The note is paid on maturity. When did the merchant realize profits?

3. A British blockade runner sold cotton during the Civil War, receiving payment in Confederate bonds. Were profits realized at the time of the sale?

4. During the Great War, American manufacturers sold merchandise for Russian bonds and for Liberty Loan bonds. Was profit realized in these transactions?

5. A buys a farm, in 1921, for $25,000. In 1926 coal is discovered, and the property is conservatively estimated to be worth $100,000. Has A made a profit? When was it made: when he bought the farm, or in 1926?

6. "Income must be accounted for, not when it is received in actual cash, but as it accrues to the corporation." Defend this statement, and illustrate. (Friday, 129.)

7. How should a reappraisal of capital assets be treated on the books of a going concern (*a*) when it involves appreciation, (*b*) when it involves depreciation?

(American Institute of Accountants, 1918.)

8. A construction company has a number of contracts partly completed at the close of the fiscal year. Would you carry any portion of the anticipated profit on these contracts into Revenue account? If so, why? (Friday, 134.)

9. Is it possible to make a profit on a purchase? It is said that in the early days of trading with Japan it was possible to exchange silver coins for gold of practically equal weight. Was profit made on such a purchase of gold by an American, gold in this country being worth approximately sixteen times an equal weight of silver?

10. A corporation purchases a tract of land for $25,000 and after holding it for three years sells half of it for $20,000, using the remainder for an extension of its plant. The president of the company favors crediting Profit and Loss with $7,500, crediting Real Estate account with $12,500. The directors ask your opinion. Write out the letter you would submit. **(Friday, 137.)**

CHAPTER XI

1. The principal objects of a corporation were to buy, rent, and sell land. The articles of incorporation provided that dividends should be paid out of net earnings. In 1882 the company had a bad debt of $350,000 and they met this by writing up in the balance sheet of that year the value of their lands some $350,000 above cost price, and brought down such increased value into the credit side of the Profit and Loss account as a set-off against the bad debt, which was in this way treated as written off. Was this legitimate accounting?

(Friday, 143.)

2. How should the following transaction be treated in the accounts?

A corporation buys a mine for $100,000, funds having been secured by the issue of $100,000 capital stock at par. One quarter of the deposit is mined at a cost of $20,000 and sold for $60,000.

3. How should the following transactions be treated in the accounts?

A company organized for the purpose of making investments, the income from the investments to be distributed as dividends to the stockholders, receives $1,000,000 as subscriptions to capital stock. This is invested, and in the first year the investments yield $80,000, expenses of management being $10,000. In the second year $250,000 of the investments are proved to be altogether worthless. Income from the other investments amounts to $65,000. Expenses are $7,000.

In discussing the above transaction, give arguments and discuss varying opinions and decisions, if such there be.

4. Discuss the distinction between the decisions in Lee *v.* Neuchatel Asphalte Company and Verner *v.* General and Commercial Investment Trust.

5. A corporation was formed which acquired several plants, issuing therefor $17,000,000 bonds and $24,000,000 stock. It was well known at the time that this capitalization exceeded the true value of the assets (including goodwill) acquired, to an extent of $11,000,000. In the first year, after paying expenses and interest on bonds, the business yielded considerable net income. May such net income be used to pay dividends, or must it be first applied towards making up the $11,000,000?

6. A leaves an estate worth $1,000,000 with provision that the income is to go to his widow during her life, the principal going to a university on her death. The estate is all invested in an office building yielding $50,000 net income. The trustees later sell the building for $1,200,000 which is invested in another building which yields $60,000 per annum. Is the increase of $200,000 capital or income? If the new investment yielded only $48,000, would the situation be altered?

7. A beneficiary was entitled to the income from $100,000, 5 per cent bonds which had been bought at par. It was possible later to sell the bonds at 90 and to invest the $90,000 at 7 per cent. If the trustees make this deal, can the loss on the bonds be charged against income so that it would be gradually amortized out of the additional return of $1,300 per annum, or must the entire $6,300 go to the beneficiary?

8. Discuss the following statement from the decision of the United States Supreme Court in the case of Eyster *v.* Centennial Board of Finance:

> The receipts of the exhibition, over and above its current expenses, are the profits of the business. . . . They are, in fact, the net receipts, which, according to the common understanding, ordinarily represent the profits of the business. The public, when referring to the profits of the business of a merchant, rarely ever take into account the depreciation of the buildings in which the business is carried on, notwithstanding that they may have been erected out of the capital invested. Properly speaking, the net receipts of a business are its profits. So here, as the business to be carried on was that of an exhibition and its profits were to be derived only from its receipts, to the popular mind the net receipts would represent the net profit.

CHAPTER XII

1. How should premium received on the sale of bonds and premium received on the issue of capital stock be treated in the accounts of the issuing corporation?

2. A bank with capital stock of $1,500,000, having surplus and undivided profits of $802,500, issued $500,000 new stock at 170. This as soon as sold had a market value of 200. Current earnings applicable to old stock, when new was sold, was $295,828.84. How much might be paid out as dividends?

(Miller *v.* Payne, 136 N. W. 811.)

3. Barley is bought at 50 cents per bushel. In process of malting this increases 15 per cent in bulk. The company buys 1,050,000 bushels. Expenses of manufacture are $100,000. It has on hand 50,000 bushels of barley and 50,000 bushels of malt. It sold, during the year, all the malt at the uniform price of 60 cents per bushel. What profits are available for distribution? Suppose the company had a contract to furnish 200,000 more bushels of malt at the same price, what would be the result?

(Hutchinson *v.* Curtiss, 92 N. Y. S. 70.)

4. A corporation organized with $300,000 capital stock, invested $200,000 in a lease and $100,000 in investment securities. Later it sold the lease for $1,050,000, reduced capital stock to $100,000, and distributed $850,000 among stockholders. Was this legitimate?

(People *v.* Sohmer, 143 N. Y. 313.)

5. No dividends can be declared before the expenses of running the business are paid. These expenses include payment of bills payable that are due because a bill payable is merely written evidence of an account due. A bond is a promissory note and, therefore, of the same category as bills payable. Since a bond is equivalent to a bill payable, no dividend can be paid out before the bond is paid off.

Examine critically the above statement. (Friday, 107.)

6. Discuss the following statement from the decision of the United States Supreme Court in Warren *v.* King: "Net earnings is what is left after paying current expenses and interest on debt and everything else the company is liable to pay."

7. A gas company with a capital of $5,000,000 and a surplus of $1,000,000 had made no provision for the depreciation of its property till the directors reviewed the valuation of the property accounts and decided to write off $2,000,000, thus creating an apparent deficit of $1,000,000. The net earnings during the year following the writing down of the assets amounted to $1,250,000 before any depreciation was charged, and the directors proposed to pay out as dividends $1,000,000. What opinion would you express as to this proposition, if called on by the board before final action was taken?

(Friday, 199.)

8. The company referred to in the last problem, five years subsequent to the time of writing down its assets, reconsidered the action taken at that time and instructed its accounting officer to write back the valuation of the assets and thus apparently add $2,000,000 to its surplus.

(*a*) What entries would be required?

(*b*) If you were auditing the accounts of a corporation which owned practically all of the capital stock of this gas company, how would you regard both the writing down and the writing up of the assets of the subsidiary company on the accounts of the company you were auditing?

(Friday, 200.)

CHAPTER XIII

1. Discuss the nature of each of the items on the credit side of the following balance sheet:

Balance Sheet

Plant at cost	$ 50,000	(1) Capital Stock	$100,000
Accounts Receivable	50,000	(2) Reserve for Depreciation	5,000
Miscellaneous Assets	25,000	(3) Reserve for Extensions	4,000
		(4) Reserve for Doubtful debts	1,000
		(5) Dividends Declared	7,000
		(6) Surplus	6,000
		(7) Balance of Undivided Profits	2,000
	$125,000		$125,000

2. Explain the nature of the six reserves in Form 3. What accounts were probably credited when the last two items among reserves were debited in 1922?

3. Explain the four reserves in Form 5. If the company went out of business what would be the nature of each of these reserves, assuming no shrinkage through process of liquidation?

4. Which items of reserves are differently treated in Forms 3 and 8?

5. The balance sheet of a corporation shows the following credit balances: Reserves for Depreciation; Reserve for Extension of Plant; Reserve for Bad and Doubtful Debts; Sinking Fund Reserve; Insurance Reserve; Reserve for Pensions; Reserve for Contingencies; Reserve for Taxes. What would you assume to be the nature of each of these items? Can better terms be submitted for any of those used? In what circumstances would each of the above accounts be debited, and when debited, what would be the corresponding credit? If the business were to be sold for the amount of its net worth, as shown by the balance sheet, which of these items would represent a proper addition to the capital stock in determining the selling price?

(American Institute of Accountants, 1917.)

6. What is the nature of each of the items listed under corporate surplus in Form 13? What difference is there in the nature of accounts 771, 772, 773 in Form 13?

CHAPTER XIV

1. What, in your opinion, would be the proper accounting record for a business corporation to make of an appropriation from its surplus profits for the amount of a permanent investment in property? (Friday, 142.)

2. A banking firm with $200,000 of capital stock outstanding shows at the end of a certain year profits for that year amounting to $38,000. The directors write off $8,000 of Premium on Bonds purchased during the year, and $10,000 of the original cost of its fixtures, charging both these amounts to the Undivided Profit account. The bonds had not fallen in market value, and 5 per cent had already been charged to Expense for depreciation on fixtures. How would you describe the result of this action on the part of the directors? (Friday, 145.)

3. Discuss the question as to whether a reserve should always be represented by specific assets set aside to cover the amount of the reserve.

4. Which of the reserves appearing in the balance sheets following Chapter I gives evidence of being especially covered, either fully or in part?

5. The auditor of an incorporated company which has been accustomed to making investments in interest-paying securities, in making his statement to the directors presented a balance sheet showing a surplus of $65,000. After discussion, the directors determined that they did not wish to declare a dividend out of the surplus and gave their auditor the following order: "Decrease this surplus by investing $50,000 in the bonds of the XYZ Railroad Company." Presuming there was an item in the aforesaid balance sheet of cash $75,000, what effect will the carrying out of the directors' order have upon the surplus of $65,000? (Friday, 130.)

6. A corporation has a Reserve for Extensions of $25,000 with Extension Reserve Fund (assets) consisting of securities listed at their cost price, $25,000. The extension planned is constructed at a cost of $25,500. The bonds in the Extension Reserve Fund are sold for $26,000 in order to pay for the extension. Give all journal entries to show these facts. What would the journal entries be if the bonds sold for $24,000?

7. If in the foregoing case it had been necessary, before the extension was constructed, to sell the bonds (for $24,000) in order to pay some notes falling due, what journal entries should have been made?

CHAPTER XV

1. When a debt is paid off, for which a sinking fund reserve was provided, what entries should be made?

2. Explain, and illustrate by the use of skeleton balance sheets, the various methods in which items relating to sinking fund transactions are treated in balance sheets. Show in what way the difference in treatment indicates a difference in the protection afforded to the holder of the bonds.

3. What is the exact significance of the two accounts, Sinking Fund and Sinking Fund Reserve? What other account is affected when each of these is increased? Under what conditions does each disappear from the books? In what accounts are the counter entries made when each is thus canceled out?

4. A manufacturing corporation handling a patent device issued bonds aggregating $375,000, payable in installments of $25,000 annually for fifteen years. Having in mind possible competition and obsolescence of its property, it was provided that the sinking fund installments be charged against earnings. The president of the company had a contract under which he was to receive a bonus of 5 per cent of the net profits in addition to his salary, but it was specifically provided that as to him the charges against earnings should not include the sinking fund installments. In making up the first year's accounts the auditors decided that the depreciation reserve, as nearly as could be determined, should be stated as $25,000 and this amount was included among the operating expenses. When their report was submitted to the directors, the president referred to his contract and stated that the sinking fund provision and depreciation were synonymous and that he was entitled to 5 per cent of the earnings before any deduction was made for depreciation. The matter is referred to you as an accountant; what is your opinion?

(Friday, 178.)

5. (*a*) The Buffalo Forge Company has just issued $1,000,000, 5 per cent first-mortgage bonds. By the terms of the trust agreement the company is required to set aside each year $50,000 in order to provide a fund for the ultimate redemption of the bonds. At the end of the first year the company uses $50,000 of its profits to purchase securities of other corpora-

tions, which securities it turns over to the trustee. Name the four accounts which will be affected and give the journal entries.

(*b*) At the end of twenty years the bonds fall due. The sinking fund assets are sold for cash and the bonds retired. What are the three journal entries which should now be made on the books of the company?

(*c*) When the sinking fund assets mentioned in (*b*) are sold $1,048,500 is realized, because of a rise in the market price of the securities. To what account would the above excess of $48,500 naturally be transferred? Could it be legitimately used for the payment of dividends? (Friday, 148.)

6. A company is under obligations to pay $10,000 to sinking fund trustees "out of profits." The following transactions take place:

1914
Dec. 31 $10,000 cash paid to sinking fund trustees.

1915
Jan. 5 Trustees invest in $10,000 of the 5 per cent bonds of the company at 98 and interest (from Jan. 1).
July 1 Coupons on above bonds collected.
Dec. 31 $10,000 paid to sinking fund trustees.

1916
Jan. 1 Coupons collected.
2 $11,000 bonds bought for sinking fund at 95.
July 1 Coupons collected.
Dec. 31 $125 paid for expenses of sinking fund.
31 $10,000 paid to sinking fund trustees.

1917
Jan. 1 Coupons collected.
10 $10,000 bonds bought at 101 and interest.

Give journal entries on the company's books for the above transactions. (American Institute of Accountants, 1917.)

7. Explain the relationship between a sinking fund and an allowance for depreciation. It is claimed that in municipal enterprises the requirement that rates must be high enough to provide both for a sinking fund to pay off the bonds and also for a reserve for depreciation with which to replace the plant results in a double charge to consumers. Criticize or explain this theory.

(American Institute of Accountants, 1917.)

8. A corporation with $200,000 common stock, $100,000, 6 per cent income bonds and $100,000, 5 per cent first-mortgage bonds outstanding sets aside $10,000 a year out of profits as a sinking fund with which to retire the first-mortgage bond issue. During the last four years of the life of the bonds profits were large enough to provide interest and sinking fund on the bonds. After the sinking fund assets have been used to pay off the bonds, the income bondholders bring action to compel payment of the four unpaid dividends.

Have they any reasonable ground for action? Explain fully the reason for your answer. (Friday, 149.)

9. An individual buys a fleet of ships. He then forms a corporation to take them over at double the sum paid by him, payable one half in debenture bonds of the company, and one half in its capital stock. A sinking fund is to be provided for the gradual retirement of the debenture bonds. A public accountant is called in at the end of five years to make up the accounts. He insists on creating a depreciation fund based on the full consideration paid by the corporation. The directors argue that the depreciation fund should be based on the amount of debenture bonds issued on the theory that the capital stock issued to the vendor was in the nature of a bonus and did not represent any real value. State your views regarding the two propositions. (Friday, 201.)

CHAPTER XVI

1. Discuss the different theories as to the valuation at which manufactured goods are to be brought down from the Manufacturing account to the Trading account.

2. The following terms are used in the Income account prescribed by the Interstate Commerce Commission: "Net railway operating revenue," "railway operating income," "gross income," "net income." What is the distinction between these? How are the following items treated: "Income received on investments in sinking fund," "depreciation of equipment," "appropriation to sinking funds"?

3. Discuss the different methods of forming the trading section of the profit and loss statement.

4. Rearrange the following Profit and Loss account of a manufacturing concern, subdividing it so as best to exhibit the desired facts:

Profit and Loss

Insurance	$ 575	Raw material inventory, Dec. 31	$ 23,000
Wages of factory hands	24,000	Sales	95,000
Reserve for discounts on accounts receivable	750	Rent received for steam power	1,500
General expenses	600		
Interest on capital—			
To A	2,400		
To B	1,200		
Raw material on hand, Jan. 1	15,000		
Purchases of raw material	38,000		
Traveling expenses	2,500		
Rent and taxes on factory	3,500		
Interest	600		
Stationery and printing	1,200		
Freight on raw material	1,500		
Discounts and allowances on sales	1,250		
Salaries of general managers, etc.	6,000		
Fuel, in factory	3,000		
Depreciation on machinery	3,500		
Profits to A	9,283		
Profits to B	4,642		
	$119,500		**$119,500**

5. The following terms are used in the statements following Chapter XVII: "Net operating income," "total income," "net income," "gross profit," "profits from operations," "net profits," "net profits from operations." How far are they synonymous and in what respects do they differ? Compare their use with the terms employed in the Income account prescribed by the Interstate Commerce Commission.

6. The fiscal year of a manufacturing company ends June 30, 1908, and the bookkeeper presents a statement to the directors made up in the following form:

Gross sales	$285,000	
Increase of inventory	15,000	$300,000
Cost of sales:		
Operating expenses, material, and supplies	$257,000	
Plant expense	12,000	
Freight on returned sales	600	
Sundry purchases finished goods	10,400	280,000
Manufacturing profit		$ 20,000
Other income:		
Miscellaneous earnings	$ 1,500	
Profit on contracts	6,500	
Discount on purchases	500	8,500
		$ 28,500
Less:		
Discount on sales	$ 2,875	
Rebates and allowances	1,125	4,000
Net plant profit		$ 24,500
Less:		
General expenses	$ 5,500	
Interest	1,500	7,000
Net profit		$ 17,500

You are required to prepare a statement in report form, showing purchases, etc., and using such of the above figures as may be necessary, together with these following: Inventory June 30, 1907—Material, $115,000; Supplies, $35,000; Finished Goods, $45,000. Inventory, June 30, 1908—Material, $140,000; Supplies, $10,000; Finished Goods, $60,000. Material used in factory during the year, $75,000. Wages, $122,500, which includes $25,000 supplies used.

(Illinois, 1909.)

7. At the close of its fiscal year, December 31, 1915, the trial balance of The Nau-Pace Company was as follows:

Real Estate	$ 225,000.00	
Fixed Machinery	150,000.00	
Movable Equipment	18,000.00	
Shaftings, Pulleys, etc.	10,500.00	
Stable Equipment	3,500.00	
Office Equipment	2,915.90	
Drawings and Patterns	9,000.00	
Patents	75,000.00	
Capital Stock		$ 500,000.00
First Mortgage Bonds		100,000.00
Profit and Loss		
Surplus		86,140.28
Dividends		300.00
Interest on Bonds	5,000.00	
Other Interest Paid	1,323.10	
Interest Received		2,469.50
Cash Discount on Purchases		13,389.52
Cash Discounts on Sales	2,861.50	
Sales		1,540,816.75
Return Sales	8,258.25	
Cash	27,750.65	
Bills Receivable	50,750.00	
Accounts Receivable	298,650.25	
Raw Materials	622,190.90	
Finished Goods, January 1, 1915	62,735.06	
Goods in Process, January 1, 1915	24,747.27	
Fuel	38,688.28	
Insurance	4,000.00	
Taxes	5,000.00	
Bills Payable		40,000.00
Accounts Payable		46,585.85
Reserve for Depreciation:		
Machinery and Equipment		50,000.00
Buildings		30,000.00
Patents		22,058.80
Bad Accounts		6,240.75
Salaries, Officers and Clerks (General)	56,150.00	
General Office Supplies	2,950.75	
Postage, Telegraph, and Phone	1,560.00	
Miscellaneous General Expenses	850.00	
Advertising	35,000.00	
Salaries and Expenses, Salesmen	72,350.31	
Agents' Commissions	30,141.40	
Credit Department Salaries	7,560.00	
Miscellaneous Expenses, Selling	610.00	
Stable Expenses	3,963.46	
Direct Labor (Mfg.)	508,311.39	
Indirect Labor (Mfg.)	44,981.01	
Superintendence, Factory	6,000.00	
Factory Supplies	8,547.18	
Repairs Machinery and Equipment	7,418.52	
Repairs of Buildings	2,860.47	
Power, Heat, and Light	2,875.80	
	$2,438,001.45	$2,438,001.45

You are to take into consideration the following facts:

(*a*) Real Estate, Machinery and other factory equipment, and Patents are stated at cost.
(*b*) Of the real estate, $25,000 is for land and $200,000 is for buildings.
(*c*) All capital stock authorized has been issued and is outstanding.
(*d*) Allowances for depreciation are:
Machinery and Factory Equipment, $15,000.
Buildings, 3 per cent on cost.
Patents, 1/17 of cost.
(*e*) $15,000 is to be set aside as a reserve for bad accounts.
(*f*) Ten per cent of the book values of Stable Equipment and Office Equipment, and one sixth of the book value of Drawings and Patterns are to be charged off.
(*g*) Inventories at the close of the fiscal year were:

Raw materials	$63,580.40
Finished goods	58,864.56
Goods in process	27,024.52
Fuel	4,823.43
Factory supplies	1,525.00
Office supplies	500.00
Prepaid insurance	500.00

(*h*) The accruals are:

Taxes	$ 7,000.00
Direct labor	12,618.75
Indirect labor	2,040.50
Interest on bonds	1,000.00
Advertising	4,718.50

(*i*) The depreciation on Stable Equipment (see item *f*) is to be charged to Stable Expenses, and one-third of the latter is apportioned to Manufacturing Expenses and two-thirds to Selling Expenses.
(*j*) The cost of fuel used is to be charged to Power, Heat, and Light.
(*k*) Maintenance of Real Estate is to be charged with cost of repairs to buildings, depreciation on buildings, 20 per cent of taxes for the year, and $1,000 for insurance. The total cost of such maintenance is to be shown as an item of manufacturing expense on the statement of cost of sales.
(*l*) The portion of Insurance remaining after charging Maintenance of Real Estate is to be allocated to Manufacturing Expenses.
(*m*) Thirty per cent of the taxes for the year is to be appor-

tioned to manufacturing expenses and 50 per cent is to be charged against income.

(*n*) Of the Salaries of Officers and Clerks, General, $3,600 should be apportioned to Selling Expenses.

(*o*) Amongst the Bills Receivable is a note for $5,000, pertaining to a previous fiscal year, which is considered to be worthless. No provision was made for such loss.

(*p*) Regardless of theory, cash discounts on purchases and sales are to be treated as pertaining to income.

(*q*) On December 10, 1915, a dividend of 10 per cent on the capital stock was declared and made payable on January 10, 1916, for which no entry was made prior to taking off the trial balance.

Given the foregoing information, you are asked to prepare the following statements in approved form for the information of your clients:

1. Cost of sales.
2. Profit and loss, showing (*a*) the gross profit and the per cent of same on sales; (*b*) selling expenses and per cent of same on gross profits; (*c*) general expenses and the percentage that such expenses bear to gross profits; and
3. The net profits and the per cent of same on sales.
4. Balance sheet showing the surplus at the beginning of the fiscal year, and the amount at the close of the year.

(Ohio, 1916.)

CHAPTER XVII

1. A makes sales as follows:

To B, $100; to C, $200. He buys from D, $300, from E, $400. These are all on account and 2 per cent discount is offered in each case. B pays, less discount. C pays the full amount. A takes advantage of the discount offered by D but fails to do so with E.

(*a*) Give journal entries for all these transactions by both methods described in the text.

(*b*) State what disposition would be made of the balances in any accounts concerned with discount when the books are closed.

(*c*) Would discount appear in the balance sheet if books were closed before the term for discount had expired?

(*d*) Would it appear if closed after that period but before accounts were paid?

(*e*) Discuss the significance of each method of handling these discounts.

2. Compare the treatment of depreciation in Forms 24 and 26. Which treatment is preferable?

3. In which section of the several income accounts (Forms 16 to 28) does interest appear? Discuss the variations in treatment shown.

4. In which section of the several income accounts (Forms 16 to 28) does taxes appear? Discuss the variations in treatment shown.

5. By some accountants, interest paid to the bank on short-time loans is treated in the income account as one of the expenses of the business while interest on bonds is treated as the distribution of income. Discuss this.

6. In auditing department store A, you find that cash discounts on purchases are regularly deducted from invoices when they are entered in the books, while in store B, the invoices are entered in full and the discounts are credited to a discount account as and when received. Discuss the relative advantages and disadvantages of the two methods, and state what variations, if any, would occur in the valuing of inventories under the two methods.

(American Institute of Accountants, 1920.)

CHAPTER XVIII

1. A carefully conducted system of cost accounts showed the cost of a given product in 1925 to have been $1.00. Is it necessary to continue to keep detail costs in Jan., 1926? If so, for what purposes? Consider carefully just what assumptions are implied in your answer.

2. A machine shop in manufacturing its product needs the services of machine A one hour and of machine B ten hours. It has expanded so that it now has five machines of B type and machine A is accordingly used only half the time. Is the entire cost of operating machine A to be considered part of the machine cost of manufacturing the product or is part of it to be considered an expense of idle time which would be avoided if five more B-type machines were added? Is the disuse of all the machines during the night an idle time expense?

3. Is depreciation a part of manufacturing cost or a general expense? Would the machinery depreciate even though not used? Does this feature affect the problem?

4. Is the depreciation or expiry of a franchise or patent right (applying to machinery of production, not to the product) an expense which should enter into the cost of production? If such an item is included in the account "Rights, Privileges, Franchises, and Inventions" appearing in Form 6, to what account would an annual charge be made? What would be the counter entry? Does the excessive depreciation of this item affect the cost of production?

5. How far does a system of cost accounts determine the price at which bids will be made for contract work? If that were the sole purpose of cost accounts what items, ordinarily included, would be properly omitted?

6. What do you understand by the phrase, prime cost? What is its significance as used in cost accounts? Is material and direct labor any more essential to production than some of the other expenses incurred in production? Why is so much importance attached to prime costs?

7. (*a*) Explain in full the theoretical difficulties in regard to each of three commonly used methods of distributing overhead burden in cost accounting.

(*b*) Show how the appropriateness of each system may be affected by the nature of the business in which it is employed.
(*c*) Give briefly your views on the proper treatment of "idle time." (American Institute of Accountants, 1917.)

8. A certain factory employs 259 men. The total number of direct labor hours for the month of April is 48,000 hours and the amount of wages is $12,250. The total burden for the month amounts to $11,000.

Job No. 45 is the construction of a heavy machine. The direct labor spent on it amounted to 3,000 hours with a direct wage of $950. The material entering into the machine cost $1,128.

(*a*) What will be the total factory cost of the job according to the hourly-burden plan and the percentage-of-wages plan?
(*b*) Suppose the job required the use of three machines on which the rates are as follows:

A—1,000	hours, rate	$0.124 per hour
B— 400	" "	0.152 " "
C—1,200	" "	0.210 " "

What would be the total factory cost according to this plan?

Give reasons for the differences in the costs according to these three methods of distributing burden.

What possible conditions in the shop would account for these differences? (Friday, 311.)

9. The books of a manufacturing concern, operating under a system of cost accounts, show the following conditions at the opening of the fiscal year: Raw materials in storeroom, $15,621.42; factory pay roll, applied and distributed but not paid, two days, $831.78; partly manufactured goods at prime cost, $63,888.44, and the further value of $8,037.17, to cover factory burden, also $12,074.92 to cover management charges; finished wares in stock at total cost of $21,656.01.

The financial operations during the ensuing year include: Purchases of raw materials, $80,416.45; factory pay rolls, $125,793.90; factory expense, including wages not applied to cost accounts, $24,846; management expenses, $38,100; interest paid on loans, $1,200; income from investments, $5,004.

The manufacturing operations during the same year comprehend: Raw materials issued on requisition for consumption, $79,820.34; wages, applied and distributed to manufacturing cost, $120,250.40; and to factory expenses $5,959.39, included in the sum stated in the preceding paragraph.

Finished goods transferred from factory to warerooms, at prime cost, covering materials, $78,542.58, and labor, $118,333.75.

The trading operations during the same year comprehend: Cost of goods sold, $251,949.90; proceeds from goods sold, $302,339.88.

At the close of the year the partly completed goods included, in addition to prime cost, the further elements of value to cover factory and management expenses in the amounts respectively of $8,439.02 and $12,678.66, and the factory pay roll for three days, amounting to $1,247.67, which has been applied and distributed, though not due till the close of the current work.

The basis of the apportionment of On Cost or Overhead Charges was as follows: Factory expense, 20 per cent to materials and 80 per cent to labor; management expenses, 30 per cent to materials and 70 per cent to labor.

The transactions of the previous year in round amounts were used in calculating the current year's apportionments, viz.: Materials, $75,000; labor, $115,000; factory expense, $24,000; management expense, $36,000.

Open the general ledger accounts that control the cost accounts; show the operation of each and the net profits resulting; also calculate the percentage to be added to each $1.00 of material and of labor to give the total cost.

(Friday, 279.)

CHAPTER XIX

1. A partnership is formed with agreement that A contribute \$200,000; B, \$100,000; and C, \$100,000, profits to be shared in ratio 2:1:1. Interest on excess or deficiency in capital contributions to be figured at 5 per cent. Actual contributions are A, \$200,000; B, \$105,000; C, \$70,000.

(*a*) Give the partners' Capital accounts and Interest account, showing all changes caused by interest reckoning.

(*b*) Work same problem with partners sharing profits equally.

2. A and B are in partnership, profits being shared equally, with the following balance sheet:

Balance Sheet

Merchandise	\$5,000	A, Capital	\$2,000
		B, Capital	3,000
	\$5,000		\$5,000

They agree to admit C, he to contribute \$4,000 and (*a*) to be entitled to an equal share of the profits; (*b*) to have a one-third interest in the business, not merely one third of the profits; (*c*) to have a one-half interest in the business. Give journal entries, partners' Capital accounts, and balance sheet for each of the above arrangements.

3. X, Y, and Z are partners, sharing profits equally. Their balance sheet is:

Balance Sheet

Real Estate	\$10,000	X, Capital	\$25,000
Plant and Machinery	11,500	Y, Capital	25,000
Merchandise	25,000	Z, Capital	12,500
Loose Tools, etc.	7,500	Mortgage	7,000
Cash	38,000	Trade Creditors	27,500
Trade Debtors	5,000		
	\$97,000		\$97,000

X wishes to retire and Y and Z agree to purchase the business on the following terms: 10 per cent to be allowed off Trade Debtors; 15 per cent off Merchandise; 10 per cent off Loose Tools; Plant and Machinery to be valued at $10,000, and Real Estate at $12,500; 2 per cent to be allowed off Trade Creditors and Y and Z to take over the mortgage. Make all journal entries necessary and present balance sheet.

(Accountants' Manual, xi, p. 386.)

4. A and B are in partnership with equal interests, their balance sheet showing:

Balance Sheet

Miscellaneous Assets	$100,000	A, Capital	$ 50,000
		B, Capital	50,000
	$100,000		$100,000

They agree to admit C who is to have a third interest in the business. Give balance sheet after the admission of C, (*a*) where he contributes $50,000 cash to the partnership; (*b*) where he contributes $30,000; (*c*) where he contributes $60,000; (*d*) where he buys from A a third interest in the business, paying him personally $40,000.

5. Smith and Jones are partners, drawing equal amounts for services, and sharing profits according to capital invested, after allowing 5 per cent on capital. They require additional capital and arrange to admit the manager to the firm, he to acquire a one-quarter interest in the business. According to the balance sheet, Smith has $12,000 and Jones $6,000 invested, and goodwill is valued at $6,000. What sum must the manager contribute? How will the partnership accounts appear after payment into the firm of the new capital? How will profits be divided in the future? Show accounts in skeleton form.

(Friday, 73.)

6. The firm of A and B have the following statement:

Balance Sheet

Store	$15,000	Accounts Payable	$10,000
Accounts Receivable	12,000	Bills Payable	5,000
Cash	9,000	A, Capital	30,000
Furniture and Fixtures	2,800	B, Capital	35,000
Merchandise	37,000		
Miscellaneous Equipment	4,200		
	$80,000		$80,000

C is admitted as a special partner with the following arrangement:

C to contribute $30,000 and to be entitled to one third of the profit for one year. Before making the contribution the following changes to be made in the books: store to be marked down 5 per cent; allowance for doubtful accounts to be created amounting to 2 per cent; merchandise to be revalued at $35,000; furniture and fixtures to be valued at $2,500. At the end the amount of goodwill is to be fixed at three times the net profits for the year in excess of $20,000, this goodwill to be set up on the books, the corresponding credit being to A and B equally. A, B, and C each to draw $3,000 in cash, the remaining profits to be carried to their Capital accounts.

During the year the following transactions took place:

Merchandise bought on credit	$240,000
Cash purchases	25,000
Cash sales	125,000
Sales on credit	175,000
Accounts payable paid (face $245,000, discount 2 per cent)	240,100
Accounts receivable collected (face $170,000, all net except $50,000 on which 2 per cent allowed)	169,000
Buying expenses, paid cash	1,500
Selling expenses, paid cash	21,000
Delivery expenses, paid cash	9,000
Management expenses, paid cash	4,500
Miscellaneous expenses, paid cash	3,000
Interest on notes payable, paid cash	250
Partners each withdrew $3,000 cash as agreed.	

In closing the books for determining profits and goodwill the following were agreed upon:

Value of merchandise on hand	$60,000
Depreciation on store	285
Additional allowance for doubtful debts	165
Furniture and fixtures written down	200

Goodwill having been estimated and duly entered, C then contributes enough cash so that his Capital account equals just one third of the total capital.

Prepare statements showing how the accounts are to be adjusted and the balance sheet after the final adjustment.

(American Institute of Accountants, 1917.)

CHAPTER XX

1. With the following statement:

Balance Sheet

Accounts Receivable	1,000	A, Capital	$1,000
Merchandise	1,000	B, Capital	1,000
Cash	300	C, Capital	1,000
Loss during year	700		
	$3,000		$3,000

the firm decides to go out of business. The merchandise is sold for $380 cash, and the accounts receivable held good are sold to B for $600. A then proves to be bankrupt. Profits and losses were to be divided in the ratio 7:2:1. Give partners' accounts showing final settlement.

2. A, B, and C were in partnership, A's capital being $100,000 with 60 per cent of the profits; B's, $60,000 with 15 per cent of the profits; C's, $40,000 with 25 per cent of the profits. During the year C withdraws $5,000. Loss during the year, $10,000. The firm goes into liquidation and assets are gradually sold, yielding in successive installments $30,000, $10,000, $10,000, $12,000, $15,000, and $40,000. No more can be realized. Show proper distribution of installments as received, payments being made to partners in such a manner as to avoid overpayment. Give results in form of partners' Capital accounts.

3. P and D formed a partnership, P contributing $320.90 and D $323.26. At the time of settlement it was shown that P owed D personally the following: Cash borrowed by P, $230; rent belonging to D collected and retained by P, $70; cash borrowed by P, $20. D had taken over the merchandise valued at $450 and the fixtures valued at $196.99. Drawings from the business had been: P, $79.75; D, $20. Present partners' accounts showing how much who owes whom. (See: Oakley *v.* Cokalete, 41 N. Y. Supp. 1, 124.)

4. A, B, and C form a partnership, profits and losses to be shared equally, the capital contributions to be: A, $2,000; B, $1,000;

C, $1,000. Give Capital accounts showing final distribution of assets in each of the following cases: (*a*) Total assets after paying creditors, $7,000; (*b*) total assets after paying creditors, $1,000; (*c*) total assets 0, and $2,000 still due creditors.

If the contributions to the above partnership had been: A, $2,200; B, $1,000; and C, $700; show distribution where total assets, after paying creditors, were $1,000 and C proves bankrupt before settlement is finally made.

5. A partnership agreement is made between C, W, B, and S. C contributes $25,000, W contributes $50,000. B and S make no contribution but all are entitled to share equally in the profits. Later the firm dissolved, with B personally insolvent. The total assets consisted of $50,000 cash. Give the Capital account of each partner, showing the distribution of the cash.

(Whitcomb *v.* Converse, 119 Mass. 38.)

6. With the following:

Balance Sheet

C, Deficiency on Capital account	$ 360	A, Capital	$ 200
Cash	2,040	B, Capital	2,200
	$2,400		$2,400

C proves to be bankrupt. Division of profits and losses to be on basis of: A, 70 per cent; B, 20 per cent; C, 10 per cent. Give journal entries to close books and Capital accounts of A and B, showing final settlement.

7. G and B formed a partnership, G contributing $6,627.56 lumber and B, $7,775.65 cash. During the life of the partnership the following transactions took place: Sales, $93,471.11; purchases, $55,146.55; general expenses, $12,242.95; lime bought, $732.18; rent paid, $111.00. The business before dissolution had been attended to by G, who had made no accounting. At the end of the partnership "stock on hand, books, and accounts" were turned over to B, who collected $7,552.68 (including amounts which he had previously collected) and this left still in his hands bad and uncollected debts of $5,461.56. No other assets were left remaining. Interest due to B because of excess capital, $183.52. Present Trading account, Profit and Loss account, and Capital accounts.

(Gunnell *v.* Bird, 10 Wall. 304.)

8. A, B, and C formed a partnership, profits to be divided equally. A contributed $2,500; B contributed $3,000; and C, $1,000. During the course of business withdrawals were as follows: A, $800; B, $300; C, $200. Business proving unprofitable, they decided to dissolve. At time of dissolution the only assets on hand were: Cash $100, and merchandise inventoried at $1,000. Unpaid bills amounted to $70. It was found that during the existence of the partnership A had collected claims belonging to the firm amounting to $500, which he had not yet turned over. B had paid bills of the firm amounting to $250, for which he had not been reimbursed. B offers to take over the merchandise at a valuation of $850, which offer is accepted by A and C. It is later ascertained that C is insolvent and cannot pay any claims against him. Give the partners' accounts showing final settlement.

9. Prepare Capital accounts of A, B, and C, showing final settlement in liquidation. Balance sheet of the partnership is as follows:

Balance Sheet

Cash	$ 5,500	A, Capital	$ 5,000
Deficit	6,000	B, Capital	3,000
		C, Capital	1,000
		A, Loan	1,500
		B, Loan	1,000
	$11,500		$11,500

10. S and A formed a partnership. S agreed to contribute $14,000 cash, but actually contributed $11,848.20. A contributed $3,876.65. During the course of business S withdraw $3,036.75 and A, $2,625.28. The firm dissolved and the nominal assets (not counting deficiency in S's capital contribution) were $10,372.22. Of these S collected $3,662.99 and A collected $208.42. The receiver held $193.70. The remaining nominal assets were of no value. S paid a note of the firm for $3,125 and retained balance of cash collected. A retained cash collected. Receiver's fees amounted to $112.63. The terms of the partnership were: profits and losses to be shared equally; no interest to be figured on capital. Present full accounts showing how much who owes whom.

(See Schulte *v.* Anderson, 13 Jones & Sp. 489.)

11. A, B, and C constitute a firm engaged in a manufacturing business, which they have decided to change into a stock company with a capital of $100,000, equally divided into common and preferred stock, par value $100 for each share. Each partner is to take stock to the amount of his net investment in the business, on the basis of 75 per cent preferred and 25 per cent common stock and the remaining shares authorized are to be offered for sale.

On taking over the business the books of the firm show assets as follows: Real Estate, $25,000; Machinery and Tools, $10,000; Merchandise, $15,000; Materials and Supplies, $8,000; Cash, $5,000; Notes Receivable, $3,000; Accounts Receivable, $9,000. The liabilities are: Notes Payable, $10,000; Accounts Payable, $5,000; A, $25,000; B, $20,000; and C, $15,000.

Formulate the necessary entries to close the books of the firm and to open the books of the new corporation. (Friday, 89.)

12. A partnership after paying all debts has $3,000 cash on hand. What is the one general procedure by which it is determined how this cash is to be distributed among the partners?

13. The following is the balance sheet of a partnership:

Balance Sheet

Miscellaneous Assets	$122,000	A, Capital	$102,000
Deficit	180,000	B, Capital	100,000
		C, Capital	100,000
	$302,000		$302,000

The agreement was that profits should be shared between A, B, and C in the ratio of 3:2:1, respectively. The business having been unprofitable, the partners decide to liquidate.

(*a*) Prepare schedule showing in advance how installments should be distributed between partners.

(*b*) Show the actual amounts distributed to each partner, the miscellaneous assets being gradually realized and distributed in the following installments:

I.	$32,000
II.	60,000
III.	12,000
IV.	6,000

It is desired to make distribution in such manner that there will be no danger of any partner being overpaid, if the remaining assets at any time should prove worthless.

CHAPTER XXI

1. A receiver who has been appointed for the retail business of A. Adams, retains you to ascertain the approximate percentage which unsecured creditors will receive on their claims. From the following data you are asked to answer your client's question and also to prepare the proper statement and the proper accompanying account as preliminary thereto:

ASSETS

Cash on Hand		$ 500
Cash on Deposit		2,000
Accounts Receivable	$ 28,500	
Reserve for Bad Debts	2,500	26,000
Notes Receivable, trade		15,000
Notes Receivable, Gem Co.		60,000
Bank Stock, 200 shares at 131⅛		26,225
Stock, Gem Co.		45,000
Merchandise Inventory		20,000
Land		25,000
Buildings	$175,000	
Less Reserve for Depreciation	35,000	140,000
Machinery and Tools	$187,500	
Less Reserve for Depreciation	44,500	143,000
Automobile Trucks	$ 15,000	
Less Reserve for Depreciation	12,500	2,500
Office Furniture and Furnishings	$ 4,000	
Less Reserve for Depreciation	2,000	2,000
Unexpired Insurance		375
Accrued Interest on Trade Notes Receivable		225
		$507,825

LIABILITIES

Notes Payable	$200,000
Accounts Payable	175,725
Taxes Accrued	1,500
Wages Accrued	275
Accrued Interest on Notes Payable	12,000
Mortgage on Land and Buildings	125,000
Accrued Interest on Mortgage Loan	6,250
Total liabilities	$520,750
A. Adams, Investment	$ 50,000
A. Adams, Drawing, Dr.	62,925
	$ 12,925

The following appraisals and estimates of values have been made:

Land	$ 30,000
Buildings	135,000
Machinery and Tools	85,000
Auto Trucks	2,000
Furniture and Furnishings	1,200
Merchandise Inventory	12,000
Accounts Receivable, good	20,000
Accounts Receivable, bad	2,000
Accounts Receivable, doubtful	6,500
But estimated to realize	3,000

The following additional facts should be taken into consideration:

Trade notes receivable and accrued interest are secured by 150 shares of an industrial stock quoted at 156.

Cash on hand includes an I. O. U. of the proprietor for $75 and a salary advance ticket to the cashier of $10.

The bank stock is quoted at 150; 175 shares of this stock is pledged to secure notes payable of $20,000, with accrued interest of $1,000.

Accounts payable to the extent of $5,725 are secured by a chattel mortgage on merchandise of $3,000.

The financial statement of the Gem Company shows:

Assets	$150,000
Liabilities	85,000
Capital Stock Outstanding	50,000
Surplus	15,000
The assets have been appraised at.	135,000

Trade notes receivable, not yet due, have been discounted at the bank to the amount of $5,000; and an examination of these discounted notes shows that one of $1,000 will be dishonored.

(Wisconsin, 1919.)

2. The firm of A and B finding itself financially embarrassed is forced to go into liquidation. A statement drawn from the books shows the following:

Trial Balance

Real Estate	$ 70,000	A, Capital	$ 35,000
Investments	140,000	B, Capital	30,000
Merchandise	100,000	Bills Payable	204,500
Bills Receivable	21,250	Accounts Payable	125,000
Accounts Receivable	14,250		
Drawings, A	12,000		
Drawings, B	10,000		
Bad debts charged off	15,000		
Expenses	10,670		
Cash	1,330		
	$394,500		$394,500

A further examination of the condition of the firm discloses the following facts:

Of the Investments, all of which are good, $100,000 are pledged to secure a note of $85,000 and $15,000 are pledged with the holder of a note of $20,000.

Of the Accounts Receivable $5,000 are recognized as bad, $3,000 are doubtful with an estimated value of $1,000, the remainder are good.

The Bills Receivable are estimated as worth $15,000.

The Merchandise is estimated as worth $60,000, and the Real Estate as worth $50,000.

In addition to the liabilities shown on the books, $2,500 is due for wages, $1,000 for salaries, and $250 for taxes, all of which are preferential claims against the assets.

Prepare the statement of affairs and deficiency account.

CHAPTER XXII

1. How does a consolidated balance sheet differ from an ordinary balance sheet?

2. The balance sheets of companies A and B are as follows:

Balance Sheet of A

Notes Receivable (due from B)	$ 10,000	Capital Stock	$120,000
Miscellaneous Assets	122,000	Surplus	12,000
	$132,000		$132,000

Balance Sheet of B

Cash	$150,000	Capital Stock	$200,000
Miscellaneous Assets	100,000	Notes Payable	50,000
	$250,000		$250,000

Give consolidated balance sheets, covering each of the following suppositions:

(*a*) B acquires all of the capital stock of A, paying $132,000 cash.

(*b*) B acquires $100,000 par value of the capital stock of A, paying $110,000 cash.

(*c*) B acquires all of the capital stock of A, paying $144,000 cash.

(*d*) B acquires $100,000 par value of the capital stock of A, paying $120,000 cash.

3. A corporation X is formed to consolidate two existing corporations, A and B, whose books show the following:

Assets

	A	B
Plant	$20,000	$40,000
Merchandise	5,500	10,000
Goodwill	5,000	0
Accounts Receivable	10,000	5,000

LIABILITIES

	A	B
Capital Stock	$25,000	$40,000
Surplus	0	10,000
Notes Payable	9,500	2,000
Accounts Payable	6,000	3,000

Five shares each of common and preferred stock are subscribed for and paid in cash at par. X then buys the assets and assumes the liabilities of A, taking same at the book value less allowance of 5 per cent for bad debts, and including $10,000 for goodwill. Preferred stock at 150 is issued for net tangible assets. Common at par is issued for goodwill.

X buys from the holders the stock of B at 125, giving for each share of B one-half share preferred at 150 and one-half share common at par. Remaining stock subscribed for at same rates and one half of subscriptions paid in cash.

Give journal entries necessary in the books of each concern and resulting balance sheets.

4. A corporation C is organized with $1,000,000 capital stock for the purpose of consolidating two corporations whose statements are:

Balance Sheet of A

Plant, etc.	$500,000	Capital Stock	$350,000
		Bonds	100,000
		Surplus	50,000
	$500,000		$500,000

Balance Sheet of B

Plant	$250,000	Capital Stock	$200,000
		Surplus	50,000
	$250,000		$250,000

The new company buys the plant of A at a valuation of $550,000 (including goodwill) assuming the debt of A and issuing in purchase $450,000 of its stock. It also obtains the stock of the individual stockholders of B, giving 1½ shares of its own stock for each share of B. C further issues $150,000 for cash and holds remainder of stocks for future needs.

5. Company H is organized with $500,000 capital stock to buy control of Company A. Stock of A is purchased by issuing H stock in exchange to the amount needed in each of the six cases. The

remainder of the stock of H is issued for cash at par. H buys stock of A as follows:

(*a*)	All	at	150
(*b*)	All	"	200
(*c*)	9/10	"	150
(*d*)	9/10	"	150
(*e*)	All	"	100
(*f*)	All	"	100

The balance sheet of A at the time is as follows:

Balance Sheet

Miscellaneous Assets	$150,000	Capital Stock	$100,000
		Surplus	50,000
	$150,000		$150,000

Prepare consolidated balance sheet of H and subsidiary companies representing each of the above conditions.

6. Corporation H is organized with $700,000 capital stock, all of which it issues for cash at par. It buys stock as follows:

(*a*) All of A Stock at 125. All of B at par.
(*b*) $120,000 A Stock at 125. $190,000 B at par.
(*c*) All of A Stock at 200. All of B at 150.
(*d*) $140,000 A Stock at 150. $195,000 B at 110.

The balance sheets of A and B at time of purchase are:

Balance Sheet of A

Plant	$100,000	Capital Stock	$160,000
Cash	50,000	Surplus	40,000
Other Current Assets	60,000	Notes Payable	10,000
	$210,000		$210,000

Balance Sheet of B

Plant	$100,000	Capital Stock	$200,000
Cash	5,000		
Other Current Assets *	95,000		
	$200,000		$200,000

* Includes note of A for $5,000.

(*a*) Prepare balance sheets of H.
(*b*) And consolidated balance sheets for each of the above cases.

(*c*) Immediately after purchase, A pays cash dividend of 20 per cent. Prepare balance sheet of A, balance sheet of H, and consolidated balance sheet immediately after the payment.

7.

Balance Sheet of A

Property Leases and Goodwill	$470,133	Capital Stock	$400,000
Fixtures	81,791	Bonds	100,000
Merchandise Inventory	126,538	Sundry Creditors	59,975
Sundry Debtors	54,642	Surplus	135,886
Sinking Fund Assets	11,690	Pension Fund	5,460
Cash on Hand	20,204	Sinking Fund Reserve	11,690
		Profit and Loss	51,987
	$764,998		$764,998

Balance Sheet of B

Cash	$ 51,195	Preferred Stock	$ 800,000
Investments:		Common Stock	123,000
Short-time Loans	108,000	Surplus	160,000
Stock of A at par	100,000	Accounts Payable	141,235
Stock of C at par	20,000	Notes Payable	4,728
Bonds of Company A at par (cost)	50,000	Profit and Loss	217,254
Railroad and Other Bonds at present value	126,070		
Merchandise	366,437		
Sundry Debtors	15,563		
Prepaid Expense	12,715		
Goodwill and Trade-marks	422,900		
Plant and Machinery	173,337		
	$1,446,217		$1,446,217

Balance Sheet of C

Land and Buildings	$ 41,438	Capital Stock	$120,000
Machinery	20,577	Bonds	30,675
Merchandise	19,610	Surplus	34,000
Office Furniture	50	Dividend Declared	1,650
Cash	14,730	Accounts Payable	5,879
Accounts Receivable	21,245	Profit and Loss	12,343
Goodwill at cost	81,867		
Bonds of Company A, $5,000 at cost	5,030		
	$204,547		$204,547

Company D is organized for the purpose of consolidating the three companies whose balance sheets are given above, engaged in allied businesses. Company D is authorized to issue $2,000,000 preferred stock, and $350,000 common stock. It arranges to buy stock of the subsidiary companies on the following terms:

For Each Share of	Is Offered of	
	D Preferred Stock	D Common Stock
A stock	1 share	½ share
B preferred	2 shares	
B common		1 share
C stock	1 share	¾ share

On these terms D acquires $290,000 of A stock, all the preferred stock of B, $100,000 of common stock of B, and $100,000 of C stock. The stock bought was obtained from individual holders, the stock of A and C held by B, as well as some stock held by non-consenting stockholders, not being acquired. The remaining preferred stock of D was held by the company. The rest of the common stock authorized was sold for cash at par. The expenses of organization amounted to $5,000 and were paid in cash.

Of the accounts receivable held by C, $20,000 were due from B. Of the sundry debtors on the books of B, $5,500 were due from A.

Company D also issues $500,000 bonds which it sells at 105 and pays $500,000 cash for a plant which it buys direct.

Prepare a consolidated balance sheet.

(American Institute of Accountants, 1917.)

8. Illustrate two methods of exhibiting goodwill in a consolidated balance sheet, when 90 per cent of the stock of the subsidiary company is bought by the holding company at more than the book value.

CHAPTER XXIII

1. The following figures are taken from the statement of a national bank:

Bank Notes in Circulation	$ 25,000.00	Internal Revenue Stamps	$ 470.20
Banking House	3,300.00	Loans and Discounts	174,870.59
Bills Payable	5,000.00	Other Real Estate	34,961.28
Bills Rediscounted	23,699.00	Overdrafts	5,087.06
Capital Stock	100,000.00	Redemption Fund in U. S. Treasury	1,250.00
Cash on Hand	10,090.56	Stocks and Securities	6,800.00
Checks and Other Cash Items	72.00	Undivided Profits	3,525.41
Deposits	122,289.50	U. S. Bonds to Secure Circulation	25,000.00
Due from Other Banks	17,612.22		

The following, from the statement of a state bank:

Bonds	$ 51,862.36	Overdrafts	$ 196.08
Capital Stock	15,000.00	Reserved for Taxes and Interest	1,215.10
Cash and Due from Banks	39,408.69	Surplus	15,000.00
Deposits	239,170.02	Undivided Profits	4,774.88
Loans and Discounts	183,692.87		

Construct balance sheets for each, and discuss the relative standing of the two banks (*a*) as to security to creditors; (*b*) as to profitableness of business.

2. The following show the condition of the books of A and B respectively on November 1, 1914:

Balance Sheet of A

Machinery	$ 9,500	A, Capital	$ 5,000
Real Estate	2,700	Accounts Payable	8,200
Merchandise	3,000	Allowance for Bad Debts	100
Accounts Receivable	2,100	Bills Payable	4,500
Cash	1,000	Reserve for Depreciation:	
Interest, etc., paid in advance	200	Machinery	500
		Real Estate	200
	$18,500		$18,500

Balance Sheet of B

Accounts Receivable	$ 4,700	Accounts Payable	$11,500
Bills Receivable	5,000	Allowance for Bad Accounts	400
Cash	5,800	B, Capital	5,000
Interest, etc., paid in advance	400	Bills Payable	3,000
Machinery	6,300	Reserve for Depreciation	300
Merchandise	3,000	Mortgage due Nov. 1, 1918	5,000
	$25,200		$25,200

Arrange each of the above in a form which will better bring out the important facts, and discuss the relative standing of the two merchants.

3. Prepare statement of sources and disposition of funds from the balance sheet in Form 3.

4. Prepare a statement from the balance sheet in Form 6 showing the seven ratios. The sales amounted to $9,993,751.74. Discuss the significance of the ratios.

5. Prepare a statement from the balance sheet of the Goodrich Rubber Company printed above, page 460, showing the seven ratios. The sales for the year were $39,509,346. Discuss the significance of the ratios.

TABLE OF CASES

INDEX